# THE NEW CAMBRIDGE SHAKESPEARE

GENERAL EDITOR
Brian Gibbons, *University of Münster*

ASSOCIATE GENERAL EDITOR
A. R. Braunmuller, *University of California, Los Angeles*

From the publication of the first volumes in 1984 the General Editor of the New
Cambridge Shakespeare was Philip Brockbank and the Associate General Editors were
Brian Gibbons and Robin Hood. From 1990 to 1994 the General Editor was Brian
Gibbons and the Associate General Editors were A. R. Braunmuller and Robin Hood.

## KING HENRY V

For this updated edition of Shakespeare's most celebrated war play, Professor Gurr has added a
new section to his introduction which considers recent critical and stage interpretations, especially concentrating on the 'secret' versus 'official' readings of the play. He analyses the play's
double vision of Henry as both military hero and self-seeking individual.

Professor Gurr shows how the patriotic declarations of the Chorus are contradicted by the
play's action. The play's more controversial sequences are placed in the context of Elizabethan
thought, in particular the studies of the laws and morality of war written in the years before
Henry V. Also studied is the exceptional variety of language and dialect in the play.

The appendices provide a comprehensive collection of source materials, while the stage history
shows how subsequent centuries have received and adapted the play on the stage and in film. An
updated reading list completes the edition.

# THE NEW CAMBRIDGE SHAKESPEARE

*All's Well That Ends Well*, edited by Russell Fraser
*Antony and Cleopatra*, edited by David Bevington
*As You Like It*, edited by Michael Hattaway
*The Comedy of Errors*, edited by T. S. Dorsch
*Coriolanus*, edited by Lee Bliss
*Cymbeline*, edited by Martin Butler
*Hamlet*, edited by Philip Edwards
*Julius Caesar*, edited by Marvin Spevack
*King Edward III*, edited by Giorgio Melchiori
*The First Part of King Henry IV*, edited by Herbert Weil and Judith Weil
*The Second Part of King Henry IV*, edited by Giorgio Melchiori
*King Henry V*, edited by Andrew Gurr
*The First Part of King Henry VI*, edited by Michael Hattaway
*The Second Part of King Henry VI*, edited by Michael Hattaway
*The Third Part of King Henry VI*, edited by Michael Hattaway
*King Henry VIII*, edited by John Margeson
*King John*, edited by L. A. Beaurline
*The Tragedy of King Lear*, edited by Jay L. Halio
*King Richard II*, edited by Andrew Gurr
*King Richard III*, edited by Janis Lull
*Macbeth*, edited by A. R. Braunmuller
*Measure for Measure*, edited by Brian Gibbons
*The Merchant of Venice*, edited by M. M. Mahood
*The Merry Wives of Windsor*, edited by David Crane
*A Midsummer Night's Dream*, edited by R. A. Foakes
*Much Ado About Nothing*, edited by F. H. Mares
*Othello*, edited by Norman Sanders
*Pericles*, edited by Doreen DelVecchio and Antony Hammond
*The Poems*, edited by John Roe
*Romeo and Juliet*, edited by G. Blakemore Evans
*The Sonnets*, edited by G. Blakemore Evans
*The Taming of the Shrew*, edited by Ann Thompson
*The Tempest*, edited by David Lindley
*Timon of Athens*, edited by Karl Klein
*Titus Andronicus*, edited by Alan Hughes
*Troilus and Cressida*, edited by Anthony B. Dawson
*Twelfth Night*, edited by Elizabeth Story Donno
*The Two Gentlemen of Verona*, edited by Kurt Schlueter

## THE EARLY QUARTOS
*The First Quarto of Hamlet*, edited by Kathleen O. Irace
*The First Quarto of King Henry V*, edited by Andrew Gurr
*The First Quarto of King Lear*, edited by Jay L. Halio
*The First Quarto of King Richard III*, edited by Peter Davison
*The First Quarto of Othello*, edited by Scott McMillin
*The Taming of A Shrew: The 1594 Quarto*, edited by Stephen Roy Miller

# KING HENRY V

*Updated edition*

*Edited by*
ANDREW GURR
*Professor of English, University of Reading*

CAMBRIDGE
UNIVERSITY PRESS

CAMBRIDGE UNIVERSITY PRESS
Cambridge, New York, Melbourne, Madrid, Cape Town, Singapore, São Paulo

Cambridge University Press
The Edinburgh Building, Cambridge CB2 2RU, UK

Published in the United States of America by Cambridge University Press, New York

www.cambridge.org
Information on this title: www.cambridge.org/9780521612647

First published 1992
Updated edition 2005
Third printing 2006

Printed in the United Kingdom at the University Press, Cambridge

*A catalogue record for this book is available from the British Library*

ISBN-13 978-0-521-84792-6 hardback
ISBN-10 0-521-84792-3 hardback
ISBN-13 978-0-521-61264-7 paperback
ISBN-10 0-521-61264-0 paperback

# CONTENTS

List of illustrations                                          *page* vi

Preface                                                              viii

Acknowledgements                                                      x

List of abbreviations and conventions                               xi

Introduction                                                         I

   The play and its date                              I

   The coercive Chorus                                6

   Context and sources                               15

   Structure and language                            30

   Staging and stage history                         35

   Recent critical and stage interpretations         52

Note on the text                                                    64

List of characters                                                  74

THE PLAY                                                            78

Textual analysis                                                   221

Appendices                                                         234

   Theatre sources: *The Famous Victories*          234

   Historical sources: Holinshed's *Chronicles*     239

   Background sources: Richard Crompton,            243
      *The Mansion of Magnanimitie*

Reading list                                                      247

# ILLUSTRATIONS

1  Henry V, an effigy in the Rood screen at York Minster (By kind                    *page* 3
   permission of the Dean and Chapter of York Minster)

2  Henry V, a restored effigy of his coronation (The Dean and                           5
   Chapter at Westminster Abbey)

3  Chorus speaking the Prologue. Drawing by C. Walter Hodges                             8

4  An illustration from Rowe's 1709 edition of *Henry V* (the Folger                    28
   Shakespeare Library)

5  Elizabethan soldiers trailing versions of the 'puissant pike', actually             31
   halberds (4.1.40). A detail from Henry Peacham's sketch of *Titus Andronicus*
   on stage in 1595 (The Marquess of Bath)

6  The French nobles before Agincourt. Drawing by C. Walter Hodges                      36

7  Strait Irish strossers (3.8.49–50), a border illustration from John                 38
   Speed, *Theatre of the Empire of Great Britain*, 1611 (The British Library)

8  Henry in armour (Act 3, Scene 4), at the gate of Harfleur with his                   39
   army. Drawing by C. Walter Hodges

9  The set for Charles Kean's production of 1859, the pageant of Henry's                43
   return to London after Agincourt, from the prompt-book for his 1859
   production (The Folger Shakespeare Library)

10  Charles Kean's set for Act 1, Scene 2, from the prompt book                          45
    (The Folger Shakespeare Library)

11  Queen Elizabeth on her throne for the opening of Parliament in 1586,                 46
    in Robert Glover, *Nobilitas Politica vel Civilis*, 1608 (The British
    Library)

12  Llewellyn (Ian Holm) approaches Henry (Kenneth Branagh) on the                      51
    battlefield of Agincourt after Henry has named it (4.7.77–80). From Kenneth
    Branagh's 1989 film

13  Adrian Lester as Henry in the National Theatre production of 2003.                   56
    Photograph by Ivan Kynel. By permission of the National Theatre

14  William Huston as Henry in the Royal Shakespeare Company                            57
    production of 2000/2001, with his soldiers at Harfleur. Photograph by
    Malcolm Davies. Copyright Shakespeare Birthplace Trust

15   The head of a linstock (3.0.33), discovered in the wreck of the Mary          218
     Rose (The Mary Rose Trust)

16   The third Earl of Cumberland dressed as the Queen's Champion,                 219
     from a miniature painted by Nicholas Hilliard in about 1591
     (National Maritime Museum)

17a  F, 4.1.197–212 (detail)                                                       223

17b  F, 4.8.35–43 (detail)                                                         223

18   The Q title-page                                                              226

# PREFACE

Richard Burbage, the leading player of the Chamberlain's Men in the late 1590s, was the original performer of the chief roles in most of Shakespeare's plays. He almost certainly took the title parts both for *Richard II* and *Henry V*, and played Prince Hal in the two plays that came between them. If he did so, then the sun which set with Richard in Act 3 of the first play would have risen again, as promised by the young Hal at the end of Act 1, Scene 2 of *1 Henry IV*, in the later plays and with the same face. Elizabethan audiences knew their players, and would see a dramatic if not a dynastic continuity with the resurrection of the dead sun-king Richard in the living sun-king Henry. As a play about the shining new king and his famous victory at Agincourt, *Henry V* was thus a fitting finale, a grandly patriotic celebration, for the series of plays which began with an unjust king unjustly deposed and murdered. Agincourt ratified Henry's rule, and settled, however temporarily, the question of the proper dynastic line for English kings which had begun with the deposition of Richard II. *Henry V* should have made a brilliant closure to the decade through which Shakespeare wrote his account of the history and politics of English monarchy. But the play that ended the sequence can sustain a far wider range of readings than the merely patriotic.

Writing a sequence of plays over a period of years is a challenge to any author's single-mindedness. The person writing *Richard II* in 1595 was not quite the same person who wrote *Henry V* in 1599. The process of writing in itself can change the concepts which initiate the writing, and new considerations always intrude to influence the development of story, character, and ideology. Outside pressures certainly affected the composition of the two plays that came between the first and the last of the tetralogy, sometimes called the 'second Henriad', that started with *Richard II*'s setting sun and ended with *Henry V*'s rising sun. The new Lord Chamberlain in 1596 forced the company to change the traditional name Oldcastle, which had been used for Prince Hal's rude companion in the old Queen's Men's play about Henry V, to Falstaff. The immediate success on stage of Shakespeare's Falstaff may have called for a sequel that was not part of the original planning. That change of plan may consequently have altered the structure of the story of Prince Hal's growth from prodigal into king. What probably started in 1596 as a fairly straightforward set of rewrites of the old stage play about riotous Prince Hal, his conversion when king and his famous victory at Agincourt, diverged radically from the well-known sources. *Henry V* is a resetting of both the popular mythology about Henry and the standard ideology of its time.

Given the two alternative readings of Henry's character in the play, as patriotic hero or jingoistic bully, and the wealth of evidence that can be used to support either view, it has been suggested that reading the play is an exercise in seeing the same phenomenon as either of two quite different things. Its ambivalence makes it like the exercise in *Gestalt* psychology where the same outline can seem either a rabbit or a duck, depending on one's preconception of the shape. More recent comment on the play has drawn attention to the bivalence in the debates of the time, where both the soldiers and the churchmen of Protestant England, involved in a long war against Catholic Spain, had to counter the Anabaptist argument against all war which they based on the Sixth Commandment, 'Thou shalt not kill' (Deuteronomy 5.17). In the context of that debate the play's ambivalence reflects the ideology of its day. How precisely this apparent exhibition of the ideological ambivalence of its time is the main feature of the play, as the cultural materialists maintain, or how far it might display a more singular and original discomfort in its author over prevailing ideologies, is the chief question the Introduction to this edition addresses.

In the last few years my friends and colleagues across the world have often run into my preoccupation with the peculiarities of *Henry V*. To all of them I offer my grateful thanks for lending me not only their ears but their minds and the fruits thereof. T. S. Dorsch gave me the notes he had prepared for his edition of *Henry V*. To him and to Brian Gibbons especially, General and particular Editor of this series, I owe much more than is writ down.

# ACKNOWLEDGEMENTS

All editions of Shakespeare are built on their predecessors. More than twenty editors and other commentators have offered material about *Henry V* that has been incorporated in this edition, starting with the players who put together the first quarto text in 1600, and most recently reaching an individual peak with Gary Taylor's Oxford edition of 1982. To all of them I owe the kind of debt that it is normal only for scholars not to repay.

There are many other works which can help editors in settling both text and notes. The books of reference which have provided the main help for this edition are those listed in the Abbreviations and Conventions. On the language, the *Oxford English Dictionary* (*OED*), in its new form, unrivalled for study of the lexical niceties, is backed by Abbott's still-authoritative *Shakespearian Grammar* on Shakespearean syntax. Particular idioms and sayings of Shakespeare's time are listed in M. P. Tilley's *A Dictionary of the Proverbs in England in the Sixteenth and Seventeenth Centuries*, 1950. It has an appendix relating to Shakespeare which has been ably augmented and corrected by R. W. Dent's three works, the most useful of which are *Shakespeare's Proverbial Language: An Index*, 1981, and *Proverbial Language in English Drama, exclusive of Shakespeare, 1495–1616*, 1984. On pronunciation, Fausto Cercignani's *Shakespeare's Works and Elizabethan Pronunciation*, 1981, is generally reliable.

The series in which this edition appears has adopted the practice of modernising the original all-too-variable spellings. This process entails some quite substantial editorial interventions, few of which will be apparent to the reader who does not consult the early texts in the First Folio and the 1600 Quarto. Stanley Wells, *Modernising Shakespeare's Spelling*, 1979, a prolegomenon to the Oxford Shakespeare, offers a sound and intelligible set of guiding principles. Where I have not followed his preferences, as given in his book and in the Oxford text, I have sought to justify my choice.

Citations of lines and line references from other plays of Shakespeare are taken from the other New Cambridge editions. References to the Bible are by book, chapter and verse. Quotations are taken from the Bishops' Bible, for reasons given on p. 27, note 1.

The pictures for this edition have been taken from a number of sources, most of which are acknowledged in the List of Illustrations. My thanks for help in obtaining them are due to the wonderful librarians at the Folger Shakespeare Library, to the archivists at York Minster and Westminster Abbey, and to the staff at the British Library. To Walter Hodges in particular, whose superb eye for the graphic portrayal of a stage scene first alerted me to the mysteries of the Shakespearean theatre, and whose acute and wonderfully inventive sense of the possibilities inherent in the original Elizabethan staging shines on the surface of his illustrations for this edition, I owe a lasting debt of gratitude for the benefits he has given me through more than thirty years.

# ABBREVIATIONS AND CONVENTIONS

## 1. Shakespeare's plays

The abbreviated titles of Shakespeare's plays used in this edition have been modified from those in the *Harvard Concordance to Shakespeare*. All quotations and line references to plays other than *Henry V* are to New Cambridge editions of each play.

| | |
|---|---|
| *Ado* | *Much Ado About Nothing* |
| *Ant.* | *Antony and Cleopatra* |
| *AWW* | *All's Well that Ends Well* |
| *AYLI* | *As You Like It* |
| *Cor.* | *Coriolanus* |
| *Cym.* | *Cymbeline* |
| *Err.* | *Comedy of Errors* |
| *Ham.* | *Hamlet* |
| *1H4* | *The First Part of King Henry the Fourth* |
| *2H4* | *The Second Part of King Henry the Fourth* |
| *1H6* | *The First Part of King Henry the Sixth* |
| *2H6* | *The Second Part of King Henry the Sixth* |
| *3H6* | *The Third Part of King Henry the Sixth* |
| *JC* | *Julius Caesar* |
| *John* | *King John* |
| *LLL* | *Love's Labour's Lost* |
| *Lear* | *King Lear* |
| *Mac.* | *Macbeth* |
| *MM* | *Measure for Measure* |
| *MND* | *A Midsummer Night's Dream* |
| *MV* | *The Merchant of Venice* |
| *Oth.* | *Othello* |
| *Per.* | *Pericles* |
| *R2* | *King Richard the Second* |
| *R3* | *King Richard the Third* |
| *Rom.* | *Romeo and Juliet* |
| *Shr.* | *The Taming of the Shrew* |
| *Temp.* | *The Tempest* |
| *TGV* | *The Two Gentlemen of Verona* |
| *Tim.* | *Timon of Athens* |
| *Tit.* | *Titus Andronicus* |
| *TN* | *Twelfth Night* |
| *Tro.* | *Troilus and Cressida* |
| *Wiv.* | *The Merry Wives of Windsor* |
| *WT* | *The Winter's Tale* |

## 2. Editions and general references

| | |
|---|---|
| Abbott | E. A. Abbott, *A Shakespearian Grammar*, 1879 |
| Capell | *Mr William Shakespeare his Comedies Histories and Tragedies*, ed. Edward Capell, 10 vols., 1767–8, VI |
| Cercignani | Fausto Cercignani, *Shakespeare's Works and Elizabethan Pronunciation*, 1981 |
| conj. | conjectured by |
| Craik | *Henry V*, ed. T. W. Craik, 1995 (*The Arden Shakespeare*) |
| Delius | *Shakespeares Werke*, ed. N. Delius, 2 vols., 1872, I |
| Dent | R. W. Dent, *Shakespeare's Proverbial Language: An Index*, 1981 (references are to numbered proverbs) |
| Dent, *PLED* | *Proverbial Language in English Drama, exclusive of Shakespeare, 1495–1616*, 1984 (references are to numbered proverbs) |
| Dyce | *The Works of William Shakespeare*, ed. Alexander Dyce, 6 vols., 1857, III |
| *Explorations* | Hilda M. Hulme, *Explorations in Shakespeare's Language*, 1964 |
| *Famous Victories* | Anonymous, *The Famous Victories of Henry the Fift*, 1598 |
| F | *Mr William Shakespeares Comedies, Histories, and Tragedies*, 1623 (First Folio) |
| F2 | *Mr William Shakespeares Comedies, Histories, and Tragedies*, 1632 (Second Folio) |
| F3 | *Mr William Shakespeares Comedies, Histories, and Tragedies*, 1664 (Third Folio) |
| F4 | *Mr William Shakespeares Comedies, Histories, and Tragedies*, 1685 (Fourth Folio) |
| Fuzier | Jean Fuzier, 'Ie quand sur le possession de Fraunce': a French crux in *Henry V* solved?' *SQ* 32 (1981), 97–100 |
| Hanmer | *The Works of Shakespear*, ed. Thomas Hanmer, 6 vols, 1743–4, III |
| Holinshed | Raphael Holinshed, *The first and second volumes of Chronicles of England, Scotlande, and Irelande* (1587), II |
| Hudson | *The Complete Works of William Shakespeare*, ed. H. N. Hudson, 20 vols., 1864, XI |
| Humphreys | *Henry V*, ed. A. R. Humphreys, 1968 (New Penguin) |
| Jackson | MacDonald P. Jackson, '*Henry V*, III, vi, 181: an emendation', *NQ* n. s. 13 (1966), 133–4 |
| Johnson | *The Plays of William Shakespeare*, ed. Samuel Johnson, 8 vols., 1765, IV |
| Keightley | *The Plays of Shakespeare*, ed. Thomas Keightley, 6 vols., 1864, III |
| Knight | *The Pictorial Edition of Shakspere*, ed. Charles Knight, 8 vols., 1838, V |
| Malone | *The Plays and Poems of William Shakespeare*, ed. Edmund Malone, 10 vols., 1790, V |
| Maxwell | J. C. Maxwell, '*Henry V*, II, ii, 103–4', *NQ* 199 (1954), 195 |
| *MLR* | *Modern Language Review* |
| Moore Smith | *Henry V* ed. G. C. Moore Smith, 1893 (Warwick) |
| *NQ* | *Notes and Queries* |
| *OED* | *Oxford English Dictionary* |
| *Oldcastle* | Munday, Drayton, Wilson, Hathway, *The Life of Sir John Oldcastle*, 1600 |
| Oxford | *The Oxford Shakespeare*, ed. Stanley Wells and Gary Taylor, 1987 |
| Pope | *The Works of Shakespear*, ed. Alexander Pope, 6 vols., 1725, III |
| Pope² | *The Works of Shakespear*, ed. Alexander Pope, 8 vols., 1728, IV |

| | |
|---|---|
| *PQ* | *Philological Quarterly* |
| Q | *The Cronicle History of Henry the fift, With his battell fought at Agin Court in* France. *Togither with* Auntient Pistoll, 1600 |
| Q2 | *The Cronicle History of Henry the fift, With his battell fought at Agin Court in* France. *Togither with* Auntient Pistoll, 1608 |
| Q3 | *The Cronicle History of Henry the fift, With his battell fought at Agin Court in* France. *Togither with* Auntient Pistoll, 1619 |
| Rann | *The Dramatic Works of Shakespeare*, ed. Joseph Rann, 6 vols., 1787, IV |
| Riverside | *The Riverside Shakespeare*, ed. G. Blakemore Evans, 1974 |
| Rowe | *The Works of Mr William Shakespear*, ed. Nicholas Rowe, 6 vols., 1709, III |
| Rowe² | *The Works of Mr William Shakespear*, ed. Nicholas Rowe, 8 vols., 1714, IV |
| SD | stage direction |
| SH | speech heading |
| Sisson | C. J. Sisson, *New Readings in Shakespeare*, 2 vols., 1956, II |
| *SQ* | *Shakespeare Quarterly* |
| *S.St.* | *Shakespeare Studies* |
| *S.Sur.* | *Shakespeare Survey* |
| Steevens | *The Plays of William Shakespeare*, ed. Samuel Johnson and George Steevens, 10 vols., 1773, VI |
| Taylor | *Henry V*, ed. Gary Taylor, 1982 (New Oxford) |
| Theobald | *The Works of Shakespeare*, ed. Lewis Theobald, 7 vols., 1733, IV |
| *Three Studies* | Stanley Wells and Gary Taylor, *Modernising Shakespeare's Spelling, with Three Studies in the Text of 'Henry V'*, 1979 |
| Tilley | M. P. Tilley, *A Dictionary of the Proverbs in England in the Sixteenth and Seventeenth Centuries*, 1950 (references are to numbered proverbs) |
| Vaughan | Henry Halford Vaughan, *New Readings and New Renderings of Shakespeare's Tragedies*, 3 vols., 1881–6, I |
| Walter | *Henry V*, ed. J. H. Walter, 1954 (New Arden) |
| Warburton | *The Works of William Shakespeare*, ed. William Warburton, 8 vols., 1747, IV |
| Wilson | *Henry V*, ed. J. Dover Wilson, 1947 (New Shakespeare) |

Full references to other works cited in the commentary in abbreviated form may be found in the Reading List.

# INTRODUCTION

## The play and its date

Shakespeare wrote the draft of *Henry V* that became the First Folio text in the early summer of 1599. The evidence for this dating is the reasonably coherent state of the manuscript used to set the Folio text, what is almost certainly a reference to the Earl of Essex's campaign in Ireland in the fifth Chorus (5.0.29–32), the absence of any reference to the play in Francis Meres' list of Shakespeare's works in *Palladis Tamia*, which was entered for printing on 7 September 1598, and the evidence in the play itself that Shakespeare had seen books printed in 1598 or at the beginning of 1599, such as Chapman's first seven books of the *Iliad* and Richard Crompton's *Mansion of Magnanimitie*.[1] The play must have been put on stage by the Chamberlain's Men at the Globe at least a few weeks before 16 October 1599, when Philip Henslowe began a series of payments to four authors for the first part of a new play called *Sir John Oldcastle*. That play, given to the rival company performing at the Rose playhouse near the newly-built Globe late in 1599, seems to have been designed by Henslowe to rub in the Chamberlain's company's embarrassment over its forced change of the name Oldcastle to Falstaff in *1 Henry IV*. It makes some overt corrections not only to the rival company's Henry IV plays but also to *Henry V*.[2]

Shakespeare's play was written as the conclusion of his long series of plays about English history which he started near the beginning of the 1590s. It was a militaristic decade, starting with vivid memories of the Armada of 1588 heightened by a renewed Spanish attempt at invasion in 1592, and marked by the long campaigns that had begun across the North Sea in the 1580s, where English armies were aiding the Protestants of the Netherlands against their Spanish masters. London was full of news about these campaigns, and periodically full of soldiers discharged or on leave. More books about military tactics and the rightful conduct of war appeared in this decade than ever before or after. Since it was in part a religious war, Protestant England fighting Catholic Spain,

---

1 For a discussion of the manuscript behind the F text, see Textual Analysis, pp. 221–4. For a discussion of Shakespeare's use of Crompton and other source material, see Introduction, pp. 21–6. Gary Taylor's Introduction to the Oxford edition of *Henry V* indicates (pp. 52–4) some phrasings which suggest Shakespeare's familiarity with Chapman's text. They occur mostly in the Chorus and opening scene of Act 4, and come from Chapman's Books 9 and 10, which have a broadly parallel account of the Greek camp on the night before a battle. Attempts have been made to identify 'the general of our gracious empress' as the Earl of Mountjoy, who preceded and followed Essex as commander in Ireland, and to date the play in 1598 on the grounds that Essex's campaign had already been announced then, or in 1600 on the grounds that Mountjoy's prospects of success were high then, but neither is very convincing. The 1600 dating requires the Choruses to have been written and inserted after the rest of the play was on stage. For composition in 1600, see Warren D. Smith, 'The *Henry V* Choruses in the First Folio', *Journal of English and Germanic Philology* 53 (1954), 38–57, and David Bevington, *Tudor Drama and Politics*, pp. 19–20.
2 For an account of *Oldcastle*, see below, pp. 19–21.

I

the morality of war became a subject for sermons and numerous books exhorting their readers about the God-fearing man's loyal duty to his country and his monarch. The theatres took an active part in this jingoism, with imitations of conquering Tamburlaine and accounts of English seafaring heroes. On occasion they even offered colourful stage versions of recent battles. A letter-writer in October 1599 told Sir Robert Sidney, whose brother Philip had been killed in a skirmish against the Spanish forces in the Netherlands, of one such performance. He wrote that 'Two daies agoe, the overthrow of *Turnholt* was acted upon a Stage, and all your names used that were at yt; especially *Sir Fra. Veres*, and he that plaid that Part gott a Beard resembling his . . . You was also introduced, killing slaying, and overthrowing the *Spaniards* . . .'[1] That mood changed after Elizabeth's death, and some people may already have been sceptical about the jingoism of the writers and preachers by 1599. In some significant respects *Henry V* offers on its surface the patriotic triumphalism of a Chorus who glorifies Henry's conquests, while through the story itself runs a strong hint of scepticism about the terms and the nature of his victories.

The late 1590s proved a difficult time for the company and its author, and the play shows some signs of discontinuity in its composition. Characters are introduced and then abandoned (Macmorris and Jamy, and some of the nobles on both sides), the Chorus tells of the army shipping from Dover when he has already announced the port as Southampton (3.0.4), and he ignores the comic characters who open Acts 2 and 5, so that their arrival makes nonsense of his announcements about the locality and the passage of time. There also seems to have been some hesitation about which of the main sources to use over the Dauphin's presence at Agincourt. In the earlier plays about Henry V, the Dauphin was the antagonist to Henry's protagonist, and his humiliation was emphasised. Holinshed's account in his *Chronicles* makes it clear that historically there were three Dauphins in close succession through the years of Henry's war in France, and that the Dauphin of the time was not present at Agincourt. The text of the play as printed in the First Folio shows some hesitation over which of the two sources to follow. The Dauphin is written in up to the eve of Agincourt and appears briefly on stage during the battle, but vanishes from the play thereafter.[2]

1599 was a difficult time to be writing plays about English history, and some of these difficulties show up in the ways critics have read the play. For the decade before her death in 1603, Elizabeth suppressed any discussion about who should succeed her on the English throne. James VI of Scotland was the obvious choice, and the possibility that he might be the one to follow Elizabeth must have raised the possibility of England being united with Scotland, although, once Peter Wentworth had been put in the Tower for writing pamphlets urging that James should be named as Elizabeth's successor, it was not a matter for general debate. England had been officially united with Wales for centuries, whatever could be made of Henry IV's and his son's long campaigns against Glendower. More recently England had developed a policy that claimed Ireland as its lawful colony. The further possibility of Scotland also joining England when its king

1 Roland Whyte to Sir Robert Sidney, quoted in E. K. Chambers, *The Elizabethan Stage*, 1, 322, n. 2.
2 A more detailed account of these and other discontinuities is given in the Note on the Text, pp. 65–8.

1  Henry V, an effigy in the Rood screen at York Minster, made in 1422–7, within five years of Henry's death. Despite some restoration, it is the most likely representation of the real Henry in existence (By kind permission of the Dean and Chapter of York Minster)

became England's king is one of the significant absences from public debate at this time. Once James was on the English throne, through several years around 1605 it became a major political issue, the cause of an early dispute between king and parliament which Shakespeare made use of in *King Lear*. But in 1599, before James did succeed to the English throne, the presence of four captains of Henry's army in France, with an Irish and a Scots company joining the English and Welsh, might easily have been read as a not particularly subtle piece of political prophecy. It was certainly an Elizabethan rewriting of English history. Holinshed notes the presence of Welsh as well as Scottish mercenaries fighting not for the English but for the French against Henry's army.[1] To unite the different domains of Britain into one army was both unhistorical and, in 1599, politically very suggestive. That possibility, together with the awkwardness of having a Scot called Jamy on stage after 1603, is considered at more length below. The use in the play of such a variety of dialect forms of English, like the uniquely large quantity of spoken French, is a related question. Some of these considerations are examined below.

Macmorris and Jamy do seem to be late inserts in the manuscript which was used to print the First Folio text. How late, though, and why they should be added only for the one scene, is a matter for some dispute. Claims have been made that these characters, along with the Choruses, were added after James came to the throne in 1603, possibly for the performance of the play at court in the 1604–5 Christmas revels. This is less than likely. If the Choric speeches had been prepared for a court performance, not only the praise of Essex but the Prologue's overt display of modesty about the theatre would have caused difficulties.

The Chorus, with its emphatic display of modesty about the capacity of the playhouse 'cockpit' to show the 'vasty fields of France', has prompted a lot of speculation about the date of the play's first performance and which playhouse it was written for. If early in 1599, the Prologue's 'wooden O' must have been the Curtain, which Shakespeare's company used while they waited for the Globe to be built. If later in 1599, it could have been the new Globe. The Chorus is either being modest about an inferior old playhouse, built as long ago as 1577, or mock-modest about the grand new Globe playhouse.[2] The Theatre, whose timbers provided the frame for the Globe, was pulled down after Christmas 1598, and the lease for the land in Southwark on which the Globe was to be constructed was signed on 21 February 1599. The builder of the Globe was allowed twenty-eight weeks in 1600 to build its rival, the Fortune, which suggests a similar period of time for the construction of the Globe. So even if it had a shorter building time because of its prefabricated timbers from the old Theatre, the Globe could hardly have opened much before midsummer 1599. Thomas Platter, a Swiss tourist, did see *Julius Caesar*, which was written very soon after *Henry V*, at the Globe on 15 September 1599. *As You Like It*, with its celebration of the seven ages of man quoting what is thought to have been the new playhouse's motto (*Totus mundus agit histrionem*,

---

1 See below, p. 29.
2 For a circumstantial account of the fraught financial conditions which accompanied the building of the Globe, see Andrew Gurr, 'Money or audiences: the impact of Shakespeare's Globe', *Theatre Notebook* 42 (1988), 3–14.

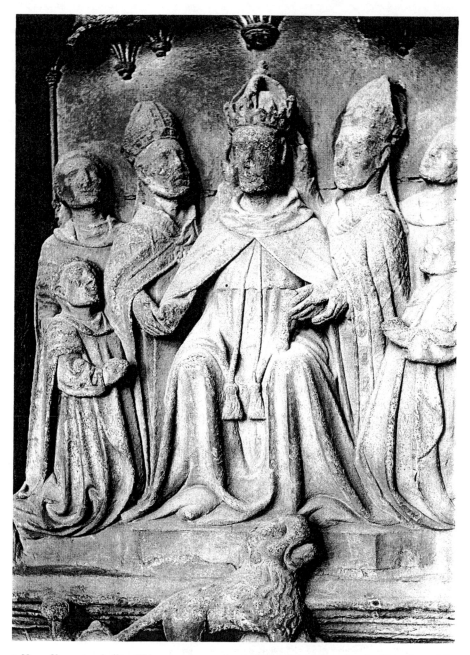

2  Henry V, a restored effigy of his coronation, on the north side of his chantry chapel at Westminster (The Dean and Chapter at Westminster Abbey)

or 'all the globe's a stage') has a good claim to be the first play definitely written for the Globe. We are unlikely ever to know for sure whether *Henry V*'s Prologue was written either to celebrate the opening or to lament the older venue. It might be better to relate the Chorus's insistent modesty about staging such a heroic subject to other questions about the oddly emphatic role of the Chorus as presenter of such a play.

### The coercive Chorus

The Shakespeare plays are not exactly abundant in choruses. Apart from the prologues to *Romeo and Juliet* and *Troilus and Cressida*, and the Ancient Gower of *Pericles*, there are only the opening Rumour painted with tongues and the apologetic Epilogue to *2 Henry IV*, and the prologue and epilogue and the other four choric prefaces to the five acts of *Henry V*. Jonson was a fellow-member of the company with Shakespeare when he made the Chamberlain's company mock its own Shakespearean repertoire in *Every Man Out of his Humour* in 1599, and later derided the use of choruses which waft you o'er the seas in a belated prologue to *Every Man In*.[1] We might speculate that it was Jonson who made Shakespeare promptly drop the practice. This may be so. It is easy to assume that Shakespeare could be overawed by his younger but more bellicose fellow-poet. But the insertion of Rumour and the Epilogue into *2 Henry IV* and the more extensive deployment of an eloquent presenter of the French war in *Henry V* were innovations, and their origin needs explaining more urgently than the brevity of their life. In different ways and perhaps for different reasons they seem to indicate discomfort with what the plays contained.

It is worth noting first the occasional, once-only nature of the *2 Henry IV* Epilogue, and of at least some parts of the chorus speeches in *Henry V*. Apologising for the Oldcastle mistake in the epilogue to the play in which he was banished was a transient requirement, and the company would hardly have gone on promising to return Sir John in the sequel once that play had been staged with nothing but a report of his death in it. *Henry V*'s Chorus, for all his magnificent verse, would also require some subsequent cutting, at least in the reference to Essex bringing rebellion broached on his sword, which was an acceptable prediction only between March and June of 1599, and became a distinct embarrassment by September of that year. Once he was put on trial for his misconduct in Ireland in 1600, any mention of him was dangerous, and after his execution in February 1601 suicidal. So the Chorus was written for his time and only for his time. He relates uniquely to the period when the play was first composed. And that raises some pressing questions about his uniquely coercive function.

It has been suggested that the Chorus was added to the play late, and that the Q text of 1600, which omits him, represents an earlier step in composition.[2] He does

1 *Every Man In His Humour*, ed. Herford and Simpson, III, 303.
2 For different theories about the function of the Chorus, see G. P. Jones, '*Henry V*: the Chorus and the audience', *S.Sur.* 31 (1978), 93–104; Eamon Grennan, 'This story shall the good man teach his son: *Henry V* and the art of history', *Papers on Language and Literature* 15 (1979), 370–82; Anthony Brennan, 'That within which passes show: the function of the Chorus in *Henry V*', *PQ* 58 (1979), 40–52; Lawrence Danson, '*Henry V*: King, Chorus, and critics', *SQ* 34 (1983), 27–47; Antony Hammond, '"It must be your

intrude on the story, ignoring the comic scenes so completely that generations of stage performances have felt obliged to reposition the first Eastcheap scene, Act 2, Scene 1, before the second Chorus, and some have done the same with Act 5, Scene 1, putting it in the immediate aftermath of Agincourt. But these features do not stand firm against the fact that the Choruses were in the manuscript prepared early in 1599, the text later printed in the First Folio. It is more likely that the Chorus was fitted to the play fairly early on, to strengthen a celebratory and patriotic reading, providing a means of coercing the audience into an emotionally undivided response to what the Chorus calls 'this star of England'.

The Chorus is certainly unique in Shakespeare in the way he does this. He operates not as a classical Nuntius but as a Prologue to each act. His opening speech ends with him describing himself as 'Prologue-like', a firm hint that he is in fact not an ordinary Prologue and that he will return to do the distinctive job of presenter before each of the succeeding acts. This he certainly does, and very eloquently. But one of the most peculiar features of his appearances is how frequently and consistently he whips up enthusiasm for his *mis*representation of what follows. The Prologue opens with the standard rhetorical trope of modesty about doing Henry's French spectacle on stage. We might expect a declaration that denies the possibility of staging spectacles to affright the air at Agincourt and speaks of imaginary horses and imaginary 'puissance' to be overstating its modesty and preparing us for some ambitious tries at achieving such a spectacle. In the event, the nearest the audience gets to a battle is Henry's speech rallying his retreating troops at Harfleur, a Chorus marked by gunfire, and drums beating the alarm. At Agincourt itself the only flourishing of swords is Ancient Pistol threatening the trembling M. Le Fer.

In varying degrees the events of each act belie the claims made by the Chorus that introduces it. The Chorus before Act 2 declares that 'honour's thought/Reigns solely in the breast of every man' in England (2.0.3–4), apart from the 'nest of hollow bosoms' (2.0.21). The act itself shows first the Eastcheap rogues and Pistol's boast that 'I shall sutler be unto the camp, and profits will accrue' (2.1.88–9), and then the Cambridge conspiracy. For Act 3 the Chorus invites us to imagine the fleet sailing to Harfleur, leaving England to be 'Guarded with grandsires, babies and old women' (3.0.20), despite the insistence at 1.2.214 that the nation's strength be divided into four, with only one quarter going to France, and the later complaint (4.3.16–18) about the small numbers at Agincourt. This Chorus promises glory, flourishing a linstock to fire a cannon, but the act then starts with the retreat from the breach at Harfleur and the failure of the renewed assault. Harfleur does not yield until the Dauphin says he cannot bring up his forces to relieve the siege in the fourth scene. The soldiers brawl amongst themselves, with Llewellyn beating the Eastcheap rogues to the battle and then picking a quarrel with Macmorris. Henry has the only honour in that act.

imagination then'": the Prologue and the plural text in *Henry V* and elsewhere', in *Fanned and Winnowed Opinions*, ed. John W. Mahon and Thomas A. Pendleton, 1987, pp. 133–50; and Sharon Tyler, 'Minding true things: the Chorus, the audience, and *Henry V*', in *The Theatrical Space*, Themes in Drama 9, ed. James Redmond, 1987, pp. 69–80.

3 Chorus speaking the Prologue standing front stage, in the centre of the yard. Drawing by C. Walter Hodges

The Chorus to Act 4 is the strangest deceiver of them all. He recounts the story of the night before Agincourt, echoing Holinshed's account of it, but adding to it above all that 'little touch of Harry in the night' (4.0.47) which revives the spirits of the English soldiers. Modestly, he echoes Sidney's *Apology*, published four years before, by mocking the 'four or five most vile and ragged foils' (4.0.50) and the 'brawl ridiculous' with which the glory of Agincourt will be represented on stage. In the event neither the little touch nor any brawl more ridiculous than Pistol's with Le Fer is shown on stage. Henry, after joking with his nobles, and hearing a better joke than his own from Erpingham about lying like a king, borrows Erpingham's cloak and goes in disguise for his encounters with Pistol and the three plain soldiers. That is hardly the way to cheer anyone up with a kingly appearance.

To these misrepresentations of the stage action in the fourth Chorus can be added the two other choric speeches which pretend that the Eastcheap rogues do not exist and cause some confusion as a result. The second Chorus tells the audience it is being transported to Southampton, immediately before the first Eastcheap scene back in London. The fifth Chorus describes all the events of the years after Agincourt, Henry's return to England and his welcome as victor in London, the visit of the Holy Roman Emperor to London, and Henry's subsequent return to France. But the act that follows opens with Llewellyn ready to repay the debt he owed Pistol from Agincourt, in a scene which ends with Pistol declaring that he will return with his cudgel-marks to England swearing he got them as wounds in the French wars. The Chorus's announcement of the events of the five years between Agincourt and the Treaty of Troyes breaks into the games belonging to the post-battle frolics.

The Chorus is a great painter of pictures, but they are never the pictures shown on stage. As Sharon Tyler puts it, 'for nearly four hundred years audiences have been seeing what is described rather than what is staged.'[1] The Choric poetry is so persuasive that the realities of the story seem to register faintly or wrongly in the mind afterwards. In Shakespeare's own time, of course, the Choric imperatives urging the audience to imagine the spectacle were certainly aimed at willingly receptive minds. In a sermon that Stephen Gosson preached at Paul's Cross on 7 May 1598 he describes the common response to spectacle in Shakespearean amphitheatres: 'in publike Theaters, when any notable shew passeth over the stage, the people arise in their seates, & stand upright with delight and eagernesse to view it well'.[2] That sort of expectation was what the Chorus in *Henry V* worked on. The fact that the stage did not meet such expectations, and yet the play is still thought of as an epic spectacle of military heroics and leadership, is the highest possible tribute to the Chorus's success as presenter. The Chorus is responsible for Olivier's and Branagh's cinema images of epic battle scenes that are not in the play.

Why, though, was the Chorus needed, when he so positively contradicts the stage actions? The one thing the Chorus does most consistently is to praise Henry. The question raised by that is why the play itself should give such ambiguous support to this glorification. Some parts of the story are altered from the sources to support the Chorus, notably the elimination of the tactic with the archers protected by stakes at Agincourt, which Holinshed makes much of and which the earlier stage-play *The Famous Victories* mentions twice.[3] Victory at Agincourt comes from Henry's morale-boosting, not from his military tactics. But the play introduces or re-emphasises other features that do not support the Chorus, most notably Henry's order to kill the prisoners. This is not mentioned in *The Famous Victories*, while Shakespeare's other main source, Holinshed, gives Henry two possible motives for his order, of which Shakespeare presents only the worse. Holinshed notes both the risk of a counter-attack by the French and the attack

---

1 *Ibid*, p. 76.
2 Stephen Gosson, *The Trumpet of Warre, A Sermon preached at Paules Crosse the seventh of Maie 1598*, C7ᵛ.
3 See Appendix 1 and Appendix 2.

on the English baggage-train, which may have led Henry to give his order in retaliation. In the play Henry gives the order the moment he hears the off-stage trumpet sounding a rally. The revenge motive is attributed to him subsequently and mistakenly by the innocent Gower.

Even more to the point than this modification of the sources is the addition of the lengthy debate with the soldiers before the battle, about the justice of the war, and Henry's subsequent soliloquy of complaint. There is no precedent for this either in the earlier plays or in the Chronicles. What causes these adjustments to the famous story, and the introduction of the cloaking Chorus, must have been some rethinking of the story, and most obviously of the Henry who has grown into this conquering role through the two preceding plays, *1* and *2 Henry IV*.

It is notable that the Chorus which ends *Henry V* makes no mention of Henry's youth. The last lines of that play in fact revert not to the Falstaff story but all the way back to the early Henry VI plays to validate this play. The English nobles after Henry's death

> lost France and made his England bleed,
> Which oft our stage hath shown – and for their sake,
> In your fair minds let this acceptance take.

'Their sake' for which we are begged to approve *Henry V* refers not to the English lords who lost France but to the early plays. The first three of the current tetralogy are completely ignored by the Chorus. In the play itself there is little reference either, except for the death of Falstaff and one reminder to God by Henry in his prayer before Agincourt about his penitence over Richard II's death. The audience is even invited by the sanctimonious Archbishop in 1.1. to regard this Henry as having undergone a conversion like the prodigal son's, a miraculous rebirth from evil ways to good. That is the view of Henry presented in *The Famous Victories*, a play which follows the full syndrome of prodigal son behaviour. Its Prince Henry starts by actually initiating the robbery at Gad's Hill, promising his companion 'Ned' that he can be Lord Chief Justice, playing at robberies with 'Jockey', or John Oldcastle, a companion of his riots, boxing the Justice's ear, and when put in prison for it protesting in high arrogance that it is no way to treat a prince. His conversion there comes suddenly and totally in his confrontation with his father on his deathbed. He then promptly banishes his low-life companions and leads England straight to glory at Agincourt and marriage with Katherine. This model career, idle prince converted into industrious king, a format popular in apprentice moral tales and plays, is plainly set out in the early play.

Shakespeare presents his idle prince differently. In *1 Henry IV* he shows Hal refusing to fall for Falstaff's temptation to become a thief, only joining the Gad's Hill exploit when Poins proposes the double game of robbing the robbers. At the end of that scene, only the second in the play and the first in which he appears, Hal declares that he knows just what he is doing. He will make use of Falstaff as a cloud to hide his sun, and rise the more gloriously as a result. By this statement he is made, explicitly and from the outset, no prodigal. He is an entirely different character from the prodigal son of the conventional and populist stories current in the 1590s, which emphasised not the Christian love of the forgiving father but the moral repentance of the battered son wandering on the primrose path. The trouble with that rewriting was that it ran into Falstaff.[1]

The first part of Shakespeare's *Henry IV* was set up explicitly for the more or less simultaneous disposal of the twin clouds of 'riot and dishonour' that darken the brow of Henry IV's young Harry. The father complains of these equal clouds in contrasting him with the other young Harry, Hotspur, in the opening scene. Whatever made Shakespeare decide to postpone the banishment of riotous Falstaff from the first play to its sequel, it was a decision that grew some complicating tendrils. The sub-plot of Part 1 turned into the main plot of Part 2, with the consequent inversion of the serious and comic lines of the original plot. The reconciliation of son with father became a two-step operation, making the combat against Hotspur at Shrewsbury a false climax and the death-bed scene more like a reprise of the old prodigal son scene than Henry's own plan for a rising-sun scene. In the two plays as we have them the sun rises in separate steps with the dying king, with the Lord Chief Justice and Henry's brothers, and finally with the banishment of Falstaff. Through all of Falstaff's scenes in the second play, in Eastcheap and in Gloucestershire, he is shielded from Hal. They only meet twice throughout the play, and for the first meeting Hal is disguised most of the time as a tapster. Falstaff has the play to himself, with the result that he throws an exceptionally long cloud. Between the announcement that Hal will overthrow the 'unyoked humour of your idleness' and the actual banishment run almost all of two plays, twice what the material was originally designed for.

This has little effect in the long run. Hal duly becomes Henry, the star of England. But the length of the run does have an effect on what has been called his 'opaque self'.[2] When it takes twice as long to dismiss riot as dishonour, the personality under scrutiny takes on a rather different character. Shakespeare had already made use of an 'opaque self', the personality whose motives are inscrutable, on whom it is impossible to pin easy moral labels, still less judgements, in *Richard II*. Henry's father as Bullingbrook never betrays any human greed or ambition, never seems human at all. He plays an inscrutable part, never admitting that he has any ambition for the crown that lay in his path. The acting, the histrionics, are all Richard's. His son is given a long history of play-acting in the Henry IV plays. He enters the 'star of England' role with a record which makes all his actions self-conscious acts of camouflage. The opaque self is made into overt role-playing.

Henry the actor through the two earlier plays learns the impossibility of establishing an honest relationship with anyone. His friends, from Falstaff through Poins to Francis the drawer, all live in expectation of profiting from him in one way or another. His brothers, like the Lord Chief Justice, fear him and his power. His enemies, like Hotspur,

1 For one interpretation of the evidence for the 'remaking' of the Henry IV plays, see Giorgio Melchiori's edition of *2 Henry IV*, New Cambridge, 1989.
2 For the concept of the 'opaque self' see for instance Anne Barton, 'The king disguised: Shakespeare's *Henry V* and the Comical History', in *The Triple Bond: Plays, Mainly Shakespearean, in Performance*, ed. Joseph G. Price, University Park, Pennsylvania, 1975, pp. 92–117, p. 102; and John D. Cox, *Shakespeare and the Dramaturgy of Power*, Princeton, 1989, p. 109.

scorn him for his personal repute and hate him for political reasons. He learns that intimate friendship is impossible. If confirmation that he can trust nobody is needed once he is king, in *Henry V*, the case of Scroop offers in personal terms what Canterbury and the nobles have already offered in the more courtly terms of political self-interest. Henry's choice of role rules the man, and isolates him.

The end of *2 Henry IV* shows the loss of humanity as it retreats into the role-playing of the opaque self through, inevitably, Henry's final speech to Falstaff. It confirms his role and his acceptance of his isolation in it. And one last twitch, one final teeter on the brink of human weakness, appears even then. As he lays on Falstaff the trite moralisings of his new role, he takes one step too far:

> I know thee not, old man, fall to thy prayers . . .
> Make less thy body hence and more thy grace,
> Leave gormandising, know the grave doth gape
> For thee thrice wider than for other men.

But as Falstaff lurches forward to pick up this invitation to more badinage, he catches himself.

> Reply not to me with a fool-born jest,
> Presume not that I am the thing I was,
> For God doth know, so shall the world perceive
> That I have turned away my former self.[1]

The new sun has risen. Henry now has to act the part of the good king, an Alexander among his captains. His three subsequent pieces of play-acting (to the conspirators in 2.2, to Pistol and the common soldiers when he is disguised in 4.1, and to Williams in 4.7 and 4.8, in pursuit of the joke with the gloves), are all explorations of the limited freedom he can enjoy when he pretends not to be his new self.

The Chorus is present in *Henry V* to advertise the new sun, the shining Burbage who died as Richard II and rose again as Prince Hal. That seems clear enough. But we need to ask why the Chorus should be introduced as a gloss on this shining sun. What is there in the body of the play that the Chorus has to misrepresent? Language and image clusters are always a strong marker in Shakespeare, and three particular sets of language may provide some clues.

The Jerusalem theme rides through all four of the plays in the second tetralogy. The choice between going to Jerusalem as militant Christian crusader or peaceful Christian pilgrim is there throughout. The first test of the opaque self is Henry IV's urging to his son to take his nobles on a crusade to busy giddy minds with foreign quarrels rather than let them fester in civil broils at home.[2] The opaque Henry IV himself ends *Richard II* by proposing to wipe Richard's blood from his soul with a penitent pilgrimage to the Holy Land, and opens the next play with a scheme to take his nobles on a crusade there instead. His death in the Jerusalem Chamber at Westminster is an ironic confirmation of the hollowness of his own promises. His son ends *Henry V* with an equally hollow

1  *2H4*, 5.5.43–54.
2  *2H4*, 4.2.325–43.

proposal to send his own son on a crusade to take the Turk by the beard. The second Henriad is set in this double frame of the just crusade and the penitent pilgrimage.

Inside this doubled frame in the final play is set the doubtfully just war against his neighbours, with which Henry busies the giddy minds of his nobles and common soldiers. His opaque self conceals awareness of his responsibility for this multi-motivated act, but the imagery is less ready to conceal the implications. The war is imaged as dog-hearted soldiers raping the daughters of France, an image which culminates in Henry's own depiction of himself as a plain dog-soldier raping Katherine from her father. And this story is set in an image of the play as an assembly of mockeries.

The dogs of war and their assaults on cities and daughters form an image running through the play up to 4.5 and recur with peculiar echoes in Henry's wooing of Katherine in 5.2. At the outset the Chorus gives us Harry behaving like the god of war with Bellona's leash of three hunting-hounds, Famine, Sword and Fire, at his heels. Images of soldiers as dogs run through the play up to Agincourt. The danger from Scotland is a matter of both 'coursing snatchers' (1.2.143), and of 'the dog' (218) who will 'worry' the English. Pistol regularly calls his enemies dogs, starting with Nym at 2.1.35 (where Nym is a 'prick-eared cur of Iceland', a lap-dog straight out of Holinshed) and 59, a 'hound of Crete'. In 2.2.80 the conspirators are hunting-dogs turning on their masters. At 2.4.50 the English kings have been 'fleshed' on the French – have tasted their blood. In his Harfleur speech ('Once more into the breach') Henry calls the English soldiers greyhounds in the slips, fast hunting-dogs ready to be unleashed in pursuit of their prey. By 3.4.11–14 they are fleshed, having tasted blood, and will range 'in liberty of bloody hand' and with 'conscience wide as hell' after the French virgins. Even the French acknowledge the English doggedness, the Dauphin calling them 'coward dogs', and again before Agincourt, when they are described not as hunting dogs but mastiffs, another passage lifted straight out of Holinshed.[1] At 4.5.16 Bourbon (the Dauphin in the Folio text) admits worse: that the English soldiers are of quite the wrong blood for their bastardising of the French. To him English victory means for the French nobles that 'by a slave, no gentler than my dog,/His fairest daughter is contaminate' (4.5.16–17).

This last claim against the English soldiery has one striking implication which reflects on Henry in his wooing of Katherine in Act 5. Behind it lies Psalm 22.20: 'Deliver my soul from the sword, my darling from the power of the dog', quoted by Canterbury at 1.2.218. Whereas the biblical commentators usually took the 'darling' to be the human soul, there seems little doubt that Shakespeare felt it applied equally well to the real daughters of French cities ransacked by English soldiers. In Act 5 the French king twice equates Henry's besieging and havocking of French cities to his conquest of the king's daughter. Henry, says the French king, sees French cities 'perspectively, the cities turned into a maid, for they are all girdled with maiden walls that war hath never entered' (5.2.286–8). Since Henry's language of love to Katherine has been entirely a matter of 'plain soldier' conquest, and of besieging her (especially 5.2.161–3), the

---

1 See Appendix 2, and Valerie Traub, 'Prince Hal's Falstaff: positioning psychoanalysis and the female reproductive body', *SQ* 40 (1989), 456–74, esp. pp. 466–9.

images of war as sex and sex as war understandably converge. Fighting is offered as sex by Henry in his speech to the defenders of Harfleur at 3.4.7 and 11–14, where Harfleur is unequivocally female (3.4.9). The same language appears at 5.2.291–3, where Henry explicitly relates Katherine to a besieged French 'maiden city'. Henry's conquest of Katherine is of a piece with his successful sieges of the French cities.

That is also of a piece with Henry's general role as a conqueror. As he says, 'I love France so well that I will not part with a village of it' (5.2.161). Henry in Act 5 is a conqueror who can afford to play the part of the plain soldier. With his soldiery and his leashed dogs of war he has won. The French king's darling daughter is not to be delivered from the sword and the dog of Psalm 22.

The Chorus's own language is distinctive in several ways. For the most part he uses the same vocabulary as Henry himself in his public orations. But he also speaks with the double tongue of *syllepsis* and *antanaclasis*. These double uses are not so much the redeployment of familiar words in new contexts, as Henry does with 'mocks' in response to the Dauphin's tennis balls in 1.2, but usual words that the Chorus employs in new and unpredictable presentations. Often they involve not so much transferred epithets as reversed expectations, a deliberate confusion of routine usage. In 1.0.13–15, for instance, the 'wooden O' of the theatre's circuit of polygonal wooden scaffolding becomes a cask, the neatly equivalent image of a barrel, which like the theatre has a round or polygonal wooden shape approximating to a circle. But this wooden cask then immediately becomes a soldier's casque, a helmet at Agincourt. The same reversal happens a few lines later when the Chorus describes itself as not a Prologue but 'prologue-like', and prays not as a humble servant (as in *Twelfth Night* 3.1.95 or the 'humble author' of the *2 Henry 4* epilogue), but for 'humble patience' from the audience. That, if a transferred epithet, is transferred with some malignancy. The same thing happens in the second Chorus, where the sword hidden with crowns, like the one in the comic by-plot of *The Famous Victories*, gets covered not with real crowns but 'crowns imperial', the country flowers specified by Perdita (see 2.0.9–10, note). The lexis of the Chorus is markedly ambivalent. And yet it is also very close to Henry's own. Five distinctive words, three of them only recorded in *Henry V*, are particularly notable. There are nouns with rare suffixes: 'portage' and 'sternage'; building terms: 'jutty' and 'abutting'; and elaborated monosyllables: 'vasty'. Any of these might be used by either speaker. The first and third are Henry's, the second and fourth the Chorus's, and the fifth is used by both of them. The Chorus consistently uses the same oratorical language as Henry, his idiosyncratic lexis and his elevated and exhortatory syntax, for much the same purpose. But where Henry uses it to excite his soldiers and to frighten the Governor of Harfleur, the Chorus uses it on the audience.

The close of the Chorus to Act 4 suggests that spectators at the play should be 'minding true things by what their mockeries be', a resonant statement to introduce the Agincourt scenes with. The word 'mock' occurs seventeen times in all through the play. It starts in a rush of *antanaclasis* and *syllepsis* in 1.2.281–6, where Henry uses it five times to stress how the Dauphin's 'mock' with his gift of tennis balls will be thrown back at him:

tell the pleasant prince this mock of his
Hath turned his balls to gun-stones, and his soul
Shall stand sore chargèd for the wasteful vengeance
That shall fly with them; for many a thousand widows
Shall this his mock mock out of their dear husbands,
Mock mothers from their sons, mock castles down.

It recurs right through to the final scene between Henry and Katherine. She protests that 'Your majesty shall mock at me' over the English conquest of France (102), and he asks Kate to 'mock me mercifully' in her closet (184), 'the rather, gentle princess, because I love thee cruelly', a neatly ambiguous sentiment for a 'plain soldier' who sees love as besieging maiden cities. The mockery of true things on stage in this form, as the Chorus tells us, is indeed something to mind.

## Context and sources

By the time he came to write the last play of his sequence about English history Shakespeare should have known exactly what he wanted to show in his mirror of all English kings. The result, as many critics have noted, is an opaque figure.[1] It is impossible to decide what generated this – whether the writing of the earlier plays in the sequence, or the rather mixed evidence from the historical sources, or other political factors in the 1590s – but it is important to hold these issues in mind while thinking about the play.

For the material facts Shakespeare was still bound by his copy of the 1587 edition of Holinshed's *Chronicles*. He was more reluctant than other writers of history plays in his time to falsify the known accounts, and closely followed Holinshed's story, sometimes versifying the precise words of his source, and only telescoping events for the sake of dramatic form, as he had done with the Northumberland rebellions of the Henry IV plays. He also used the earlier staged versions. They had taken their story from the old Chronicle of Hall rather than Holinshed, and Hall seeps into Shakespeare's play where he remembered the staged versions.[2] The general outline of the play, too, with its telescoping of everything between Agincourt and Troyes, came from the earlier stage plays, if the 1598 text of *The Famous Victories* is a good indication of what they contained.[3] But at least some of their falsifications of history he rejected. He diminished their elevation of the Dauphin into Henry's antagonist, for instance, which was a feature both of the play Nashe mentions in 1592 and of *The Famous Victories*. In *3H6* he made the Earl of March say that Henry had 'revelled in the heart of France / And tamed the king, and made the dauphin stoop' (2.2.150–1), which reflects the final act as it is shown in *The Famous Victories*. But from Holinshed he knew that the Dauphin who was dispossessed of his regal inheritance by the Treaty of Troyes, which ends the play, was not the same man as the sender of the tennis balls. So for his own *Henry V* Shakespeare

1 See above, p. 11, n. 2.
2 The most conspicuous of the memories of Hall to survive in Shakespeare's text is his 'tunne' of tennis balls where Holinshed calls it a 'barrell'. *The Famous Victories* calls it a 'tunne'.
3 For details about Shakespeare's use of *The Famous Victories*, see Appendix 1.

removed him from the final scene. In all the earlier versions the Dauphin makes his submission to Henry at the end in person, and in *The Famous Victories* the insult of the tennis balls bounces back several times, most forcefully at Agincourt.

Because of the patriotic appeal in 1599 of the battles and victories of Henry V, Shakespeare was on much safer ground than he had been with the preceding plays. *Richard II* must have made him nervous, since the part of it that concerned Richard's deposition was cut from the three editions printed in Elizabeth's lifetime. John Hayward had to remove the dedication to Essex from his book about the same piece of English history when it was published in February or March 1599. He was imprisoned in the Tower for his book in July 1600.[1] *1 Henry IV* had drawn a different sort of trouble from the new Lord Chamberlain in 1596 for its misuse of his ancestor Oldcastle.[2] Michael Drayton, writing *Englands Heroicall Epistles* over the same period, 1596–9, covered much the same ground as Shakespeare's history plays but confined them largely to romantic exchanges. Drayton's Epistles between Richard II and his queen Isabel seem to suggest that Richard's deposition was known to be an embarrassment. But by 1599 for Shakespeare the earlier versions of Henry's career as king, prominent on the stage since the days of the Queen's Men in the 1580s, must have made it a safe and a popular subject in a noisily militaristic decade. Drayton, who later wrote both a ballad and a long poem about the glory of Agincourt, clearly saw it as an easier subject. Nevertheless, in working on it, Shakespeare seems not to have found it so easy.

There are multitudes of reasons why this should be so. They range from the possibly unpremeditated extension of the story of the young prince Hal from one into two plays, which intensified the questions about his real personality and the influences on his conduct, to a growing weariness with the militarism of the time. It is only possible here to outline a few of these possible reasons. Two in particular seem worth giving some attention. One is the pair of dynastic problems, the first made explicit in the rehearsal of the question of Salic Law in 1.2, and the second suppressed from the dramatisation of the Cambridge conspiracy in 2.2. The other reason is Henry's order to kill the prisoners at Agincourt, which is given both an overt and a camouflaging treatment. What is suppressed in the writing of this play is potentially as revealing as what is proclaimed.

By the 1540s one major lesson from the long dynastic conflict in England called the Wars of the Roses was evident: primogeniture, inheritance by the eldest son, was no secure guarantee of a clear title to the succession. From the time when the childless Richard II's cousin claimed his crown down to the gamble between two equal claimants at the battle of Bosworth,[3] the question of title to rule came under pressure from the various strong right arms that contested it. Henry VIII looked for an insurance against

---

1 See Marvyn James, *Society, Politics and Culture: Studies in Early Modern England*, Cambridge, 1986, chapter 9, and J. Leeds Barroll, 'A New History for Shakespeare and his Time', *SQ* 39 (1988), 441–64, especially pp. 449–53.

2 See Gary Taylor, 'The fortunes of Oldcastle', *S.Sur.* 38 (1985), 85–100.

3 After his victory at the end of *Richard III* Richmond declares that at last the dynastic issue will be closed by his marriage to Elizabeth of York on the grounds that the two of them, now that Richard is dead, are 'the true succeeders of each royal house' (5.5.30).

such questions by making a will, supplementing primogeniture as a rule of nature with his personal expectations over the succession. His will laid down that first his son should succeed, and then his sister's children, the line of Mary Queen of Scots. It disqualified his daughters Mary and Elizabeth for illegitimacy. Parliament restored them ahead of the Scottish line in 1544. Such changes called the law of succession into question once more. By the 1570s, with Elizabeth still unmarried and nearing forty years of age, it became a cause for urgent concern. Security demanded an heir with a clear title. And then, when in 1578 she started dallying with the possibility of marrying the French king's brother, France's Salic Law denying succession through the female line emerged as a boiling issue. A combination of childlessness and what John Knox called the 'monstrous regiment of women' had called primogeniture into question in terms of gender. Now the threat of Elizabeth marrying a French prince, and the likelihood that her children would suffer the imposition of Salic Law to block their chances of inheritance, threatened England's dynastic security.

In 1578 the Duc d'Alençon came to London to offer himself for Elizabeth. He was the younger brother of the childless Henry III, and although himself a Catholic was looked on by the Protestant Huguenots in France as their leader. The marriage seemed to offer an intriguing prospect for the alliance of Protestant England with the Protestant half of France. The difficulties were, first, Alençon's Catholicism and, secondly, the dynastic implications. If Elizabeth married Alençon and had his children, the legal position that Henry V secured in 1420 with his marriage to the daughter of the French king would operate in reverse. Elizabeth's heirs would become French, and the English crown would go with them. That evidently was not the way Elizabeth herself saw it. She had a precedent in the marriage of her elder sister Mary to Philip of Spain, which had not taken Mary off the English throne. But then, Mary had no children, and an heir for Elizabeth was the crucial question for the English in 1578. It became a major plank in the case against the Alençon marriage, and Salic Law was its heartwood.

In August 1579 John Stubbs, a puritan divine, published an octavo pamphlet entitled 'THE DISCOVERIE OF A GAPING GULF WHEREINTO ENGLAND IS LIKE TO BE SWALLOWED by an other French mariage, if the Lord forbid not the banes, by letting her Majestie see the sin and punishment thereof'. A thousand copies were printed. Elizabeth immediately issued a proclamation banning its sale or possession, and Stubbs along with three others had his right hand chopped off. Despite the ban, more printed copies have survived, along with some manuscripts copying the printed text, than of less controversial works. It was widely read. The Earl of Northampton issued a formal reply to Stubbs,[1] but by then the point had been taken. Salic Law now made primogeniture as a law for inheritance even less secure. One almost immediate consequence was a famous judgement in law, based on a test-case that ran from 1579 to 1581. It established that inheritance by will took precedence over inheritance by primogeniture. Shelley's Case, as the ruling became known, at once began to determine all matters of inheritance. It

---

1 Lloyd E. Berry (ed.), *John Stubbs's 'Gaping Gulf' with Letters and Other Relevant Documents*, Charlottesville, 1968, reprints Northampton's sharp and elaborate reply, which has survived in three manuscript copies. The reply, although it goes through the history of the English and French dynastic disputes and the issue of Salic Law (pp. 158–9), avoids naming it.

was in fact not officially replaced as the law until 1926.[1] Stubbs's pamphlet, the Alençon marriage debate, and Shelley's Case effectively foreclosed on primogeniture as the first principle of dynastic succession. And Salic Law was part of the marriage question. It lay close to the heart of Stubbs's case against the marriage.

Stubbs first argued that it would be bad if Elizabeth married a Catholic, not only for Protestant England but for 'the poore orphane churches in France' (b2ʳ). Alençon was an untrustworthy leader of 'that great armie of protestants'. France was an 'alien enimy', Alençon 'a most illcome guest'. Elizabeth should 'chuse a king from emong thyne owne brethren'. Stubbs went on to rehearse 'the auncient hurts that Englande have received through royall intermariages with that nation', listing Edward II, whose marriage generated the English claim to the French crown, and all the other cases from the Hundred Years War. 'Even the last mariages we made with France were lyke unhappy to the end. Henry the fift that noble king had the alliance of Katherin daughter to Charles the seaventh of Fraunce, and after had possession of Fraunce, first by right of descent and mariage, then by conquest of sword, and lastly by covenant agreed with king Charles and his peeres. yet coulde he none otherwise hold theyr love, but having theyr necks under his yoke' (c5ᵛ). Their son Henry VI lost France and eventually lost England and his life as a result of his marriage to a French princess. All foreign marital alliances, Stubbs concludes, are unhappy, and especially marriages with the French.

He then goes on to examine the consequences if Elizabeth's marriage to Alençon were to produce any children. Elizabeth was by then forty-six, but English hopes for an heir evidently sprang eternal. Alençon, as 'brother of childles Fraunce', might become the next French king. This would make it a much more dangerous marriage than Mary's to the king of Spain. If Elizabeth had only a girl child, the French husband would

have her into Fraunce and so eyther adjoyne this land to Fraunce, or mary her to some French or other stranger at hys lyking: and all this whyle we never the neere possession of our old right in Fraunce whych we so much desired, for the Salique lawe barres hyr quite. (c7ᵛ)

Elizabeth would have no power in France because of the Salic Law. Her children would be unable to rule either. In an extended discussion of the dynastic consequences if Elizabeth had only a daughter, or only a son, or a daughter and a son, Stubbs makes his case for Salic Law having always been the great impediment to English claims to rule France, and now the great danger should England be ruled by France. After the religious difference, Salic Law as France's traditional defence against the English claim to the French crown is Stubbs's main argument against the Alençon marriage.

To Stubbs, Alençon was a serpent, 'this stinging straunger of France, we muste keepe warme in our bosom'. Elizabeth, who called him her frog, did not pursue the marriage very ardently, though she wept when she heard of his death in the Low Countries in 1584. What knowledge Shakespeare may have gained of this story we do not know. The Alençon who is mentioned as fighting Henry hand-to-hand at Agincourt is specified in Holinshed. The fact that Shakespeare himself lost his son in 1596, leaving two daughters

---

1 See W. S. Holdsworth, *An Historical Introduction to the Land Law*, Oxford, 1927, pp. 53–5.

as his heirs, is incidental. But Stubbs's pamphlet did help to lodge the Salic Law firmly in English consciousness. It became a well-known grievance. Hall's chronicle spent several pages dismissing it as a false medieval concoction. Robert Dallington's *The View of France*, published in 1604 but written before Shakespeare's play in 1598, claimed that 'As for the [Law Salique], they would needes make the world beleeve that it is of great antiquitie, wherewith they very wrongfully tromped the heires of *Edward* the third, of their enjoying this Crowne of *France*, which to them is rightly descended by his Mother, and whose claime is still good, were the English sword well whetted to cut the Labels of the Law' (E3ʳ). He adds that it was invented by Philip le Long in 1321, a different inventor from Hall's culprit.

The law of inheritance was high in people's consciousness after Shelley's Case. In its wake Salic Law became an evident case of injustice, the narrowest interpretation of an old law, one that the English could now scorn. Of Henry V's three claims to France, specified by Stubbs as descent, conquest and covenant, the first was validated by the denial of Salic Law. Agincourt assured the second. And the third was strengthened by Shelley's Case with its endorsement of the right to bequeath a title by will, as the French King Charles did when he signed the Treaty of Troyes, rather than by the old law of primogeniture. Shakespeare's play gives equal emphasis, one after the other, to the three claims.

The best account of what Shakespeare suppressed over the first of them, the dynastic issue, is in *Sir John Oldcastle*.[1] This was a play commissioned from four authors in the autumn of 1599 by Philip Henslowe, who ran the rival company to Shakespeare's at the Rose on Bankside. It was designed as a corrective to the Globe company's use of Oldcastle (Henslowe records a payment 'as a gefte'[2] which may have been an incentive to get it on stage). It certainly rubbed in the Chamberlain's Men's hasty change of his name to Falstaff, for which they had apologised in the Epilogue to *2 Henry IV*. The prologue to the new play asserted that 'It is no pampered glutton we present,/ Nor aged Councellor to youthfull sinne,/ But one, whose vertue shone above the rest,/ A valiant Martyr.' Oldcastle is represented not as a clown but as the Lollard martyr, enemy of the Catholic Church and loyal friend of the king that Foxe's *Acts and Monuments* made him.

Act 3 of *Oldcastle* launched a specific corrective to *Henry V* by setting out the lineage issue behind the Cambridge conspiracy that Shakespeare dramatised in 2.2. It begins

> *Enter Earle of Cambridge, Lord Scroope, Gray, and*
> *Chartres the French factor.*

SCROOP. Once more my Lord of Cambridge make rehersal,
    How you do stand intiteled to the Crowne,
    The deeper shall we print it in our mindes,
    And every man the better be resolv'de,
    When he perceives his quarrel to be just.

---

1 For a detailed account of this play, see *A Critical Edition of '1 Sir John Oldcastle'*, ed. Jonathan Rittenhouse, New York and London, 1984.
2 *Henslowe's Diary*, ed. Foakes and Rickert, Cambridge, 1961, p. 126.

CAM. Then thus Lord Scroope, sir Thomas Gray, & you
　　　Mounsieur de Chartres, agent for the French,
　　　This Lionell Duke of Clarence, as I said,
　　　Third sonne of Edward (Englands King) the third
　　　Had issue Phillip his sole daughter and heyre,
　　　Which Phillip afterwards was given in marriage,
　　　To Edmund Mortimer the Earle of March,
　　　And by him had a son cald Roger Mortimer,
　　　Which Roger likewise had of his discent,
　　　Edmund, Roger, Anne, and Elianor,
　　　Two daughters and two sonnes, but those three
　　　Dide without issue, Anne that did survive,
　　　And now was left her fathers onely heyre,
　　　My fortune was to marry, being too
　　　By my grandfather of King Edwardes line,
　　　So of his sirname, I am calde you know,
　　　Richard Plantagenet, my father was,
　　　Edward the Duke of Yorke, and son and heyre
　　　To Edmund Langley, Edward the third's first sonne.
SCROOP. So that it seems your claime comes by your wife,
　　　As lawful heyre to Roger Mortimer,
　　　The son of Edmund, which did marry Phillip
　　　Daughter and heyre to Lyonell Duke of Clarence.
CAM. True, for this Harry, and his father both
　　　Harry the first, as plainely doth appeare,
　　　Are false intruders, and usurp the Crowne,
　　　For when yong Richard was at Pomfret slaine,
　　　In him the title of prince Edward dide,
　　　That was the eldest of king Edwards sonnes:
　　　William of Hatfield, and their second brother,
　　　Death in his nonage had before bereft:
　　　So that my wife deriv'd from Lionell,
　　　Third sonne unto king Edward, ought proceede,
　　　And take possession of the Diademe
　　　Before this Harry, or his father king,
　　　Who fetcht their title but from Lancaster,
　　　Fourth of that royall line. And being thus,
　　　What reason ist but she should have her right?
SCROOPE. I am resolv'de our enterprise is just.
GRAY. Harry shall die, or else resigne his crowne.

This laborious account confirms that the Cambridge conspiracy of *Henry V* was a renewal of Northumberland's long campaigns in Shakespeare's Henry IV plays, the rebellion which aimed to put Edmund Mortimer, the fifth Earl of March, on the throne in place of the Lancastrian line of Bullingbrook. Descent through the third son of the eldest son of Edward III took precedence over descent through the fourth son of the eldest son.[1]

1 For the genealogical issues concerning Henry IV's acquisition of the crown from Richard II, see the New Cambridge *Richard II*, pp. 20, 28. On the incomplete acknowledgement of Cambridge's claim to the crown, see Karl P. Wentersdorf, 'The conspiracy of silence in *Henry V*', *SQ* 27 (1976), 264–87.

Except for one enigmatic statement in his confession, Shakespeare's Cambridge makes no mention of any of this, and nobody else in the play acknowledges it either. He puts the point only by a negative:

> For me, the gold of France did not seduce
> Although I did admit it as a motive
> The sooner to effect what I intended.                                    (2.2.150–2)

Even the fact that Cambridge was younger brother to the York who dies at Agincourt is omitted from Shakespeare's play, although it is specified in Holinshed. Since York's identity as the Aumerle of *Richard II* is also omitted, a minor irrelevance given the exclusively symbolic function of York's valour in the battle, that may simply have been streamlining, polishing out irrelevant details. But the elimination of an alternative dynastic claim to the English crown in favour of Henry's claim to the French crown cannot have just been streamlining.

There are many possible reasons for this additional opacity in the play. The most positive one is the way it helped to narrow the focus of Henry's titular claim to France. Stubbs's three justifications for Henry's claim are presented one after the other in the play. The genealogical claim is rehearsed in the first act, the conquest is completed in the fourth, and the covenant, whereby the marriage left the French crown to Henry's heirs, is completed in the final act. Undue emphasis on the doubtful nature of Henry's claim to the English crown, which itself was the basis for his claim to the French, would have redoubled the other doubts that are discreetly implied in the first act.

Actually, in the play as a whole, each of the three claims is put in doubt even before it is properly established. The Archbishop's expedient reason for urging the genealogical claim on Henry is presented in 1.1, before he makes the case against Salic Law in 1.2. His misuse of Erasmus's parable of the beehive underlines the point (the pacifist Erasmus had argued that in the kingdom of the bees the leader alone had no sting, and never left the hive. To him, as to Saint Augustine, any attack on a neighbouring kingdom was no better than 'brigandage').[1] Other features of the questionable character of Henry's conquest are dealt with below. Most pointedly, the third claim, the marriage and covenant signed at Troyes, is undermined by a further opacity: between Act 1 and Act 5 Henry's initial demand for the French crown quietly shifts to his final demand only to be named as heir. And that reintroduces the dangers of the Salic Law.

This weakness in the treaty (quoted directly from Holinshed at 5.2.300–5), with its restoration of the legal position that Edward III had fought for, is camouflaged in the play by the game of Henry's betrothal to Katherine. But it remains as a feature to justify the final Chorus lamenting the brevity of Henry's triumph. And the Dauphin's absence from the final act as the dispossessed heir, despite his presence in the earlier versions and his pre-existing return on stage in *1 Henry VI* at Rheims to reclaim the French crown, makes the omission as pointed as the omission of the Cambridge claim. Dynastic title was an insoluble and recurrent problem. It is worth bearing in mind that *Henry V* was the last of the nine plays Shakespeare wrote about English history and the problems of dynastic title. Immediately after *Henry V* he turned to the Rome of Julius

1 See '*Henry V* and the Bees' Commonwealth', *S.Sur.* 30 (1977), 61–72.

Caesar, where power rather than title was the issue. He never again touched on title to rule as a political subject.

The second large factor in the background of the play was the military propaganda that was published in extraordinary quantities through the 1590s. The Armada in 1588, and the later threats of invasion or of Spanish-financed insurrection in Ireland, the long wars against Spanish Catholicism in the Low Countries, the Jesuit-led subversion of English Catholics after the Council of Trent and the Papal Bull freeing Catholics from the duty of obedience to heretical princes all meant danger, and danger provoked militarism. The theoretical aspect was highlighted by the publication of Alberico Gentili's *De Jure Belli*. It was the first to appear with a dedication to the Earl of Essex, an aim followed by almost all the books about war at this time. Gentili was an Italian Protestant refugee in England, professor of law at Oxford and a theorist of international renown. The Privy Council consulted him over the Spanish ambassador's right to immunity after his involvement in the plot to rescue Mary Queen of Scots and depose Elizabeth was discovered in 1584. In the next year he lectured and published widely about the laws protecting ambassadors. He became involved in the academic debate with John Rainolds in 1597 about performing plays at university. Gentili's great book, a minutely detailed examination of international law, the 'law of nations' as it applied to war, appeared in London in 1588–9.[1] In the 1590s it inspired a large number of English treatises about the conduct of war, by William Segar, John Eliot, Matthew Sutcliffe, William Fulbecke, Barnabe Rich, John Norden, and Richard Crompton among others.[2]

---

1 Alberico Gentili, *De Jure Belli, Libri Tres*, 1589. It was written in Latin and dedicated to the Earl of Essex. Gentili arrived in England in 1580 as an Italian exile. He met the Leicester clique, including Sidney, and became a teacher of international law at Oxford and in London, where he was admitted to Gray's Inn in 1600. He died in 1608 and was buried alongside his father in St Helens, Bishopsgate. Shakespeare was living in the St Helens parish, near the Theatre and Curtain playhouses, in 1597–8.

2 Lily B. Campbell, *Shakespeare's 'Histories': Mirrors of Elizabethan Policy*, San Marino, 1947, devotes a long section (chapter 15) to the writings about war in the 1590s. One of the volumes she does not deal with is Eliot's *Discourses of Warre and single combat*, a double volume translated from a French original in 1591. It leans heavily on the Old Testament in order to controvert the Anabaptists, who cite 'Thou shalt not kill' as an argument for pacifism. In a passage closely parallel to the debate in 4.1 between Henry and the soldiers, it quotes Matthew 26.52, arguing that war is God's beadle. The arguments, if not the phrasing, are modelled on Gentili, with a heavy overlay of biblical citations. Much of it reflects Henry's attitudes at Agincourt in the play. Other evidence for Gentili's pervasive influence can be found in Stephen Gosson's sermon *The Trumpet of Warre*, given at Paul's Cross on 7 May 1598. He makes one point which might have influenced Shakespeare to alter his sources by presenting the Dauphin's insult with the tennis balls to Henry only after the decision to wage war against France had been taken. Had Henry's decision been motivated by revenge, the justice of his cause would have been at risk, according to Gosson. It is a question of the proper use of authority. 'As in a common weale it is requisite there should be an authoritie to punish offences, and to keepe the same in order: so in the wide worlde, that all kingdomes and commonweales might be preserved, it is requisit there should be a power & authority to punish injuries, this power resting in no one Prince in the worlde as superiour to all other Princes, war steps in in the place of just vindicative judgement, God hath left no other meanes unto Princes to flie unto. Howsoever, this may seeme to be controlde by scripture, and reason, in that *Rom* 12, the Apostles councell is, *Render to no man evill for evill*. And if private revenge is not to be admitted, because the selfe and same person is both a Judge and an actor in his owne cause, it may peradventure be thought as unfitte for a Prince to be a Judge and an actor in his owne cause' (B8). Gosson also, in a passage which Henry would not have liked, claimed that soldiers have only to obey authority, because 'souldiers are of the nature of executioners' (C2).

Much of the debate hung on a peg of theology, since among Catholic recusants the Jesuit Parsons and Cardinal Allen were raising basic questions about the necessity for subjects to obey their rulers in unjust wars. Most of the books rooted themselves in the Bible, and most of them explicitly addressed themselves to the question whether loyalty to the sovereign came before religious obedience.[1]

Gentili's position, set out in his first seven chapters, was that war is necessary because, unlike individuals, sovereign rulers cannot be ruled by the laws of others, and therefore have only the sword as their means of enforcing justice. Wars are sovereign against sovereign, when all other recourses have failed. Pirates and brigands, not having sovereign authority, are subject to the criminal laws of the states they operate against, and cannot be counted as an equal 'enemy' as if they were fighting wars. 'The necessity which justifies war, says Baldus, arises when one is driven to arms as the last resort.'[2] In the fifth chapter of the first book, entitled 'It is just to wage war', he begins by rehearsing the early writings against all war, citing Cicero, Seneca and Erasmus among others. Then he puts the opposite case, which he says has been the orthodoxy since Augustine. Cicero and Seneca, he points out, were objecting to unjust wars. Augustine defined certain kinds of war as just, and the justice of wars, and just conduct in them, are his subject. He does not go into the theology of a 'just war', which Augustine defined as a war to convert the heathen, a crusade. Gentili draws delicate distinctions between cases, most pointedly over the division in religious attitudes to war, but he invokes Old Testament militarism and New Testament pacifism without discrimination. The balance for him lies between Erasmus's outright pacifism and Augustine's acceptance of just crusades. 'What shall I say of Erasmus, who in a long digression in his *Proverbs* assails the injustice of war?', he writes (p. 28), and answers the question with Augustine: 'Others perhaps would not condemn every war, but only one which is undertaken for another motive than honour or defence.'[3] Four chapters are given to religious wars, four to defensive wars, and the rest of the first book to the 'necessity' for honorable offensive wars.

The second of the three books is largely based on Roman practices, since Roman law was the basis for international law or 'the law of nations'. Gentili was principally concerned in it to draw lines about what was proper conduct in war with regard to such niceties as ambushes, truces and the treatment of prisoners. He drew his case histories from recent examples as well as ancient history. It is in the last context that he cited Henry's killing of the prisoners at Agincourt. He did not read English. His sources

---

1  Richard Crompton's *Mansion of Magnanimitie*, for instance, gave its seventh chapter to denouncing the Pope's 'plots and practises' against Elizabeth, citing Papal Bulls that promised heaven to the recusant, 'to move, stirre up, and perswade as many of her highnesse sujects as they dare deale withall, to renounce their allegeance due to her Majestie and her Crowne, & upon hope by forreyn invasion to be inriched'. See Appendix 3.

2  *De Jure Belli, Libri Tres*, translated by John C. Rolfe, Oxford, 1933, chapter 3, p. 15.

3  He opens chapter 7 at the end of the introductory section by denying gold as a just reason for war and invoking Augustine: ' "To make war upon one's neighbours and thence to proceed to other wars, and merely from a lust for power to trample under foot nations which have done one no harm, what else should this be called than brigandage on a grand scale?" '

were Latin works such as Polydore Virgil's history of England, the *Historia Anglica*, and George Buchanan's *History of Scotland*.[1] Over the treatment of prisoners taken in battle, he wrote

At this point I must commend the Scots, who at one time did not slay their captives, no matter how great danger threatened them. Also the French general who nobly set free all his prisoners, in order to relieve his camp of their great numbers. I cannot praise the English who, in that famous battle in which they overthrew the power of France, having taken more prisoners than the number of their victorious army and fearing danger from them by night, set aside those of high rank and slew the rest. 'A hateful and inhuman deed', says the historian, 'and the battle was not so bloody as the victory.' In like terms another writer speaks of the barbarous savagery of the Turk, who slew four thousand prisoners, to relieve himself of their burden.     (pp. 211–12)

Gentili's version of Henry's act of slaughter is different from Holinshed's, whom he had evidently not read. Shakespeare did not read Polydore Virgil's Latin, and may not have read Gentili's account either. But his own version of the killings is markedly different from Holinshed's, and may reflect some of the discomfort that Gentili generated about the act, and that led to other defences of the killings.

   Holinshed's account is more detailed than the accounts Gentili had access to. It cites the attack on the baggage train and offers that as one motive for the order, together with the danger of the French reassembling:

But when the outcrie of the lackies and boies, which ran awaie for feare of the Frenchmen thus spoiling the campe, came to the kings eares, he doubting least his enimies should gather togither againe, and begin a new field; and mistrusting further that the prisoners would be an aid to his enimies, or the verie enimies to their takers in deed if they were suffered to live, contrarie to his accustomed gentlenes, commanded by sound of trumpet, that everie man (upon paine of death) should incontinentlie slaie his prisoner. When this dolorous decree, and pitifull proclamation was pronounced, pitie it was to see how some Frenchmen were suddenlie sticked with daggers, some were brained with pollaxes, some slaine with malls, other had their throats cut, and some their bellies panched, so that in effect, having respect to the great number, few prisoners were saved.     (p. 554)

In the play the Chorus makes no mention of the incident, but Gower, entering for the next scene immediately after (4.7), provides his own gloss. He assumes that the order was given in revenge for the attack on the boys and the baggage train:

There's not a boy left alive, and the cowardly rascals that ran from the battle ha' done this slaughter. Besides, they have burned and carried away all that was in the king's tent, wherefore the king most worthily hath caused every soldier to cut his prisoner's throat. Oh, 'tis a gallant king!

This attribution of the motive for the order follows immediately on the actual event, which is presented in a form quite different from Gower's assumption:

1 In Book 3 (p. 364), from Buchanan he deplores the English capture and imprisonment of the Scots King James and approves the refusal of the Scots serving the French at Melun when Henry sent young James to order them to change sides. See Appendix 2.

*Alarum.*

[HENRY]   But hark, what new alarum is this same?
The French have reinforced their scattered men.
Then every soldier kill his prisoners.
Give the word through.                                              *Exeunt.*

In the play Henry has only Holinshed's second reason for giving the order. It is Gower
who attributes to him Holinshed's notion of revenge, a reattribution of motive that has
confused centuries of readers of the play.

Other points are quietly grouped around this incident in ways that imply a sense of
discretion as well as complexity in the evaluation of the morality of Henry's order. The
boy who was Falstaff's boy in Eastcheap is evidently one of those killed in the French
attack on the baggage train. He has already warned of the possibility at the end of 4.4: 'I
must stay with the lackeys with the luggage of our camp. The French might have a good
prey of us if he knew of it, for there is none to guard it but boys.' So Gower's outrage
has some personal point for an audience prepared to sympathise with the boy. But his
other statement, that the prisoners were killed by having their throats cut, points to a
feature calling for a more complex response. References to war as a matter of cutting
throats are made frequently up to this moment in the play. Pistol's 'couple a gorge' is a
comic catchphrase from Act 2. In 4.4 he has captured a French prisoner and has been
seen revelling in the prospect of 'egregious ransom'. When we next see him in 5.1, after
the throat-slitting, he is as penniless as ever. M. Le Fer is one of the prisoners who
has his throat cut.[1] The fact that Henry's order has fortuitously deprived Pistol of his
profit is another of the unemphasised but distinct consequences of Henry's order.

One in particular of the many writers about war in the 1590s is worth noting because
of his proximity to Shakespeare. There is room for doubt and even scepticism over
many of the sources that Shakespeare is thought to have consulted for his plays, largely
because so many of them were either rare or costly. Without libraries of any kind, let
alone public libraries, Shakespeare must have been entirely dependent on his own purse
and loans from his friends for his books. Unless he found ready access, as Jonson did,
to the great collectors such as Camden or Stow, the limited number of books available
in print must have restricted his resources severely, and access to manuscripts was
almost inconceivable. Most likely he had his own copy of Holinshed. Equally possibly
his fellow-Stratfordian Richard Field, the printer who issued his poems, gave him the
run of his books. It may have been Field's Huguenot wife who introduced him to the
Mountjoys with whom he lodged at the turn of the century and who must have helped
with his French. Certainly Field was one contact who had books in his house. And of
those, one was certainly Richard Crompton's *Mansion of Magnanimitie*, because Field
printed it at the beginning of 1599.[2]

---

1  Q1 adds 'Couple gorge' by Pistol in response to Henry's order at the end of the scene. It might be regarded
   as a nice comic twist, but it forgets the financial disaster that order became for Pistol through his loss of
   the ransom money.
2  It was entered to R. Blower in the Stationers' Register on 15 May 1598, transferred to W. Ponsonby on
   13 December, and printed by Field for Ponsonby with the date 1599 on the title page. A more detailed
   account of Crompton's book is given in Appendix 3.

Crompton's book was dedicated, like almost all of its predecessors, to the Earl of Essex. It hails his 'late valiant service at CALES [sic] in SPAINE, and else where', and begins with a model oration by the general to his army which was evidently designed for Essex at Cadiz, since the enemy is Spanish. The Shakespearean connection, apart from the coincidence that both were soon to be embarrassed by Essex's failure in Ireland, comes in a passage about Henry's slaughter of his prisoners tacked on to the end of the sixth chapter, which is about sedition. It does not belong there, and its overly defensive tone implies some self-consciousness about the question. He writes

When king Henry the fift, not having above fifteene thousand men, gave a great overthrow to the French king at Agincourt in Fraunce, where he had assembled to the number of forty thousand of the flower of all his countrey, & had taken many prisoners of the french, both Nobles and others, the french as they are men of great courage and valure, so they assembled themselves againe in battell array, meaning to have given a new battell to king Henry, which king Henry perceiving, gave speciall commaundement by proclamation, that every man should kill his prisoners: whereupon many were presently slaine, whereof the French king having intelligence, dispersed his army, and so departed: whereby you may see the miseries of warre, that though they had yeelded and thought themselves sure of their lives, paying their ransom, according to the lawes of armes, yet uppon such necessary occasion, to kill them was a thing by all reason allowed, for otherwise the king having lost diverse valiant Captaines and souldiers in this battell, and being also but a small number in comparison of the French kings army, & in a strange countrey, where he could not supply his neede upon the sudden, it might have bene much daungerous to have againe joyned with the enemy, and kept his prisoners alive, as in our Chronicles largely appeareth. (G2$^v$–G3)

Crompton's version echoes Holinshed, but it ignores the attack on the boys and the king's camp and pleads necessity in a distinctly defensive tone. Since two chapters later he assails Spanish 'bloudie inhumanitie' for the slaughter of English prisoners at Resendale and Gravelines, this defensiveness is understandable. After a decade of military atrocities in the Low Countries sensitivity to such acts is not surprising. It would be more surprising if such sensitivity did not communicate itself to Shakespeare.

Salic Law and the debate about justice in war were potent issues in Shakespeare's time. Neither of them necessarily influenced his writing directly. The frontal sources were the early plays that prompted *The Famous Victories*, and Holinshed's detailed account. These sources are examined in Appendices 1 and 2. But the play's direct use of these sources needs to be placed in this larger context if the concept of the play when it was written is to have any potency. For this the omissions from the sources, and additions such as the debate about justice in war between Henry and his soldiers, are as weighty as the direct uses.

Some of the omissions are obvious streamlining. The Oldcastle story and the associated Lollard rebellion was one such, though Shakespeare also had special reasons for keeping Oldcastle out of the play. The French king's name and his periodic bouts of madness, which Holinshed calls 'his old disease of frensie', is a rather more substantial omission. Holinshed notes that the king's illness put the Dauphin in charge when Henry was besieging Harfleur. This may have prompted Shakespeare to allocate responsibility for Harfleur's fall to the Dauphin. That, along with the uniform depersonalisation of the French king, is consistent with Shakespeare's reappropriation of the Dauphin's role. Altered from the versions in the early plays, it was one of the three major omissions, each of which relates to one of Stubbs's three reasons for Henry's claim to France. Each of these three omissions characterises the play in distinct ways.

The first of Stubbs's reasons, title, has to justify the omission of Cambridge's alternative claim to the English crown. In some degree this was streamlining, since it would have intermixed the Salic Law issue with doubts about who in England should be the proper claimant to the French crown. Lesser omissions – York as Aumerle, and as Cambridge's brother – follow from this first one. The second of Stubbs's reasons, conquest, is notable in the play not so much for the omission of any large-scale battle scenes but for the complete absence of any reference to Henry's most celebrated weapon and tactic, the archers and the hedge of stakes that protected them from the French cavalry. To Holinshed the stakes were Henry's great invention: 'This devise of fortifieng an armie, was at this time first invented: but since that time, they have devised caltraps, harrowes, and other new engins against the force of horssemen; so that if the enimies run hastilie upon the same, either are their horsses wounded with the stakes, or their feet hurt with the other engins, so as thereby the beasts are gored, or else made unable to mainteine their course' (p. 553). Neither archers nor stakes appear in the play. They are mentioned twice in *The Famous Victories*, so it was not an accidental omission. The only two reasons for the victory offered in Shakespeare's play are Henry's 'band of brothers' speech, and the killing of the prisoners. The third area where things are omitted is Stubbs's claim by 'covenant', the Treaty of Troyes and the peace agreed in the fifth act. Removing the Dauphin was one major change from the early stage versions. Elevating Henry's marriage to Katherine also muted the fact that Henry had dropped his claim to the French crown by Act 5. It must have been for this that the French king was made impassively regal, unlike his son, with no name and no madness.[1]

Each of these three categories of omission can carry a different set of explanations. The dynastic issue is given added weight by the fact that the writers of *Sir John Oldcastle* laid special emphasis on it, as if they had fastened on a weakness in Shakespeare's version. That prompts speculation whether it was cut simply for streamlining, or more substantially because Henry's reign had to be kept free of the rebellious claims

---

1 One further source used by Shakespeare, the Bible, is worth a note because of the evidence that this play supplies about which version Shakespeare was familiar with in 1599. It is generally assumed that Shakespeare knew best the translation into English known as the Geneva Bible. It was much more widely sold than its rival the Bishops' Bible, appearing in 81 editions between 1576 and 1611 compared to only 11 of the Bishops' Bible. If Shakespeare owned his own copy of the Bible it would probably have been a Geneva text. But the Bishops' Bible was the one read in churches, and the heard text seems to have lodged far more firmly in Shakespeare's mind when writing *Henry V* than the Geneva translation. Six expressions peculiar to the Bishops' Bible occur compared with only one from the Geneva Bible, and the Geneva reference most likely came indirectly through *Tamburlaine*. From the Bishops' Bible come 'the grave doth gape' (2.1.49–50, used also in *2H4* 5.5.48–9); 'excess of wine' (2.2.42); 'fierce tempest . . . In thunder and in earthquake' (2.4.100–1); 'men of mould' (3.2.20); 'the latter day' (4.1.125); and 'death . . . to him advantage' (4.1.162). Geneva has the reference to 'Assyrian slings' (4.7.52), an echo which recurs three times in *Tamburlaine*.

4  An illustration from Rowe's 1709 edition of *Henry V*, showing the field at Agincourt, including the stakes and arrows (the Folger Shakespeare Library)

that dominate the two preceding plays. The omissions from the conquest issue seem designed to minimise Henry's professionalism as a soldier and to give credit to his talent for raising his soldiers' morale. The omissions from the covenant issue relate to the position of the Dauphin as antagonist to Henry's protagonist, and more weightily to the care Shakespeare took with Holinshed's account, privileging it over the stage versions. How one interprets the omissions depends in part on how much weight is also given to the various additions to the sources offered by the stage texts and the chronicles.

In between the omissions and the additions there are some revealing changes made to the sources. The most notable of these are the images of the dogs of war, the transposition of the tennis balls insult from before the decision to invade France until after, Henry's order to his soldiers to have mercy on Harfleur, and the order to kill the prisoners, which is put before the news of the attack on the baggage train. These all make Henry a cooler and more rational being than the sources made him. The additions to the sources work similarly, but add an edge which can cut both ways. Centrally, there is Henry's debate with his soldiers about the justice of war. An inversion of the usual disguised king topos, where the ruler as judge learns the truth by hiding his identity, like the Duke in *Measure for Measure*, it opens up Henry's mind in its public and, in soliloquy, its private aspects. This is the only time the 'opaque self' is put on display. It also puts a value on the 'reckoning' (4.1.124), the imagery of accounting that runs through the play from 1.0.17 onwards. Related in complex ways to this debate is the exceptionally broad array of soldiers that the play as a whole exhibits, from the nobles like Exeter and York, through the four linguistically-comic captains, to the common soldiers, who range from Pistol, Bardolph and Nym to John Bates, Michael Williams, and Alexander Court. In all of these, the most intriguing insertions are the Irish Macmorris and the Scots Jamy.

The last of these is the most puzzling, especially in view of the emphasis given to the threat from Scotland in 1.2, and the fact that while the English and Welsh were subjects of Henry's, the Irish were more doubtfully so, and the Scots were certainly not. Jamy must have been technically a mercenary in the English army, a point that may help to explain the emphasis on the mercenaries in the French army at Agincourt.[1] A further comment on this addition to the play is given in Appendix 2.

One other addition to the play is worth noting because of its links with the multitude of different languages in the play, and with the dogs of war. The scene in which the French princess starts to learn English is a wonderfully comic insertion in the otherwise intensely warlike Act 3. Some preparation for it might be found in the Chorus to that act, which says that the French king has offered Henry his daughter Katherine (3.0.29–30), but that 'the offer likes not' (32), and sets off the war. Act 3 also highlights the linguistic comedy of the four captains as part of the general emphasis given in that act to the quarrelsome division of soldier from soldier in Henry's army. Act 3, Scene 5 prepares for the linguistic games between Henry and

1 See 'Why Captain Jamy in *Henry V*?', *Archiv* 226 (1989), 365–73.

Katherine in 5.2. Language which emphasised difference in Act 3 becomes the basis for union in Act 5. By then the French king has given up his daughter to the dog of Psalm 22.

## Structure and language

Omissions have many possible explanations. Additions to the story, especially when it was one so famous, so well documented, handled so often before, and so dependent on the factual evidence of the Chronicles, bring a sharper focus. Some of these have been discussed above. The closest focus comes from the patterns of situation and language, those structural images and words which run and grow throughout the play and, in their most narrowly linguistic manifestations, give a particular colouring to the shape of the story.

When Alexander Court enters in 4.1.81 and addresses his companion as 'brother John Bates' he gives emphasis to a feature of this play which is unique in all Shakespeare. Court is one of the three English soldiers who are given curiously ordinary and yet full names. There is no Wart or Mouldy in 4.1, nor any anonymous 'soldiers' or mere surnames in their entry direction. And they have the longest talk with Henry in the play. These three brother-soldiers, whose names signify that they are brothers in misfortune rather than true brothers, highlight a special concept in the play. Henry has talked with one group of three of his subjects already. Addressing the three conspirators in 2.2 had involved Henry in some acting, but it was a mask he soon threw off as he threw off theirs. His dismissal of his bedfellow Scroop to death in Act 2 matches the death of Falstaff in the same act as the closing of the last doors on his solitary self. His talk with the three plain soldiers in 4.1 reverses the earlier scene. Where with the conspirators he had acted himself as he threw off their disguises, in this scene with the honest men Henry's mask stays on. He is not one of this band of brothers.

The term Alexander Court uses to John Bates has already recurred through the play. Court's term is a pointer to and a preparation for Henry's most celebrated claim in his Crispin's Day speech, to be brother with all his army. Henry's assertion of brotherhood at that point makes Agincourt unique in the play. It marks what was probably designed to be the most potent single factor in the English victory. His trenchant proclamation, that everyone who 'sheds his blood with me / Shall be my brother; be he ne'er so vile / This day shall gentle his condition' (4.3.61–3), is carefully set up by a host of other claims to brotherhood and kinship in the play, before and after the battle. Pistol might have had reason to regret that Le Fer did not scratch him first before surrendering.

The whole play is notable for the stress that it puts on differentiations in social status. From 1.2.180, where Exeter explains government by the 'high, and low, and lower' through his analogy of musical harmony, which is then amplified by the Archbishop's analogy of the bees, to Pistol's enquiry at 4.1.37–8 whether the disguised Henry is an officer or merely 'base, common and popular', the distinction between what the Chorus to Act 4 calls 'mean and gentle' is upheld consistently and emphatically. When Henry is upset before Agincourt he refers to 'lackeys' and 'slaves', the word the French nobles use when they talk of their 'gentle' daughters being raped by the English soldiers

5  Elizabethan soldiers trailing versions of the 'puissant pike' (4.1.40), actually halberds. A detail from Henry
Peacham's sketch of *Titus Andronicus* on stage in 1595 (The Marquess of Bath)

(4.5.16–17). Henry declares at Agincourt that all social distinctions must disappear. In
the rest of the play, both before and after the battle, they are forcibly reaffirmed.

   These social differentiations give some support to Terry Hands' reading of the play
in his 1975 production for the Stratford centenary. Concerned to develop a feeling of
brotherhood and battle-readiness in his actors at a time of great social dissension and
danger to the national subsidised theatre, he offered a play where the English start as
a divided people and only unite for Agincourt. The play, he wrote, has three battles.
'The first is Harfleur, fought from externals, revealing the deep divisions in Henry's
army and consequently his country. The second is Agincourt, fought by a renewed and
re-united band of brothers. Henry . . . abandons privilege and rank, the final offer of
ransom. He awakens interdependence and trust, he speaks to all as equals, and accepts
equality with them for himself . . . "I am not covetous for gold . . . All things be ready if
our minds be so." '[1] The third battle, rather less obviously, Hands defined as Henry's
courtship of Katherine, which he thought was also an equalising process.

   It is true that the uniqueness of Henry's claim to brotherhood in the Crispin's Day
speech is emphasised by its difference from his equivalent speech in the previous battle,
at Harfleur, and by the weaknesses in the English army that are put on show at Harfleur.
There the soldiers, retreating from the breach they have made, are heartened by the
king's urging to return to the breach, although their renewed attack has no better effect
than the previous one. Harfleur does not fall to any attack by the English. It only falls
when the Governor, after listening to Henry's threats, admits that his hope of relief by
the Dauphin's forces has failed. And that victory ends with Henry admitting that his

---

1  Quoted in Sally Beauman, *The R.S.C.'s Production of 'Henry V' for the Centenary Season at the Royal
   Shakespeare Theatre*, Oxford, 1976, p. 19.

forces are weak and that he must retreat to Calais. It is hardly a promising precursor for Agincourt.

Brotherhood, however, grows in importance before that battle. The Eastcheap clowns have already sworn their own pact of brotherhood and fellowship after their quarrel in 2.1. Bardolph tries to make Pistol and Nym friends with the logical plea 'We must to France together; why the devil should we keep knives to cut one another's throats?' (73–4). Like horseleeches (2.3.43–4), they must thrive on French blood, not each other's. But in 3.7.44–7 Llewellyn refuses Pistol's request to intercede for the condemned Bardolph in terms which call this easy concept of brotherhood into question. Llewellyn takes up a rank-conscious posture, upholding virtue and saying 'For if, look you, he were my brother I would desire the duke to use his good pleasure and put him to execution.' The duke, followed by Henry himself when he hears of Bardolph's punishment, does not yet have any feeling of blood-brotherhood with the vile. That must wait for the battle speech itself.

The chief difference in the Agincourt speech from the Harfleur speech is its insistence that the whole English army is a single brotherhood. Before Harfleur Henry addresses each social rank separately, speaking first to 'you noble English', and only eight lines later turning to 'you, good yeomen'. Not until Agincourt does he propose equality. First in a neat pun that puts friendship against fear he offers comradeship:

> We would not die in that man's company
> That fears his fellowship to die with us. (4.3.38–9)

And then, fellow-feeling assured, he offers the ultimate bond, the blood that will rank the common soldier with his king:

> We few, we happy few, we band of brothers –
> For he today that sheds his blood with me
> Shall be my brother; be he ne'er so vile
> This day shall gentle his condition. (60–3)

It is a cohesive moment. The noble (commonly identified by a false etymology as the 'non-vile') will be united with the vile in blood. The social divisions emphasised in the Harfleur scenes, where Henry's rallying speech to the separate nobles and yeomen is followed by Llewellyn beating the Eastcheap rogues to the breach and then enjoying a violent quarrel with his fellow-captain Macmorris, distinct marks of a divided army, are now forgotten[1].

---

1 Shakespeare began negotiating over his father's coat of arms, originally drafted twenty years before, in October 1596. It is possible that such comic allusions as Slender's claim in *The Merry Wives of Windsor* that Shallow is 'a gentleman born . . . who writes himself "Armigero" in any bill' (1.1.8–10) arose out of the addition put in the draft of the proposal that Shakespeare's grandfather Arden was an esquire, or *armigero*, not just *generosus* or gentleman. C. W. Scott-Giles, *Shakespeare's Heraldry*, London, 1950, p. 29, declares that 'an interesting feature of the two drafts of 1596 is that the terms, and particularly the alterations and additions, probably represent information given and suggestions made by William Shakespeare in conference with the heralds.' These negotiations, and particularly the motto 'Non Sanz droict' (Not Without Right), were evidently talked about in the Chamberlain's company, given Jonson's joke in *Every Man Out* about a coat of arms showing a boar's head and the motto 'Not

The grandeur of Henry's offer of brotherhood to all his soldiers at Agincourt is given a further context by the insistent acknowledgements of kin in the levels of social ranking that have gone before. In Act 1 brotherhood is exclusively royal or noble. Exeter speaks of Henry's 'brother kings', his ancestors, at 1.2.122. The French king three times calls the threatening Henry 'our brother of England' in 2.4. Henry himself is careful in the early acts to designate his nobles as 'uncle' (Exeter) and 'cousin' (Westmorland, who probably secured his position in the F1 text and was placed at Agincourt by his kinship with Henry, which Henry stresses several times: he is 'cousin' at 1.2.4 and 4.3.19). Henry specifies Gloucester as his 'brother' in 3.7, and at 4.1.3 he greets the arrival who joins him and Gloucester as 'brother Bedford'. After his argument with Bates and Williams, he acknowledges the sound of 'my brother Gloucester's voice', arousing him from prayer before the battle. Only after that does his oration before the battle make every social rank a brother.

The victory allows Henry to adjust his attitude back again to its former strong sense of the differences in degree. When Williams goes to fetch Gower to the king he eagerly predicts that it is to make him a knight (4.8.1), to 'gentle' him as Henry promised, but it is not. Montjoy at 4.7.64 renews the traditional social distinctions when he asks leave to separate the noble corpses of the French from the blood of the 'vulgar' and the mercenaries.

> For many of our princes – woe the while –
> Lie drowned and soaked in mercenary blood,
> So do our vulgar drench their peasant limbs
> In blood of princes . . .
>
> (4.7.65–8)

This divisiveness of social rank is perhaps an understandable French attitude, but it is also Henry's. While the listing of French prisoners divides them precisely by class and 'name', deploring the mingling of bloods, so does Henry's own recital of the English dead. His list ends 'none else of name'. At 4.7.152 it is 'my brother Gloucester' again. By then Williams is a 'fellow' and no longer of the royal fellow-ship. Henry reaffirms the social distinctions by suggesting that the swaggerer who exchanged gloves with Williams might have been 'a gentleman of great sort' (4.7.121), of too high degree to accept the common soldier's challenge. And Williams is once again the other kind of socially lower-class 'fellow' at 4.8.51. By then even Llewellyn, technically a gentleman like all the other captains (5.1.66), can patronise him as a common 'fellow'.

---

without Mustard'. This being so, we might wonder whether Shakespeare's contact with the College of Heralds extended to a note of the entry about the right to bear arms after Agincourt. Scott-Giles (p. 121) notes:

Agincourt became a landmark in heraldic history. In 1418, Henry V issued a writ referring to the fact that heretofore 'divers men . . . assumed unto themselves Arms and Coats of Arms, called Coat-Armours, in cases where neither they nor their ancestors in times gone by used such Arms;' and proclaiming 'that no one, of whatsoever rank, degree, or condition he may be, shall assume such Arms or Coats of Arms, unless he possess or ought to possess the same in right of his ancestors, or by the gift of some person having adequate power for that purpose; and that he shall plainly shew forth, on the day of his mustering, by whose gift he hold those Arms . . . those excepted who bore arms with us at the battle of Agincourt.'

Act 5 goes even higher up the social scale, renewing the claims of a purely royal brotherhood that Agincourt might have called in question. In 5.2 Henry matches the French king's formal 'our brother of England' with his own 'our brother France' (2), and his more cursory 'brother' at 83, which are met by the French 'most worthy brother England' (10), and the queen's echoes of her husband at 12 and 92. Henry invites his family, 'brother Bedford, and you brother Gloucester' (84), to negotiate the terms of the treaty while he goes on to guarantee the diplomatic and marital alliance and to arrange the succession of his own children to both crowns. Blood relations at the end of the play are a matter of marriages and dynasties, not of the blood shed by brothers in arms.

The patterning of blood kin and brothers, which makes its presence felt first at Harfleur, is counterpointed with the proliferation of different accents and languages. From early in Act 3 the different dialects of the four captains and the scenes spoken in alien French offer an aural challenge to the claims for brotherhood. No play of Shakespeare's makes so much use of differences in language and has more language barriers. With one entire scene in French, another half in French, and the French nobles regularly starting their scenes by making use of French phrases, plus Llewellyn's, Macmorris's and Jamy's non-standard English, Pistol's theatrical and old-fashioned quasi-verse, together with Mrs. Quickly's malapropisms, the play puts up a considerable show of non-communication. When all these communication problems are set in a play uniquely supplied with six visits by an explanatory Choric voice which regularly misrepresents what happens on stage, confusion is to be expected. From the moment when the Prologue describes itself as only 'Prologue-like', the audience's thoughts are set to piece out a lot of evident imperfections in communication.

There are several precedents for foreign speech on the popular stage in the 1590s, besides the Latin used to confuse Jack Cade in *2 Henry VI*. *The Wounds of Civil War* (1589) and *James IV* (1590) both have a murderer who speaks comic franglais. Soon after the doubtfully comic Welsh of Glendower and his daughter in *1 Henry IV* there came (if we can accept 1597 as the play's date) the certainly comic Welsh parson and French physician of *The Merry Wives of Windsor*. In 1598 William Haughton wrote a comedy for Henslowe at the Rose with three gulls as lovers who speak comic French, Dutch, and Italian.[1] And in 1599 Rose audiences also enjoyed the romantic hero's pseudo-Dutch in *The Shoemaker's Holiday*. The Rose in the same year, not long after *Henry V* was first on stage, included in its parodically imitative *Sir John Oldcastle* a similar comic Irishman, in accent and in 'strait strossers'. With so many precedents and imitations, one of the main questions about *Henry V* is what specific function other than incidental comedy the language divisions were designed to fulfil.

There is no doubt that the language scenes were designed as comedy. In a play making careful use of the division of prose from verse, all the lower-class scenes and all the comic scenes are in prose. Apart from the isolated phrases in French used by the French nobles, the three French scenes, Katherine's two and Le Fer's one,

---

1 *Englishmen for my Money*, bought by Henslowe for the Rose early in 1598.

are comic. The French nobles on the night before Agincourt (3.8) chat in prose. No French and no prose are used in the scenes showing the French king. The play is in part structured on a basic dichotomy. The comic scenes emphasise linguistic differences, one of the clearest evidences that the people in the play are not brothers, while in the 'serious' scenes of verse Henry lays stress on the concept of brotherhood amongst the English.

This dichotomy, the evidence for which develops through Act 3, comes to its climax and to what ought to be its dissolution at Agincourt. There Henry promises his act of union to make brothers of the English and Welsh, mean and noble, throughout his army. His purpose is still to defeat the French and so to unite them into one nation under the one English king, as he had declared at the end of 2.2: 'No king of England if not king of France'. Act 5 does make Henry a member of the French royal family, son-in-law to the king and heir to his crown. Brotherhood thus seems to have replaced the alienation signalled by the different accents. The only French in 5.2 is spoken not by the French nobles but by Henry and by Katherine in her half-English attempts to meet his franglais gallantries. In reality, as the epilogue acknowledges, this union of the alien families and alien languages proved short-lived. The dichotomy prevails. Williams is no more Henry's brother than Pistol is Llewellyn's. The French do not become English brothers.

## Staging and stage history

To a remarkable degree *Henry V* has been a paradigm for the debate about Shakespeare on stage or page. If you take seriously the view that a stage production is a 'reading' of the play, a director's or a small group's interpretation, then almost the whole history of the play as performed amounts to a series of patriotic and emotional readings rather than the analyses of its ambivalence that reading the play in private study has evoked. Until very recently, all stage readings presented the play as an emotional voyage into patriotism, with Henry as the heroic helmsman that the Chorus makes him. Hazlitt's condemnation of his jingoism in 1830, John Masefield's in 1901, Yeats's in 1907 and Gerald Gould's in 1919 made no impact on the stage versions of their time. Most critiques of the play as performed amounted to judgements of how successful the actor playing Henry was in portraying a heroic personality. The play became a vehicle for rousing patriotic spirits. The greatest successes on stage were not often in time of war, but usually they were inspired by thoughts of war. Not until the 1960s and 1970s did anti-war feeling enter into the production of the play. The one consistent feature of stage productions has been the emotional charge, wherever it was directed.

France has by far the best claim to rival Scotland as the old enemy of England. Between 1599 and the twentieth century there were three major wars and a number of lesser demonstrations of enmity between England and France. The three major conflicts ended in English (or British) victories: Blenheim, the Heights of Abraham, Waterloo. And yet the periods when *Henry V* had its greatest successes on the English stage do not correspond precisely to those times of conflict. It certainly was staged successfully in times of war, but that success seems more related to a general mood of

6 The French nobles before Agincourt. Drawing by C. Walter Hodges

belligerence, no matter who the enemy, than to any specific hostility towards France. Olivier's film in 1944 and its subsequent success owed more to this belligerence than to a feeling in audiences that Henry's invasion of France was any sort of model for current military enterprises such as the D-Day landings. The need that the play seems to serve in asserting social cohesiveness, a justifiable team spirit, can crop up on unexpected occasions. Its function in a narrower context than patriotism can be seen, for instance, in productions at Stratford in 1951 and 1975, at times when the war was social, economic, and internal to Britain.

It is true that the play was popular in London during Britain's Seven Years War with France in the mid-eighteenth century, up to 1773, and again during the Napoleonic Wars at the beginning of the next century. In 1804 in Manchester a newspaper critic reported that the actor playing Henry there had cried 'God for Harry, England and

King George!', and was unsure whether it was not a deliberate mistake.[1] It triumphed again in both World Wars. National bellicosity has always helped it on stage. Of its first success little is known, but the ebb tide of militarism soon after it was first staged cannot have helped much. The 1600 Quarto's title-page says, without excitement, that it had already been 'sundry times played by the Right honorable the Lord Chamberlaine his servants'. The company staged it at court on 7 January 1605,[2] but under a new king who wanted peace the easy jingoism of the 1590s and its applause for stage heroes like the Talbots became less fashionable.

Its first staging must have been in part affected by the Chamberlain's Men's triumph with Falstaff. The first audiences had been promised in the epilogue to *2 Henry IV* that 'if you be not too much cloid with Fat Meate, our humble Author will continue the Story (with Sir John in it) and make you merry, with faire Katherine of France, where (for any thing I know) Falstaffe shall dye of a sweat'. Their disappointment at the off-stage death has been a lasting grievance. Both Olivier's and Branagh's films had to insert a portrayal of the deathbed scene more graphic and less comic than the Hostess's account. A much more positive reaction, though, is recorded in *Sir John Oldcastle*, a two-part play written late in 1599. The first part, the only text surviving, starts with a prologue which declares that it is correcting the rival company's misrepresentation:

> It is no pampered glutton we present,
> Nor aged Councellor to youthful sinne,
> But one, whose vertue shone above the rest,
> A valiant Martyr . . .

Foxe's 'Book of Martyrs' gave the four authors the story of Oldcastle's fight against the Catholic Church in an account which rubs several times against the story of Henry's life told in the three Shakespeare plays. It has comic scenes that echo the Falstaff antics, including a 'John Ostler' who is told 'well said old Jacke, thou art the old lad still', echoing Hal's allusion at 1.2.34 of *1 Henry IV* to 'my old lad o'the castle'. It also has a comic Irishman who loses his clothes, and has to demand the return of 'my strouces' in 'the Irish fashion', the 'strait strossers' mentioned by Bourbon at 3.8.49–50 in *Henry V* and worn by Macmorris. Apart from the performance at court at the Christmas season 1604–5, itself a mark of its success in the eyes of the Master of the King's Revels, this is the only firm indication of the play's reception on stage in Shakespeare's time.

The original requirements for staging the play are surprisingly modest. The few ragged foils which the Chorus derides at 4.0.50 were not called on for combat, except when Pistol wielded his old 'fox' broadsword in 4.4. The most demanding requirement must have been for the French and to a lesser extent the English nobles' costumes. These would have changed from spectacular scarlets in the court scenes such as 1.2, to armour for the battle scenes, and back again for the final scene. In the battles the nobles would have worn gorgets and breastplates (Henry's 'aspect of iron', 5.2.207) and iron helmets (1.0.13, 4.6.6, 4.7.139, 4.8.25, 5.0.18) decorated with 'plumes' (4.5.5). The captains and plain soldiers wore woollen caps or bonnets (4.1.185, 190, 4.8.27), and Llewellyn wore

7 Strait Irish strossers (3.8.49–50), a border illustration from John Speed, *Theatre of the Empire of Great Britain*, 1611 (The British Library)

8 Henry in armour (Act 3, Scene 4) at the gate of Harfleur with his army. Drawing by C. Walter Hodges

a 'Monmouth cap' (4.7.89, 138, 4.8.29). Besides the 'chair of state' for royal Henry in his one court scene, 1.2, and for the French king's court in 2.4, 3.6, and 5.2, the only major properties needed were the items of military apparatus. These amounted to nothing beyond the costumes and arms of war, except for the wall of Harfleur in 3.1 and 3.4 and the related siege weapons. The wall must have been the tiring-house front. For the attack the scaling ladders, specified in the Folio stage direction to be carried on by the English soldiers in 3.1, were easily portable properties. Their removal is a little puzzling, but it is likely that they were drawn up by the soldiers who climbed them after setting them against the tiring-house balcony.[1] The same balcony would serve as the wall on which the Governor appears in 3.4, and the curtained doorway or recess below it the gates through which Henry and his victorious army enter at the end of the scene. The 'devilish cannon', a small chamber for ceremonial gunfire which the Chorus hails with a flourish of a linstock at 3.0.33, would have jutted from the gabled superstructure over the stage. The chamber that was fired during a performance of *Henry VIII* on 29 June 1613 landed its smouldering wadding in the thatch that roofed the galleries, as we know from the accounts of the subsequent fire. The chamber must therefore have been positioned near the topmost level of the stage structure.

1 In the 1630s, when the Globe's stage balcony had been curtained and was routinely used by the Blackfriars musicians as their music room, Jasper Mayne praised Jonson's avoidance of military exhibitionism by declaring 'thou laidst no sieges to the *Musique Roome*' (*Jonsonus Virbius*, E4ʳ).

No other major or special properties were needed. Henry might have worn his dented helmet (5.0.18) for his entry at 4.6.1, and the English soldiers in 4.7 might have worn some 'gay new coats' from the French soldiers promised them by Henry at 4.3.118. No stage blood was necessary unless the victorious soldiers and their prisoners in 4.7 were marked with red, and unless we accept the spectacular throat-cutting as an act performed on-stage at the end of 4.6. Gloves are exchanged at 4.1.189 and produced again at 4.7.138 and 4.8.5. Papers are called for at 4.8.66 and 94. The leek, a seasonal vegetable, might have caused some problems of supply out of season, but at a pinch one can imagine Pistol chewing coloured paper in 5.1.

The opening Chorus, with its over-assertive modesty about the stage's inability to mount the crowded pageant of Agincourt, has provoked a great deal of speculation about how inadequate the original venue must have been. Either the Chorus was making an honest apology for a venue that was shortly to be surpassed by the newly painted Globe or he was offering a mock-modest apology for a magnificent new venue, which was enough of a glory on the Bankside to force the rival enterprise to flee to the northern suburbs which the Globe company had just abandoned, as the Rose company had to do.[1] Neither of these interpretations of the inadequate evidence is wholly acceptable. I suspect that the imprecision of the demands that Shakespeare wrote into the play for the staging are one indication that he was unsure which venue the play would eventually appear at. The false modesty of the Chorus over the staging relates more to the exercise of 'counterfeiting' any sort of heroic reality than to doubt about the quality of the theatrical venue.

After the early appearances, it seems to have been a long time before *Henry V* returned to the London stage. Pepys reported seeing Betterton play Henry in July 1668, but otherwise there are no records of any performance between 1605 and 1738. Even the famous victory against the French at Blenheim did not evoke a revival. Only when a combination of the new Shakespeare editions of Pope and Theobald, the Shakespeare Ladies' Club, and Pope's campaign to erect a Shakespeare monument in Westminster Abbey were helping to raise the poet's status in the licensed theatres did it reappear. Before that, the fashion can best be gauged by Aaron Hill's thoroughgoing adaptation of the play in 1723.[2]

Designed partly to compensate for the shortage of parts for women in the original, but also possibly to eliminate the unfashionable military heroics, Hill's rewrite chose to abstract the conspiracy of Act 2 for its main story. Hill's Act 1 begins with the first 19 lines of the Chorus to Act 2 and picks up dialogue from all three of the first acts to set the historical background for a story of romantic intrigue. Scroop has a niece, Harriet, who has been seduced by Henry, and now wants revenge. In Act 2 she discusses the conspiracy with the Dauphin and poisons Princess Katherine's mind against Henry. In Act 3 her mood changes from hatred of Henry to love, and she decides to warn him about the conspiracy. In Act 4 he learns of it and placates Harriet, who stabs herself. Act 5 is a dextrous knitting together of fragments from Acts 3 to 5 of the original play,

---

1 See above, p. 4.
2 Hill's version was published in 1723.

with an additional Song by the Genius of England. The play closes with the final 50 lines from the original, including the French acceptance of their defeat and Henry's betrothal to Katherine. The comic scenes are cut completely.

Aaron Hill's version was first staged in 1723 and appeared again at Goodman Fields in 1735 and 1736. In part an assault on the predominance of comedy at the time, the published text was headed by a Preface in which Hill declared that 'the Experience of both our Theatres might have taught any Writer, but so dull a one as I am, that the *Harlequins* are Gentlemen, of better Interest than the *Harrys*.' But, he went on, 'After all, I am sanguine enough to hope, that a Taste for *Tragedy* may be restor'd.' It was later adapted into a one-act play with the name *The Conspiracy Discovered*, in which form it was played at Drury Lane in August 1746. Its subtitle for that performance, 'French Policy Defeated', indicates that its staging was an attempt to capitalise on the current trial of Lords Kilmarnock, Cromarty and Balmerino after the Jacobite Rebellion of 1745. In the meantime Shakespeare's version had arrived at Covent Garden in a scene-divided text which included the Chorus, and otherwise was not greatly altered. First performed in 1738, it returned in 1739, 1740, 1744 and 1745. In 1746, before the one-act version was staged, aware of the recent 'main intendment of the Scot', Covent Garden played the original text twice, in January and March, and the Hill version also in March. In the years following, as hostilities against the French began to grow, the original version reappeared almost every year until 1773.[1]

Scenic and illusionistic staging required more spectacle, fewer words, and not too many breaches of the picture-frame by an intervening choric speaker. The Chorus, spoken by Garrick in 1747, 1748 and 1752, was taken out in 1759, and a good deal more vanished subsequently, according to Bell's text of the Covent Garden prompt-book published in 1773. That version lacks all the Chorus speeches, the bulk of Canterbury's Salic Law speech and his tale of the bees from 1.2, some of Henry's rage against the conspirators in 2.2, the babbling about green fields from 2.3, most of Henry's Harfleur speech, the Boy's speech about his three masters from 3.2, the whole language scene of Kathcrine and her lady in 3.5, the first 150 lines from 3.7, from 4.1 Henry's argument about his responsibility for wicked soldiers, and from 5.2 most of Burgundy's speech about the garden of France and the bawdy joking about Katherine. In 1761 its value as a play of scenic pageantry was enhanced by adding at the beginning the coronation scene from *2 Henry IV*. Initially inserted to celebrate the accession of George III, it remained as part of the patriotic pageantry which was increasingly seen as the play's great strength. Increasingly the Eastcheap scenes were cut.

Between 1773 and 1789 it appeared only three times. After that, with the aid of an adaptation by Charles Kemble, its popularity revived, and it appeared in London in 1789, 1790, 1791, 1792, 1793, and 1794. It then vanished, reviving at the turn of the century when the war with Napoleon and fears of an invasion dominated the mood of the country. Kemble's version, which ruled the stage completely through these years, on the whole followed the Covent Garden text but made still more cuts and some

---

1 For detailed records of performances see *The London Stage, 1660–1800*, ed. W. Van Lennep and others, 11 vols., New York, 1964–8.

switches of scene.[1] The Choruses stayed out. Henry's reform was cut from 1.1, and the Llewellyn–Macmorris quarrel was cut from 3.3. Henry's 'Once more unto the breach' at Harfleur was reduced to four lines and the later part transferred to the end of 4.3, at Agincourt. The threats to Harfleur in 3.4 were cut to ten lines, the French contempt for the English cut from 3.8. Ancient Pistol, a favourite in the eighteenth century in a performance style established by Theophilus Cibber, had lost his swagger, and dwindled accordingly. Kemble removed the whole scene between Pistol and Le Fer (4.4), including the Boy's last speech. Act 4, Scene 2 was rewritten as prose, and the lines naming the dead after Agincourt were cut. Altogether Kemble's text was shorter by one-third than the Folio text.

The last of Kemble's own stagings appeared in 1811. After Waterloo, apart from a single disastrous and expensive attempt at the Kemble version by the ageing Edmund Kean in 1830 at Drury Lane,[2] there was little interest until Macready's great production at the end of the 1830s rode in on the back of the new enthusiasm for 'historical' realism, which, allied to Macready's own reverence for Shakespeare, restored much of the original.

Macready in fact played Henry five times between 1819 and 1839. The five productions are a record of consistent development and growing ambition. He started in the Kemble mould, using costume rather than armour for the battle scenes, but grew unhappy with the Kemble text, wanting to try a version more his own. His 1837 Covent Garden production was derided for its crudity, having, as *The Times* critic put it, not an archer in sight. Static pageant was due to change into historical tableau. This Macready supplied in 1839. It was his farewell production as manager at Covent Garden, and was, in the words of one commentator, 'a kind of summary of all his ideals and ambitions'.[3] Dickens and Forster and other friends were summoned to help at rehearsals. A scenic diorama backed a Chorus dressed as Time, with scythe and hourglass. The third Chorus was backed by the fleet sailing to France, then a panoramic battle with noises off merging into an on-stage siege. The fifth Chorus spoke against a diorama with scenes showing Henry's triumphant return to London. Realistic scenic staging reached a new height and was duly acclaimed by London audiences.

From then on Victorian productions aimed at increasingly lavish and realistic historical spectacles. They were loaded with static tableaux, colourful in sets, banners and heraldic emblems, full of cheering crowds. Samuel Phelps at Sadler's Wells, who had played Exeter and later Burgundy in Macready's productions, was Macready's

---

1 The prompt-books of Kean's productions were regularly published between 1806 and 1859. For one of his earlier productions Macready used a Kemble text of 1815, marked in ink and pencil, which is now in the Folger Shakespeare Library (PROMPT HV 7). It lacks the choruses, which were restored in 1839, and has an ink note at the end saying 'The Play 2 hours 50 minutes'.

2 Kean had played Henry in 1806 and 1815. But by 1830 Hazlitt's and Leigh Hunt's attacks on the play's jingoism had cooled some enthusiasm for it, and the years before the Great Reform Bill were far from jingoistic. More dangerously Kean's health had gone, and with it his memory. The opening scheduled for 22 February was postponed until 8 March, and when it was put on his incompetent performance evoked such a protest from the audience that he was forced to close the play before the end. In *The Times* of 10 March he apologised, saying 'my heart is willing, but my memory has flown'. That was the last drop of the squeezed eighteenth-century versions of the play.

3 Alan S. Downer, *The Eminent Tragedian William Charles Macready*, Cambridge, Mass., 1966, p. 184.

9 The set for Charles Kean's production of 1859, showing the southern gate to London Bridge for the pageant of Henry's return to London, Act 5, Chorus (The Folger Shakespeare Library)

named heir, and his production in 1852 followed its model loyally. Charles Kean at the Princess's seven years later borrowed even more heavily from Macready's 1839 version, adding pageants of the battle at Agincourt and making Henry's return to London a massive set-piece. Trying to make it a companion piece to his celebrated *Richard II*, and remembering the pageant of Bullingbrook's welcome to London that he had inserted in that text, he used a set of London Bridge gateway approached from the south with a cast of six hundred to applaud Henry's return after Agincourt. Kean's two productions sowed seeds in England. It was reported in 1906 that the two plays most studied in schools were *Richard II* and *Henry V*.[1]

In 1852 Phelps worked from a carefully thought-out text, altering the Prologue's 'cockpit' to an 'area', and the 'wooden O' to a 'little space', and breaking the Act 2 Chorus into two parts, using it to lead up to the Eastcheap scene that opens Act 2 but holding back the Southampton lines to preface the conspiracy scene, 2.2. This adjustment, a device to cope with the awkwardness of the Chorus taking the audience to Southampton and then following it with a scene in Eastcheap, became standard in later years. Phelps's breach scene at Harfleur was as much active spectacle as pageant. The Chorus launched the scene, not into Henry's exhortation to his troops, but straight into the fighting. The first spoken words were Bardolph's, and Henry did not give his

1 Reported by Sprague, *Shakespeare's Histories*, p. 99 note 2.

speech until after Llewellyn's assault on the laggards. The stage manager's notes in the prompt-book describe what happened between the Chorus and the Eastcheap second thoughts:

*Reports.*
*Loud Shouts – Drums – Cannon.*
4 large shields with Archers behind also 4 men with Storming Ladders. The whole of the English troops – Soldiers Officers. Westmorland – Bedford – Exeter – Salisbury – Warwick – Williams – Bates – Gower – Erpingham &c – & in a body down platform L3E and off R3E. The Shouts partially outside, Enter King on platform (The army (with Flags) as in a retreat looking off LUE). The King rallies them, and they again rush to attack. Loud shouts – Cannon – Drums – Trumpets. The platform and Panorama move. The men shouting cross platform from L off R3E. 4 of the troops, seen fighting thro' opening in Panorama LUE. when Panorama worked to C. Enter Nym. Bardolph. Fluellen. Pistol and Boy –
Subdue shouts &c a little.

In this production the background music for Agincourt included 'The British Grenadiers'.

Charles Kean's 1859 production outdid the Sadler's Wells version as a historical spectacle. The Prologue, played by Mrs. Kean, became Clio, the Muse of History. She appeared for later choruses in red and blue as Britannia, wearing a crown. The second chorus was backed by a tableau of the three conspirators receiving French gold. Kean's address at the end of the 1859 season, reprinted in his prompt-book, proclaimed the values he looked for:

The period thus recalled is flattering to our national pride; and however much the general feeling of the present day may be opposed to the evils of war, there are few amongst us who can be reminded of the military renown achieved by our ancestors on the fields of Crécy, Poictiers, and Agincourt, without a glow of patriotic enthusiasm.

The descriptive poetry assigned to the 'Chorus' between the acts is retained as a peculiar feature, connecting and explaining the action as it proceeds. This singular personage, so different from the Chorus of antiquity, I have endeavoured to render instrumental to the general effect of the play . . . For the figure of Time, under the semblance of an aged man, which has been heretofore presented, will now be substituted Clio, the muse of History.

Between the fourth and fifth Acts I have ventured to introduce, as in the case of *Richard the Second*, a historical Episode of action, exhibiting the reception of King Henry on returning to his capital after the French expedition.[1]

For the music Kean took a *Te Deum* of 1310 and medieval songs from the recently published Chappell collection. All details scrupulously represented what was thought to be historical reality. The throne room for Act I was based on an engraving of Elizabeth opening Parliament in 1586. His 'Historical Episode. Old London Bridge from the Surrey side of the river. Reception of King Henry the Fifth on entering London, after the Battle of Agincourt' was another impressive piece of Victorian medievalism. The illusionist theatre was nearly ready to turn into cinema.

One trouble with pageants was that like all scenic staging they reduced the time for the words. According to French's edition of 1875, the mid-century texts still left out nearly

1 *Henry V*, (Lacy edition), 1859, p. 7.

10  Charles Kean's set for Act 1, Scene 2, from the prompt-book for his 1859 production (The Folger
Shakespeare Library)

one-third of the original. The pageant aspect was increased in 1876 in John Colman's
adaptation, which, like some earlier versions, started the play with the coronation from
the end of *2 Henry IV*. A long-running and much-travelled production of the 1870s
starred George Rignold as Henry. It used the shortened text and had the now-standard
female Chorus, dressed first as Rumour, with a golden trumpet, and successive changes
to suit the different occasions. It started at Manchester in 1872, went on to New York
in 1875 and then crossed America, reaching London in 1879. It was chiefly famous,
not inappropriately, given all the company's travels, for the white horse named Crispin
which Rignold rode on stage. Henry James disliked its crude realism in New York,[1]
and an account of one performance in a tiny theatre in Colorado Springs may help to
explain his reaction:

When Crispin appeared on the scene, his tail touched the back of the stage, and his forefeet were
firmly planted among the footlights. The climax was reached when King Henry, animating his
dispirited troups with hot, impassioned words, waved above his head the royal standard. The spear
head on the staff became implanted in the low ceiling, and could not be disentangled. Rignold
stopped, completely overcome, saying: 'This is really too ridiculous, ladies and gentlemen. You
must be content simply with the beautiful words of Shakespeare, for I've nothing more to offer
you.'[2]

1  Henry James, *The Scenic Art*, ed. Allan Wade, London, 1948, pp. 26–7.
2  Levette J. Davidson, 'Shakespeare in the Rockies', *SQ* 4 (1953), 39–49, p. 45.

11 Queen Elizabeth on her throne for the opening of Parliament in 1586, in Robert Glover, *Nobilitas Politica vel Civilis*, 1608 (The British Library)

In the first half of the twentieth century, as the theatre began to react against cinematic realism, the words did get more attention. In 1900 the Boer War evoked a production by Frank Benson which, given the insistence on spectacle, was a triumph over adversity. Benson's company lost all its properties in a fire at a Newcastle theatre on 24 November 1899, but he opened with an energetic *Henry V* on the huge stage of the Lyceum on 15 February 1900. The Lyceum had been vacated by Henry Irving, then touring in America, and Benson, after years of touring in Britain, probably saw his chance to make his mark in the metropolis with a play for the times. He certainly made good use of his main assets, the large stage area and his own athletic personality. He deleted the Chorus, added dancing girls to the French camp before Agincourt, and as Henry he pole-vaulted in full armour onto the walls at Harfleur. A similar opportunism in time of war took him back to London with a production of *Henry V* at Christmas 1914.

Lewis Waller's version, also staged at the Lyceum in the winter of 1900–1, was scenically more colourful than Benson's. It had static tableaux, a woman Chorus, and sets so strongly asserting historical realism that their display of heraldry provoked an article in *The Genealogical Magazine*. It offered some corrections to the design of details in the royal arms, and concluded

this play shows a distinct and decided advance in accuracy . . . to any of its predecessors which have come within our notice. The one bare fact, that neither of the two heralds represented in this play either blows or carries a trumpet, is portentous, and augurs, if we may so dare hope, that the hardy race of trumpet-blowing heralds will soon, like the white rhinoceros of South Africa, become altogether extinct in 'Stageland', where they have so often been found.[1]

Richard Mansfield's production in New York in 1900 was also done in what has been called the 'upholstered, heroic manner'.[2] Mansfield's notes to his acting text, printed in 1901, speak of Henry as 'Godly'. He gave him a white horse, too.

By this time, though, Shakespeare in scenic staging was being challenged by William Poel's Elizabethan Stage Society. In 1901 Poel staged *Henry V* at Stratford in the open air without sets or interval, and with only a slight musical backing. The Chorus was an Elizabethan student. It was far from popular, but it was the first step in a shift towards staging which emphasised the language before the spectacle and eventually inspired the first apron-stage performance in December 1936. Poel's arguments against illusionist theatre led E. K. Chambers to invoke *Henry V*'s Prologue and its apology for inadequate staging against him. This in turn prompted Beerbohm Tree to claim that had Shakespeare enjoyed modern resources he would have used them. Tree went so far as to claim that Shakespeare 'not only foresaw, but desired, the system of production that is now most in public favour'.[3] The other side, including Sidney Lee, Granville Barker, and George Bernard Shaw, maintained that the Prologue, as an exhortation to

1 G. Ambrose Lee, 'The heraldry of Shakespeare's "King Henry the Fifth" at the Lyceum Theatre', *The Genealogical Magazine*, February 1901, p. 449.
2 Sprague, *Shakespeare's Histories*, p. 96.
3 E. K. Chambers, 'The stage of the Globe', in *The Works of Shakespeare*, Stratford, 1907, p. 10; Beerbohm Tree, *Thoughts and Afterthoughts*, London, 1915, p. 60. The debate is described by Cary M. Mazer, *Shakespeare Refashioned: Elizabethan Plays on Edwardian Stages*, Ann Arbor, 1981, pp. 50–2. One of the better critiques of this debate over how to stage Shakespeare, with some comments on the *Henry V*

the imagination, was anti-illusionistic. Poel's kind of staging was tried again during the war period, in full-text versions by Martin Harvey at His Majesty's in 1916, using the theory of alternate inner- and outer-stage scenes, at Stratford by W. Bridges-Adams in 1920, and by Robert Atkins at the Old Vic in 1921.

Little attention was paid to *Henry V* between the Boer War and the First World War, and not much to it between the two world wars. There were two productions besides Benson's during the First World War, one of them by an all-woman cast, and there was another by an all-woman cast in 1921. Nigel Playfair produced it at the Lyric, Hammersmith in the winter of 1927 with a variation on the woman Chorus in the form of Sybil Thorndike acting it as an Elizabethan boy. Otherwise it sank again until war fever began to mount in 1936 and 1937.

Three productions were mounted in London between December 1936 and the lull that followed the Munich agreement in the summer of 1938. First Robert Atkins, who was the mainspring of the Regent's Park Open Air Theatre, opened at the Ring in Blackfriars. The Ring had been a boxing stadium, and Atkins, a keen follower of Poel, set up a thrust stage with a form of Elizabethan tiring house as backdrop. His *Henry V* was an athletic production which galvanised the actors as they found themselves for the first time speaking in the middle of their audience. It may have had some covert influence on the use of an Elizabethan theatre setting as the 'frame' for Laurence Olivier's film in 1944. The film, though, was more directly influenced by Olivier's own stage performance in 1937 at the Old Vic, where several of the actors cast for the film played with Olivier, including Leo Genn as Burgundy, and Harcourt Williams as the French king. The third production of this period was Lewis Casson's in the summer of 1938 at Drury Lane. Making spectacular use of banners, armour and cannon fire, it renewed the device of having a woman play the Chorus as a boy.

In the 1940s the bombing of London made theatre runs more hazardous than in the previous war. Robert Atkins did *Henry V* in Regent's Park in the Battle of Britain summer of 1941, but otherwise the great staging was Olivier's film. It is in the nature of films to be scenic, and in a way Olivier's version might be seen as the apotheosis of the nineteenth-century trend to historical realism. Brilliantly inventive, Olivier coped with the double problem that a realistic medium set him, the non-realistic Chorus and the equally non-realistic verse, by starting the play in the frame of an Elizabethan stage performance, as a play within a film. Doing so admitted verse-speaking from the outset and allowed Olivier to follow the tradition started by Tyrone Guthrie at the Old Vic in 1937 of making the Salic Law speeches comic. It was an ingeniously metatheatrical trick. The film dissolves gradually, step by step, into cinematic realism, becoming a film within a play within a film. It starts being realistic before Harfleur, where Henry appears on horseback, and completes the transformation in the Agincourt scenes.

Inevitably, given that it was filmed in the months up to the D-Day landings, it was one of the last versions to present an unambiguously heroic Henry. Because of that and because it was cinema, the Agincourt scenes take up a disproportionate space. The

productions of the period, is Gordon Crosse, *Shakespearean Playgoing 1890–1952*, London, 1953. Poel's career is described in Robert Speaight, *William Poel and the Elizabethan Revival*, London, 1954.

use of County Wicklow's open hills in Ireland and a large assembly of Irish soldiers, farmers, and Dublin cabmen was the boldest as well as the costliest single feature of the adaptation.[1] The central section of the film, the realistically portrayed battle, almost completely abandons speech (the whole script at 1,500 lines is not much above half the full text) for visual effects. Since there is no battle scene in the play itself apart from Pistol and Le Fer, that was an inevitable adjustment. It is all Hollywood, with a great charge of French horsemen taken from Griffiths, an Eisenstein-like flight of arrows through the sky, and English soldiers dropping from branches to pull the French knights from their horses as in Errol Flynn's Robin Hood films. The re-transformation into theatre at the very end, when we see Henry's stage make-up, and Katherine turns back into a boy actor, works more as a joke, a reminder of the theatrical frame which the sensational Agincourt scenes had made the audience forget, than as a post-modernist renewal of the narrational frame.

Since the war Britain has seen rather more productions than in the past. Partly this reflects the growth of theatre in education, partly the trend to mark festivals and anniversaries with a sequence of plays. And in part it gained new life as an anti-war play. The full course of the Henriad opened the new Stratford theatre in 1932. The sequence reappeared there in 1951 during the Festival of Britain, in 1964 for the Shakespeare quatercentenary (the first truly sceptical production), and in a four-play variant, with *Merry Wives* instead of *Richard II*, for the Memorial Theatre centenary season in 1975. The Falklands conflict did not bring a revival, although more warlike Henries appeared in 1984–5. Not surprisingly, the general shift of attention from Henry as hero to a self-doubting man acting the part of a king loosened the patriotic fervour while still holding its focus on the charisma of the central character.

Outside Britain *Henry V* has rarely been staged in non-English-speaking countries, although a similar pattern to Britain's can be found in North America. Joseph Papp's New York Festival production in 1960 was notable for 'dash and splendor and spectacle',[2] but Michael Langham's 1966 production at Stratford, Ontario had photographs of the Vietnam War in its programme, and Michael Kahn's 1969 American Shakespeare Festival version was both anti-illusionist and anti-militaristic, as was Gregory Boyd's production for the Great Lakes Festival at Lakewood, Ohio in 1983. Stratford (UK) and New York both saw more heroic Henries in 1984, with Kevin Kline in Wilfred Leach's production at the New York Festival in 1984 and Kenneth Branagh's youthfully valiant Henry in Adrian Noble's version in Stratford and London.

Easing away from illusionist staging in postwar Henries has strengthened the function of the Chorus as a means of emphasising the theatricality of the story. He (now male again) is usually made a compère or 'presenter'. The Chorus at Stratford Ontario in 1966 was called 'an animated playbill'.[3] This interceding figure has been made to

1 During the location shooting the cost overruns led to the film's producers, London Films, being taken over by the emergent J. Arthur Rank Corporation.
2 *Shakespeare Around the Globe: A Guide to Notable Postwar Revivals*, ed. Samuel L. Leither, New York, 1986, p. 214. An overview by Daniel J. Watermeier of the major performances of *Henry V* is given on pages 213–31.
3 *Ibid.*, p. 215.

offer the play with, increasingly, some scepticism towards its heroics, either in the story as spectacle or in Henry play-acting his heroic role. The Chorus in Adrian Noble's production at Stratford in 1984–5 remained on stage throughout, like the ghostly figures of Revenge and Don Andrea in the National Theatre's *Spanish Tragedy* of the previous year. Terry Hands at Stratford, in a celebrated production for its centenary year, 1975, put the Chorus (who had played Henry's father, and who also played Burgundy) into modern dress, as had John Neville at the Old Vic in 1960. The problem of the awkward fit that the Chorus's commentaries make in the narrative sequence has generally been ignored since the nineteenth century, though it evoked some old-fashioned adjustments in Arthur Lithgow's production for the Great Lakes Shakespeare Festival in 1963. He put the second Chorus between Eastcheap in 2.1 and Southampton in 2.2, as Macready and Phelps had done and as the 1975 Stratford production also did. Lithgow also split the fourth Chorus before Agincourt, putting the French camp scene (3.8) in between.

The anti-illusionism strengthened by the Chorus function has emerged in varying ways since Olivier's film. Open-stage productions were mounted at Harvard in 1956 and at Stratford Ontario in the same year, where Christopher Plummer played Henry, later transferring to Edinburgh. Peter Hall's 1964 Henriad at Stratford used a thrust stage. The most adventurous though not the most well-received innovation was in the 1975 Stratford production. It started on a bare set with all the cast in track suits, as if rehearsing, and only gradually allowed the costumes and the spectacular hung cloths of the set to come in. Henry became a neurotically anxious actor who gradually learns his part as a conqueror while the story unfolds. Alan Howard, who played Henry and has some searching comments about the play,[1] pointed out that Henry uses the word 'soldier' five times in his speech to the Governor of Harfleur, linked with images of hell, as if to remind himself about the role he is now taking on.

Post-war concern about war's horrors prompted the introduction of added business over the killing of the prisoners at Agincourt. In the 1950s it became standard to show the Eastcheap Boy being killed by French soldiers on stage, sometimes with Henry's order to kill the prisoners following his discovery of the body, as Gower's interpretation of the events suggests he does. At the Great Lakes Festival in 1963 the business was curiously fudged. The 'formal battle' of Agincourt was followed by 4.4, between Pistol and Le Fer, ending with the Boy's speech. As the Boy left he met the Constable of France, who stabbed him on stage. The account of the deaths of York and Suffolk and the order to kill the prisoners were cut, but when Henry re-entered to speak the 'I was not angry' speech he had a dead 'child' in his arms. The 1975 Stratford production, playing *Henry V* along with the two Henry IV plays in a Falstaff season, also killed the Boy on stage. It, though, made the Boy not Falstaff's boy from *2 Henry IV* but Francis the drawer from *1 Henry IV*, giving a personal edge to Henry's reaction. Kenneth Branagh's 1989 film used a similar device to emphasise Henry's ambivalence and sensitivity to the horrors of war, ending the battle with Henry walking off, the dead Boy in his arms.

1 Sally Beauman, *The R.S.C.'s Production of 'Henry V' for the Centenary Season at the Royal Shakespeare Theatre*, Oxford, 1976, *passim*.

12   Llewellyn (Ian Holm) approaches Henry (Kenneth Branagh) on the battlefield of Agincourt after Henry has named it (4.7.77–80). From Kenneth Branagh's 1989 film

At Stratford in 1975 the horror was emphasised by the now-usual reordering of the sequence relating to the order to kill the prisoners, following Gower's version of the story. The Boy was killed on-stage before the entry of the disordered French in 4.5, who were followed by Llewellyn entering with his comments on the 'poys and the luggage'. Henry arrived a few lines later to say he had not been angry till that moment, whereupon Exeter announced that the French had reinforced their scattered men. Henry's prompt order to kill the prisoners thus became both retaliation and expedience. Pistol cut Le Fer's throat on stage, anticipating Gary Taylor's augmentation of the Folio text with the Quarto in the Oxford edition.

Given the rise of anti-war feeling, it is not surprising that a sensitive Henry has been standard in post-war productions. Always hesitant about the brutalities of war, and the price of renouncing Falstaff and his fellows, he has been varied more in his disguises and role-playing than in his heroism. Ian Holm's Henry at Stratford in 1964, the first production to make him a calculating politician, played the entire wooing scene (5.2) as a wearisome diplomatic manoeuvre, made wonderfully comic by the fluttering Alice's archly romantic interventions. Richard Burton's tight-lipped portrayal at Stratford in 1951 made much of the naming of Bardolph for execution in 3.7, as did David Gwillim in the 1979 BBC television film. Branagh in his film showed Bardolph being hanged in Henry's presence. The camera's command of close-ups puts a premium on shows of mutely conflicting emotions in the faces of the cinematic Henries.

Terry Hands has said that he started the 1975 Stratford centenary season with *Henry V* because it was the play which most thoroughly embodied the Stratford company's problems and their needs. He saw it as the study of an army of radically diverse people gradually uniting into a brotherhood. 'It is a play of great vitality, with a surging up-beat text: potentially, it has all the impact necessary to herald such a crucial double season. Second, it is about improvisation, interdependence, and unity: three essential qualities if the company was to surmount its present difficulties.' This unity, Hands went on to say, was not the patriotism of Olivier's film but the theatre company's team spirit: 'individuals aware of their responsibilities, both to themselves and to each other . . . a real brotherhood.'[1] In uses like this, perhaps, the play as a problematic work for the student and yet the producer of potent emotional responses in performance is beginning to receive more serious attention than it has ever yet had.

## Recent critical and stage interpretations

NEW THOUGHTS

Since this edition first appeared in 1992, a lot of rethinking has been registered in views of the play, some of it by the editor. Mostly it has intensified the idea that when Shakespeare first wrote the text that was used to print the First Folio version, he was well aware of its ambivalent character. Norman Rabkin's idea that the play stands like a black silhouette which can be seen either as a rabbit or as a duck, but never as both, has come to seem the play's most challenging feature.[2] Readers and directors have to choose whether their Henry is either a Christian king and heroic leader of his nation or a ruthless self-seeker who acts the role of good king for his own profit. He cannot be both. Under pressure from the swell of anti-war feeling, most recent stage and screen productions have tried, unsuccessfully, to give him something of both aspects.

Study of the first Quarto of 1600 suggests that Shakespeare knew his company would never try to stage the ambivalent text he gave them. Two features of the Folio text affirm that quite clearly. The first is the pair of authorial stage directions that launch the third act. The Chorus speaks of 'the ordnance on their carriages / With fatal mouths gaping on girded Harfleur', and how 'the nimble gunner / With linstock now the devilish cannon touches / *Alarm, and chambers go off /* And down goes all before them.' Off-stage explosions signal the attack. Henry and his nobles enter, followed by soldiers carrying '*scaling ladders at Harfleur*', as he launches his celebrated exhortation, 'Once more unto the breach, dear friends, once more, / Or close the wall up with our English dead!', a speech that closes with another order for chambers to be fired. The 1600 Quarto text removed the speech along with the Chorus and all three stage directions.

---

1 *Ibid.*, pp. 14–15.
2 Norman Rabkin, 'Rabbits, ducks, and *Henry V*', *SQ* 28 (1977), 279–96, reprinted in revised form as 'Either/or: responding to *Henry V*', chapter 2 of *Shakespeare and the Problem of Meaning*, 1981.

This means that almost certainly they were kept out of the first staged version of the play, the version that the Quarto derived from, for reasons that were clearer to Shakespeare's fellow-players than they have been to subsequent commentators. Readers of the play, and stage and film directors, have been slow to realise that the attack Henry inspires in the Folio was a failure.

In Shakespeare's original version, the soldiers who were to bring on the ladders to scale the walls damaged by Henry's ordnance would have put them against the stage balcony before climbing them to enter the upper level of the tiring house, as if they were entering the town. Three scenes later, however, Henry stands in front of the same balcony ordering the governor to surrender. The governor replies to him from the place the soldiers climbed up to on their ladders, above the central opening, now the city gates which he invites the English army to enter. The Quarto's compressed version does not have the soldiers invade the town. All that its version puts on stage is the Eastcheap laggards being beaten off stage by Llewellyn, and some of the debate from the Folio's lengthy argument about the problems with the mines. For the company rewriters to keep the original version with Henry's speech of exhortation would have shown it leading to the deaths of the ladder-carrying English. As Annabel Patterson argued in 1989, the Quarto streamlines Shakespeare's ambivalence into a simpler play showing Henry exclusively as a hero.

Assertions about the dual character of the Folio text raise serious doubts about its viability on stage. A hero play like the Quarto's simplification could be staged, but not both rabbit and duck. Stephen Greenblatt in *Shakespearean Negotiations* (1988), facing the upsurge of anti-war versions of the play, was the first to raise the question whether the Folio text 'can be successfully performed as subversive'.[1] Graham Bradshaw has argued against the early audiences having any shared preconceptions about Henry, and identifies a complex ambivalence in the author. Trying to keep a balance between Tillyardian royalists and subversive readers, he occupies a middle position, objecting to 'prematurely politicized readings that short-circuit the genuinely exploratory process of Shakespeare's dramatic thinking'.[2] Harry Berger Jr, in an article published in 2003,[3] claims that the Folio text denies its own capacity to stage a heroic vision of Henry through its 'anti-theatricalism'. If there is substance in the necessarily brief reassessment we give here of the most recent trends in thinking about the play, it does seem to make the ambivalence of the Folio text an almost intolerably difficult challenge to any stage or film director.

TEXTUAL EMENDATIONS AND NOTES
First, though, we should note some reconsideration of details in the text and small features of the staging in the Folio text. The only fresh edition has been T. W. Craik's

---

1 Stephen Greenblatt, *Shakespearean Negotiations: The Circulation of Social Energy in Renaissance England*, Oxford, 1988, p. 63.
2 Graham Bradshaw, *Misrepresentations: Shakespeare and the Materialists*, Ithaca, 1993, p. 38.
3 Harry Berger Jr, 'Harrying the stage: *Henry V* in the tetralogical echo chamber', *The Shakespearean International Yearbook* 3, 2003, pp. 131–55.

Arden 3 *King Henry V* in 1995.[1] Conservative in its view of the play and its text, it is notable for a few well-argued new readings. Rather too often, however, it denies the Shakespearean characteristic of admitting multiple meanings for words such as 'quarrels' (4.1.198), or 'uncoined' (5.2.145). Denying Shakespeare the capacity to play with his words is not a popular approach. The new ideas about possibly fresh readings of the text by Craik and others are noted here.

Of the more substantial proposals, Williams and Berger[2] argue that 1.2.307, 'God before' should be taken as a succinct prayer. In Exeter's speech at 2.4.118–20, for F's version of line 118 'Scorne and defiance, sleight regard, contempt', they prefer Capell's placing of a semi-colon after 'defiance' in order to differentiate the direct words of feeling from the words by which the king prizes the Dauphin. For the much-debated term at 4.2.9–10, where the blood of the French horses will 'spin in English eyes', they conjecture 'spit'. At 4.5.21–3, where the same word is repeated in 'throngs . . . throng', they think a compositor anticipated the correct word, because both come at the end of adjacent lines. They conjecture that the first of the two should have been 'swarmes'. Similarly in Burgundy's long speech about peace, at 5.2.54–8, they argue that 'for want of time' makes no sense, and suggest that 'time' might be a compositor's misreading of the manuscript's 'care'. They also suggest that the second of the two rhyming couplets closing the Chorus speech at 2.0.39–42 may be a non-Shakespearean intrusion, since all the other choruses end with just one. Each couplet addresses the auditors direct, but the first is jocular, and would make a good ending to the speech, while the final couplet is contrastingly formal and informative.

Norman Blake's notes on the language include a comment on the neologism 'vasty', used by the Prologue (1.0.12), Henry at 2.2.120, and Exeter at 2.4.106. He notes (p. 28) that adding a terminal 'y' is not necessarily poetic, and was chiefly used to make adjectives insulting.[3] Other views, including some features of T. W. Craik's Arden 3 edition, favour the original spelling of words such as 'vaward' (4.3.130) rather than the standard modernisations used in this edition, on the ground that they are distinct in meaning from modern usage.

Williams and Berger also have a note about the handling of the gloves at the meeting between Williams the soldier and Llewellyn with gloves in their caps. Where the gloves are is marked for us by the gestures accompanying the two uses of the word 'this' at 4.8.5–7, when Llewellyn, wearing Williams the soldier's glove in his cap, meets Williams wearing Henry's glove in his. When Williams says 'know you this glove?' at line 5 he takes the king's glove from his cap and flourishes it. When Llewellyn fails to recognise it, Williams gestures to his own glove now fixed in Llewellyn's cap and strikes it, boxing his ear in the process. In this edition, the glove belonging to Williams that Henry gave Llewellyn to wear is the one filled with gold and returned to Williams. The Williams and Berger team feel this to be unnecessary. They claim, rightly, that the

1 T. W. Craik, ed., *King Henry V*, The Arden Shakespeare. Third Series, London, 1995.
2 Thomas L. Berger and George Walton Williams, 'Notes on Shakespeare's *Henry V*', *Analytical and Enumerative Bibliography* 12 (2001), 264–87.
3 Norman Blake, 'Shakespeare's text: introduction and commentary', *Studies in English Language and Linguistics* 4 (2002), 23–36, esp. 28–9, 32–4.

soldier Williams's first 'this' refers to the glove in his own cap, his second (line 7) to the one in Llewellyn's. They approve of Craik's argument about the subsequent exchanges, following Taylor, that at line 35 Henry asks Williams to give him the glove in Williams's cap, and shows him its fellow in his own hand. Llewellyn's 'this' at 33 must mean the glove under discussion, the one belonging to Williams which he exchanged for Henry's at 4.1.189 and which now is in Llewellyn's cap. At 4.8.35 Henry asks Williams for the glove he is wearing, and matches it with his own. In my reading Henry has to take the glove that Williams is wearing from him at 35 in order to return it to Williams filled with gold at 51. The Williams and Berger team claim that this leaves the king's glove in Llewellyn's cap, which it does not. They find this edition's reading of the gestures less 'economical' than Taylor's or Craik's, which requires the glove returned to Williams full of gold to be Henry's, he keeping the other to wave at Williams when telling him to wear the royal glove in his cap until the king should challenge it. He clearly has both gloves in his hands at line 35, when he shows Williams that they match. Hence the inserted stage direction at line 34. Craik's point, that it must be the king's glove with the crowns in it that Henry tells him to wear henceforth until Henry challenges it, is a good one, however. Berger and Williams also argue that the blow Williams gives to Llewellyn is a more general blow than the threatened box on the ear where the Williams glove was lodged.

Craik also re-examines the game between Nym and Pistol in 2.1 when they keep drawing and sheathing their swords. Specifically at line 54, Craik argues, Nym, Pistol, and Bardolph must all three sheathe their swords before Pistol offers his hand as a peace-making gesture to Nym. When he says 'Give me thy fist', his right hand must be free, since up to then it would have held his sword. When Nym scorns Pistol's offer, Pistol draws his sword again. Alternatively, Nym might not have sheathed his sword along with Pistol and Bardolph at line 54, when Pistol says 'and fury shall abate'. That would allow him to reject Pistol's offer of peace by waving the sword he still holds. On Bardolph's second order, at lines 80–1, he is again slower than Pistol to sheathe his weapon.

Other details in Craik's edition include 3.4.8, where he offers as a new pronunciation an emphasis in 'half-achievèd Harfleur', stressing the first syllable of 'Harfleur', and making the line eleven syllables with a feminine ending. At 3.4.47, he proposes 'dread king' for the Folio 'great', on the grounds that the compositor may have repeated 'great' by dittography from 'so great a siege' earlier in the same line.

A notable addition to the study of songs in Shakespeare is Ross W. Duffin, *Shakespeare's Songbook*.[1] On *Henry V*, he notes that Pistol's exclamation 'Colin o custure me' (4.4.3) is the refrain of a love song, the words and music of which he reproduces (p. 86). He also notes that the tune 'Nutmegs and Ginger', referred to in the Dauphin's reply to Orleans at 3.8.18–19, appears in early manuscripts under the name 'Kemp's jig' (p. 277). The clown Will Kemp left the Shakespeare company some time in 1599 to dance his way from London to Norwich for a bet, most likely while Shakespeare was writing the play.

---

1 Ross W. Duffin, *Shakespeare's Songbook*, New York, 2004.

13  Adrian Lester as Henry in the National Theatre production of 2003, with members of the company as his soldiers. Henry has a pistol and a microphone in his hands

## STAGE HISTORY

Two excellent books about the play's stage history have appeared in recent years: James N. Loehlin's history in the 'Shakespeare in Performance' series,[1] and Emma Smith's edition in the 'Shakespeare in Production' series,[2] which registers what individual actors and productions did at each section of the play. Both of them take careful note of the distinction between the two views of Henry set out in the play. Loehlin offers a pointed version of the 'rabbit and duck' alternatives by starting with John Arden's comment that a 'secret' play lurks inside the 'official' play. The actions of Henry and others subvert and even contradict the official story told us by the Chorus. The two books record a wide variety of responses in the theatre to the play's ambivalence, noting how the 'secret' version has been given more and more account since the Second World War. In the process they show how difficult the Folio text is to stage in all its ambivalence without introducing drastic changes. The first fourteen pages of Loehlin's introductory chapter give us a concise and lucid summary of the major features of the play as 'official' and 'secret'. He reckons, for instance, that what he calls the 'celebration of heroic individualism' in Kenneth Branagh's film of the play makes it an official version disguised as a secret one (p. 145). Both books emphasise the drastic choices necessary to produce any stageable version of the Folio text.

1 James Loehlin, *Shakespeare in Performance: Henry V*, Manchester, 1996.
2 Emma Smith, *King Henry V*, Shakespeare in Production, Cambridge, 2002.

14 William Huston as Henry in the Royal Shakespeare Company production of 2000–1, with his soldiers at Harfleur

Since Loehlin's and Smith's books appeared, no major innovatory productions have appeared on stage. Nicholas Hytner's production starring Adrian Lester at the Royal National Theatre in London in 2003 followed the wartime tradition by using desert war uniforms and military weapons and vehicles on stage familiar from television images of that year's invasion of Iraq. The play's war speeches were given on large-screen television. Henry himself executed Bardolph on stage with an impatient pistol shot to the head. Edward Hall (son of Peter, producer of the most 'secret' version of the play yet seen, in 1964 at Stratford) adopted a comically referential approach in 1997 at the Watermill Theatre in Newbury. He took the audience out of doors for Harfleur, mounting his Henry on a bay horse to deliver his 'Once more unto the breach' oration, in an oblique burlesque of Olivier's film, where Henry speaks from a white horse in the first of the film's openly cinematic scenes. Like all Shakespeare, especially in the subsidised English theatre, no production can ever escape its predecessors. Hall directed a more subtle version of the play as part of a series including the Henry IV plays, with William Huston in the title role, at Stratford in 2001.

RECENT BOOKS AND ARTICLES
Fresh criticism of the play has matched the stagings in its struggle between providing an 'official' or a 'secret' reading of the play. The older view, set out by Tillyard and

others, still rears its anglophile head, especially when critics look at *Henry V* as the concluding work of the four plays in the whole cycle beginning with *Richard II*. Tom McAlindon's essay in his book *Shakespeare Minus 'Theory'*,[1] sets out what is probably the most articulate case for continuing to view Henry as hero–king. In an essay in *The Shakespearean International Yearbook* 3 he scans the wooing scene as an act of mutual admiration, and argues that the dual Henry, hard warrior and gentle wooer, is a model of Renaissance concepts of manliness.[2] In the process, though, he passes over all the hints about Henry's exercise of self-interest such as the order to kill the prisoners.

Tillyard's providentialist reading of the philosophy lying behind the history plays is rarely heard now, in the wake of Stephen Greenblatt's 'Invisible bullets', the second chapter of *Shakespearean Negotiations* an essay first published in 1981.[3] The more radical critics tend to favour the machiavellian view of history as based on human self-interest that Bacon and other Tudor philosophers upheld, and that dominates modern thinking about history. Hugh Grady, *Shakespeare, Machiavelli, and Montaigne*,[4] surveys the history plays from *Richard II*, with *Hamlet* as a postlude, in this light. Machiavelli, wrote Bacon approvingly, affirms what men do, not what they ought to do, an apt position for writers of drama. Such a position presents a special challenge to the reader. Graham Bradshaw's *Misrepresentations* devotes ninety pages to the problems the play presents for any historicist reading.

On the context and sources of the play, Annabel Patterson's *Reading Holinshed's Chronicles*,[5] in its analysis of the political eclecticism of the authors who were Shakespeare's chief source, takes issue persuasively against Phyllis Rackin's reading in *Stages of History: Shakespeare's English Chronicles*.[6] Her argument implicitly sets up the form of drama, showing what men do and not what they ought to do, as analogous to Holinshed's approach to his historical data. The view that a similarly pragmatic approach was the essence of Machiavelli is now generally accepted as the basis for most Tudor histories. In her book Patterson also gives a full account of the issues behind the Oldcastle story, which reverberates through the last three plays of the *Henry IV–V* cycle.

In *Shakespeare's Arguments with History*, Ronald Knowles takes a 'secret' play approach, opening his chapter (6) on *Henry V* by asserting 'the action is war, which culminates in Agincourt, and the argument is its justification, which is challenged immediately before the battle'.[7] Richard Hillman (*Shakespeare, Marlowe and the Politics of France*) underwrites and complicates Knowles's point about the argument being the justice of war by bringing in Nashe's references to Talbot, along with *Edward III*'s account of the Crécy story. He embeds these in the historiographical question, especially

1 Tom McAlindon, *Shakespeare Minus 'Theory'*, Aldershot, 2004.
2 'Natural closure in *Henry V*', *The Shakespearean International Yearbook* 3, 2003, pp. 156–71.
3 *Shakespearean Negotiations*, pp. 21–65; originally published in *Glyph* 8 (1981), 40–61.
4 Hugh Grady, *Shakespeare, Machiavelli, and Montaigne: Power and Subjectivity from 'Richard II' to 'Hamlet'*, Oxford, 2002, chapter 5.2.
5 Annabel Patterson *Reading Holinshed's Chronicles*, Chicago, 1994, pp. 16–32, 131–53.
6 Phyllis Rackin, *Stages of History: Shakespeare's English Chronicles*, Ithaca, 1990.
7 Ronald Knowles, *Shakespeare's Arguments with History*, Basingstoke, 2001, p. 87.

of old versus new historicism, notably the killing of the prisoners (pp. 191–2).[1] Theodor Meron, in *Bloody Constraint: War and Chivalry in Shakespeare*,[2] looks into contemporary accounts of the laws of war for what they say about a ruler's responsibility for waging war. Jean Howard and Phyllis Rackin's *Engendering a Nation: A Feminist Account of Shakespeare's English Histories* lays out the patriarchal assumptions vested in the plays.[3] Chapter 12 on *Henry V* compares Henry's approach to his Kate with Hotspur's to his wife Kate in *1 Henry IV*, seeing the name itself as 'an act of domestication', as in *The Taming of the Shrew*. They uphold Lance Wilcox's view of Henry's wooing as a rape,[4] and trace the contrast of the play's 'performative masculinity' with its representations of female vulnerability. 'The entire French kingdom is represented as a woman to be conquered by the masculine force of the English army' (p. 213). Nina Taunton makes the now-familiar comparison of Henry's threats to Harfleur with Tamburlaine's. She argues persuasively that Henry's words with his soldiers before Agincourt 'problematize Henry's generalship'.[5] Like Meron, she registers the early views about the moral codes of war.

Concern with the language games of the different accents in the play continues, best summarised in Janette Dillon's neat account.[6] Michael Neill's essay in *Putting History to the Question*[7] extends these implications into the broader frame of English colonialist thinking at the end of the century. Sarah Werner reconsiders the role of Princess Katherine, and the related imagery of the rape of France and English soldiers. She develops the arguments of Wilcox and this Introduction (pp. 13–14) by asking what the effect of a boy actor playing the role would be.[8]

Harry Berger Jr, chiefly celebrated for insisting that Shakespeare when read at leisure on the page is superior to encounters through the three hours' traffic of the modern stage, has an essay based on the Folio text, claiming that it denies its own capacity to be staged.[9] Arguing for what he calls 'Shakespeare's anti-theatricalism', Berger reckons that 'the staged play is reductively framed' by the Folio's Chorus as a pageant for the royal triumph. He makes the point that the Folio text emphasises the play's continuity with its predecessors, whereas the Quarto stands alone in upholding Henry's heroism. He also notes, though, that 'taken by itself, [the Folio] *Henry V* solicits an objective response to its protagonist; either praise or something else for this mirror of all Christian kings'. He underlines the ambivalence of Henry's 'concern for moral solvency', and his wholly personal pursuit of success in the war. In effect, Berger attempts to maintain a balance between the official and the secret play by arguing that the reader can keep

1 Richard Hillman, *Shakespeare, Marlowe and the Politics of France*, Basingstoke, 2002, pp. 191–2.
2 Theodor Meron *Bloody Constraint: War and Chivalry in Shakespeare*, Oxford, 1998, pp. 157–60.
3 Jean Howard and Phyllis Rackin, *Engendering a Nation: A Feminist Account of Shakespeare's English Histories*, Routledge, 1997.
4 Lance Wilcox, 'Katherine of France as victim and bride', *S.St.* 17 (1985), 61–76.
5 Nina Taunton, *1590s Drama and Militarism: Portrayals of War in Marlowe, Chapman and Shakespeare's Henry V*, Basingstoke, 2001, p. 66.
6 Janette Dillon, *Language and Stage in Medieval and Renaissance England*, Cambridge, 1998, pp. 177–82.
7 Michael Neill, *Putting History to the Question: Power Politics, and Society in English Renaissance Drama*, New York, 2002, pp. 357–72.
8 'Firk and foot: the boy actor in *Henry V*', *Shakespeare Bulletin* 21 (2003), 19–27.
9 'Harrying the stage', pp. 131–55.

the ambivalence in mind, whereas the stage version denies itself through its Choric disclaimers as its author's own denial of the play's theatricality.

Patterson's comparison of the Folio text with the Quarto finds in their differences a set of adjustments made in the Quarto for, she claims, entirely political reasons.[1] It has to be said that such critics, when they argue in favour of either the official or the secret version, are unlikely to give their readers much sense of the complex interactions between the two that are there in the Folio version of the play. The whole story, if set out in its full complexity by the author, as I believe it was, needs a more broadly holistic approach than modern political convictions can afford to give us.

One book with substantial implications for any reading of *Henry V* as an ambivalent play is Lukas Erne's *Shakespeare as Literary Dramatist*.[2] The title's emphasis is on 'literary', because Erne's chief argument is that the printing of the early Quartos and the Folio was designed for a new market, the reading of printed play-texts. This approach to the plays, which underrates the controlling status of the companies as owners of all the Shakespeare playbooks rather than the author, leads Erne to study the early market for the Quartos and the distinct origins of different play-texts. He insists, rightly, that the company was happy to have its plays published, usually a couple of years after their first appearance on stage. He goes on, less plausibly, to dismiss the standard idea that Shakespeare himself took no interest in getting his plays into print, arguing that the 'corrected' Quartos of *Romeo and Juliet*, *Hamlet*, perhaps *Love's Labour's Lost*, and *Troilus and Cressida*, were issued at the author's instigation.

The second part of Erne's book is the most relevant to *Henry V*. He argues that the so-called 'bad' Quartos were unlikely to have been shortened for performance in the provinces, and that their relationship to performed texts should not discount their character as texts issued for the reader. In chapter 8 he studies three of these so-called 'bad' play-texts, including Q1 *Henry V* (the others are Q1 *Romeo and Juliet* and Q1 *Hamlet*). Erne makes a strong case for the prints of these three plays being prepared for the reader from a performance text that was not the manuscript the company originally bought from the author. Noting the relative brevity of each text, and denying the old assumption that they were shortened for performance in the provinces, he claims (p. 241) that these shorter performance texts differ from their longer originals because they were designed for different media. Shakespeare, in other words, meant his original scripts from the start for readers, while the players routinely shortened and reshaped them for their playhouse audiences.

I would argue that the variety in the origins of the longer texts does not support this idea with much consistency. We know the company chose to give the press such spare copies of the authorial manuscripts as they had, retaining their own key manuscript, the 'allowed book', for themselves because it contained the vital signature by the Master of the Revels authorising it for performance. What the company gave the printer was whatever version was at hand that they did not need for company use. Very few manuscripts

---

1 'Back by popular demand: the two versions of *Henry V*', *Renaissance Drama* n.s.19 (1988), 29–62, revised in *Shakespeare and the Popular Voice*, Oxford, 1989, chapter 4.
2 *Shakespeare as Literary Dramatist*, Cambridge, 2003.

ever survived the heavy process of use as printer's copy, and certainly no playbooks. So authorial manuscripts preceding the transcript sent to the Master of the Revels for authorisation as an acting text were the kind of copy most likely to be used to print the Folio.[1]

While not accepting the ambition and control over his plays that Erne assumes Shakespeare had, I do believe that the Quarto version of *Henry V* represents as closely as any playscript can what the company did with the manuscript Shakespeare sold them. That the original manuscript was later printed in the Folio version we all know. The fact that Q1 contains three occurrences of the rare accident in which characters who have just left the stage re-enter immediately for the next scene may support Erne's case for Q1 as a reader's text, since only one such re-entry exists in any of the Folio plays. That is in *The Tempest*, where it spreads across an act-break of the sort introduced after 1608 when the company acquired the indoor Blackfriars for winter use.

If we accept that the Folio text, and perhaps the Quarto text too, were printed to be read rather than performed on stage, Erne's book offers a means to identify the different versions of the text as designed for readers as well as for audiences, but coming to the press from drastically different sources. Erne does makes some use of the edition of Q1 *Henry V* that I prepared for the New Cambridge Quarto series. The final section here offers an amended version of Erne's argument set out in the light of the findings in my 2000 edition of the Quarto.

## Q *HENRY V* AND THE MEDIUM OF THE STAGE

The most distinctly fresh reading of the play can be found by reconsidering the Quarto *Henry V*, and its relationship with the Folio text. The implications of *Henry V* as a rabbit and duck play, and how we might read the Folio text in relation to the Quarto and how we might think of Shakespeare as author of his plays at large, are quite considerable.

Transfixing a Shakespeare text as an edition in one version only for reading has to turn the naturally plastic stage script into marble, and the process of such editorial fixation incurs substantial losses. Fixity denies the flow from author's mind to staged event. That fluid movement, with all the effects of individual needs impacting on it, is exemplified vividly with *Henry V*. The long processes that brought the products of Shakespeare's quill to paper, and that made the company rewrite what he sold them, eventually produced the two sets of words which put on record all the evidence we have of that complex flow for *Henry V*. The Folio text gives us a version of what Shakespeare originally wrote, while the Quarto gives us what the company made of it, whether for the play's first staging or for its first readers. This text, based on the Folio, tries to turn into marble the version that Shakespeare originally composed before throwing it into the fluid processes of readying it for the stage. The Quarto edition marmorealises, making marble out of the natural plastic, what the company then prepared for the stage out of the raw material that Shakespeare had sold them. The least it does is to offer a mine of suggestions about what Shakespeare's fellows found unmanageable in his intolerably two-faced script.

---

1 See my 'Maximal and minimal texts: Shakespeare v. the Globe', *S.Sur.* 52 (1999), 68–87.

The Quarto text is the first in a long line of adaptations made in order to bring Shakespeare's play onto the stage in some form more feasible for the stage than the original manuscript as we have it in the Folio version. Above all it reflects discomfort with the *gestalt* 'rabbit or duck' feature of the original, John Arden's 'secret play' lurking inside the 'official' reading upheld by the Chorus. Note has been made here (pp. 6–15) of the way the Chorus announces things that the following scenes contradict. The Quarto text, by deleting the Chorus altogether, removed those anomalies, but at the same time it cut out almost all the features that raise any doubts about Henry's thinking. It removed, for instance, the entire opening scene, where the Archbishop of Canterbury speaks of bribing Henry to invade France, together with all the references to Henry having killed Falstaff by rejecting him at the end of *2 Henry IV*. It streamlined the whole play, in the process eliminating almost all the signs of the 'secret' play.

Some of its adjustments do indicate a less than perfect grasp of Shakespeare's ideas. It kept, for instance, both Henry's order to kill the prisoners and Gower's subsequent misinterpretation of that order as an act of revenge for the massacre of the boys, and even added a gratuitous 'Couple gorge' from Pistol when he hears the order, thus losing its consequence, requiring him to kill M. Le Fer, whose ransom Pistol was looking forward to and which he has evidently lost when he reappears penniless in Act 5. The general effect of the company's changes show clearly their conclusion that Shakespeare's manuscript with its ambivalent Henry could not be staged, and that a simply heroic Henry was the only practicable alternative.

The effects of this rewriting are most evident in the Quarto's version of Act 3 at the siege of Harfleur, as noted above. For modern readers and playgoers the most startling cut of all in the Quarto text must be the complete removal of the first of Henry's two most quoted speeches, 'Once more unto the breach, dear friends, once more, / Or close the wall up with our English dead!' (3.1.1–34). The company must have found it necessary to make that cut because they recognised more clearly than any director has since what was intended by the extraordinary stage direction that in the Folio accompanies Henry's arrival on stage to address his army: '*Alarum: Scaling Ladders at Harflew*' (3.1.10). This unique direction shows that Shakespeare wanted ladders to be set against the tiring-house wall, the traditional way of staging sieges at the Globe. He must have expected that after Henry's exhortation some soldiers would climb up them onto the stage balcony, representing the city walls, and disappear into the tiring house as if they were entering the city.

With such a requirement, the company would have realised its effect when Henry returns in 3.4 to address the Governor of the city. At that point he would speak from stage level to the Governor standing on the stage balcony. The Folio entry direction (3.4.0) says '*Enter the King and all his Traine before the gates.*' After Henry has issued his threats the Governor admits that the Dauphin cannot raise the siege, and invites the English army to 'enter our Gates' (3.4.49). The company knew that the Governor must speak from the balcony above the central opening, representing the city gates. That is, he would have to stand exactly where we had recently seen the soldiers climbing up their ladders at the end of Henry's exhortation to reach the same balcony. The obvious inference must be that the attack on the breach failed, and the soldiers who mounted their scaling ladders were now supposed to be enacting Henry's alternative, their dead filling the breach. The absence of any stage direction for the removal of the ladders in 3.1 even left open the possibility that they were still there when the Governor appeared on the walls they leaned against. Second thoughts would say that if the attack on the breach had succeeded there would have been no need to threaten the Governor on his walls. Not having such second thoughts has meant that the magic of Henry's 'Once more' speech has misled readers and directors over the attack's failure.

The Quarto's version of Act 3 is the most severely trimmed of all from the original Folio text. It reduces the Folio's 249 lines to 40, cutting out not only the Chorus and Henry's speech but the entire scene of the four captains apart from a brief exchange between Gower and Llewellyn about the mines, further affirmation that the attack had not secured the city for Henry. It also trims Henry's 43 lines of threats addressed to the Governor down to 12, and cuts the discussion with Exeter about the ailing troops altogether. The main object of the company rewriters was obviously to minimise the siege of Harfleur in order to maximise the impact of the second battle, at Agincourt, preceded as that is in both Folio and Quarto by Henry's more successful speech about his band of brothers. The Quarto's version of the Harfleur siege chooses a far less ambivalent staging than exists in the Folio.

One rather alarming implication of this revelation about how drastically the company revamped Shakespeare's original manuscript is that Shakespeare must have known they would change his text, and was prepared for it. If he was, it becomes possible to believe that he installed the features of the Folio text that show his own ambivalence over Henry quite deliberately, knowing that such a delicate balancing act was unlikely to survive the rescripting process the company would impose on his manuscript before staging the play. It suggests that Shakespeare was writing for himself, well aware that his own version would not be staged. When the copy for the Folio text was chosen, the senior surviving company members, Heminges and Condell, opted to print from the manuscript the company had discarded, the raw material out of which they had made their own version of the concluding text in the history sequence. Shakespeare's expectation of what the company would do to his original copy was a prophecy as accurate as his inclusion of four captains representing the four countries soon to become the united kingdom that was Scottish King James VI's gift to the English in 1603.

Every one of the many stagings of the play through the four hundred years since 1599 has failed to cope with the play's ambiguities, as Loehlin's and Smith's studies of the productions show. It seems that Greenblatt is right, and that what Shakespeare sold his company in 1599 was, knowingly or not, incapable of being fully realised on stage. All performed scripts of the play, from the first Quarto onwards, have made alterations to Shakespeare's impossibly ambivalent original. We might conclude like Harry Berger, therefore, that the play's duplicity is more easily grasped by reading than by anyone sitting in a modern theatre audience. Moreover, if we want access to the first of the many plastic versions of the original that reached the stage in 1599 and keep it in the marble of an edition, we should look at the Quarto's text, not the Folio's.

# NOTE ON THE TEXT

Plays are put on stage by team-work. The producers who commission the writer, the stage managers and actors who prepare it for performance, the book-keeper who records changes made to the text as it is being rehearsed for the stage, even the early audiences whose reactions tell the company what needs improving, all make their mark by adjusting the writer's original concept. There is no halt to this process. The dynamics of theatre production subject the collective endeavour to a process of constant change and adjustment, from the starting idea through every rehearsal and every performance.

Shakespeare's plays have been undergoing adjustment for four hundred years, and are still moving. In this dynamic process there is no single moment of perfection, no still point in the evolution of the script when the play can be seen as perfectly finished. Unfortunately, with the technology of the printed book, editions have to pretend that there is such a moment. It is like using a single snapshot to represent a lifetime. The text exists like a freeze-frame from a moving picture, pretending fixity while in reality it offers only one moment from a process. On the moderately well-justified assumption that Shakespeare's own concept of the play, so far as that can be fixed, is worth more than any other frame from the movie, editors have tried to freeze the text at a point just before the author released his manuscript into the hands of the production team. The texts are then most purely authorial, authoritative, and least adjusted by the theatre team that Shakespeare worked with and the shape of the theatre and the players that he wrote for.

Recently the target has shifted a little, taking the not unreasonable opinion that Shakespeare's team knew its job and that Shakespeare wrote exclusively for the stage, not for the page. The preferred freeze-frame now, the play in its prime, is the script that was used for the first performances, the first staged text. Unfortunately, no such scripts have survived. Identifying the text as originally performed is a matter of inference and deduction from the various printed texts. Most of the Shakespeare plays survive in versions which appear to have been printed from manuscripts that had not progressed so far as the staging process. *Henry V* is to some extent an exception.

The target text for this edition is what we might loosely call the play-script, the text of the play as it was originally performed. For that purpose, neither of the two primary texts, F and Q, is completely satisfactory on its own, since one stands before and the other some time after that moment in the production process which is the edition's target. F1 certainly precedes the script of the play as staged. It has a number of slips and irregularities that must have been corrected before the play was first performed. Q's text stands at some distance on the other side of the target. It was mediated through what seems to have been a transcript of the performed play written and adjusted from memory by some of the original players. The memories may represent the original staging, or more likely they may entail adaptations and cuts made by the scribes without any firm basis in the performed text. For this edition F has been used as the basic text, on the grounds that it is a printed copy of the manuscript submitted to the company before the play went into rehearsal. It has been altered by reference to what appears to have survived in Q from the modifications made to the performed text.

The Folio text (F) has a disconcerting number of inconsistencies. Some are merely verbal slips or inconsistencies that seem to indicate a change of mind in the course of writing. Others are matters of the structure, where we are told what is to happen and it does not. At the outset we are told that the arrival of the French ambassadors has interrupted the exposition of the Salic Law issue by the Archbishop, in 1.1. That visit, however, is held back until after the Archbishop has completed his account in 1.2. The Chorus to Act 2 announces the audience's arrival at Southampton, but first we go to Eastcheap in London. The same Chorus announces Southampton as the port where they embark for Harfleur, but the Chorus at 3.0.4 sends them out from Dover. At the end of 3.3 Llewellyn promises to renew his dispute with Macmorris later, but Macmorris never reappears. The Chorus to Act 5 describes Henry's triumphant return to England, the arrival in London of the Holy Roman Emperor, and Henry's eventual return to France, but then takes us back to Llewellyn settling his pre-Agincourt score with Pistol in the immediate wake of the battle. The French princess is seen learning English immediately after the English have captured Harfleur (3.5), long before any mention is made that she is Henry's 'capital demand, comprised / Within the forerank of our articles' (5.2.96–7). The only previous hint is the Chorus's brief statement at 3.0.29–32 that the French king has offered Henry his daughter, and that 'the offer likes not'. Similarly the English nobles come and go with an irregularity which cannot be explained simply by reference to Holinshed. Above all, there is the question of the Dauphin's presence at Agincourt. At 3.6.64–6 the French king orders him to remain in Rouen, as Holinshed reports. But he is present with the French nobles before Agincourt in 3.8, although he is not mentioned at or after the battle, nor in the rest of the play. His insult with the tennis balls in 1.2 is never mentioned again, though it gets several later mentions in *The Famous Victories*. And lastly there is the peculiar twist in Pistol's final words at the end of 5.1, when he makes no mention of his new wife Mistress Quickly and her tavern, but only laments the death of 'my' Doll and the renewal of his old life of bragging pretence.

There are several ways of reading these F inconsistencies. The references to Dover and to Doll may be momentary forgetfulness. The intrusion of the second and fifth Choruses on the comic scenes may be a consequence of later writing and insertion where they do not make a perfect fit. Alternatively, since the fifth Chorus seems to provide a necessary break between Llewellyn's and Gower's presence on stage at the end of Act 4, when they join the processional departure of the army from the field of Agincourt, and their re-entry to start Act 5, it may be that the comic scenes such as 2.1 at Eastcheap and 5.1 after Agincourt are deliberately ignored by the Chorus as beneath his notice. The Dauphin's appearance and disappearance may be signs of authorial hesitation over whether to follow Holinshed or the early stage version reported by Nashe, where the Dauphin appears in the final scene to pay homage to Henry. Possibly the Quarto text, which displaces the Dauphin from Agincourt and gives his lines to

another French noble, shows the final choice.¹ The scene where Katherine and Alice
rehearse their French may be a late insertion, like the addition of Jamy in 3.3, although
it is in the 1600 Quarto from which Macmorris and Jamy are cut.²

Some of these inconsistencies cannot be resolved. The reference to diseased Doll,
for instance, from her 'malady of France' in the Spital (mentioned already at 2.1.60)
may have been designed as a mark of Pistol's final return to being a bawd in England
instead of to the relative respectability of being 'mine host' with Mistress Quickly, as
he is in 2.1. Still, the consequence of the new status that he gains with his marriage
in 2.1 does not easily fit his departure in 5.1. If 'Doll' was an absent-minded slip for
'Nell', his new wife, Pistol's loss would be the more complete, though he could still
be expected to take possession of his dead wife's tavern on his return to London.
Neither death fits comfortably with his new role as mine host. Choosing the F name
'Doll' in 5.1 has to involve some specious reasoning about Pistol's use of Mrs. Quickly.
Emending it to 'Nell' brings it closer to the story of 2.1, but leaves his evident poverty
unexplained. He has to be poor at the end. He has not only lost all his thieving friends
but the 'egregious' ransom promised by M. Le Fer, thanks to the king's order to cut
all the prisoners' throats. So the comedy of Nym's insulting 'mine host' in 2.1, with its
implication that Pistol has acquired an Eastcheap home to return to, has to be forgotten
in 5.1.

A similar inconsistency runs through F with the naming of the lords, both English
and French. Warwick, for instance, is given an entry in 1.2 but has nothing to say. He
has no place in Acts 2, 3, and the first six scenes of Act 4, although his name is cited
as one to be made famous at Agincourt in 4.3. He is next named in 4.7, where he is
not given an entry stage direction, to accompany Gloucester in pursuit of Llewellyn.
His only words occur in the following scene. In Act 5 he has an entry and is named
by Henry, but again has nothing to say. Westmorland has a larger part at the outset,
where Henry addresses him as 'cousin', and he is present among the band of brothers
and kinsmen for the conspiracy scene, 2.2. He is added (unhistorically) to the English
nobles at Agincourt, where he is given the wish that there might be more Englishmen at
the battle. He is not named for any of the later scenes, except for a single speech heading
in 5.2. With similar inconsistency, Henry's three brothers, Bedford, Gloucester and
Clarence, all enter for 1.2 but appear only intermittently thereafter. Clarence never
reappears. Bedford is present with Westmorland for 2.2, Gloucester is mentioned in
3.1 and 3.3, and the two brothers enter together with Henry in 4.1. They return with
Westmorland in 4.3, where Salisbury specifies both of them plus Westmorland in his
farewell. Bedford is named, but not the others, in Henry's Crispin's Day speech in 4.3,
and Gloucester returns to pursue Llewellyn at the end of 4.7 and 4.8. Bedford but not
Gloucester is named as entering among the English nobles in 5.2.

It is not possible to explain all of these comings and goings in F by reference to
doubling. In the Q version, which is more economical with the lords, Gloucester stays,
Clarence replaces Bedford throughout, and Warwick replaces Westmorland. Warwick,

1 Gary Taylor canvasses this possibility at length in the Introduction to his 1982 edition of the play, pp. 24–6.
2 See Keith Brown, 'Historical context and *Henry V*', *Cahiers élisabethaines* 29 (1986), 77–81.

named in the text and more famous than Westmorland as a warrior, could easily have assimilated the original need for Westmorland as Henry's kinsman, but there is no obvious reason why Clarence should swallow Bedford. Q does not give much help with the inconsistencies. Its change of Westmorland into Warwick gives him the false title of 'kinsman' to Henry, although since the reporter Exeter is not only 'uncle' to Henry but also 'cousin' in the opening lines we may feel that the reporters of Q did not take the king's family connections seriously. (Q was at least more consistent than Kemble, who made Exeter into Henry's 'brother' in his 1789 version.) Q, however, is not much use as a pointer to economies of staging in the original performances. Its streamlining of the flow of minor players does not seem to reflect any substantive alterations made to the play as performed. In the F text as a whole, which is exceptionally demanding over minor parts – forty-six in all – a total of twenty-three adult players are needed for the eighteen main speaking parts, and five boys for the four principal female parts and the Boy. Q, which reduces the minor parts from 42 to 26, still requires twenty men and four boys.

Doubling makes no major difference to these totals. W. A. Ringler thought that a minimum of sixteen players would have been needed for the F version,[1] as does T. J. King, who posits eleven men and five boys.[2] Thomas L. Berger[3] thinks as few as thirteen possible, though with considerable and unlikely 'poetic' pointing and some straining of credulity. The difficulty with Berger's doubling can be seen in its multiplication of the on-stage presences for the player of Henry, who has to add Berri in 2.4 and in 4.2 Grandpré, with his 18 additional lines of verse. His assignations of Q's reported parts also create problems for this kind of 'poetic' doubling, where Gower has to add Bedford and Brittany, Exeter has to add Macmorris, and Pistol has to take on the Chorus, Montjoy, and the English Herald. In any case, judging by the evidence of its three awkward scene breaks, the shortened Q version can hardly have altered its allocation of the minor roles for the purpose of performance by a smaller touring cast.

The cumulative inconsistencies in the F text seem to indicate that it was the product of discontinuous composition, and possibly some imperfect revisions, before the perhaps rather hasty copying out of the final draft for the company. This copy was the text used to print F.[4] The difficulty these inconsistencies create for a coherent edition is what choices to make in regularising them. It would be possible either to keep the Dauphin at Agincourt or to replace him with Bourbon as Q does; to keep Doll as the last deprivation for Pistol or to substitute Nell Quickly; to split up the second Chorus, as many productions have done, so that the Eastcheap scene (2.1) follows the first part and the announcement that the audience is to be transported to Southampton precedes the conspiracy scene, 2.2, which is set at Southampton; to replace the third Chorus's

1 W. A. Ringler, 'The number of actors in Shakespeare's early plays', in *The Seventeenth-Century Stage*, ed. G. E. Bentley, Chicago, 1968, p. 123.
2 See T. J. King, *Casting Shakespeare's Plays: London Actors and their Roles, 1590–1642*, Cambridge, forthcoming.
3 Thomas L. Berger, 'Casting *Henry V*', *S. St.* 20 (1988), pp. 89–104.
4 The question of rewriting as a cause of what he calls 'unconformities' in the F text is examined by Kristian Smidt, *Unconformities in Shakespeare's History Plays*, New Jersey, 1982, chapter 8, 'The Disunity of *King Henry V*', pp. 121–44.

'Dover' with 'Hampton', or indeed to cut out the choruses altogether, as Q does, and to merge some of the lords as Q also does. The choice that has been adopted here is based on the aim of providing a text as close as possible to the play as it was originally staged, and in the fullest form. It was thought wrong to demote the choruses, magnificently persuasive verse as they are, to a place only in the footnotes. The reasons for some other choices, particularly the replacement of the Dauphin with Bourbon in 3.8 before Agincourt and the retention of 'Doll' for 'Nell', are explained below.

Against this evidence for some lack of cohesion in the play's original composition, it is worth noting the consistent patterns, particularly in the language. Reasons for the play's extraordinary assembly of speakers of non-standard English have been considered above. In the predominant patterns of imagery the 'music' of war in the play has been widely noted. Less obvious perhaps are the images of dogs applied to the English army and the comparison of the storming of cities to sexual rape, described above.[1] The play's language is more consistent and coherent than its plot.

Q is in significant respects a version of the text that was performed in London in 1599 as several of the players remembered it. A number of its features which differ from the F text may therefore be changes approved by the author for the staged version. Of these possible changes, though, only one is backed by evidence which suggests it was made by, or with the approval of, the author. It has been suggested above that Shakespeare was uncertain whether to retain the Dauphin on stage for Agincourt and the final scene at the French court, as the old versions of the story did, or to remove him from the play altogether before Agincourt. His removal in Q and his replacement by Bourbon with some rewriting and reallocation of speeches indicates that the final decision was to remove him. In accordance with the principle of trying to reproduce the script as first acted, this edition has followed suit.[2]

The different languages used in the play have caused some peculiar problems for the modernising of the spellings in this edition, especially the French. Shakespeare may have acquired his French from the Mountjoy family, with whom he is known to have lodged in 1604 and probably for some time before that. His French contacts probably began early with the Huguenot wife of Richard Field, the Stratford-born man who printed *Venus and Adonis* and *The Rape of Lucrece* in 1593 and 1594. His command of the language was evidently quite good. But in French as in English, sixteenth-century pronunciation differed in several ways from modern French. Henry's response to Pistol's question about his name at 4.1.48, for instance, where he turns 'Harry the king' into 'Harry le Roy', which Pistol hears as Cornish 'Leroy', and Pistol's mishearing of M. Le Fer's '*moi*' as 'moys' at 4.4.17 both reflect the old French pronunciation of '*oi*', now changed. Similarly, the modern *été* and *écolier* still had their 's' in 1600: 3.5.1 '*este*' and 12 '*escolier*' echo the French pronunciation of the time, as do '*nostre*' and '*vostre*' at 5.2.229 and 302 for the modern '*notre*' and '*votre*'. A similar change has happened to '*Le François*', modernised as '*le français*', and '*l'Anglois*' as '*anglais*' in 5.2.

A further complication is the question whether Shakespeare's own French was accurate or not. The use of 4.4.44 '*j'ai tombé*' for '*je suis tombé*' and 5.2.109 '*à les anges*' for

---

1 See Introduction, p. 13.
2 For a detailed account of the changes relating to the Dauphin, see Textual Analysis, pp. 223–5.

'*aux anges*' are common enough mistakes in English translation today, and are more likely to have been made in the original manuscript than misprinted by the F compositor. The same may be true of 4.4.13 and 42, where '*le*' appears when it should agree with its noun as '*la*'. The F compositors, however, did struggle with the French, some of which they set nearly as phonetically as the Q version. For this edition, the choice has been made to correct the French so far as possible and to present it in modernised spelling. Where the original pronunciation of the French affects what a character on stage hears (for instance Henry's 'Harry *le roi*' to Pistol at 4.1.48), the original pronunciation is indicated by Pistol's response, as is his translation of Le Fer's 'tun of moys' (4.4.17). Such instances are recorded in the notes.

Related to the problem of regularising and transcribing the early French in a modernised edition is the question of regularising the dialect speech of Llewellyn, Macmorris, and Jamy. There is every likelihood that modern Welsh, Irish, and Scottish dialect pronunciation has altered as much as standard English and French. Since some effort was evidently made to produce a reasonably phonetic transcription of each regional mode of speech, the question of modernising the distinctly old French forms should apply also to the regional dialects. So far as Llewellyn's speech is concerned, the problems are not great. His use of unvoiced plosives for the standard voiced forms – p for b, f for v, and ch for j – are marked in both F and Q, though not with perfect consistency in either. It is not easy to hear any distinctively Welsh lilt in his speech rhythms, but his lengthy sentences full of syntactical inversions, as well as the insistent 'look you' (which occurs even more frequently in Q), probably indicate something not entirely different from the modern use of English in southern Wales. Some other distinctive spellings may be marks of more remote pronunciations, notably F's 'aunchient', which occurs five times in 3.7, in contrast with Bardolph's 'ancient' in 2.1. A middle position between F's novel orthography and Q's phonetic transcription seems best, with an improvement in the consistency of the idiomatic spellings. This edition, for instance, consistently uses 'woreld' as a phonetic compromise between Q's 'worell' and F's 'Orld'. The distinctive plosives are also regularised. It might be added that twice F uses the unique spelling 'doo's' for 'does' in Llewellyn's speeches at 4.7.143 and 5.1.23. This seems both too rare and not sufficiently distinctive as a pronunciation to use in the text.

Macmorris's sibilants are usually given as 'sh' sounds. He too has a characteristic set of exclamations, notably 'be Chrish' for 'by Christ', and an exclamatory style that was also clearly designed to convey non-standard speech forms. The only point where it is really uncertain whether the F spelling was designed to signal his pronunciation is 3.3.48, where F spells 'besieged' as 'beseech'd'. This is one of Llewellyn's consonant shifts, from voiced to unvoiced, but it is not a pronunciation that Macmorris uses elsewhere. Jamy, probably a late addition to the round-up of the regions, has an even more distinct set of spellings than the others. The guttural first vowel in his 'gudday' (3.3.27) is stressed by the repetition of 'gud' four times in his next speech, which is only twenty-seven words long. He also has 'sall' for 'shall', which appears three times, nearly as often as 'gud', 'bath' for 'both', 'ligge' for 'lie', 'breff' for 'brief', and 'wad' for 'would'. Some adjustment of these idioms seems desirable, for instance 'gud' to the familiar 'guid', and 'bath' to 'baith', though it should be stressed that both of these modernisations may misrepresent the pronunciations which Shakespeare heard. Holinshed's history of Scotland transcribes a letter from the King of the Scots to Henry IV about the captivity of his son James, who was later to accompany Henry V to fight in France. The letter uses distinctive word forms such as 'sike' for 'such', 'mair' and 'maist' for 'more' and 'most', 'monie' for 'many', 'thame' for 'them', 'amang' and 'warld' for 'among' and 'world', and 'na' for 'no'; but from these only *Henry V* 's 'baith' and 'wad' get much support. The play's regional speeches evidently came to Shakespeare by ear, not eye. Given the variety and diversity of modern forms of the three regional dialects, this edition has tried to stay close to Shakespeare and to present a systematised version of the pronunciations that the F spellings seem to indicate.

There are other problems with modernisation, too. The names of French towns and of some French lords were pronounced by Elizabethans in distinct ways which do not correspond to the familiar modern pronunciation. Calais was spelled 'Callis' or 'Callice', sounding the final sibilant. Harfleur was 'Harflew' in Hall, Holinshed, and Shakespeare. The French Dauphin was spelled 'Dolphin' by the same three authors, and probably pronounced accordingly. At the price of some strain, and possibly some misrepresenting of the pronunciation, all of these spellings have been silently modernised.

A more complex question is Pistol's military title. The 'Ancient' of Henry V's and Othello's armies was the stock spelling and pronunciation for the rank of Ensign, the standard-bearer of a company commanded by a captain. Below the lieutenant in rank, he was something like a modern sergeant-major. Honesty and practical leadership were his most important attributes. He did not need to be the arithmetician that Cassio's lieutenancy in Othello's troop required him to be, but he might well act as 'sutler' or provider of his men's food, as Pistol expects to be in France. Pistol's choice of military title belies his character as much as it signals his age. In the interests of their principles for modernising the text, Taylor and the Oxford edition alter the original spelling to 'Ensign'. This edition retains it not just because of its familiarity as an Elizabethan title but chiefly because the old 'Ancient' was not equivalent to the modern army rank of 'Ensign', which usually survives in ex-cavalry regiments as a junior or cadet rank. The modern title also removes the connotation of age and maturity.[1] It might be argued that to call Pistol 'Ensign' would at least distinguish him from the other meaning of the word, marked by 'Ancient Gower' in *Pericles*, whose title is not a military rank. But the use of the modern 'Ensign' for Pistol loses precisely that additional connotation. His last words, after all, play on his false title when he admits 'Old I do wax' (5.1.73) as he decides to leave the English army. He is at last growing truly ancient.

A slightly different difficulty concerns Llewellyn. The Shakespearean spelling of his name, which F renders as 'Fluellen' and which Q makes into 'Flewellen', is phonetically very close to the modern 'Llewellyn', which must therefore be the appropriate form to use in a modernised-spelling edition. Although for nearly three centuries editors of modernised-spelling editions have retained the F form, a modern-spelling edition ought to make the adjustment. It is more difficult to resist such a change than with

---

1 See the discussion between Jennifer Krause and Gary Taylor on this question, *SQ* 36 (1985), 523–7.

Pistol's title, since it is almost exclusively orthographic. This edition gives the name in modern spelling.

The patterning and the different function of verse and prose in the play are generally clear. The very few mislineations of verse in F indicate that the setting-out was made distinct as verse or as prose in the author's manuscript. The only major problem in a modernised edition is the form that should be given to Pistol's speeches. Strongly rhythmical, and sometimes ending in rhyming couplets, they are still not quite verse. F sets them as prose, although Q makes them verse. They do not follow an entirely regular decasyllabic beat and were evidently written out as prose in the manuscript from which F was set. Q spasmodically tried to make them into verse. Most editors, starting with Pope, have broken them into more plausible lines of verse. The problem in making a choice over this is that the distinctions between verse and prose in the rest of the play are so clear. Every comic scene, including the French princess's two scenes attempting to speak English and Burgundy's heavy-handed joking over Henry's wooing of Katherine in 5.2, is in prose. All the Llewellyn and Gower scenes are in prose, and even Henry drops into it when with them or other ordinary soldiers. The idle scenes before Agincourt, first the backchat between the nobles of the French camp, and later the more tense but still low-key debate in the English camp between the disguised Henry and the common soldiers, are likewise in prose. Verse is reserved for the Chorus, the public scenes of Henry and the nobility, and for Henry in soliloquy. The prose of Henry's debate with his common soldiers turns to verse as soon as they leave. His prose exchanges with Katherine continue as jesting prose when the French nobles return, and verse re-enters suddenly only when he turns to serious business and asks Exeter about the terms of the treaty. The only apparent exception to this firm rule is the French Herald's speech at 3.7.102–17, where he gives a verbally precise report of the French king's trenchant address to Henry before the battle. Curt and formal, it contrasts emphatically with the prose that has gone before and with Henry's verse reply. Given such a clear patterning of speech rhythms, it was thought best to set Pistol's speeches as prose. The poetic rhythms, syntactical inversions, and archaisms are clear evidence of his manner of speaking and do not need any extrinsic patterning.

*King Henry V*

# LIST OF CHARACTERS

in order of appearance

CHORUS
CANTERBURY
ELY
KING
GLOUCESTER
BEDFORD
EXETER
WESTMORLAND
AMBASSADOR
BARDOLPH
NYM
PISTOL
HOSTESS
BOY
SCROOP
CAMBRIDGE
GRAY
FRENCH KING
DAUPHIN
BERRI
BOURBON
CONSTABLE
MESSENGER
LLEWELLYN
GOWER
MACMORRIS
JAMY
GOVERNOR
KATHERINE
ALICE
MONTJOY
RAMBURES
ORLÉANS
ERPINGHAM
BATES
COURT
WILLIAMS
BEAUMONT
GRANDPRÉ
SALISBURY
YORK
FRENCH *Soldier*
WARWICK

74

*English* HERALD
QUEEN *Isabel*
BURGUNDY
*Attendants, soldiers*

## Notes

Neither F nor Q supplies a list of characters. Most are named in the opening dialogue of the scenes in which they appear, and all the attendant nobles in the English and French courts are named in Holinshed. The notes which follow are mainly about the historical figures.

CANTERBURY Henry Chichele, Archbishop of Canterbury from 1414.

ELY Holinshed names no accompanying Bishop in his account of Chichele's speech about the Salic Law. The reason for using a Bishop of Ely is given in the commentary note to 1.1.8.

KING Henry V, born in 1387, crowned king in succession to his father Henry IV in 1413, died in France in 1422.

GLOUCESTER Prince Humphrey, Duke of Gloucester, younger brother of the king. At Agincourt he was in the middle battle-line with the king, who stood over him and defended him when he fell from a sword cut to his 'hams'. It was in this defence of his brother that Henry fought Alençon (4.7.140).

BEDFORD John of Lancaster in *2H4*, younger brother of the king.

EXETER Thomas Beaufort, Duke of Exeter, uncle to the king.

WESTMORLAND Earl and Warden of the northern Marches, husband of Joan Beaufort, daughter of John of Gaunt and therefore the king's cousin by marriage.

AMBASSADOR In *The Famous Victories* and Holinshed he is specified as the Archbishop of Bourges.

BARDOLPH First appearing, with his colourful nose, in *1H4* 2.2 with Falstaff in Eastcheap.

NYM First appearing in *Wiv.* 1.1 with Falstaff. A small man, his part may have been written for the player John Sinklo, who was noted for his small, thin stature.

PISTOL First appearing in *2H4* 2.4 as a 'swaggerer'.

HOSTESS Mistress Nell Quickly, hostess of the Boar's Head tavern in Eastcheap, first appearing in *1H4* 2.4, where she has a husband. In *2H4* she is a 'poor lone woman'. In *Wiv.* she is Caius's housekeeper.

BOY Possibly Falstaff's boy, first appearing in *2H4* 1.2.

SCROOP Henry, third Lord Scroop of Masham, Treasurer of the Royal Household.

CAMBRIDGE First Earl of, brother to the Duke of York (Aumerle in *R2*), and godson to Richard II. He was married to the sister of the Earl of March, alternative heir to Henry V. For his dynastic ambition, see Introduction, pp. 19–21.

GRAY A northern noble, son-in-law to Westmorland. His eldest son was married to Cambridge's daughter.

FRENCH KING Not named in this play, although he is in *The Famous Victories*; historically he was Charles VI, who reigned from 1380 until 1422, dying only six weeks after Henry. From 1392 onwards he suffered from recurrent bouts of insanity, which left the government in the hands of various regents, mostly Burgundians.

DAUPHIN Historically the name Dauphin, heir to the throne of France, covers at least three figures in the period of the play. The Dauphin whom Holinshed identifies as sender of the tennis balls, an incident he relates more confidently than do modern historians, he calls Charles. In fact, before Harfleur and at the time of Agincourt it was the fat and idle nineteen-year-old Louis. Louis was followed in December 1415 by his brother Jean, who renewed the fight against the English after Agincourt. Charles became Dauphin in 1417. Leader of the Armagnac cause against the Burgundians, his supporters assassinated John of Burgundy in 1419, and he was thereafter kept from the French court by the Burgundians. He became Charles VII in 1422. Holinshed records each change of Dauphin and much of the Armagnac–Burgundian struggle.

BERRI Historically leader of the Armagnac faction in France, sometimes acting as regent during the king's fits of insanity. The celebrated Book of Hours, the *Très Riches Heures*, was made for him.

BOURBON A duke of the Armagnac faction, along with the Duc d'Orléans. In the play he is elevated to take the Dauphin's role as chief boaster and antagonist to Henry before Agincourt. The historical Bourbon was in the first rank of battle at Agincourt and was captured along with Orléans.

CONSTABLE Charles D'Albret, Constable of France and the General of the French army. One of the less hot-headed French nobles, he was killed at Agincourt.

LLEWELLYN F's 'Fluellen', Q's 'Flewellen', a captain in the English army. Historically Henry had many Welshmen in his army, some of whom he had fought with in his long campaigns in Wales before he became king. Davy Gam, cited as one of the English dead at Agincourt, was a leading Welsh soldier. Some Welshmen fought on the French side at Agincourt.

GOWER The English captain. There is a 'Master Gower' in *2H4* 2.1 who brings news to the Lord Chief Justice in his second scene with Falstaff.

MACMORRIS The Irish captain. Historically there were several contingents of Irish soldiers with Henry in France. See Appendix 2.

JAMY The Scottish captain. The only Scot known to be with Henry in France according to Holinshed was his prisoner, King James I of Scotland, a captive of the English since he was eleven. Henry brought him to France some years after Agincourt. See Appendix 2.

GOVERNOR The Governor of Harfleur. Historically the commander of the defences was Lord Jean d'Estouteville. On 18 September 1415 he sent envoys to the besiegers offering to surrender if no relief had come by 22 September.

KATHERINE Daughter of Charles VI of France. Marrying Henry after the Treaty of Troyes in May 1420, she bore him a son who became Henry VI in 1422.

ALICE Katherine's waiting-woman, addressed by name in 3.5.

MONTJOY The official title of the French herald, named after the French war-cry, 'Montjoie! Saint Denis!' Holinshed calls him 'Montjoy king at armes'.

RAMBURES Named in Holinshed as Master of the Crossbows at Agincourt, where he is amongst those killed.

ORLÉANS A duke of the Armagnac faction, he was captured at Agincourt and held in the Tower of London along with Bourbon. His father had been murdered by the Burgundians.

ERPINGHAM Sir Thomas Erpingham, a member of Henry's Royal Household, is named by Holinshed as commander of the English archers at Agincourt.

BATES John Bates is named on his entrance at 4.1.81 but otherwise only in the F entry stage direction. There is no apparent reason why the three soldiers should have been named so precisely in this entry. See Introduction p. 30.

COURT Alexander Court is named in the entry stage direction in F, at 4.1.81, when he identifies 'brother John Bates' by name, but otherwise Court takes no part in the ensuing debate.

WILLIAMS Michael Williams is identified by his full name at the entry at 4.1.81, but not named in the text. On his reappearance in 4.7 and 4.8 he is known only by the glove he wears in his cap. His part in Branagh's film was played by Michael Williams.

BEAUMONT Listed by Holinshed among the French nobles killed at Agincourt.

GRANDPRÈ Holinshed names him in the middle ward of the French battle lines and amongst the dead at Agincourt.

SALISBURY Thomas Montacute, fourth Earl. Historically he started his career as a soldier with Prince Henry in Wales. Along with Warwick he became one of the most famous commanders of the English campaigns in France.

YORK Henry's cousin, the senior English noble to die at Agincourt. Historically the Aumerle of *R2*, he was a fat man who, leading the English van, was trampled and suffocated in the press of the first confrontation. The account in the play of his death is fanciful.

FRENCH *Soldier* M. Le Fer (the iron man), according to 4.4.

WARWICK Richard Beauchamp, Earl of Warwick. A famous warrior, he was at Agincourt, though not named there by Holinshed. In later years he captured and burned Joan of Arc.

QUEEN *Isabel* Isabella of Bavaria, who married Charles VI in 1385.

BURGUNDY His father Duke John the Fearless was assassinated by the Dauphin in 1419. This duke, Philip, became an ally of the English and was made co-regent of France with Henry at the Treaty of Troyes.

# THE LIFE OF HENRY THE FIFTH

**Prologue** *Enter* CHORUS

CHORUS  O for a muse of fire, that would ascend
      The brightest heaven of invention,
      A kingdom for a stage, princes to act,
      And monarchs to behold the swelling scene.
      Then should the warlike Harry, like himself,     5
      Assume the port of Mars, and at his heels
      (Leashed in, like hounds) should famine, sword and fire
      Crouch for employment. But pardon, gentles all,
      The flat unraisèd spirits, that hath dared,
      On this unworthy scaffold, to bring forth     10

**Act 1, Scene 0**

**1.0 CHORUS** The Folio text sets '*Enter Prologue*' centred, and puts the whole speech in two columns of italics, before marking '*Actus Primus. Scoena Prima*' within rules across the page. F's setting of the Chorus speeches is not wholly consistent. Three of them it sets with *Enter Chorus* centred (Acts 2, 3, and 5), while Act 4 has only *Chorus* centred. None has a speech heading. Since this Chorus compares itself to a regular Prologue (33), the description of himself by the second Prologue in Heywood's *Four Prentices of London* is worth noting: 'Do you not know that I am the Prologue? Do you not see this long black velvet cloak upon my back? Have you not sounded thrice? Nay, have I not all the signs of a Prologue about me?' The three 'sounds' were more likely to have been the knocks which traditionally introduce plays in France than three blasts of a trumpet.

**1 muse** i.e. inspiration.

**1 fire** One of the two elements that by its nature rises.

**2 invention** In rhetorical theory, the spirit of creativity. The ending -ion was pronounced as a dissyllable.

**3–4 princes . . . behold** As in the description of the battle of Crécy in 1.2.105–10, where the Black Prince 'played a tragedy' while his father Edward III watched.

**4 swelling** Compare *Mac.* 1.3.127–8: 'happy prologues to the swelling act / Of the imperial theme'.

**5 like himself** An early introduction for the 'acting' element in Henry's conduct. He is to be 'like' his real warrior self.

**6 port** deportment; posture and appearance. It may also signify an actor's 'part'. In *LLL* 5.2.56–7 'part' rhymes with 'short'.

**7 Leashed in** Hunting-dogs were held in threes on a single leash.

**7 famine, sword and fire** Holinshed (p. 567) reports Henry's oration to the besieged people of Rouen in 1418, where he declared 'that the goddesse of battell called *Bellona*, had three handmaidens . . . blood, fire, and famine'. See Appendix 2.

**8 gentles** gentlemen and gentlewomen.

**9 flat** not rising to heaven, as fire does. The image of unrisen bread is probably in the background.

**9 unraisèd spirits** not conjured up like demons.

**9 hath** A singular verb for a plural subject is not an uncommon feature of Henry's and the Chorus's syntax.

**10 unworthy scaffold** the stage platform. Whether this is real modesty or mock-modesty has been much debated, as has the question whether it refers to the Curtain or the Globe. See Introduction, p. 4.

So great an object. Can this cockpit hold
The vasty fields of France? Or may we cram
Within this wooden O the very casques
That did affright the air at Agincourt?
Oh, pardon: since a crooked figure may                        15
Attest in little place a million,
And let us, ciphers to this great account,
On your imaginary forces work.
Suppose within the girdle of these walls
Are now confined two mighty monarchies,                       20
Whose high uprearèd and abutting fronts
The perilous narrow ocean parts asunder.
Piece out our imperfections with your thoughts.
Into a thousand parts divide one man,
And make imaginary puissance.                                 25
Think when we talk of horses that you see them
Printing their proud hooves i'th'receiving earth,
For 'tis your thoughts that now must deck our kings,
Carry them here and there, jumping o'er times,

---

**Act 1, Prologue**   17 And] F; So *Taylor*   17 account] F (Accompt)

**11 cockpit** ring, arena, a deliberate diminutive. Pits for cock-fighting were far smaller than amphitheatres such as the Curtain and the Globe.

**12 vasty** spacious. For the inflated lexis used by the Chorus, see Introduction p. 14.

**13 casques** This seems to be the first of many uses of the rhetorical figure *syllepsis*, the same word with different senses, of which the most conspicuous example is Henry's redeployment of 'mock' in 1.2.285–6. The commonest 'wooden O' for cramming things into is a barrel or cask, not the casque or helmet of Agincourt. The wooden 'casks' of the first half of the sentence are swallowed by the iron 'casques' of the second half.

**15 a crooked figure** (1) a curved number, (2) an old and bent human figure. Sycorax in *Temp.* is said to have grown into a hoop (1.2.259). It is difficult to see how a single figure can signify one million, which is seven figures, but the allusion is to the addition of zeros which multiply the total.

**16 Attest** Vouch for, signify.

**17 ciphers** (1) numbers, (2) nonentities. A proverbial usage (Dent C391), the term is employed similarly in *LLL* 1.2.56 and *AYLI* 3.2.246.

**17 account** F's 'Accompt' emphasises the sense (1) of a 'reckoning', a sum in figures; it is also (2) a great story. The play is pervaded with images of money, mostly in accounting and reckoning (4.1.124), but also in gambling (3.7.96–7).

**18 imaginary forces** (1) powers of imagination; (2) fictional armies.

**19 girdle** A term with human associations, as in 'figure', (15). It recurs in the French king's reference to his daughter as a 'maiden city', 5.2.287.

**20 confined** in a prison, restricted (as of the imagination).

**21 abutting** Normally used of buildings constructed against one another.

**21 fronts** (1) the cliffs of Calais and Dover, (2) foreheads, (3) frontiers.

**22 perilous** Usually pronounced 'parlous', as a dissyllable.

**23 Piece out** Add to, augment.

**25 imaginary puissance** fictional armed force. See line 18.

**28 deck** clothe, equip.

**29 jumping** i.e. as on horseback.

Turning th'accomplishment of many years                    30
Into an hour-glass. For the which supply
Admit me Chorus to this history,
Who, Prologue-like, your humble patience pray,
Gently to hear, kindly to judge our play.              *Exit*


**1.1** *Enter the two Bishops of* CANTERBURY *and* ELY


CANTERBURY My lord, I'll tell you, that self bill is urged
          Which in th'eleventh year of the last king's reign
          Was like, and had indeed against us passed
          But that the scambling and unquiet time
          Did push it out of farther question.              5
ELY But how, my lord, shall we resist it now?
CANTERBURY It must be thought on. If it pass against us
          We lose the better half of our possession,

---

Act 1, Scene 1   1.1 *Actus Primus. Scoena Prima* F   4 scambling] F; scrambling *Taylor*

**30 th'accomplishment . . . years** This is the only acknowledgement that more than six years, from 1414 to 1420, have been compressed into the two-hour hour-glass of the play.

**31 the which supply** i.e. to support this effort of travel and time.

**32–3 Chorus . . . Prologue-like** An indirect statement that, although appearing merely as a Prologue, he will return to make choric comments on each act. For normal Prologues and their dress, see headnote to Act 1, Scene 0.

**33 humble patience** A striking inversion. Normally 'humble' precedes words such as 'servant', 'suitor', or 'suppliant', as in *3H6* 3.1.19, *R3* 1.1.74, *TN* 3.1.80. Here, after the identification of the 'Prologue-like' speaker, we might expect a term like the 'humble author' of *2H4*'s Epilogue. The transferred epithet works like the syllepsis of line 13.

**34 to hear** After inviting imagination to evoke the sights of war, the Chorus now emphasises the play as something to be listened to.

**Act 1, Scene 1**

**0 SD the two Bishops** F does not differentiate between the Archbishop and the Bishop, either here or at their entry in 1.2.7. Q omits this scene, but in Act 1, Scene 2 it also calls them '2 *Bishops*'. The Archbishop of Canterbury's tactic in the scene is described at length by Holinshed. The choice of

Ely as the second bishop arose from an Elizabethan precedent. See note to line 8.

**1 that self bill** the self-same bill in Parliament. In 1410 the Commons raised the perennial question of the Church's huge and untaxable property holdings, and with strong support from the Lollards proposed to sequestrate much of them. See note to line 8.

**3 like . . . passed** was likely to be, and would have been, passed.

**4 scambling** violent; cognate with 'scrambling'. It is repeated by Henry with reference to his capture of Katherine at 5.2.187, and also used in *Ado* 5.1.93.

**4 unquiet time** Holinshed's term for the reason why the bill was shelved.

**8 the better . . . possession** Church property before the Reformation was enormous. Kings and Parliaments had argued over it since before the Statute of Mortmain, the first attempt to get lands away from the 'dead hand' of the Church, passed under Edward I. It was still a major issue in 1599. The Elizabethan Bishop of Ely, Richard Cox, had fought to retain his episcopal property from 1558 until 1581, so strongly that after his death Elizabeth kept the see of Ely vacant for eighteen years, up to February 1599. See John D. Cox, *Shakespeare and the Dramaturgy of Power*, pp. 106–8.

For all the temporal lands, which men devout
By testament have given to the Church                           10
Would they strip from us, being valued thus:
As much as would maintain to the king's honour
Full fifteen earls and fifteen hundred knights,
Six thousand and two hundred good esquires,
And to relief of lazars and weak age                            15
Of indigent faint souls, past corporal toil,
A hundred alms-houses, right well supplied;
And to the coffers of the king beside
A thousand pounds by th'year. Thus runs the bill.

ELY  This would drink deep.
CANTERBURY                'Twould drink the cup and all.          20
ELY  But what prevention?
CANTERBURY  The king is full of grace, and fair regard.
ELY  And a true lover of the holy Church.
CANTERBURY  The courses of his youth promised it not.
The breath no sooner left his father's body                     25
But that his wildness, mortified in him,
Seemed to die too. Yea, at that very moment
Consideration like an angel came,
And whipped th'offending Adam out of him,
Leaving his body as a paradise                                  30
T'envelop and contain celestial spirits.
Never was such a sudden scholar made,
Never came reformation in a flood
With such a heady currance scouring faults,

**9 temporal** secular. The issue at heart was one of taxation. Land bequeathed to the Church became exempt.

**13–19 Full . . . by th'year.** See Holinshed, p. 545: 'fifteene earles, fifteene hundred knights, six thousand and two hundred esquiers, and a hundred almesse-houses, for reliefe onelie of the poore, impotent, and needie persons, and the king to have cleerlie to his coffers twentie thousand pounds'.

**15 lazars** lepers or seriously diseased and disfigured invalids. The name originally came from the story of Lazarus in Luke 16.20.

**19 the bill** (1) the proposed act of Parliament, (2) the cost.

**22 grace** (1) Christian goodness, (2) beauty.

**22 fair regard** (1) highly respected, (2) respectful of the Church.

**26 mortified** (1) killed (as in his father's body), (2) thwarted, frustrated.

**28 Consideration** (1) spiritual contemplation, (2) careful thought.

**29 th'offending Adam** This account of Henry's conversion is phrased in the language of the baptismal service in the Book of Common Prayer, which speaks of 'the old Adam'. The 'Adam' of original sin was proverbial (Dent A 29).

**30 a paradise** i.e. unfallen, like Adam in Eden.

**33 in a flood** More likely the Herculean labour of cleaning the Augean stables than Noah's flood. See line 35.

**34 currance** *OED* acknowledges 'currence' as a variant of 'currency', flowing. Walter wrongly calls it a 'nonce word'.

Nor never Hydra-headed wilfulness                          35
So soon did lose his seat, and all at once,
As in this king.
ELY                         We are blessed in the change.
CANTERBURY Hear him but reason in divinity,
And all-admiring, with an inward wish,
You would desire the king were made a prelate.           40
Hear him debate of commonwealth affairs,
You would say it hath been all in all his study.
List his discourse of war, and you shall hear
A fearful battle rendered you in music.
Turn him to any cause of policy,                          45
The gordian knot of it he will unloose,
Familiar as his garter, that when he speaks
The air, a chartered libertine, is still,
And the mute wonder lurketh in men's ears
To steal his sweet and honeyed sentences,                50
So that the art and practic part of life
Must be the mistress to this theoric.
Which is a wonder how his grace should glean it,
Since his addiction was to courses vain,
His companies unlettered, rude and shallow,              55
His hours filled up with riots, banquets, sports,
And never noted in him any study,
Any retirement, any sequestration
From open haunts and popularity.

**35 Hydra-headed** The many-headed monster, another labour of Hercules. See Dent H278.

**42 You would** The metre seems to require this to be an ellipsis.

**43 List** Pay attention to. The imperative mood of 'listen to'.

**44 in music** The discourse is musical, not the battle, though it has been suggested that this phrase starts a refrain of military music that runs through the play.

**45 cause of policy** judicial argument about politics.

**46 gordian knot** A proverbial phrase (Dent G375). An oracle prophesied that whoever could untie the knot would rule all Asia. Alexander the Great cut it with his sword. See 4.7.10–40.

**47 his garter** A more accessible knot than Alexander's. The Order of the Garter was established by Edward III in 1348.

**48 chartered** licensed. A proverbial image (Dent A88). In *AYLI* 2.7.48 Jaques speaks of having 'as large a charter as the wind'.

**49 the mute wonder** i.e. the tongueless being called wonder.

**50 sentences** maxims, *sententiae*.

**51 art and practic** practical, as opposed to 'theoric', line 52. The Archbishop sets up Henry's practice as the mistress of his theory, instead of the reverse, which was more usual.

**53 his grace** (1) the king (see 4.8.98–100), (2) his Christian goodness (22 above).

**55 companies** companions.

**56 riots** This is the term used by Henry IV of his son's conduct at *1H4* 1.1.84, *2H4* 4.2.62, and 4.2.263–4.

**58 sequestration** withdrawal into privacy (to read), away from 'popularity', public society, as in 4.1.38.

ELY  The strawberry grows underneath the nettle,                    60
          And wholesome berries thrive and ripen best
          Neighboured by fruit of baser quality.
          And so the prince obscured his contemplation
          Under the veil of wildness, which, no doubt,
          Grew like the summer grass fastest by night,               65
          Unseen, yet crescive in his faculty.
CANTERBURY  It must be so, for miracles are ceased,
          And therefore we must needs admit the means
          How things are perfected.
ELY                                But my good lord,
          How now for mitigation of this bill                        70
          Urged by the Commons? Doth his majesty
          Incline to it or no?
CANTERBURY              He seems indifferent,
          Or rather swaying more upon our part
          Than cherishing th'exhibiters against us,
          For I have made an offer to his majesty                    75
          Upon our spiritual convocation
          And in regard of causes now in hand
          Which I have opened to his grace at large,
          As touching France, to give a greater sum
          Than ever at one time the clergy yet                       80
          Did to his predecessors part withal.

66 crescive] *Rowe;* cressive F

**60 strawberry** The strawberries of Ely House were famous. See *R3* 3.4.32.
**62 baser quality** Being undamaged by neighbouring plants, strawberries were used as a symbol of righteousness. See Florio's *Montaigne*, 1603: 'some gardners say . . . that those Roses and Violets are even the sweeter & more odiferous that grow neere under Garlike and Onions'.
**63 contemplation** spiritual thought (see line 28).
**66 crescive** increasing. *OED* cites *crescence*: 'obs . . . 1602 . . . in their crescence in the wombe'.
**66 in his faculty** by means of its own power.
**67 miracles are ceased** A Protestant dogma, anachronistic here. It is also mentioned in *AWW* 2.3.1.
**68 admit the means** find the natural cause.
**69 perfected** The metre indicates that the word should be stressed on the first syllable.
**69 my good lord** The metre requires this to

be emphasised by putting the stress on 'my' and 'lord'.
**72 indifferent** impartial.
**74 exhibiters** the parliamentary sponsors of the bill.
**75–81 an offer . . . withal** Holinshed (p. 546) ascribes this to Archbishop Chichele as the conclusion of his speech about the Salic Law and Henry's claim to the French crown: 'And to the intent his loving chapleins and obedient subjects of the spiritualtie might shew themselves willing and desirous to aid his majestie, for the recoverie of his ancient right and true inheritance, the archbishop declared that in their spiritual convocation, they had granted to his highnesse such a summe of monie, as never by no spirituall persons was to any prince before those daies given or advanced.'
**76 Upon** On behalf of.
**77 causes** legal questions, as at line 45.

ELY  How did this offer seem received, my lord?

CANTERBURY  With good acceptance of his majesty,
    Save that there was not time enough to hear,
    As I perceived his grace would fain have done,        85
    The severals and unhidden passages
    Of his true titles to some certain dukedoms,
    And generally to the crown and seat of France
    Derived from Edward, his great-grandfather.

ELY  What was th'impediment that broke this off?        90

CANTERBURY  The French ambassador upon that instant
    Craved audience, and the hour I think is come
    To give him hearing. Is it four o'clock?

ELY  It is.

CANTERBURY  Then go we in, to know his embassy,        95
    Which I could with a ready guess declare
    Before the Frenchman speak a word of it.

ELY  I'll wait upon you, and I long to hear it.

                               *Exeunt*

**1.2**  *Enter the* KING, GLOUCESTER, BEDFORD, CLARENCE,
WESTMORLAND *and* EXETER [*and attendants*]

KING  Where is my gracious lord of Canterbury?

---

Act 1, Scene 2  0 SD *Enter . . . and attendants*] *Enter the King, Humfrey, Bedford, Clarence, Warwick, Westmerland, and Exeter.* F; *Enter King* Henry, Exeter, 2 *Bishops,* Clarence, *and other Attendants.* Q

**86 severals** separate details.

**86 unhidden passages** clear lines of inheritance (see 2.4.91).

**88 seat** throne, property, basis of title.

**89 great-grandfather** For Henry's genealogy, see Introduction, p. 21.

**93 four o'clock** There is no special reason for naming the hour, except to indicate the precise scheduling of the royal time. On-stage it would have been about two o'clock.

**95 embassy** the ambassador's message.

**Act 1, Scene 2**

**0 SD GLOUCESTER** Henry's brother, the Duke of Gloucester, generally known as 'Duke Humphrey', especially in the *H6* plays, is called Gloucester everywhere else in this play. A similar initial uncertainty over how to name him occurs with the other Gloucester, Woodstock, at the start of the second scene of *R2*.

**0 SD BEDFORD** Taylor follows Q in deleting Bedford (John of Lancaster in *2H4*), on the grounds of streamlining the characters (*Three Studies*, p. 101).

**0 SD CLARENCE** Henry's third brother has no speaking part and does not appear in any other scene. He figures more largely in Q, where he takes on Bedford's lines. He is retained here because of the play's emphasis on brotherhood. See Introduction, p. 66.

**0 SD** *attendants* Q has '*other Attendants*'. Somebody has to leave at line 221 to fetch the French ambassador.

**1 SH KING** On entering, Henry seats himself on the chair of state, or throne. See 7, 35, and especially 269–75.

EXETER  Not here in presence.

KING                              Send for him, good uncle.

WESTMORLAND  Shall we call in th'ambassador, my liege?

KING  Not yet, my cousin. We would be resolved,

Before we hear him, of some things of weight                    5

That task our thoughts, concerning us and France.

*Enter* [CANTERBURY *and* ELY]

CANTERBURY  God and his angels guard your sacred throne,

And make you long become it.

KING                              Sure, we thank you.

My learnèd lord, we pray you to proceed,

And justly and religiously unfold                              10

Why the law Salic that they have in France

Or should or should not bar us in our claim.

And God forbid, my dear and faithful lord,

That you should fashion, wrest, or bow your reading,

Or nicely charge your understanding soul                       15

With opening titles miscreate, whose right

Suits not in native colours with the truth.

For God doth know how many now in health

Shall drop their blood in approbation

Of what your reverence shall incite us to.                     20

Therefore take heed how you impawn our person,

How you awake our sleeping sword of war.

We charge you in the name of God take heed,

6 SD *Enter . . . ELY*] *Enter two Bishops* F

2 **presence** i.e. the royal presence: 'no man speaketh to the prince nor serveth at the table but in adoration and kneeling, all persons of the realme be bareheaded before him: insomuch that in the chamber of presence where the cloath of estate is set, no man dare walke, yea though the prince be not there, no man dare tarrie there but bareheaded'. Thomas Smith, *De Republica Anglorum*, Book 2, Chapter 3.

4 **cousin** Westmorland was related to Henry by marriage.

6 **task** give labour to.

10 **justly and religiously** with law and morality. 'Religiously' had the additional connotation of 'accurately'.

11 **the law Salic** A notorious law of the Salian Franks forbidding inheritance through the female. See Introduction, pp. 17–19.

12 **Or . . . or** Either . . . or.

14 **fashion** give a false shape to. See *Ado* 1.3.21.

14 **bow** distort.

15 **nicely charge** lay a burden on (your soul) with niceties.

15 **understanding** (1) comprehending, learned, (2) standing under God.

16 **opening** raising the question of.

16 **miscreate** An archaic form. See Spenser, *Faerie Queene*, 2.10.38.

17 **Suits . . . colours** Is economical with, does not match.

19 **in approbation** to support, prove.

20 **your reverence** a form of address for Canterbury, but also a potential sarcasm.

21 **impawn** put under an obligation, into debt.

For never two such kingdoms did contend
Without much fall of blood, whose guiltless drops                25
Are every one a woe, a sore complaint
'Gainst him whose wrongs gives edge unto the swords
That makes such waste in brief mortality.
Under this conjuration speak, my lord,
For we will hear, note, and believe in heart                     30
That what you speak is in your conscience washed
As pure as sin with baptism.
CANTERBURY  Then hear me, gracious sovereign, and you peers
    That owe your selves, your lives and services
    To this imperial throne. There is no bar                        35
    To make against your highness' claim to France
    But this which they produce from Pharamond:
    *In terram Salicam mulieres ne succedant*,
    – No woman shall succeed in Salic land –
    Which Salic land the French unjustly glose                       40
    To be the realm of France, and Pharamond
    The founder of this law and female bar.
    Yet their own authors faithfully affirm
    That the land Salic is in Germany,
    Between the floods of Sala and of Elbe,                          45
    Where Charles the Great, having subdued the Saxons,
    There left behind and settled certain French,
    Who, holding in disdain the German women
    For some dishonest manners of their life,
    Established then this law: to wit, no female                     50

---

38 *succedant*] F2; *succedaul* F  40 glose] F; gloss *Taylor*  45 Elbe] F (Elue); Elme Q  46 Great] F; fift Q  50 then] F; there Q

**27 wrongs** wrongdoings.

**27–8 gives . . . makes** Singular verbs were used with plural nouns, especially when the concept behind the verb was singular.

**28 brief mortality** This issue is confronted (and left unanswered) in Henry's dispute with his soldiers. See 4.1.111–64.

**32 sin with baptism** Baptism cleansed the flesh of original sin. As Canterbury did at 1.1.29, Henry evokes the baptismal service.

**35 imperial throne** 'Empire' meant absolute sovereignty, as also at 196, 2.0.10, 3.7.107, 4.1.234, 5.2.26, and 5.3.8.

**35 There is no bar** The Archbishop starts without making the point that Henry's claim

depended on his descent through a female, Queen Isabella, the mother of Edward III and daughter to Philip IV of France. Holinshed omits this point, too, although it is specified in Hall and *Famous Victories*.

**37 Pharamond** The legendary ancestor of the Frankish kings.

**40 glose** i.e. gloss, translate. It rhymes with 'close' in *R2*, 2.1.10–12.

**42 female bar** bar against descent through the female, the key to Henry's claim.

**46 Charles the Great** Charlemagne, A.D. 742–814. He is named again at 61, 71, 77, and 84.

**47 There . . . French** i.e. Charlemagne colonised Salia with Frenchmen.

Should be inheritrix in Salic land,
Which Salic (as I said) 'twixt Elbe and Sala
Is at this day in Germany called Meissen.
Then doth it well appear the Salic law
Was not devisèd for the realm of France.                    55
Nor did the French possess the Salic land
Until four hundred one-and-twenty years
After defunction of King Pharamond,
Idly supposed the founder of this law,
Who died within the year of our redemption,                60
Four hundred twenty-six, and Charles the Great
Subdued the Saxons and did seat the French
Beyond the River Sala in the year
Eight hundred five. Besides, their writers say
King Pepin, which deposèd Childeric,                        65
Did as heir general, being descended
Of Blithild, which was daughter to King Clothair,
Make claim and title to the crown of France.
Hugh Capet also, who usurped the crown
Of Charles the Duke of Lorraine, sole heir male            70
Of the true line and stock of Charles the Great,
To fine his title with some shows of truth,
Though in pure truth it was corrupt and naught,
Conveyed himself as th'heir to the Lady Lingard,
Daughter to Charlemagne, who was the son                    75
To Louis the emperor, and Louis the son
Of Charles the Great. Also King Louis the Ninth,
Who was sole heir to the usurper Capet,
Could not keep quiet in his conscience,
Wearing the crown of France, till satisfied                80
That fair Queen Isabel, his grandmother,

---

59 Idly] F; Godly Q   72 fine] Q; find F   74 Lingard] *Sisson;* lingare F; Inger Q   77 Ninth] *Pope;* Tenth F

**57 four . . . years** Holinshed's dating. It was actually A.D. 379. Holinshed's arithmetic allows him to substract 426 from 805 (line 64) and make the result 421. Shakespeare accepts Holinshed's calculation.
**58 defunction** i.e. death.
**59 Idly** Carelessly.
**60 the year . . . redemption** Anno Domini, the year of our Lord's birth.
**66 heir general** legitimate heir (through the female).

**72 fine** i.e. refine, make perfect.
**72 shows** appearance.
**74 Conveyed himself** Pretended to be, with the legal connotation of acquiring a title.
**75 Charlemagne** Charles II, not the Charlemagne of 61, 71, 77 and 84.
**77 Ninth** Shakespeare copied Holinshed's slip. Hall had correctly made him the tenth Louis.

Was lineal of the Lady Ermengard,
Daughter to Charles the foresaid Duke of Lorraine;
By the which marriage the line of Charles the Great
Was reunited to the crown of France.                              85
So that, as clear as is the summer's sun,
King Pepin's title, and Hugh Capet's claim,
King Louis his satisfaction, all appear
To hold in right and title of the female.
So do the kings of France unto this day.                          90
Howbeit, they would hold up this Salic law
To bar your highness claiming from the female,
And rather choose to hide them in a net
Than amply to embar their crooked titles
Usurped from you and your progenitors.                            95
KING  May I with right and conscience make this claim?
CANTERBURY  The sin upon my head, dread sovereign,
For in the Book of Numbers is it writ
'When the man dies, let the inheritance
Descend unto the daughter.' Gracious lord,                        100
Stand for your own, unwind your bloody flag,
Look back into your mighty ancestors.
Go, my dread lord, to your great-grandsire's tomb,
From whom you claim. Invoke his warlike spirit,

---

82 Ermengard] *Sisson;* Ermengare F   88 Louis] F (*Lewes*); Charles Q   90 day.] F;–, Q   94 embar] *This edn;* imbarre F;
imbace Q; imbare *Warburton conj;* unbar *Steevens conj.*   94 titles] F; causes Q   99 man] F; sonne Q

**82 lineal of** in direct line of descent from.

**86 as clear ... sun** Proverbial (Dent s969). The sun image that Henry has used of himself since *1H4* 1.2.147 is latent here.

**88 Louis his** The French 'Louis' was pronounced 'Lewis'. The possessive 'his' thus could be elided to it.

**91 Howbeit** However much, however it be that. The French uphold the Salic Law against succession through the female in spite of the fact that the French succession itself is through the female.

**93 a net** a network, a web, rather than a lineal tree. There may be a proverbial usage in the background, too: 'You dance in a net and think nobody sees you' (Dent N130).

**94 amply** openly.

**94 embar** (1) make bare, (2) hide, to prevent discovery of the crookedness of their title. A heraldic 'bar' was a pair of broad horizontal bands

across a shield. The spelling and the meaning of the word have provoked considerable speculation.

**98–100 Book ... daughter** The Bishops' Bible, quoted in Holinshed, says 'And thou shalt speake unto the children of Israel, saying "If a man dye, and have no sonne, ye shall turne his inheritance unto his daughter".' See Introduction, p. 18.

**99 dies** Holinshed adds 'without a son'. Q tries to make sense of the quotation, but too compressedly.

**103 great-grandsire** Edward III, whose son, the Black Prince, won the battle at Crécy.

**104 From ... claim** Holinshed, p. 545: 'not onelie the duchies of Normandie and Aquitaine, with the counties of Anjou and Maine, and the countrie of Gascoigne, were by undoubted title apperteining to the king, as to the lawfull and onelie heire of the same, but also the whole realme of France, as heire to his great grandfather king Edward the third'.

And your great-uncle's, Edward the Black Prince,                105
Who on the French ground played a tragedy,
Making defeat on the full power of France,
Whiles his most mighty father on a hill
Stood smiling to behold his lion's whelp
Forage in blood of French nobility.                            110
O noble English, that could entertain
With half their forces the full pride of France,
And let another half stand laughing by,
All out of work and cold for action.

ELY     Awake remembrance of these valiant dead,              115
        And with your puissant arm renew their feats.
        You are their heir, you sit upon their throne.
        The blood and courage that renownèd them
        Runs in your veins, and my thrice-puissant liege
        Is in the very May-morn of his youth,                 120
        Ripe for exploits and mighty enterprises.

EXETER  Your brother kings and monarchs of the earth
        Do all expect that you should rouse yourself,
        As did the former lions of your blood.

WESTMORLAND  They know your grace hath cause, and means,
                and might;                                     125
        So hath your highness. Never king of England
        Had nobles richer and more loyal subjects,
        Whose hearts have left their bodies here in England

---

110 Forage in] F; foraging Q   115 these] F; those *Taylor conj.*

**106 a tragedy** i.e. Crécy, fought in 1346. See 2.4.54–62.

**108 on a hill** Holinshed, p. 372: 'When the Frenchmen were clearlie overcome, and those that were left alive fled and gone, so that the English men heard no more noise of them, king Edward came downe from the hill (on the which he stood all that day with his helmet still on his head) and going to the prince, imbraced him in his armes, and kissed him.'

**110 Forage** Feed on, engorge himself with (used of armies taking food from local resources).

**111 entertain** The word develops the image of 'played a tragedy' at line 106.

**119 thrice-puissant** triply powerful, as (1) the heir, (2) the occupant of the throne, and (3) courageous, the three points made in lines 117–19.

**120 May-morn** A proverbial allusion (Dent M768.1).

**123 rouse** A hunting term; provoking a wild beast to leave its lair.

**124 lions** The lions here are the beasts referred to in the hunting image of line 123, but principally they are the heraldic lions of Henry's coat of arms. Edward II quartered the Plantagenet lions (of Richard I, the lion-heart) along with the French fleur-de-lis on his arms to denote his claim to the French crown. The earlier Henriad makes several references to these royal blazons. The Black Prince is the 'lion's whelp' at line 109.

**125 They** An intensified form, stressed in speaking.

**125 cause** legal justification. See 1.1.45, 77.

**126 So hath** As you do.

And lie pavilioned in the fields of France.

CANTERBURY  Oh, let their bodies follow, my dear liege,                    130
With blood and sword and fire, to win your right.
In aid whereof we of the spirituality
Will raise your highness such a mighty sum
As never did the clergy at one time
Bring in to any of your ancestors.                                        135

KING  We must not only arm t'invade the French
But lay down our proportions to defend
Against the Scot, who will make road upon us
With all advantages.

CANTERBURY  They of those marches, gracious sovereign,                    140
Shall be a wall sufficient to defend
Our England from the pilfering borderers.

KING  We do not mean the coursing snatchers only,
But fear the main intendment of the Scot,
Who hath been still a giddy neighbour to us.                              145
For you shall read that my great-grandfather
Never went with his forces into France
But that the Scot on his unfurnished kingdom
Came pouring like the tide into a breach
With ample and brim fullness of his force,                               150
Galling the gleanèd land with hot assays,
Girding with grievous siege castles and towns,

---

131 blood] F3; bloods F   138 road] F(roade), Q (rode); raid *Taylor*   142 England] Q; in-land F   147 Never . . . France]
F; neuer my great grandfather / Vnmaskt his power for *France* Q; Never unmasked his power unto France *Taylor*   **151**
assays] F, Q; essays *Malone*

**129 pavilioned** Pavilions were the tents of the
nobility used in jousting tournaments.
**132 the spirituality** Holinshed's term for the
clergy.
**136–9** In Holinshed it is not Henry but Westmorland, Warden of the northern Marches, who
raises the question of the danger from Scotland.
See note to line 140.
**138 road** inroads.
**140 marches** the border territories. The Lords
of the Marches, bordering Scotland and Wales, kept
a military retinue and a quasi-regal authority there
until the seventeenth century.
**142 England** In the manuscript copy for F it
must have been written 'Ingland', misread by the
F compositor. At 5.2.12 the same word was read as
'Ireland'.
**143 coursing snatchers** fast-galloping raiders.

'Coursing' was the sport of running hounds after
hares, and the 'snatch' was the capture of a hare.
**144 main** an army set for battle.
**145 still** constantly.
**146 you shall read** Henry here confirms one
of the Archbishop's claims about his studies
(1.1.41–2).
**147** F's reading is much less colourful than Q's,
and consequently Q is preferred by Taylor, with
support from Jackson. But that is not sufficient
reason for abandoning F here. The Q reading does
not make it clear that Edward III left England along
with his army.
**151 Galling** Wounding, making sores in.
**151 gleanèd** i.e. with its harvest of soldiers
lodged elsewhere.
**151 assays** ventures, sallies.

That England, being empty of defence,
Hath shook and trembled at th'ill neighbourhood.
CANTERBURY  She hath been then more feared than harmed,
    my liege.                                                                                       155
For hear her but exampled by her self:
When all her chivalry hath been in France
And she a mourning widow of her nobles,
She hath herself not only well defended
But taken and impounded as a stray                                          160
The king of Scots, whom she did send to France
To fill King Edward's fame with prisoner kings,
And make their chronicle as rich with praise
As is the ooze and bottom of the sea
With sunken wreck and sumless treasuries.                            165
WESTMORLAND  But there's a saying, very old and true,
    *'If that you will France win,*
    *Then with Scotland first begin.'*
For once the eagle England being in prey,
To her unguarded nest the weasel Scot                                    170
Comes sneaking, and so sucks her princely eggs,
Playing the mouse in absence of the cat
To 'tame and havoc more than she can eat.

154 th'ill neighbourhood] F; the brute hereof Q, *Taylor*  163 And make their chronicle] F; Filling your Chronicles Q; And make her chronicle *Capell*; And make your chronicle *Taylor*  165 wreck] *Theobald*; Wrack F; wrack Q  165 sumless treasuries] F (sum-lesse); shiplesse treasurie Q  166 SH WESTMORLAND] *Capell*; Ely. F; *Lord.* Q  168 begin] F (*begin*)  170 her unguarded] F; his unfurnish Q  173 'tame] *Wilson (conj. Greg)*; tame F; spoyle Q; tear *Rowe*[2]; taint *Theobald*

**154 th'ill neighbourhood** Bad neighbours have already been mentioned at 1.1.62. Henry jokes about them at Agincourt (4.1.6).

**155 She** Not England in the form of Henry, as elsewhere, but a widowed state without men, as at line 158. A state or city that is at risk from an invader is usually female, as at 3.4.9. The female to be invaded is imaged as a city at 5.2.286–8.

**155 feared** i.e. made afraid. It echoes the proverb 'more afraid than hurt' (Dent A55).

**160 impounded as a stray** lawfully locked up like straying cattle.

**161 The king of Scots** David II, captured at Neville's Cross in 1346 while Edward III was in France. In *Edward III* 5.1.63 the captured Scots king appears (unhistorically) in the king's camp at Calais. For Henry V's captive Scots king see Appendix 2.

**163 their** i.e. England's and Edward's.

**164 ooze and bottom** A hendiadys, the ooze of the seabed.

**165 sumless treasuries** immeasurable riches.

**166 SH WESTMORLAND** Holinshed gives this speech to Westmorland. F's allocation of the speech seems unlikely, since it is odd that Ely should contradict his Archbishop. He does have one other speech, at 115–21, but that only endorses Canterbury. Possibly F's 'Ely' was a misreading of 'Exe', who speaks next. Q's ascription to a 'lord' justifies the correction based on Holinshed.

**167–8 'If . . . begin'** Quoted by Holinshed, this was a proverbial saying (Tilley D43, Dent F663), first recorded in 1548.

**169 in prey** in search of prey.

**172 mouse . . . cat** A familiar proverb (Dent C175).

**173 'tame** aphetic for 'attame', to break in. Greg's conjecture seems better than Rowe's or Theobald's, since it is closest to F. Cats do not usually tame the mice they catch.

EXETER  It follows, then, the cat must stay at home.
Yet that is but a crushed necessity,                                    175
Since we have locks to safeguard necessaries
And pretty traps to catch the petty thieves.
While that the armèd hand doth fight abroad
Th'advisèd head defends itself at home.
For government, though high and low and lower,                          180
Put into parts, doth keep in one consent,
Congreeing in a full and natural close
Like music.
CANTERBURY        Therefore doth heaven divide
The state of man in diverse functions,
Setting endeavour in continual motion,                                  185
To which is fixèd as an aim or butt
Obedience. For so work the honey bees,
Creatures that by a rule in nature teach
The act of order to a peopled kingdom.
They have a king, and officers of sorts,                                190
Where some like magistrates correct at home,
Others like merchants venture trade abroad,
Others like soldiers, armèd in their stings,
Make boot upon the summer's velvet buds,
Which pillage they with merry march bring home                          195
To the tent royal of their emperor,
Who, busied in his majesties, surveys
The singing masons building roofs of gold,

---

175 crushed] F; curst Q   182 Congreeing] F; Congrueth Q   183 Therefore] F; True: therefore Q, *Taylor*   184 state] F;
fate Q   189 act] F, Q; art *Pope*   197 majesties] F; maiestie Q, *Rowe*   197 surveys] F; behold Q

**175 crushed** distorted.
**177 pretty . . . petty** A *paronomasia*, using
words of similar sound.
**179 advisèd** prudent.
**181 parts** The image is from music. 'Parts' are
different melodic lines, and 'one consent' is singing
in harmony. This analogy for government faintly
echoes Thomas Elyot's *The Boke of the Governor*
(1531), Book 1, Chapter 7. The Archbishop's beehive image (187–204) is more evidently from Chapter 2 of Elyot's book.
**182 Congreeing** Co-operating.
**182 close** The cadence at the end of a musical
phrase.

**184 state** estate, social rank.
**186 butt** target (in archery).
**187 the honey bees** See note to line 181.
**189 act** Pope's emendation to 'art' creates a false
antithesis between art and nature. See *Explorations*,
p. 289.
**190 king** i.e. a queen bee. Aristotle and later
writers were unclear about generation and gender
in bees.
**190 of sorts** of different ranks. See 4.7.121,
4.8.67, 5.0.25, and Introduction, p. 30.
**191 correct** dispense justice.
**194 Make boot** ransack, take booty.
**197 majesties** the royal duties of his kingdom.

The civil citizens kneading up the honey,
The poor mechanic porters crowding in                    200
Their heavy burdens at his narrow gate,
The sad-eyed justice with his surly hum
Delivering o'er to executors pale
The lazy yawning drone. I this infer,
That many things, having full reference                  205
To one consent, may work contrariously.
As many arrows loosèd several ways
Come to one mark; as many ways meet in one town,
As many fresh streams meet in one salt sea,
As many lines close in the dial's centre,                210
So may a thousand actions, once afoot
End in one purpose, and be all well borne
Without defeat. Therefore to France, my liege.
Divide your happy England into four,
Whereof take you one quarter into France,                215
And you withal shall make all Gallia shake.
If we with thrice such powers left at home
Cannot defend our own doors from the dog
Let us be worried, and our nation lose
The name of hardiness and policy.                        220
KING  Call in the messengers sent from the Dauphin.
                                        [*Exit attendant*]
Now are we well resolved, and by God's help

---

199 kneading] F; lading Q  204 yawning] F; caning Q  208 Come] F; flye Q  209 salt] F; selfe Q  212 End] Q, *Pope;*
And F  212 purpose] F; moment Q  213 defeat] F; defect Q  219 worried] F; beaten Q  221 SD *Exit attendant*] *Exeunt
some Attendants / Capell*

199 **civil** orderly, well-mannered.

200 **mechanic** artisan, working-man.

202 **sad-eyed** serious-minded.

203 **executors** punishers, executioners.

206 **one consent** See note to line 181.

206 **contrariously** by contraries. The underlying image is probably musical counterpoint.

207 **As** i.e. just as.

208 **many . . . town** Proverbial (Dent W176, L305.1). The same proverb is amplified in 211–12.

209 **many . . . sea** Proverbial (Dent R140; not in Tilley).

210 **dial** i.e. a sundial.

214 **into four** This proposal answers Henry's concern expressed in 136–8 about the English

'proportions'. Here it appears as a first indication of the size of the English army in France and the small numbers present at Agincourt. Henry renews the point about the army's size in 2.2.15–18.

216 **Gallia** i.e. Gaul, the standard word for ancient France. 'Gallia' is used in *1H6* and *3H6*, and in *Wiv.* it is specified as 'Gallia and Gaul'.

218 **the dog** A paraphrase from Psalm 22. The 'dog of war' is a recurrent image in the play. See Introduction, p. 13.

219 **worried** (1) toyed with by a hunting-hound, (2) made anxious.

222 **well resolved** (1) freed from doubt, (2) determined on action.

And yours, the noble sinews of our power,
France being ours, we'll bend it to our awe,
Or break it all to pieces. Or there we'll sit,                    225
Ruling in large and ample empery
O'er France and all her almost kingly dukedoms,
Or lay these bones in an unworthy urn
Tombless, with no remembrance over them.
Either our history shall with full mouth                          230
Speak freely of our acts, or else our grave
Like Turkish mute shall have a tongueless mouth,
Not worshipped with a waxen epitaph.

*Enter* AMBASSADOR *of France* [*with attendants*]

Now are we well prepared to know the pleasure
Of our fair cousin Dauphin; for we hear                           235
Your greeting is from him, not from the king.
AMBASSADOR  May't please your majesty to give us leave
Freely to render what we have in charge,
Or shall we sparingly show you far off
The Dauphin's meaning, and our embassy?                           240
KING  We are no tyrant, but a Christian king,
Unto whose grace our passion is as subject
As are our wretches fettered in our prisons.

---

230 history] F; Chronicles Q   230 with full mouth] F; with full mouth speake Q   233 waxen] F; paper Q   233 SD
*Enter . . . attendants*] Enter Ambassadors of France F; Enter thambassadors from France Q   240 meaning] F (meauing)   243
are] Q, *Rowe;* is F

**223 noble sinews** The body politic image has already been broached at 178–9. This address is to the nobility attending in the king's 'presence', not the commons.

**224 awe** An image of authority. Like a bow, France will either be made to bend out of respect or be broken.

**224–5 awe . . . Or** Another *antanaclasis.*

**225–8 Or . . . Or** Either . . . Or.

**227 almost kingly dukedoms** The Chorus at 3.0.31 calls the French offer to Henry 'some petty and unprofitable dukedoms'.

**230 history** Pronounced with two of the three syllables stressed.

**230 with full mouth** i.e. wide-stretched, wide open.

**232 Turkish mute** tongueless slave.

**233 waxen** i.e. easily perishable.

**233 SD** The F stage direction makes the ambas-

sador plural, but Henry and Exeter at 3–5 speak only of one. He would have had attendants, and English attendants are also needed, both to deliver them on-stage and to obey the order to 'convey them' away at line 297.

**235 cousin** Henry's claim to the French crown made him kin to the French king and therefore also related to the Dauphin as the king's heir.

**240 embassy** the message carried by the ambassadors. The practice of keeping ambassadors regularly resident in a foreign country was new in Shakespeare's time.

**242–3 grace . . . prisons** As with his confirmation of the Archbishop's claim about his reading, Henry now affirms the 'grace' awarded him at 1.1.21. Since at the end of *2H4* he had committed Falstaff to the Fleet prison, however temporarily, this simile echoes the Archbishop's praise of his reform.

Therefore with frank and with uncurbèd plainness
Tell us the Dauphin's mind.

AMBASSADOR                      Thus then in few:                    245
Your highness lately, sending into France,
Did claim some certain dukedoms, in the right
Of your great predecessor, King Edward the Third.
In answer of which claim the prince our master
Says that you savour too much of your youth,        250
And bids you be advised: there's naught in France
That can be with a nimble galliard won;
You cannot revel into dukedoms there.
He therefore sends you, meeter for your spirit,
This tun of treasure, and in lieu of this            255
Desires you let the dukedoms that you claim
Hear no more of you. This the Dauphin speaks.

KING  What treasure, uncle?

EXETER                        [*Opens tun*] Tennis balls, my liege.

KING  We are glad the Dauphin is so pleasant with us.
His present and your pains we thank you for.          260
When we have matched our rackets to these balls
We will in France, by God's grace, play a set
Shall strike his father's crown into the hazard.
Tell him he hath made a match with such a wrangler
That all the courts of France will be disturbed       265
With chases. And we understand him well,

254 spirit] F; study Q    256 claim] F; craue Q

247 **some certain dukedoms** Holinshed reports this original claim, which preceded the claim to the French crown itself.

252 **galliard** A gay and lively dance.

255 **tun** A tun was a heavy casket or box, with the transferred meaning of a heavy weight. Holinshed calls it a 'barrell', but Shakespeare took the word, which is more appropriate to a 'treasure', from one of the earlier versions of the play, probably *Famous Victories*, which used Hall's 'tun'. See Appendix 1.

259 **pleasant** Henry's 'grace' controls his 'passion' (242) over the insult.

261–6 **When . . . chases** An extended image from 'royal' tennis, or 'jeu de paume', the game in which the tun of balls would be used. France was noted for the popularity of the game and the number of its courts. The early courts were of variable design. One reconstructed in Falkland Palace in Fife reproduces the kind of court Shakespeare refers to. A ball when served could be bounced off any of the walls of the court.

262 **play a set** play a game.

263 **crown** (1) the French crown, (2) the final point scored in the game.

263 **hazard** A hole in the wall of the real tennis court. Hitting the ball into the hazard scores a winner.

264 **wrangler** debater, especially in law courts.

265 **courts** (1) royal courts, (2) tennis courts.

266 **chases** (1) returns of the ball, (2) hunting with dogs. In royal tennis if the server allows the ball to bounce twice on his side, no point is scored. Laying a 'chase', a term which must have come into tennis from hunting, was a challenge to return the ball before the second bounce. The name 'tennis' may have derived from the call 'tenez' used before serving when a chase is being laid, though if so it reached England before the time of the medieval *Gawaine*, which also mentions tennis balls.

How he comes o'er us with our wilder days,
Not measuring what use we made of them.
We never valued this poor seat of England,
And therefore, living hence, did give ourself                          270
To barbarous licence, as 'tis ever common
That men are merriest when they are from home.
But tell the Dauphin I will keep my state,
Be like a king, and show my sail of greatness
When I do rouse me in my throne of France,                             275
For that I have laid by my majesty
And plodded like a man for working days.
But I will rise there with so full a glory
That I will dazzle all the eyes of France,
Yea, strike the Dauphin blind to look on us.                           280
And tell the pleasant prince this mock of his
Hath turned his balls to gun-stones, and his soul
Shall stand sore chargèd for the wasteful vengeance
That shall fly with them; for many a thousand widows
Shall this his mock mock out of their dear husbands,                   285
Mock mothers from their sons, mock castles down,
And some are yet ungotten and unborn
That shall have cause to curse the Dauphin's scorn.
But this lies all within the will of God,
To whom I do appeal, and in whose name                                 290

276 I have] F; have we Q; have I *Taylor*   284 with] F; from Q   285 husbands] F (hnsbands)   287 And] F; Ay Q

**267 comes o'er us** throws in our face.

**269 this poor seat** (1) this poor estate, (2) the throne (on which Henry is seated: see note to line 1) from which he lived 'hence' (270).

**272 merriest** The word had a narrower meaning than it has now, with a strong connotation of bawdiness. 'Merry tales' were usually bawdy jokes.

**273 keep my state** (1) stay on my throne, (2) observe the ceremonies of royalty. In 2.4.32 his reception of the French ambassador is described as carried out with 'great state'.

**274 my sail of greatness** The image of a sail may gesture towards a military banner, but it also marks the canopy and the cloth of estate with the royal arms on it which hung behind the chair of state.

**275 my throne** This is the first explicit declaration of Henry's claim to the French crown.

**278 I will rise there** The image recalls the use in the preceding plays of the Henriad as a rising

sun. See especially *R2* 3.3.62–7, *1H4*, 1.2.157–63, and Preface, p. x.

**281 pleasant** joking.

**282 gun-stones** cannon-balls. The larger calibres were made from stone until the sixteenth century.

**283 vengeance** This threat to take revenge for the Dauphin's insult stands against the careful weighing of the legal case for Henry's title to the French crown. Revenge is a strong motive in *Famous Victories*.

**284 with** The Q reading normalises, missing the point about the flying cannon-balls and fleet vengeance for the tennis balls.

**285 mock** The most conspicuous of a series of uses of *syllepsis* and *antanaclasis* in the play. See Introduction, p. 14.

**289** This halt to the announcement of revenge makes grace once again overrule passion.

Tell you the Dauphin I am coming on
To venge me as I may, and to put forth
My rightful hand in a well-hallowed cause.
So get you hence in peace. And tell the Dauphin
His jest will savour but of shallow wit                                    295
When thousands weep more than did laugh at it.
[*To attendants*] Convey them with safe conduct. Fare you well.
                              *Exeunt Ambassador [and attendants]*

EXETER  This was a merry message.
KING  We hope to make the sender blush at it.
Therefore, my lords, omit no happy hour                                    300
That may give furtherance to our expedition,
For we have now no thought in us but France,
Save those to God that run before our business.
Therefore let our proportions for these wars
Be soon collected, and all things thought upon                             305
That may with reasonable swiftness add
More feathers to our wings. For, God before,
We'll chide this Dauphin at his father's door.
Therefore let every man now task his thought
That this fair action may on foot be brought.                              310
                                             *Flourish. Exeunt*

---

297 SD *Ambassador] Ambassadors* F    310 SD *Flourish. Exeunt] Exeunt* F

293 **well-hallowed cause** a righteous legal case upheld by God.
298 **merry** (1) comic, (2) indecent. See note to line 272. Henry picks up the secondary meaning when he says he will make the sender blush.
300 **happy** fortunate and favourable.
301 **expedition** (1) invasion of France, (2) speed.
303 **that run before** i.e. only thoughts of God take precedence over the invasion.
304 **proportions** (1) resources, (2) the fraction of one-quarter assigned to France (137, 215).
307 **God before** i.e. with God as our leader.
308 A reaffirmation of the posture of revenge for the insult, with no direct attack on the French king. The Dauphin is made the immediate target.
309 **task** lay the task on.
310 **fair action** The normal phrase for good stage acting. Bringing it 'on foot' means making it move, from sitting to walking. The latter phrase also hints that the movement will not be by horses (1.0.26) or by ship (2.0.37–40).

310 SD **Flourish** F, which should have inserted an act-break here, moves the trumpet flourish to the Chorus's entrance, not to Henry's exit. The same thing happens at the end of 2.4 on the French king's exit. None of the other entrances by the Chorus are heralded by a flourish, but F does mark flourishes for the king's other exits at 2.2.188 and 3.4.58. Normally, trumpets were used to announce the arrival or departure of royalty, although in *MND* and in *Ham.* a flourish marks the arrival of a troupe of players. Following Dyce's conjecture, this edition regularises the flourishes for the kings and takes them away from the Chorus. Continuous staging would have run entrances on the heels of the exits, of course. Flourishes were trumpet-calls, or fanfares. Four of the Folio plays specify cornets, because substituting woodwinds for brass was standard when plays transferred from the open amphitheatre to a hall theatre. The trumpets specified in the F text of this play indicate that it was prepared for performance at an amphitheatre.

**2.0** *Enter* CHORUS

CHORUS  Now all the youth of England are on fire
And silken dalliance in the wardrobe lies.
Now thrive the armourers, and honour's thought
Reigns solely in the breast of every man.
They sell the pasture now to buy the horse,                            5
Following the mirror of all Christian kings
With wingèd heels, as English Mercuries.
For now sits expectation in the air,
And hides a sword from hilts unto the point
With crowns imperial, crowns and coronets                              10
Promised to Harry and his followers.
The French, advised by good intelligence
Of this most dreadful preparation,
Shake in their fear, and with pale policy
Seek to divert the English purposes.                                   15
O England: model to thy inward greatness,
Like little body with a mighty heart,

---

**Act 2, Scene 0    0** SD *Enter* CHORUS] *Flourish. Enter Chorus.* F

**Act 2, Scene 0**
  **2.0** Johnson introduced the act division here.
Pope transposed Act 2, Scene 1 to before the
Chorus, in order to eliminate the Chorus's confus-
ing announcement of arrival at Southampton when
the first scene of the act is in London.
  **1 on fire** Proverbial (Dent F287.1). The image
picks up the first Chorus's 'Muse of fire'.
  **2 wardrobe** A dressing-room. Metal clothing is
replacing the silks of lovers.
  **5** A paradox. Horses normally need pasture. One
is fixed, the other a means to travel.
  **6 the mirror of all Christian kings** The term
is a conflation of *A Mirror for Magistrates* and
Erasmus's *Institutio Principis Christiani*, the Institution of the Christian Ruler. Hall called Henry
the 'mirror of Christendom'. A 'mirror' is a model
or paragon, not a looking-glass.
  **7 Mercuries** Mercury was the Roman god with
winged heels and hat.
  **9–11 hides . . . followers** One of Edward
III's heraldic devices was a sword ringed by three
crowns. Here the sword which buys military conquest will be concealed from view by the crowns
which will be its reward. The lines also carry
a distinctly incongruous memory from *Famous
Victories*, where in a comic incident at Agincourt

the clown Dericke is threatened by a French soldier. He offers to buy his life by covering the
soldier's sword with gold crowns (coins). When
the soldier puts the sword down so that Dericke
can more easily cover it with the crowns, Dericke
snatches it up and threatens the Frenchman with
it. See Appendix 1.
  **9 hilts** the cross-piece at the base of the handle.
  **10 crowns imperial** The flower known as the
crown imperial is named in *WT* 4.4.126, along
with 'bold oxlips'. There is something sylleptic,
as in 1.0.13, about the transition from crowns to
flowers.
  **10 coronets** Variously pronounced with two or
three syllables. In *Ham.* 4.7.172 F spells it 'coronet',
in *Ant.* 4.12.27 'crownet'.
  **12 intelligence** news, spying.
  **14 pale policy** i.e. timid plotting, not fiery mil-
itancy. It stands on Hamlet's side with the 'pale
cast of thought' rather than the 'native hue of
resolution'.
  **16 England** It is deliberately left unclear at this
point whether the Chorus means Henry or his
country.
  **16 model** paragon, exemplar.
  **17** The first recorded use of this saying. See
Dent B501.

What mightst thou do, that honour would thee do,
Were all thy children kind and natural?
But see, thy fault France hath in thee found out,                    20
A nest of hollow bosoms, which he fills
With treacherous crowns, and three corrupted men –
One, Richard, Earl of Cambridge, and the second
Henry, Lord Scroop of Masham, and the third
Sir Thomas Gray, knight of Northumberland –                          25
Have for the gilt of France (oh, guilt indeed)
Confirmed conspiracy with fearful France,
And by their hands this grace of kings must die,
If hell and treason hold their promises,
Ere he take ship for France, and in Southampton.                     30
Linger your patience on, and we'll digest
Th'abuse of distance, force perforce a play.
The sum is paid, the traitors are agreed,
The king is set from London, and the scene
Is now transported, gentles, to Southampton.                         35
There is the playhouse now, there must you sit,
And thence to France shall we convey you safe
And bring you back, charming the narrow seas
To give you gentle pass, for if we may
We'll not offend one stomach with our play.                          40

---

20 fault France] F; fault! France *Capell*   32 force perforce] *Taylor;* force F

18 **would thee do** i.e. would do to thee.

19 **kind** i.e. naturally filial.

21 **nest** Normally used of vipers.

21 **hollow bosoms** (1) empty of heart, (2) hungry for gain.

21 **he** i.e. the French king ('France' at line 20).

22 **crowns** the French *écu*, a gold coin.

23 **Cambridge** Cambridge's claim to the crown, or specifically his plan that it should descend through his wife to his son, the York of the *H6* plays, is conspicuously omitted here. This omission was evidently noted by the four authors of *Oldcastle*, who spelled it out in detail. See Introduction, pp. 19–20.

26 **gilt . . . guilt** A *paronomasia*.

28 **grace** Canterbury and Ely emphasise this term for Henry at 1.1.22 and 53.

30 **Southampton** Historically Henry did ship his forces from Southampton, which was where the conspiracy was uncovered. The Chorus's triple emphasis on the locality, at 30, 35, and 42 has caused confusion, since the first scene of Act 2 is back in London and the Chorus to Act 3 in the F text sends him out from Dover. Many productions have followed Pope's precedent and transferred the whole Chorus to follow Act 2, Scene 1. Others have split the Chorus into two at line 32, putting the Southampton transfer at the beginning of Act 2, Scene 2. See note to line 41, and Introduction, pp. 65, 67–8.

31–2 **digest . . . distance** (1) absorb the offence, (2) compress the length.

32 **force perforce** 'Force' is force-feeding or cramming, an image developed from 'digest' in the previous line. Both the pun and the metre are improved by Taylor's addition.

38 **And bring you back** A slightly arch comic afterthought.

38 **charming** Like a magician.

40 **offend one stomach** make sick, either by the sea journey or poor taste.

But when the king come forth, and not till then,
Unto Southampton do we shift our scene.                *Exit*


**2.1** *Enter Corporal* NYM *and Lieutenant* BARDOLPH


BARDOLPH Well met, Corporal Nym.

NYM Good morrow, Lieutenant Bardolph.

BARDOLPH What, are Ancient Pistol and you friends yet?

NYM For my part, I care not. I say little, but when time shall serve
there shall be smiles, but that shall be as it may. I dare not            5
fight, but I will wink and hold out mine iron. It is a simple one,
but what though? It will toast cheese, and it will endure cold as
another man's sword will, and there's an end.

BARDOLPH I will bestow a breakfast to make you friends, and we'll

---

41 when] *This edn* (*Blayney conj.*); till F   **Act 2, Scene 1**   3 Ancient] F; Ensign *Taylor*   8 there's an end] F; theres the
humor of it Q

---

**41 when the** Peter Blayney's conjecture resolves
much of the discomfort registered by Pope and
others over the contradiction between the Chorus
announcing arrival at Southampton and the immediate entry of the Eastcheap clowns. F's 'till the'
must be a compositor error by anticipation of 'till
then' at the end of the line. An F manuscript
reading 'when the' allows the Chorus to adjust
his previous announcement about the transfer to
Southampton, making allowance for the arrival of
the clowns but avoiding explicit acknowledgement
of their existence.

**Act 2, Scene 1**

**0 SD** *Corporal* Barnabe Rich, in *A Pathway
to Military Practise*, 1587, says 'Of the Corporall
or Launce-*prezado*: It is much beneficiall for the
redines for service, that a company of men should
be devided into fower squadrons, the weapons
equally devided, and to be committed to the charge
of foure Corporalls.' (G3).

**0 SD** NYM In F Compositor B spells the name
'Nym' for this scene and 4.4, while Compositor
A elsewhere spells it 'Nim'. Nym, a notably small
and skinny man, does not appear in *2H4*, but he
is in *Wiv.* In thieving slang, to 'nim' meant to
steal.

**0 SD** *Lieutenant* BARDOLPH He is a corporal
at *2H4* 2.4.120, and at 3.2.2 below. Here the rank
places him above 'Ancient' Pistol as well as Nym.

**3 Ancient** A rank below that of lieutenant but

above corporal. Originally bearer of a company's
flag or ensign, it was the senior non-gentlemanly
rank. Rich says 'As the Ensigne in the fielde is the
honour of the bande, so the Ensign bearer in like
case should be honoured by his company, and this
reputation is best attained, by his owne curteous
demeanour towards ye soldiers, the loove of them
concerneth greatly his owne safety, in all perrilles
and attempts' (G1ᵛ). Usually he was responsible for
feeding the company, the 'sutler' post that Pistol
claims for himself in line 88, for which honesty was
an important qualification. In *Oth.* 'honest' Iago is
Othello's 'ancient'. For the spelling, see Introduction, p. 70.

**3 Pistol** The name was pronounced 'pizzle'.
Mrs. Quickly in *2H4* 2.4.128 calls him 'Captaine
Peesell'. See Cercignani, p. 345.

**3 friends** The reason for the quarrel between
Nym and Pistol only becomes clear at 15–17.

**4–5 shall . . . shall . . . shall be as it may**
The emphatic 'shall' leads up to a very ordinary
proverbial saying (Dent T202), which Nym repeats
as a catchphrase at 13, 18 and 101. His main comic
idiom is the repetition of banal proverbial sayings.

**6 wink** close my eyes.

**6 iron** sword, useful for toasting cheese on.

**7 endure cold** Toasting cheese would make it
hot, but not fighting.

**8 there's an end** Another proverbial catchphrase (Dent E113.1). Q's alternative, 'there's the
humour of it', is used by Nym more commonly in
*Wiv.*

be all three sworn brothers to France. Let't be so, good   10
Corporal Nym.

NYM Faith, I will live so long as I may, that's the certain of it, and
when I cannot live any longer I will do as I may. That is my
rest, that is the rendezvous of it.

BARDOLPH It is certain, corporal, that he is married to Nell   15
Quickly, and certainly she did you wrong, for you were troth-
plight to her.

NYM I cannot tell. Things must be as they may. Men may sleep,
and they may have their throats about them at that time,
and some say knives have edges. It must be as it may. Though   20
patience be a tired mare, yet she will plod. There must be
conclusions. Well, I cannot tell.

*Enter* PISTOL *and* QUICKLY

BARDOLPH Here comes Ancient Pistol and his wife. Good
corporal, be patient here.

NYM How now, mine host Pistol?   25

PISTOL Base tyke, call'st thou me host? Now by this hand I swear I
scorn the term, nor shall my Nell keep lodgers.

HOSTESS No, by my troth, not long, for we cannot lodge and board

---

21 mare] Q; name F   22 tell] F; tell, and there is the humour of it Q   25 SH NYM] Q, *not in* F   26 tyke] F; slaue Q; tick *Taylor*

**10 sworn brothers** Bardolph means a brother-hood of thieves who swear loyalty to one another in blood. 'France' makes it an anticipation of Henry's declaration at Agincourt, 4.3.61–3.
**13 I will do as I may** A perversion of the proverb used in 4–5. Here it compounds the more usual expression 'I will die as I may.' In view of the cause of the quarrel over which Nym is grieving here, 'do' probably means sexual doing.
**14 rest** (1) musically, a pause, (2) in primero (a card game), the reserved stake, the last chance.
**14 rendezvous** The first use of French in the play. It meant not so much a meeting place as a refuge.
**15–16 Nell Quickly** The Hostess of the Eastcheap tavern in *2H4*.
**16–17 troth-plight** to engaged to marry.
**18 I cannot tell** Proverbial (Dent T85.1). Nym repeats it at the end of this speech.
**19–20 throats . . . knives** The first of several

references to cutting throats. See Introduction, p. 27.
**21 mare** Q's reading uses the old proverb. E. A. J. Honigmann, in *MLR* 50 (1955), 197, argues for the F 'name' on the ground that the puns Nym / name, plod / plot are deliberate distortions of the proverb. But Nym's other proverbial phrases are plodding and undistorted.
**25 SH NYM** Q's attribution of this line must be right, since Nym is far more likely than the peace-making Bardolph to replace Pistol's military title with the insulting name of a taverner. The form of address is a derisive allusion to his marriage to the Hostess.
**26 tyke** a mongrel or cur. Malone notes a 'tick' as a parasite, which would lodge on a 'host', and a pun may be intended. But on the strength of the frequent references to dogs in the play, F's 'tike' seems preferable. F *Lear* has a 'bobtail tike or trundle-tail' in a list of dogs at 3.6.27.
**27 lodgers** By extension from the insulting 'host' of the previous line.

a dozen or fourteen gentlewomen that live honestly by the prick
of their needles but it will be thought we keep a bawdy house          30
straight. [*Nym draws his sword*] Oh, welladay, Lady, if he be not
hewn now, we shall see wilful adultery and murder committed.
[*Pistol draws his sword*]

BARDOLPH Good lieutenant, good corporal, offer nothing here.

NYM Pish.

PISTOL Pish for thee, Iceland dog, thou prick-eared cur of Iceland.     35

HOSTESS Good Corporal Nym, show thy valour, and put up your
sword.
[*They sheathe their swords*]

NYM Will you shog off? [*To Pistol*] I would have you *solus*.

PISTOL *Solus*, egregious dog? O viper vile! The *solus* in thy most
mervailous face, the *solus* in thy teeth, and in thy throat, and in    40
thy hateful lungs, yea, in thy maw, perdy, and, which is worse,
within thy nasty mouth! I do retort the *solus* in thy bowels, for I
can take, and Pistol's cock is up, and flashing fire will follow!

NYM I am not Barbason, you cannot conjure me. I have an humour

32 hewn] F; drawn *Theobald;* here *Walter*

31 **straight** at once.

31 SD *Nym draws his sword* Judging from the
Hostess's cry about her new husband being 'hewn',
Nym must draw his sword first. Neither F nor Q
marks these actions.

32 **hewn** cut by a sword, reaped like corn. The
word has behind it the figure of Death with his
reaper's scythe.

32 SD *Pistol draws his sword* Bardolph's words
at line 33 indicate that both Nym and Pistol have
their swords out by now.

33 **lieutenant** A promotion, possibly as an
appeasement for the stigma of 'mine host'. At
3.7.10 Llewellyn calls him an 'ancient lieutenant',
or sub-lieutenant, a more precise designation.

33 **offer** make no challenge to combat.

35 **Iceland dog** a small, hairy, quarrelsome
lap-dog. Harrison's 'Description of England' (in
Volume I of Holinshed), p. 231, states of English
dogs that 'The last sort of dogs consisteth of the
currish kind, meet for manie toies: of which the
whappet or prickeared curre is one . . . Besides
these also we have sholts or curs dailie brought out
of Iseland, and much made of among us, bicause of
their sawcinesse and quarrelling.' Pistol's slur picks
up the quarrelsomeness.

36 **show . . . put up** reveal . . . sheathe. The
Hostess is either being verbally sophisticated or
typically self-contradictory.

37 SD This is the moment for the swords to
be put back in their carriages, in obedience to
Bardolph's plea. The game of constant drawing and
sheathing continues for the next forty lines.

38 **shog off** Slang addressed to the Hostess: go
away.

38 **solus** A standard Latin stage direction, as
with *exit* and *manet*. It means 'alone', though to
Pistol it evidently means single, unmarried.

40 **mervailous** The original spelling for
'marvellous' was retained by Humphreys, on the
grounds that it indicates a distinctive pronunciation. Taylor suggests that it was stressed on
the second syllable. Holinshed spells it in Pistol's
form.

40–2 **face . . . bowels** Pistol verbally takes
Nym's insulting word step by step through his
digestive system.

41 **maw** stomach.

43 **take** catch fire.

43 **Pistol's cock** (1) the striking-lever of a
hand-gun, (2) his penis, or pizzle.

44 **Barbason** A devil. He is listed among the
names of fiends in *Wiv.* 2.2.233.

44 **conjure** control by a magic spell.

44 **humour** Up to now Nym has not used the
comic catchphrase he uses regularly in *Wiv.* He
renews it at the end of this speech. Q redoubles his
use in this and other scenes.

to knock you indifferently well. If you grow foul with me, Pistol,    45
I will scour you with my rapier, as I may, in fair terms. If you
would walk off I would prick your guts a little in good terms, as
I may, and that's the humour of it.

PISTOL O braggart vile, and damnèd furious wight, the grave doth
gape and doting death is near. Therefore exhale!                      50

               *[They draw their swords]*

BARDOLPH Hear me, hear me what I say. *[Draws his sword]* He
that strikes the first stroke, I'll run him up to the hilts, as I am a
soldier.

PISTOL An oath of mickle might, and fury shall abate. Give me thy
fist, thy forefoot to me give. Thy spirits are most tall.             55

NYM I will cut thy throat one time or other in fair terms, that is the
humour of it.

PISTOL Couple a gorge, that is the word. I defy thee again! O
hound of Crete, thinkst thou my spouse to get? No, to the
Spital go, and from the powdering tub of infamy fetch forth the       60
lazar kite of Cressid's kind, Doll Tearsheet, she by name, and

---

50 exhale] F; exall Q    58 Couple a gorge] F (*Couple a gorge*); Couple gorge Q; Coup la gorge *Taylor*

**45 grow foul** (1) speak of turds, (2) as a pistol, become fouled by firing.

**46 scour** clean a gun barrel with a ramrod.

**46 in fair terms** i.e. not foul terms, as Pistol has been doing. He repeats the phrase at line 56.

**49–50** F sets these lines as verse, the only time it versifies Pistol in the play.

**49 damnèd** Pronunciation as a poetic double-syllable seems appropriate even if the lines are not formal verse.

**49–50 the grave doth gape** Ultimately from the Bishops' Bible, Isa. 5.14, 'Therefore gapeth hell'. See Introduction, p. 27, note 1. It became proverbial (Dent GG2). The newly crowned Henry uses precisely this phrase to Falstaff as a half joke ('Know / The grave doth gape for thee thrice wider . . .') in his speech banishing Falstaff.

**50 exhale** An extravagant word for drawing a sword. Taylor suggests 'ex-hale', from 'hale' or 'haul', to heave. Cercignani (p. 336) suggests that Q's 'exell' reflects the pronunciation.

**51 SD** *Draws his sword* By the time he makes his threat to skewer them up to the hilt of his sword (52), Bardolph too must have drawn.

**54 mickle might** great power. Used in *2H6*

5.1.174 and elsewhere, the adjective's emphatically poetic character is marked by its use in *The Faerie Queene*, 2.4.7.

**55 tall** brave (contrasting Nym's 'spirits' with his small stature).

**58 Couple a gorge** Pistol is practising his French (strictly *couper la gorge*, or *coupez la gorge*). The cutting of French throats looms large at Agincourt. See Introduction, p. 25.

**58 defy thee** F makes prosaic the poetic word order adopted in Q.

**60 Spital** The lazar hospital, a charitable institution for treating the poor, especially lepers.

**60 powdering tub** (1) a barrel for salting beef, (2) a sweating tub for treating venereal disease.

**61 lazar kite of Cressid's kind** a diseased carrion bird like Cressida. Leprosy was thought to be a venereal disease. See 1.1.15 n. The phrase is probably a memory of one in Barnabe Rich's book of stories, *Rich's Farewell to the Military Profession*, 1581, which provided the story on which *TN* is based, and which is alluded to in *Wiv*. It mentions 'these Kites of Cressides kind' on sig. R2ᵛ. See also 4.8.57–8 n.

**61 Doll Tearsheet** She first appears in *2H4* 2.4.

her espouse. I have, and I will hold the quondam Quickly for
the only she, and *pauca*, there's enough. Go to.

Enter the BOY.

BOY Mine host Pistol, you must come to my master, and your
    hostess. He is very sick, and would to bed. Good Bardolph, put          65
    thy face between his sheets and do the office of a warming pan.
    Faith, he's very ill.
BARDOLPH Away, you rogue.
HOSTESS By my troth, he'll yield the crow a pudding one of these
    days. The king has killed his heart. Good husband, come home          70
    presently.

Exeunt [Hostess and Boy]

BARDOLPH Come, shall I make you two friends? We must to
    France together. Why the devil should we keep knives to cut
    one another's throats?
PISTOL Let floods o'erswell, and fiends for food howl on!          75
NYM You'll pay me the eight shillings I won of you at betting?
PISTOL Base is the slave that pays.
NYM That now I will have. That's the humour of it.
PISTOL As manhood shall compound. Push home.

[They] Draw [their swords]

BARDOLPH [Draws his sword] By this sword, he that makes the first          80
    thrust, I'll kill him, by this sword I will.

---

63 enough. Go to] *Rowe; there's enough to go to* F; *there it is inough* Q    64 your] F; *you* Q, *Hanmer*    66 face F; *nose*
Q    71 SD *Exeunt*] *Capell; Exit.* F, Q

**62 I have . . . hold** A paraphrase of the wedding
service.
  **62 quondam** former (Latin).
  **63 *pauca*** A Latin tag, *pauca verba*, in few words.
  **63 enough. Go to** F's reading appears to be a
compositorial error.
  **63 SD BOY** Falstaff's boy from *2H4* 1.2.
  **64 Mine host** The boy confirms Nym's taunt.
  **64 my master** i.e. Falstaff.
  **64 your** Q and Hanmer normalise, but F's reading is acceptable given the boy's reference to
Pistol as a 'host' and the fight over possession of
the Hostess.
  **66 face** Bardolph's spectacular face looked red
and heated, according to the boy at 3.2.28 and
Llewellyn's more detailed description at 3.7.87–
91. It features in jokes at *1H4* 3.3.20–33 and *2H4*
2.4.269–71.

**69 yield . . . pudding** A proverbial periphrasis
for dying (Dent c860).
  **71 presently** at once.
  **71 SD *Exeunt*** Neither F nor Q gives any notice
of the boy's departure. He may either leave with
the Hostess or stay to witness the next bout of
bravado and leave with the others at the end of
the scene, where F gives no indication of how
many leave. Since Falstaff is the boy's master, and
since respectable women did not walk the streets
unescorted by a male, it seems likely that the boy
would accompany her to Falstaff. But see note to
line 92.
  **77 Base . . . pays** A poetic perversion of the
proverb 'the poor man pays for all' (Dent M357).
  **79 As . . . compound** real men fight rather than
pay up.

PISTOL Sword is an oath, and oaths must have their course.

[*Sheathes his sword*]

BARDOLPH Corporal Nym, an thou wilt be friends, be friends. An
thou wilt not, why then be enemies with me too. Prithee put up.

[*Nym sheathes his sword*]

PISTOL A noble shalt thou have, and present pay, and liquor          85
likewise will I give to thee, and friendship shall combine, and
brotherhood. I'll live by Nym and Nym shall live by me; is not
this just? For I shall sutler be unto the camp, and profits will
accrue. Give me thy hand.

NYM I shall have my noble?                                           90

PISTOL In cash, most justly paid.

NYM Well, then that's the humour of it.

*Enter* HOSTESS [*and* BOY]

HOSTESS As ever you come of women, come in quickly to Sir
John. Ah, poor heart, he is so shaked of a burning quotidian
tertian that it is most lamentable to behold. Sweet men, come       95
to him.

NYM The king hath run bad humours on the knight; that's the even
of it.

PISTOL Nym, thou hast spoke the right, his heart is fracted and
corroborate.                                                        100

---

83–4 BARDOLPH . . . put up F; *Nym.* I shall haue my eight shillings I wonne of you at beating? Q    88 profits] F; profit
Q    92 that's] F2; that F    92 of it] Q; of't F    93 come of] F; came of Q, F2

82 **Sword** i.e. God's word.

83 **an** if.

84 Q's addition is a renewal of the demand made
at line 76. Most editions include it on the grounds
that Pistol's next speech is a direct reply. But the
sword-waving has only interrupted Pistol's answer
to the original demand, which he now gives.

85 **a noble** a coin worth one-third of a pound,
or six shillings and eightpence, which is distinctly
less than eight shillings.

85 **present day** cash immediately.

87 **by Nym** Possibly an allusion to nimming as
theft.

88 **sutler** seller of food.

92 If the boy leaves with the Hostess at line
65, he should return here. Along with Nym and
Bardolph he should be present to hear Pistol
declare '*we* will live' at line 103, since the three
of them do not.

93 **come of** Q normalises the F reading, which
has a bawdy edge to it, as in 'come off'. In *2H4*
2.4.40 and 41 Falstaff says 'to serve bravely is to
come halting off', and in the next line 'to come off
the breach with his pike bent'.

94–5 **quotidian tertian** A quotidian fever
recurred daily, a tertian every third day. When
joined, it was thought that both regimes prevailed,
which made it the worst kind of sickness. See
A. A. Mendilow, 'Falstaff's death of a sweat', *SQ*
9 (1958), 479–83.

97 **run bad humours** Nym's idiom means (1)
that Henry made Falstaff melancholy, or (2) that
he vented his bad temper on Falstaff.

97 **the even** the plain truth.

99–100 **fracted and corroborate** fractured and
made secure. Like most of Pistol's poetical lexis,
each word sounds stronger than it means.

NYM  The king is a good king, but it must be as it may. He passes
  some humours and careers.
PISTOL  Let us condole the knight, for, lambkins, we will live.

                                                          *Exeunt*


2.2  *Enter* EXETER, BEDFORD *and* WESTMORLAND


BEDFORD  'Fore God, his grace is bold to trust these traitors.
EXETER  They shall be apprehended by and by.
WESTMORLAND  How smooth and even they do bear themselves,
      As if allegiance in their bosoms sat,
      Crownèd with faith and constant loyalty.                          5
BEDFORD  The king hath note of all that they intend
      By interception which they dream not of.
EXETER  Nay, but the man that was his bedfellow,
      Whom he hath dulled and cloyed with gracious favours;
      That he should for a foreign purse so sell                       10
      His sovereign's life to death and treachery!

      *Sound trumpets. Enter the* KING, SCROOP, CAMBRIDGE
          *and* GRAY [*and* OFFICERS]

KING  Now sits the wind fair, and we will aboard.
      My lord of Cambridge and my kind lord Masham,
      And you my gentle knight, give me your thoughts.


103 SD *Exeunt.*] Q; *not in* F  **Act 2, Scene 2**  0 SD BEDFORD] F; Gloster Q  1 SH BEDFORD] F; *Glost.* Q  11 treachery!
F; treachery / *Exe.* O the Lord of Massham. Q  13 lord Masham] *This edn;* Lord of *Masham* F

**102 careers** full gallops. Nym means that he has
moods which include some made gallops.

**103 we will live** An emphatic affirmation that
Falstaff's companions will outlive him. In fact, only
Pistol lives beyond Act 4.

**Act 2, Scene 2**
**3–5** Q omits this speech, together with Henry's
reference to Westmorland in line 67, as one of its
economies over the English lords. In Q Gloucester
continues with 8–11, and Exeter interjects Scroop's
name as Masham.
**5 Crownèd** The Chorus has already declared
that the 'hollow bosoms' have been filled with gold.
**8 bedfellow** close friend. It was not unusual for
friends to share a bed. Iago claims to have done so

with Cassio in *Oth.* 3.3.414. In *A Knack to Know
a Knave* the king says 'thou wast once bedfellow
to the king . . . I loved thee as my second selfe'
(line 549). In *Oldcastle* Scroop is named as Henry's
bedfellow and offers to assassinate him while in bed
(line 2095).
**9 cloyed** clogged with sweetness.
**10 a foreign purse** The French money is noted
by Holinshed, but so is the link of Cambridge with
Mortimer and the alternative line to the crown,
which is omitted here.
**11 sovereign's** The word-play on crowns makes
this second pun on gold sovereigns inevitable.
**13 lord Masham** The second 'of' was
probably a Compositor B repetition from the earlier use. Usually Shakespeare varies the syntax in
such cases.

Think you not that the powers we bear with us            15
Will cut their passage through the force of France,
Doing the execution and the act
For which we have in head assembled them?

SCROOP  No doubt, my liege, if each man do his best.

KING  I doubt not that, since we are well persuaded          20
We carry not a heart with us from hence
That grows not in a fair consent with ours,
Nor leave not one behind that doth not wish
Success and conquest to attend on us.

CAMBRIDGE  Never was monarch better feared and loved       25
Than is your majesty. There's not I think a subject
That sits in heart-grief and uneasiness
Under the sweet shade of your government.

GRAY  True. Those that were your father's enemies
Have steeped their galls in honey, and do serve you        30
With hearts create of duty and of zeal.

KING  We therefore have great cause of thankfulness,
And shall forget the office of our hand
Sooner than quittance of desert and merit,
According to the weight and worthiness.                     35

SCROOP  So service shall with steelèd sinews toil
And labour shall refresh itself with hope,
To do your grace incessant services.

KING  We judge no less. Uncle of Exeter,
Enlarge the man committed yesterday                         40
That railed against our person. We consider
It was excess of wine that set him on,

---

26 a] F; *one Taylor*   29 SH GRAY] *Kni* F   29 True. Those] F; *Even those* Q

15–18 See note to 1.2.214.
18 in head as a force or army.
20–4 Henry's first explicitly deceitful speech. As play-acting, it contains a concealed threat.
23 Nor . . . not A double negative used as an intensifier.
29 Those . . . enemies The chief agent for the rebels of the *H4* plays now is Cambridge. For his position, see Introduction, pp. 19–21.
30 galls in honey Proverbial (Dent G11.1, H55.1).
31 create of created by.
33 the office . . . hand what my hand should do.

34 quittance rewards, payment.
36 So . . . toil Scroop's first line is full of sibilants, as might fit the most snake-like betrayer. In Stubbs's *Discoverie of a Gaping Gulf*, 1581, A2ᵛ, Elizabeth is urged 'neither to trow a Frenche man nor once here speake a dayly hearer of masse (for she may know him by his hissing and lisping) but that some English mouthes professing Christ are also perswaders of the same'.
40 Enlarge Set free.
42 excess of wine A phrase from the Bishops' Bible, 1 Pet. 4.3.

> And on his more advice we pardon him.

SCROOP  That's mercy, but too much security.

> Let him be punished, sovereign, lest example          45
> Breed by his sufferance more of such a kind.

KING  Oh, let us yet be merciful.

CAMBRIDGE  So may your highness, and yet punish too.

GRAY  Sir, you show great mercy if you give him life

> After the taste of much correction.                   50

KING  Alas, your too much love and care of me

> Are heavy orisons 'gainst this poor wretch.
> If little faults, proceeding on distemper,
> Shall not be winked at, how shall we stretch our eye
> When capital crimes, chewed, swallowed, and digested,  55
> Appear before us? We'll yet enlarge that man,
> Though Cambridge, Scroop and Gray, in their dear care
> And tender preservation of our person
> Would have him punished. And now to our French causes.
> Who are the late commissioners?

CAMBRIDGE                            I one, my lord.      60

> Your highness bade me ask for it today.

SCROOP  So did you me, my liege.

GRAY                              And I, my royal sovereign.

KING  Then Richard, Earl of Cambridge, there is yours.

> There yours, Lord Scroop of Masham, and sir knight,
> Gray of Northumberland, this same is yours.           65
> [*Gives them papers*]
> Read them and know I know your worthiness.
> My lord of Westmorland and uncle Exeter,
> We will aboard tonight. Why, how now, gentlemen?

67–8 My lord . . . tonight] F; Uncle *Exeter* I will aboord to night Q

**43 on . . . advice** after hearing more from him.

**44 security** over-confidence. Hecate uses the term of Macbeth at 3.5.32.

**46 his sufferance** the indulgence towards him.

**50 correction** punishment.

**52 orisons** prayers.

**53 distemper** a disordered state of mind. From Henry's description in line 42 this must be counted a euphemism.

**54 winked at** Proverbial (Dent F123).

**54 stretch** open wide. If a minor fault cannot be viewed with closed eyes, the far greater 'monster' treason would require even more than wide-eyed horror.

**55 capital crimes** major crimes involving the taking of life.

**57 dear** See *R2* 1.3.151.

**60 late** recently appointed, with a faint innu-endo about mortality.

**60 commissioners** the regents appointed to rule in England during the king's absence in France. The game with the official papers which follows is not in the sources.

**61 ask for it** Confirmation that Henry has stage-managed this exposure.

What see you in those papers, that you lose
So much complexion? Look ye how they change.                    70
Their cheeks are paper. Why, what read you there,
That have so cowarded and chased your blood
Out of appearance?
CAMBRIDGE                         I do confess my fault,
And do submit me to your highness' mercy.              [*Kneels*]
GRAY *and* SCROOP   To which we all appeal. [*They kneel*]     75
KING   The mercy that was quick in us but late
By your own counsel is suppressed and killed.
You must not dare for shame to talk of mercy,
For your own reasons turn into your bosoms,
As dogs upon their masters, worrying you.                       80
See you, my princes and my noble peers,
These English monsters. My lord of Cambridge here,
You know how apt our love was to accord,
To furnish him with all appurtenants
Belonging to his honour, and this man                           85
Hath for a few light crowns lightly conspired
And sworn unto the practices of France
To kill us here in Hampton. To the which
This knight, no less for bounty bound to us
Than Cambridge is, hath likewise sworn. But oh,                90
What shall I say to thee, Lord Scroop, thou cruel,
Ingrateful, savage and inhuman creature?

72 have] F; hath Q   73 appearance] F (apparence)   84 him] Q, F2; *not in* F   84 appurtenants] F (appertinents)   85 this
man] F; this vilde man Q

71 **paper** i.e. the colour of the scrolls they have
been given.
72 **have** A plural because it refers to what *words*
(understood).
73 **appearance** The whole scene is about
deceptive appearances.
74 SD *Kneels* A visible gesture of submission
is needed here. The conspirators should probably
remain on their knees until Exeter arrests them at
line 142. Neither F nor Q supplies stage directions
for actions that can be inferred from the text, such
as the handing out of the papers at 63–5. Scroop
should be kneeling at 116–18 when Henry speaks
of 'dubbing' him traitor as if he was kneeling to be
knighted.
76 **quick** alive.
80 **dogs . . . masters** A proverbial saying (Dent
M258), with perhaps a hint of Actaeon, who was

turned into a stag by Diana and torn to pieces by
his own hunting-hounds.
82 **English monsters** i.e. monsters and
therefore not English.
84 **appurtenants** fittings, things appropriate
for.
87 **practices** secret plots.
88 **in Hampton** See Introduction, p. 65.
91 **Lord Scroop** The first clear revelation of
which of the three had been Henry's bedfellow.
Possibly Q's addition at line 11 was designed on
stage to make it clear which one was the principal
traitor.
92 **Ingrateful** Ungrateful, a word with more
kick than the modern usage. An 'ingrate', the term
used at *1H4* 1.3.135 and *TN* 5.1.102, was worse
than merely discourteous. *OED* admits 'ingrateful'
as an obsolete form current between 1547 and 1754.

Thou that didst bear the key of all my counsels,
That knew'st the very bottom of my soul,
That almost mightst have coined me into gold,                    95
Wouldst thou have practised on me for thy use?
May it be possible that foreign hire
Could out of thee extract one spark of evil
That might annoy my finger? 'Tis so strange
That though the truth of it stands off as gross                  100
As black on white my eye will scarcely see it.
Treason and murder ever kept together,
As two yoke-devils sworn to either's purpose,
Working so grossly in a natural cause
That admiration did not whoop at them.                           105
But thou 'gainst all proportion didst bring in
Wonder to wait on treason and on murder,
And whatsoever cunning fiend it was
That wrought upon thee so preposterously
Hath got the voice in hell for excellence.                       110
All other devils that suggest by treasons
Do botch and bungle up damnation
With patches, colours, and with forms being fetched
From glistering semblances of piety;
But he that tempered thee bade thee stand up,                    115
Gave thee no instance why thou shouldst do treason,
Unless to dub thee with the name of traitor.
If that same demon that hath gulled thee thus

---

101 on] *Maxwell;* and F; from Q   104 a natural] F2; an naturall F   105 whoop] F (hoope)   111 All] *Hanmer;* And F

**95 coined . . . gold** turned me into money, as in counterfeiting by using the king's image.

**96 use** commercial advantage. It generally had a sexual association.

**101 black on white** Maxwell's conjecture matches proverbial usage (Dent B438).

**104 a natural** What is natural for devils is monstrous for humans. The F compositor seems to have wavered between 'natural' and 'unnatural'.

**105 admiration . . . whoop** amazement was beyond the power to exclaim.

**109 preposterously** unnaturally, as at lines 82, 104.

**110 voice** vote.

**111 All** A misreading by the F compositor.

**111 suggest** i.e. tempt, used of devils' tricks as in *Oth.* 2.3.319. A closely similar use occurs in *R2* 1.1.101.

**113 fetched** stolen.

**114 glistering** falsely shining, glistening and glittering.

**115 tempered** i.e. the tempting devil.

**115 stand up** i.e. rebel.

**117 dub thee** The whole of this section represents the devil parodying the act of a king knighting a subject. Scroop is kneeling before Henry, as a knight would when dubbed with his title.

**118 gulled** fooled.

Should with his lion gait walk the whole world
He might return to vasty Tartar back                                    120
And tell the legions 'I can never win
A soul so easy as that Englishman's.'
Oh, how hast thou with jealousy infected
The sweetness of affiance? Show men dutiful?
Why, so didst thou. Seem they grave and learnèd?                       125
Why, so didst thou. Come they of noble family?
Why, so didst thou. Seem they religious?
Why, so didst thou. Or are they spare in diet,
Free from gross passion, or of mirth or anger,
Constant in spirit, not swerving with the blood,                       130
Garnished and decked in modest complement,
Not working with the eye without the ear,
And but in purgèd judgement trusting neither?
Such and so finely bolted didst thou seem.
And thus thy fall hath left a kind of blot                             135
To mark the full fraught man, and best endowed
With some suspicion. I will weep for thee,
For this revolt of thine, methinks, is like
Another fall of man. Their faults are open.
Arrest them to the answer of the law,                                  140
And God acquit them of their practices.
EXETER I arrest thee of high treason, by the name of Richard Earl
    of Cambridge. I arrest thee of high treason, by the name of

125 Seem] F; *or* seem *Pope*   136 mark] *Theobald;* make F   136 the] *Pope;* thee F   136 endowed] F (indued)   137 suspicion. I] *Pope;* –, I F

119 **lion gait** 'Be sober, & watch, for your adversarie the devyll, as a roaring Lion walketh about seeking whom he may devour.' 1 Pet. 5.8 (Bishops' Bible).

120 **vasty** waste or desolate. This enhancement of the monosyllabic form is not known except in Shakespeare. It is used by the Chorus at 1.0.12.

120 **Tartar** i.e. Tartarus, a name for hell, from 2 Pet. 2.4.

121 **legions** 'And he asked hym, what is thy name? And he aunswered and sayd unto hym: my name is legion, for we are many.' Mark 5.9 (Bishops' Bible).

123 **jealousy** mistrust, suspicion.

124 **affiance** trust, as in betrothal.

125 **Seem** Pope's smoothing of the metre does not suit the stark catechism here.

130 **swerving . . . blood** The hot and moist humours, present in the blood, provoked lechery and related disorders of morality.

131 **complement** personal qualities.

133 **but in** except in.

134 **bolted** sifted, like flour.

136 F's line is awkward and seems to call for emendation. 'Full fraught', meaning fully equipped or burdened, is a mercantile image. It requires a 'mark', as on a bill of lading. The burden may thus become an endowment of suspicion.

139 **Another fall** Eve was tempted by the devil Satan.

140 **to the answer** so that they may be answerable.

Henry, Lord Scroop of Masham. I arrest thee of high treason,
by the name of Thomas Gray, knight of Northumberland.                   145
SCROOP  Our purposes God justly hath discovered,
    And I repent my fault more than my death,
    Which I beseech your highness to forgive,
    Although my body pay the price of it.
CAMBRIDGE  For me, the gold of France did not seduce               150
    Although I did admit it as a motive
    The sooner to effect what I intended.
    But God be thankèd for prevention,
    Which I in sufferance heartily will rejoice,
    Beseeching God and you to pardon me.                        155
GRAY  Never did faithful subject more rejoice
    At the discovery of most dangerous treason
    Than I do at this hour joy o'er myself,
    Prevented from a damnèd enterprise.
    My fault, but not my body, pardon, sovereign.               160
KING  God quit you in His mercy. Hear your sentence.
    You have conspired against our royal person,
    Joined with an enemy proclaimed, and from his coffers
    Received the golden earnest of our death;
    Wherein you would have sold your king to slaughter,          165
    His princes and his peers to servitude,
    His subjects to oppression and contempt,
    And his whole kingdom into desolation.
    Touching our person seek we no revenge,
    But we our kingdom's safety must so tender,                  170
    Whose ruin you have sought, that to her laws
    We do deliver you. Get you therefore hence,

---

144 Henry] *Theobald;* Thomas F   144 Masham] *Rowe;* Marsham F, Q   154 I . . . heartily] F2; in sufferance heartily F; heartily in sufferance *Taylor*   163 proclaimed] F; proclaimed and fixed Q; *not in Pope*   170 must] F (wust)   171 have] Q, *Knight; not in* F; three F2   172 Get you] F, Q3; Get ye Q

**144 Henry** F took up 'Thomas' by eyeskip from the next line.

**146 discovered** uncovered.

**150–2** This is the nearest the play comes to an explicit acknowledgement of the non-commercial motive that Cambridge had for the conspiracy. The intention is explained in *3H6* 1.1, especially 26–7.

**154 sufferance** (1) enduring, (2) suffering.

**161 quit** (1) punish, (2) acquit ('quit), (3) requite.

**164 earnest** part payment made in advance.

**168 desolation** A strong term for a change of kings. Henry is predicting that the French would have invaded England with the help of the conspirators and laid the country waste.

**172 Get you** The Oxford editors note that this is the only 'ye' in Q and conjecture influence from Q3 on F. The source in Holinshed has 'ye'. But see Textual Analysis, pp. 222–4.

Poor miserable wretches, to your death,
The taste whereof God of His mercy give
You patience to endure, and true repentance                    175
Of all your dear offences. Bear them hence.
              *Exeunt Cambridge, Scroop and Gray [and Officers]*
Now lords, for France, the enterprise whereof
Shall be to you as us, like glorious.
We doubt not of a fair and lucky war,
Since God so graciously hath brought to light                   180
This dangerous treason lurking in our way
To hinder our beginnings. We doubt not now
But every rub is smoothèd on our way.
Then forth, dear countrymen. Let us deliver
Our puissance into the hand of God,                             185
Putting it straight in expedition.
Cheerly to sea, the signs of war advance.
No king of England if not king of France!

                                    *Flourish. Exeunt*

**2.3** *Enter* PISTOL, NYM, BARDOLPH, BOY *and* HOSTESS

HOSTESS Prithee, honey-sweet husband, let me bring thee to
    Staines.
PISTOL No, for my manly heart doth yearn. Bardolph, be blithe.
    Nym, rouse thy vaunting veins. Boy, bristle thy courage up, for
    Falstaff he is dead, and we must earn therefore.               5

---

188 SD *Exeunt*] Q (*Exit omnes*); *not in* F   Act 2, Scene 3   1 honey-sweet] F (honey sweet); honey, sweet F3   3 yearn]
F (erne)   5 earn] F (erne)

176 **dear** Compare line 57. The word here may
also have an echo of 'dire'.
183 **rub** hindrance, obstacle.
185 **into . . . God** At 4.1.152 Henry declares
that war is God's beadle.
187 **the signs . . . advance** Raise the army's
banners. In the scenes through the next two acts
where the army charges or marches on stage, it
would have been led by banner carriers and accompanied by drummers.

Act 2, Scene 3
1 **honey-sweet** This double adjective could be
divided as F3 has it, but the linked form was proverbial (Dent H544.1) and is therefore a little more
likely.

2 **Staines** A town with a bridge over the
Thames, on the road from London to Southampton, about twenty miles from the city.
3 **yearn** (1) grieve; (2) feel desire. The F spelling
also relates it to 'earn' in line 5. In *A Woman
Killed with Kindness* 2.1.84, Nicholas says 'my heart
still ernes', using the unambiguous first meaning. The double meaning is in *Wiv.* 3.5.34, where
Mrs. Quickly's 'yern your heart' is linked both to
Falstaff's grief and his erection. See Hulme,
*Explorations*, pp. 125, 139–40. The second use,
at line 5, has a different innuendo and has been
modernised accordingly.
5 **earn** Implying that after Falstaff's death the
need for cash is the more urgent.

BARDOLPH Would I were with him, wheresome're he is, either in
  heaven or in hell.

HOSTESS Nay, sure, he's not in hell. He's in Arthur's bosom if
  ever man went to Arthur's bosom. A made a finer end, and
  went away an it had been any christom child. A parted e'en just    10
  between twelve and one, e'en at the turning o'the tide, for after
  I saw him fumble with the sheets, and play with flowers, and
  smile upon his finger's end, I knew there was but one way. For
  his nose was as sharp as a pen, and a babbled of green fields.
  'How now, Sir John,' quoth I, 'what man, be o' good cheer!' So    15
  a cried out 'God, God, God' three or four times. Now I, to
  comfort him, bid him a should not think of God; I hoped there
  was no need to trouble himself with any such thoughts yet. So a
  bade me lay more clothes on his feet. I put my hand into the
  bed, and felt them, and they were as cold as any stone. Then I    20
  felt to his knees, and so up-peered and upward, and all was as
  cold as any stone.

9 finer] F  10 christom] F (Christome)  14 a babbled of green fields] *Theobald;* a Table of greene fields F; And talk of
floures Q  21 up-peered] F (vp-peer'd); upward Q, Rowe

9 **Arthur's bosom** More properly Abraham's
(Luke 16.22: 'And it came to passe, that the beggar
dyed, and was caryed by the Angels unto Abrahams
bosome'). It conflates a good Christian death with
the Arthurian knights sleeping in Avalon.

9 **A** A common form for 'he' and a likely
indication of the pronunciation.

9 **finer** Since no direct comparison is made, this
should possibly read 'fine'. But the comparative
form carries with it the implication that his death
was better than his life.

10 **christom** The Hostess mixes 'Christian' and
'christom', the white baptismal cloth. A 'christom
child' was one who died soon after birth. Early
christenings were normally held within three days
of the birth because infant mortality was so great.

11 **between twelve and one** Midnight rather
than midday. In *Wiv.* 4.6.19 'just twixt twelve and
one' is the time for Falstaff's midnight meeting
with Herne the hunter in the forest.

11 **at . . . tide** Traditionally the time when
travellers died.

13 **but one way** Proverbial (Dent W148). See
*TN* 3.2.31 and *Oth.* 5.2.354–5.

14 **a babbled** For all the attempts to justify
F's reading or emend it, Theobald's conjecture
still has the most support. Q's version is a rough
equivalent, up to the general standard of its
reporting in the Eastcheap scenes. Giles Dawson,
'Shakespeare's handwriting', *S.Sur.* 43 (1990),
119–28, argues for the likelihood of 'babld' on the

basis of its capacity to be misread as 'table' if written in the script of Hand D in *Sir Thomas More.*
For similar instances of the d / e error in the F
text of this play see Textual Analysis, p. 222. On
the other hand Hulme argues at length for the F
reading in *Explorations* pp. 133–49. A more likely
story is the linkage of 'greene fields' with 'Babil-
lards' in a book Shakespeare used for its French
dialogues, *Ortho-epia Gallica,* 1593. See Joseph A.
Porter, 'More echoes from Eliot's *Ortho-epia Gallica,* in *King Lear* and *Henry V*, *SQ* 37 (1986),
486–8.

19–22 Emrys Jones, *The Origins of Shakespeare,*
p. 20, says that the account of Falstaff's death par-
odies the account in Plato's *Phaedo* of the death of
Socrates. He cites the poisoner, who 'pressed his
foot hard, and asked if he could feel, and he said,
No; and then his legs, and so upwards and upwards,
and showed us that he was cold and stiff' (*The
Four Socratic Dialogues of Plato,* trans. B. Jowett,
Oxford 1903, p. 273). But this translation may
in its turn have echoed the account of Falstaff's
death.

21 **up-peered** Possibly the F compositor
betrayed his interest in his text by interpreting
the meaning here. More likely it was taken from
a manuscript spelling designed to emphasise the
pronunciation.

22 **stone** Both the familiar object and a testicle,
in another of the Hostess's inadvertent pieces of
bawdy.

NYM They say he cried out of sack.

HOSTESS Ay, that a did.

BARDOLPH And of women.                                              25

HOSTESS Nay, that a did not.

BOY Yes, that a did, and said they were devils incarnate.

HOSTESS A could never abide carnation, 'twas a colour he never
    liked.

BOY A said once, the Devil would have him about women.           30

HOSTESS A did in some sort, indeed, handle women. But then he
    was rheumatic, and talked of the Whore of Babylon.

BOY Do you not remember a saw a flea stick upon Bardolph's nose,
    and a said it was a black soul burning in hell?

BARDOLPH Well, the fuel is gone that maintained that fire. That's   35
    all the riches I got in his service.

NYM Shall we shog? The king will be gone from Southampton.

PISTOL Come, let's away. My love, give me thy lips. Look to my
    chattels and my moveables. Let senses rule: the word is, pitch
    and pay. Trust none, for oaths are straws, men's faiths are   40
    wafer cakes, and Hold-fast is the only dog, my duck. Therefore
    *caveto* be thy counsellor. Go, clear thy crystals. Yoke-fellows in
    arms, let us to France, like horseleeches, my boys, to suck, to
    suck, the very blood to suck!

---

28 HOSTESS] *Woman* F   39 word] Q; world F, F2, *Rowe, Taylor*

23 **of sack** against sherry.
25 **of women** against women.
26 **a did not** The Hostess accepts that Falstaff's
'finer end' made him renounce one of his vices, but
not all.
28 **SH HOSTESS** F's Compositor A makes this
speech heading into the generic 'Woman', although
all the other F speech headings are '*Hostess*'. The
irregularity probably originated in the manuscript.
28 **carnation** The colour 'carnation' was pink
like white flesh, which makes it an apt misunder-
standing.
32 **rheumatic** Malone suggests 'lunatic'. The
Hostess' grasp of polysyllables is better than
Dogberry's, but she is not so much better with
their meanings.
32 **the Whore of Babylon** A term used by
Protestants of the Pope. It ultimately came from
a commentary on Revelation in the Geneva Bible.
It extends the pun on Rome in 'rheumatic', since

Rome was pronounced as 'Room' or 'rheum'.
35 **That's** i.e. his nose. See *1H4* 3.3.61–2: 'What
call you rich? Let them coin his nose.'
37 **shog** See 2.1.38, note.
39 **Let senses rule** Be alert. The plural is
ambiguous. See Sonnet 35.9. The singular meant
reason, the plural, seeing, hearing, and feeling.
39–40 **pitch and pay** i.e. no credit (Dent P360).
40 **oaths are straws** Proverbial (Dent S918).
41 **wafer cakes** Proverbial (Dent W1.1).
41 **Hold-fast** Proverbial (Dent B588). The
original proverb was a word play, 'Brag is a good
dog, but Holdfast is a better', both referring to
varieties of large nail. The binding element in
Pistol's punning is 'dog', a spike, with 'holdfast', a
clamp.
42 *caveto* From the Latin, 'beware'. Pistol presumably intends '*cavete*', be careful, the imperative
plural.
42 **clear thy crystals** wipe your eyes.

BOY And that's but unwholesome food, they say.                        45
PISTOL Touch her soft mouth, and march.
BARDOLPH Farewell, hostess. [*Kisses her*]
NYM I cannot kiss, that is the humour of it, but adieu.
PISTOL Let housewifery appear. Keep close, I thee command.
HOSTESS Farewell, adieu.                                             50

*Exeunt*


**2.4** *Flourish, Enter the* FRENCH KING, *the* DAUPHIN, *the Dukes of* BERRI *and* BOURBON, [*the* CONSTABLE *and other Lords*]

FRENCH KING Thus comes the English with full power upon us,
          And more than carefully it us concerns
          To answer royally in our defences.
          Therefore the Dukes of Berri and of Bourbon,
          Of Brabant and of Orléans, shall make forth,            5
          And you, Prince Dauphin, with all swift despatch
          To line and new repair our towns of war
          With men of courage and with means defendant,
          For England his approaches makes as fierce
          As waters to the sucking of a gulf.                     10
          It fits us then to be as provident
          As fear may teach us, out of late examples
          Left by the fatal and neglected English

---

49 Let . . . appear] F; Keepe fast thy buggle boe Q   **Act 2, Scene 4   0** SD BOURBON] Q; Britaine F   **4** Bourbon] Q; *Britaine* F

**49 housewifery** good household management.
**49 Keep close** Stay concealed indoors.
**49 Keep . . . command** Q's alternative invokes the 'bugle bow' of Cupid, which by extension seems to have been made an image not only for the shape of female lips but also the female genitals.

**Act 2, Scene 4**
**0** SD BOURBON Q substitutes 'Bourbon' for F's '*Britaine*', whom the French king calls on in line 4. It helps prepare for his taking the place of the Dauphin at Agincourt.
**0** SD CONSTABLE The Lord Constable was head of the royal household, and commander of the army.

**4 Bourbon** F's 'Britaine' was pronounced in two syllables, making the substitution of 'Bourbon' easy.
**6 And . . . Dauphin** The sequence of names here makes the Dauphin into an afterthought. His status as heir to the throne should have led the king to name him first. The afterthought may be in anticipation of the king's insistence at 3.6.64–6 that the Dauphin stay with the king in Rouen while all the other French princes, listed at 40–45 of that scene, go off to battle. See Textual Analysis, pp. 231–3.
**7 To line** To strengthen.
**10 gulf** whirlpool. Compare Montjoy at 4.3.82.
**13 fatal and neglected** i.e. fatally neglected, killing because we neglected the danger.

Upon our fields.

DAUPHIN                    My most redoubted father,
It is most meet we arm us 'gainst the foe,                          15
For peace itself should not so dull a kingdom,
Though war nor no known quarrel were in question,
But that defences, musters, preparations
Should be maintained, assembled and collected
As were a war in expectation.                                      20
Therefore I say 'tis meet we all go forth
To view the sick and feeble parts of France.
And let us do it with no show of fear,
No, with no more than if we heard that England
Were busied with a Whitsun morris dance.                           25
For, my good liege, she is so idly kinged,
Her sceptre so fantastically borne,
By a vain, giddy, shallow, humorous youth,
That fear attends her not.

CONSTABLE                      Oh peace, Prince Dauphin,
You are too much mistaken in this king.                            30
Question, your grace, the late ambassadors,
With what great state he heard their embassy,
How well supplied with noble counsellors,
How modest in exception, and withal
How terrible in constant resolution,                               35
And you shall find his vanities, forespent,
Were but the outside of the Roman Brutus,

---

32 great state] F; regard Q   33 noble] F; aged Q

18–19 defences . . . collected Each of the three
verbs in the second line matches the equivalent
noun in the first.

25 a Whitsun . . . dance The folk-dance
with hobby horse, performed at May festivals in
England. See Alan Brissenden, *Shakespeare and the
Dance*, pp. 19–22. On the references to dancing in
the play at large, see Brissenden, pp. 28–33.

26 she 'England' is normally masculine, whether
personified in Henry or in the state at large.
See 1.2.155 n. Here the Dauphin makes 'her' the
queen of the May to Henry's clownish May king,
in the Whitsun festival. The Dauphin's speech,
not unlike Hotspur's comments on the unre-
formed Hal in *1H4*, underlines the reality of his
reformation.

28 humorous capricious.

29 attends Royalty always had a large retinue.

31 late ambassadors The singular ambassador
of Act 1, Scene 2 is here conflated with his
attendants.

32 great state Jackson notes that Q's 'regard' is
lifted by the reporters from a similar context, not
actually used in the Q text, at 1.1.22.

34 exception the expression of disagreement.

36 vanities, forespent past frivolities, now
exhausted.

37 the Roman Brutus An early Brutus, not the
assassin of Caesar, freed Rome from Tarquin and
the Etruscan kings. Under Tarquin he pretended
to be stupid, as the meaning of the Latin name
'Brutus' indicates.

Covering discretion with a coat of folly,
As gardeners do with ordure hide those roots
That shall first spring and be most delicate.                           40
DAUPHIN Well, 'tis not so, my Lord High Constable.
But though we think it so, it is no matter.
In cases of defence, 'tis best to weigh
The enemy more mighty than he seems,
So the proportions of defence are filled,                               45
Which of a weak and niggardly projection
Doth like a miser spoil his coat, with scanting
A little cloth.
FRENCH KING          Think we King Harry strong,
And, princes, look you strongly arm to meet him.
The kindred of him hath been fleshed upon us,                           50
And he is bred out of that bloody strain
That haunted us in our familiar paths.
Witness our too-much memorable shame
When Crécy battle fatally was struck,
And all our princes captived, by the hand                               55
Of that black name, Edward, black Prince of Wales,
Whilst that his mountant sire, on mountain standing,
Up in the air, crowned with the golden sun,
Saw his heroical seed, and smiled to see him
Mangle the work of nature and deface                                    60

---

57 mountant] *Taylor;* mountain F; mounting *Theobald*   59 heroical] F; heroic *Rowe*

---

**38 a coat of folly** the fool's coat, seen at May games.
**39 ordure** mulch.
**42 though** even if.
**45 So** So long as.
**46 projection** prediction of scale. 'Proportions' are a fair allocation and also the full measurement. A weak projection is an under-estimate of scale.
**47 scanting** economising, cutting the cloth too short.
**50 fleshed** i.e. tasted the meat from. Hawks and hunting-dogs were given an advance taste of their prey.
**52 haunted** pursued, a term from hunting.
**52 familiar** (1) usual, (2) familial.
**56 black Prince** See *AWW* 4.5.33–4: 'The black prince, sir, alias the prince of darkness, alias the devil'.
**57 mountant** Taylor argues for 'mountant' as a correction of an F misreading by assimilation of

the following word. As 'ascendant', climbing but not yet at the peak of success, it fits here. The F reading probably obscures a play on two related words. The minim error posited by Taylor seems more likely than Theobald's conjecture. At Crécy Edward III was both in the ascendant and standing on a hill.
**58 crowned** Edward's crest was a lion guardant, not a sun. The image relates him to the sun imagery of *R2* in the form of a sun rising.
**59–64** The French king's speech reapplies the biblical reference to God smiling on Christ's baptism: Luke 3.22: 'And the holy ghost came downe, in a bodily shape lyke a Dove, upon hym: and a voyce came from heaven, which said, "thou art my beloved sonne, in thee I am well pleased."' This 'heroical seed' mangles God's work. Edward smiles on destruction, not loving creation.

The patterns that by God and by French fathers
Had twenty years been made. This is a stem
Of that victorious stock, and let us fear
The native mightiness and fate of him.

*Enter a* MESSENGER

MESSENGER Ambassadors from Harry, king of England,                    65
    Do crave admittance to your majesty.
FRENCH KING We'll give them present audience.
    Go, and bring them.

                            *[Exit Messenger]*

    You see this chase is hotly followed, friends.
DAUPHIN Turn head and stop pursuit, for coward dogs                    70
    Most spend their mouths when what they seem to threaten
    Runs far before them. Good my sovereign,
    Take up the English short, and let them know
    Of what a monarchy you are the head.
    Self love, my liege, is not so vile a sin                          75
    As self neglecting.

*Enter* EXETER

FRENCH KING            From our brother of England?
EXETER From him, and thus he greets your majesty:
    He wills you in the name of God almighty
    That you divest yourself, and lay apart
    The borrowed glories that by gift of heaven,                       80
    By law of nature and of nations, 'longs
    To him and to his heirs, namely, the crown,
    And all wide-stretchèd honours that pertain

By custom and the ordinance of times
Unto the crown of France. That you may know                    85
'Tis no sinister nor no awkward claim
Picked from the wormholes of long vanished days,
Nor from the dust of old oblivion raked,
He sends you this most memorable line
                              [*Delivers scroll*]
In every branch truly demonstrative,                          90
Willing you overlook this pedigree,
And when you find him evenly derived
From his most famed of famous ancestors,
Edward the Third, he bids you then resign
Your crown and kingdom, indirectly held                       95
From him, the native and true challenger.
FRENCH KING  Or else what follows?
EXETER  Bloody constraint, for if you hide the crown
Even in your hearts, there will he rake for it.
Therefore in fierce tempest is he coming,                     100
In thunder and in earthquake, like a Jove,
That if requiring fail, he will compel,
And bids you, in the bowels of the Lord,

---

103 And] F; He *Rowe*; A *Oxford conj.*

---

**84 the ordinance of times** customary law, tradition.
**86 sinister** (1); dishonest, (2) drawn through a bastard line.
**86 awkward** perverse.
**87 Picked** Selected, plucked.
**89 this . . . line** (1) a written paper, (2) a lineage or pedigree. See 1.2.84.
**90 SD** A written document must accompany such a declaration. Exeter presumably hands it over at 'this' rather than waiting to the end of his speech, although the king's reaction at line 97 is to his words, not the paper. Probably he takes it but refuses to read it on the spot.
**90 branch** i.e. of the genealogical tree on the paper.
**91 Willing** Insisting.
**91 overlook** read through, study.
**91 pedigree** i.e. a true line, not a bastard one.
**92 evenly derived** directly descended.
**95 indirectly held** i.e. unevenly derived, and also crookedly or unfairly withheld from Henry.
**96 native** rightful and natural. Exeter unknowingly echoes the king's own term for

Henry's 'native mightiness' at line 64.
**96 challenger** i.e. claimant to the title.
**100–1 in fierce . . . earthquake** From the Bishops' Bible, Isa. 29.7: 'Thou shalt be visited of the Lord of hostes, with thunder, earthquake, and with a great noyse, with storme and tempest.' The Geneva Bible has 'shaking' for 'earthquake'.
**101 like a Jove** like Jupiter, whose weapon was the thunderbolt.
**103 And** Many editors stop the sentence at the end of the previous line and alter the connective to 'He' or 'A' to begin a new sentence. This is a possible correction to F, though it interrupts the flow of Exeter's speech. Q halts it in a different way by cutting lines 103–6, which, since Exeter was one of the compilers of the Q text, may reflect a cut in the staged version.
**103 in . . . Lord** by God's compassion, a stock injunction from Phil. 1.8: 'in the bowels of Jesus Christe'. The whole passage is taken directly from Holinshed, p. 548: The pursuivant 'exhorted the French king in the bowels of Jesu Christ, to render him that which was his owne, whereby effusion of Christian bloud might be avoided'.

Deliver up the crown, and to take mercy
On the poor souls for whom this hungry war            105
Opens his vasty jaws, and on your head
Turning the widow's tears, the orphan's cries,
The dead men's blood, the privèd maiden's groans,
For husbands, fathers, and betrothèd lovers
That shall be swallowed in this controversy.          110
This is his claim, his threatening, and my message –
Unless the Dauphin be in presence here,
To whom expressly I bring greeting to.

FRENCH KING For us, we will consider of this further.
Tomorrow shall you bear our full intent               115
Back to our brother of England.

DAUPHIN                            For the Dauphin,
I stand here for him. What to him from England?

EXETER Scorn and defiance, slight regard, contempt,
And anything that may not misbecome
The mighty sender, doth he prize you at.              120
Thus says my king, and if your father's highness
Do not, in grant of all demands at large,
Sweeten the bitter mock you sent his majesty,
He'll call you to so hot an answer of it
That caves and womby vaultages of France             125
Shall chide your trespass and return your mock

---

107 Turning] F; Turns he Q    108 privèd] *Walter;* priuy F; pining Q, *Pope*    113 greeting to] F; greeting too Q    124 of]
F; for Q, *Taylor*

**106 vasty** The third use of this neologism in
this play.

**107–8 widow's . . . groans** As at lines 18–19,
the three terms used in 109 each reflect one of the
three that precede them.

**108 privèd** Walter's conjecture is attractive
because it requires minimal misreading by the F
compositor, privie for prived, an i/e and a d/e error
as elsewhere in this text. The maiden's groans do
not need to be 'privy' if her lover is betrothed to
her, but she is deprived, like the widow and the
orphan.

**110 swallowed** i.e. in the 'vasty jaws' of the
hungry war.

**112 in presence** in the royal presence room. See
1.2.2 n.

**113 greeting to** Q's reading is attractive since

Exeter has already offered his greeting to the
French king. The 'express' greeting is the reply
to the Dauphin's embassy in Act 1, Scene 2. But
F is not incorrect. A double preposition is quite
usual. See Abbott p. 293.

**120 prize you at** The pronoun is stressed.
Exeter evidently sees through the Dauphin's
attempt at aloof anonymity.

**122 at large** (1) open, not yet settled, (2) the
total of the demands.

**125 caves** both cellars and hollows. The
'womby' vaults hint at the children yet unborn
mentioned in Henry's reply to the Dauphin's
ambassador at 1.2.287.

**126 trespass** sin, with a hint that the Dauphin
is trespassing on Henry's property.

In second accent of his ordinance.
DAUPHIN Say, if my father render fair return
It is against my will, for I desire
Nothing but odds with England. To that end,                    130
As matching to his youth and vanity,
I did present him with the Paris balls.
EXETER He'll make your Paris Louvre shake for it,
Were it the mistress-court of mighty Europe.
And be assured, you'll find a difference,                    135
As we his subjects have in wonder found,
Between the promise of his greener days
And these he masters now. Now he weighs time
Even to the utmost grain. That you shall read
In your own losses, if he stay in France.                    140
FRENCH KING Tomorrow shall you know our mind at full.

                              *Flourish*

EXETER Dispatch us with all speed, lest that our king
Come here himself to question our delay,
For he is footed in this land already.
FRENCH KING You shall be soon dispatched, with fair conditions.    145
A night is but small breath and little pause
To answer matters of this consequence.

                         [*Flourish*] *Exeunt*

---

130 England. To] *Rowe; –. / To* F    133 Louvre] F (*Louer*)    141 SD *Flourish*] F; *not in Dyce*    147 SD *Flourish*] *Dyce; not in* F

127 **second accent** echo.
127 **ordinance** (1) artillery, (2) law and authority. Strictly, the modern 'ordnance', meaning
artillery, is a disyllable. The longer form has been
retained here for the metre.
130 **odds** (1) a quarrel, (2) a bet, as in tennis.
131 **matching** As in tennis, but also matched to
his youth and lightness.
131 **his** i.e. the king of England's.
132 **Paris balls** French tennis balls were famous
for their light weight.
133 **Paris Louvre** (1) the royal palace, (2) lovers
in Paris. The F spelling 'Lover' indicates that the
two words were close to being homonyms.
134 **mistress-court** the best royal and tennis
court.
137 **greener** more immature.
139 **grain** of sand, as in an hour-glass.
139 **read** (1) recognise, (2) regret (rede).

141 The king repeats the statement of lines 115–
16.
141 SD Dyce shifts the trumpet fanfare marking the king's rising to depart to the end of the
scene. Capell keeps it here on the grounds that the
king rises to dismiss the embassy, but is checked
by Exeter's refusal to go quietly. If Dyce's transfer
of the flourish from the Chorus entry in 3.0 to the
king's departure at the end of this scene is correct,
which other examples make most likely, then there
should be the two flourishes, thanks to Exeter's
interruption.
142 **our** i.e. the king of England and of the
French.
144 **footed** Historically Exeter's embassy
preceded Henry's invasion by six months.
146 **small breath** little time for taking a breath.
147 SD *Flourish* See note to 1.2.310 SD.

**3.0**  *Enter* CHORUS

CHORUS  Thus with imagined wing our swift scene flies
        In motion of no less celerity
        Than that of thought. Suppose that you have seen
        The well-appointed king at Hampton Pier
        Embark his royalty, and his brave fleet          5
        With silken streamers the young Phoebus feigning.
        Play with your fancies, and in them behold
        Upon the hempen tackle ship-boys climbing.
        Hear the shrill whistle, which doth order give
        To sounds confused. Behold the threaden sails,    10
        Borne with the invisible and creeping wind,
        Draw the huge bottoms through the furrowed sea,
        Breasting the lofty surge. O do but think
        You stand upon the rivage, and behold
        A city on th'inconstant billows dancing,    15
        For so appears this fleet majestical,
        Holding due course to Harfleur. Follow, follow!
        Grapple your minds to sternage of this navy,

Act 3, Scene 0   3.0] Pope; *Actus Secundus* F   0 SD *Enter* CHORUS.] *Dyce; Flourish. Enter Chorus.* F   1 SH CHORUS] *Not in* F   4 Hampton] *Theobald;* Dover F   6 feigning] F (fayning); fanning *Rowe*

**Act 3, Scene 0**
**3.0** The act division is Pope's. F marks it 'Actus Secundus'.

**1 swift scene** i.e. the locality to be imagined.

**2–3 motion . . . thought** Hamlet describes exceptional speed as like meditation or the thoughts of love. It was proverbial (Dent T 240).

**3** F makes this two lines, divided at 'thought / Suppose'.

**4 Hampton** The army has been placed at Southampton in 2.0.30, 2.2.88, and 2.3.37. Here the F text gives a clear indication of uncertainty about which English port it should be. Act 3 seems to suppose a different route from that of Act 2. In 3.2.38 the boy says that Nym and Bardolph have been in Calais, and at 3.4.56 Henry himself speaks of 'retiring' from Harfleur to Calais. Dover is a much more appropriate port than Southampton for landing at Calais. This edition adopts Theobald's correction on the grounds both of the evidence in Act 2 and of the historical source. Holinshed set the landing at 'Caur' or 'Kidcaur', near Harfleur.

**5 brave** spectacular, brightly dressed (in the silks of the next line).

**6 the young Phoebus** i.e. the morning sun. Phoebus was the Roman sun god.

**6 feigning** F's word generates an appropriate image of the English fleet pretending to be rising Phoebus in his colourful clothing. Rowe's conjecture is based on *Mac.* 1.2.50, where the Norwegian banners 'fan our people cold'.

**9 order** (1) control, (2) instructions.

**10 threaden** This adjective is a puzzle. It means either the stitched-in cords strengthening the sails themselves, marginally the more likely image, or the 'hempen tackle' attached to them.

**12 bottoms** ships (literally hulls, by synecdoche).

**13 Breasting** The first known use of this image for ships at sea.

**14 rivage** shore.

**17 Harfleur** Stressed on the first syllable. Holinshed's and the F spelling 'Harflew' probably reflects the pronunciation.

**18 Grapple** Attach with grappling irons.

**18 sternage** the rear end. A ship that fixed itself to the stern of another ship would be towed along behind it. 'Sternage', like other amplified terms used by the Chorus, does not occur elsewhere.

And leave your England as dead midnight, still,
Guarded with grandsires, babies and old women,                    20
Either past or not arrived to pith and puissance.
For who is he whose chin is but enriched
With one appearing hair that will not follow
These culled and choice-drawn cavaliers to France?
Work, work your thoughts, and therein see a siege.                 25
Behold the ordnance on their carriages
With fatal mouths gaping on girded Harfleur.
Suppose th'ambassador from the French comes back,
Tells Harry that the king doth offer him
Katherine his daughter, and with her to dowry                      30
Some petty and unprofitable dukedoms.
The offer likes not, and the nimble gunner
With linstock now the devilish cannon touches
              *Alarm, and chambers go off*
And down goes all before them. Still be kind,
And eke out our performance with your mind.          *Exit*   35

*cut in both films*

35 eke] F (eech)

19 **as** as if it were.

19 **dead midnight** 'As still as midnight' was proverbial (Dent M919.1).

24 **culled** selected, a term often used of beasts for slaughter.

24 **choice-drawn** Implying careful selection, and the drawing of straws.

26 **ordnance** See note to 2.4.127. Henry V's siege cannon, originally developed for his assaults on the great castles in Wales, were a celebrated feature of his successful tactics in France.

27 **fatal** (1) deadly, (2) hungry for food.

27 **girded** dressed defensively. The first Chorus speaks of the 'girdle of these walls' at 1.0.19, and the French king speaks of 'maiden walls' being 'girdled' at 5.2.287.

29–31 This offer is what Henry accepts in 5.2. Taylor notes that 'petty and unprofitable dukedoms' is an oxymoron, since dukedoms were never petty, except in comparison with a crown. They are in fact Henry's 'almost kingly dukedoms' of 1.2.227.

32 **likes not** is not pleasing.

33 **linstock** a stick for holding a lighted fuse. See Illustration 15, p. 218 below.

33 **devilish** Fireworks were regularly associated with devils, especially in the Elizabethan theatre.

33 SD *Alarm* A military signal. For cavalry, the instruments used to transmit battlefield messages were trumpets, and for infantry drums. A trumpet has already been used for flourishes in the royal scenes, but, given the pedestrian nature of the army that enters at 3.1, a drumbeat is more likely here, despite Henry's reference to the 'blast of war' at 3.1.5. In Barnabe Rich's *A Pathway to Military Practise*, he writes 'It is necessary that every company have two drums, the one to be stil resident with the Cullours the other to marche with the Troupes, as upon occasion they shall be drawne forth. These Drummes must be perfect to sounde a call, a march, a charge, a retrait, a larum, and such lyke poyntes of warre' (G2).

33 SD *chambers* small cannon, positioned on the superstructure over the stage. See Introduction, p. 39. The deliberate shock effect of this cannon-shot anticipates the second cannonade called for in the stage direction at 3.1.34.

34 **Still** Continue to. This repeats the plea made at 1.0.23.

35 **eke** F1's 'eech' indicates the pronunciation. In *Per.* 3.0.13 it rhymes with 'speech'.

**3.1** *Enter the* KING, EXETER, BEDFORD *and* GLOUCESTER

*Alarm. [Enter soldiers with] scaling ladders at Harfleur*

KING  Once more unto the breach, dear friends, once more,
          Or close the wall up with our English dead!
          In peace there's nothing so becomes a man
          As modest stillness and humility.
          But when the blast of war blows in our ears,                    5
          Then imitate the action of the tiger:
          Stiffen the sinews, conjure up the blood,
          Disguise fair nature with hard-favoured rage.
          Then lend the eye a terrible aspect,
          Let it pry through the portage of the head,                    10
          Like the brass cannon. Let the brow o'erwhelm it
          As fearfully as doth a gallèd rock
          O'erhang and jutty his confounded base,
          Swilled with the wild and wasteful ocean.
          Now set the teeth and stretch the nostril wide,              15
          Hold hard the breath, and bend up every spirit

Act 3, Scene 1    7 conjure] *Walter;* commune F; summon *Rowe*

Act 3, Scene 1

0 SD *Alarm* See note to 3.0.33.1.

0 SD *scaling ladders* If the first cannon at 3.0.33 brought down a wall at Harfleur, as the Chorus declares, ladders to enter by the breach are appropriate here. It should be noted, though, that this army is in retreat. Henry exhorts them to return to the assault.

1 **breach** a break in the walls of 'girded Harfleur' (3.0.27). The ladders indicate that only the parapet has been smashed, allowing access to the top of the walls.

5 **blast** cannon-shot, or possibly trumpet-call.

6 **imitate the action** Theatrical terminology: act as if on stage.

7 **conjure** F does not make much sense. Hulme, *Explorations*, pp. 158–9, argues for 'commune' as an irregular derivation from the Latin *communire*, to fortify, but it is not convincing. Rowe normalises. Walter's conjecture supposes a minim error in F (coniure), and has the advantage of connecting warfare with sex. To 'conjure' the blood was normally a form of bawdy magic, as in Mercutio's conjuration of Romeo in *RJ* 2.1.16 and 26. Given the links between battles and sex elsewhere in the play,

such as 3.4.11–14 and 5.2.287–8, it seems the best choice here.

8 **fair nature** a naturally handsome appearance.

8 **hard-favoured** (1) stern-faced, (2) unkind.

9 **aspect** Stressed on the second syllable.

10 **pry** (1) see, (2) stick out.

10 **portage** openings, portholes. As with 'sternage', 3.0.18, this is the only occurrence of this term.

11 **o'erwhelm** i.e. dominate the eye's aspect by its frowning.

12 **gallèd** worn, eroded.

13 **jutty** project over – a building term like the Chorus's 'abutting', 1.0.21.

13 **confounded** worn away.

14 **Swilled** Vigorously washed.

15 Henry now moves on to the expression on the rest of the face.

16 **bend up** force, as in bending a bow in archery. When the bow has been bent and the bow-string notched onto it, the string is stretched to its full length. See Ann and John O. Thompson, *Shakespeare: Meaning and Metaphor*, p. 143. This image is almost the only reference to the long-bow, the weapon which largely won the battle at Agincourt for the English.

To his full height. On, on, you noble English,
Whose blood is fet from fathers of war-proof,
Fathers that like so many Alexanders
Have in these parts from morn till even fought,                      20
And sheathed their swords for lack of argument.
Dishonour not your mothers. Now attest
That those whom you called fathers did beget you.
Be copy now to men of grosser blood,
And teach them how to war. And you, good yeomen,                     25
Whose limbs were made in England, show us here
The mettle of your pasture. Let us swear
That you are worth your breeding, which I doubt not,
For there is none of you so mean and base
That hath not noble lustre in your eyes.                             30
I see you stand like greyhounds in the slips,
Straining upon the start. The game's afoot.
Follow your spirit, and upon this charge
Cry 'God for Harry, England and Saint George!'

*Alarm, and chambers go off* [*Exeunt*]

17 noble] *Malone;* noblish F; noblest F2   24 men] F4; me F   32 Straining] *Rowe;* straying F   34 Harry,] F; – !
*Warburton*   34 SD *Exeunt*] not in F

**17 his** i.e. its.
**17 noble** F by eyeskip sets the ending of the next
word. F2 normalises the mistake. Henry specifically addresses the nobles first, although none
are recorded in the entry direction as accompanying him on stage. He goes on to the yeomen at
line 25.
**18 fet** inherited (fetched).
**18 of war-proof** tested in war.
**19 Alexanders** The Archbishop at 1.1.46
and Llewellyn at 4.7.10–43 compare Henry to
Alexander the Great.
**20 even** evening.
**21 argument** (1) opposition, (2) reason, (3) a
subject for debate.
**24 copy** example.
**24 men . . . blood** the yeomen whom Henry
turns to in the next line.
**27 pasture** grazing grounds. Yeomen were the
rural equivalent of citizens, self-employed freemen
farmers, in the account of English classes given

in Harrison's 'Description' which appeared in
Volume I of Holinshed. The line puns on placing
metal (swords rather than ploughshares) in grass.
**30 noble** i.e. capable of imitating the nobles,
whom he has ordered to make their eyes glare
fiercely.
**31 greyhounds in the slips** hunting-hounds
held on a slip-leash by their lords. See 1.0.7.
**32 Straining** Hunting-dogs would not be
allowed to stray, as F makes them.
**32 The game's afoot** The quarry is out of its
lair and running.
**33 charge** (1) order, (2) advance.
**34 Harry . . . George** The punctuation is
indefinite, but the three names together, King
Henry, the country (also Henry personified), and
Henry's favourite saint, comprise a standard battle-
cry. Holinshed notes that one of Henry's first pious
acts after his coronation was to make St George's
day a feast-day. He adds that the Archbishop of
Canterbury had wanted St Dunstan.

**3.2** *Enter* NYM, BARDOLPH, PISTOL *and* BOY

BARDOLPH  On, on, on, on, on, to the breach, to the breach!
NYM  Pray thee, corporal, stay. The knocks are too hot, and for
    mine own part I have not a case of lives. The humour of it is
    too hot, that is the very plain-song of it.
PISTOL  'The plain-song' is most just, for humours do abound.    5
    Knocks go and come, God's vassals drop and die,
      [*Sings*] And sword and shield,
      In bloody field,
      Doth win immortal fame.
BOY  Would I were in an ale-house in London. I would give all my    10
    fame for a pot of ale, and safety.
PISTOL  And I.
      [*Sings*] If wishes would prevail with me,
      My purpose should not fail with me,
      But thither would I hie.    15
BOY  [*Sings*] As duly
      But not as truly
      As bird doth sing on bough.

*Enter* LLEWELLYN

**Act 3, Scene 2**

**0 SD** This, a new entry, marks a new scene in this edition. Most editions add it to the previous scene, but only if there is a brief gap between the real soldiers' exit and the arrival of the Eastcheap rogues could Nym's interruption of the charge be given the hearing it needs. The staging is awkward, since the scaling ladders at the charge that ends 3.1 would have to be placed against the tiring-house wall, and Nym and the others must emerge from the tiring house. But the ladder-carriers emerged from there too. They probably ascend the ladders placed against the 'above' or balcony, and pull them up after them. In Jasper Mayne's encomium to Ben Jonson, *Jonsonus Virbius*, written in 1638, he wrote 'Thou laidst no sieges to the *Musique-Roome*' (E4). After the company took over the Blackfriars playhouse and its musicians in 1608, the central room on the stage balcony at the Globe was made into a music room. That place (Juliet's balcony) would also have served as the wall of Harfleur.

**2 corporal** Bardolph was called lieutenant at 2.1.2, when the corporal was Nym. The new title is more likely to be Bardolph's demotion than a misattribution of the speech headings.

**3 a case** a package.
**4 plain-song** simple melody, or truth.
**5 most just** i.e. a *mot juste*, the right (French) word.
**5 humours** After firing the 'chambers' twice, there would be smoke in the theatre, which would qualify as mists or 'humours'.
**7–9** The rhymes indicate that Pistol starts singing here, prompted by Nym's reference to 'plain-song'. Johnson thought these lines and Pistol's and the boy's following at 13–18 are fragments of old songs.
**17 truly** i.e. melodiously, in tune.
**18 As . . . bough** Either this line echoes the proverb 'as blithe as bird on bough' (Dent B359) or the proverb echoes an old refrain.
**18 SD LLEWELLYN** For the spelling of the F name 'Fluellen', see Introduction, pp. 70–1. A William Fluellen was a resident in Stratford, according to a list of nine recusants drawn up in 1590, one of whom was Shakespeare's father. See F. W. Brownlow, 'John Shakespeare's recusancy: new light on an old document', *SQ* 40 (1989), 186–91. This is Llewellyn's first and briefest appearance. His Welsh accent ('preach' for 'breach'),

LLEWELLYN  Up to the preach, you dogs! Avaunt, you cullions!

PISTOL  Be merciful, great duke, to men of mould! Abate thy rage,     20
abate thy manly rage! Abate thy rage, great duke! Good
bawcock, bate thy rage. Use lenity, sweet chuck.

NYM  These be good humours! Your honour wins bad humours!

*Exeunt [Pistol, Bardolph and Nym, pursued by Llewellyn]*

BOY  As young as I am, I have observed these three swashers. I am
boy to them all three, but all they three, though they would     25
serve me, could not be man to me, for indeed three such antics
do not amount to a man. For Bardolph, he is white-livered and
red-faced, by the means whereof a faces it out but fights not.
For Pistol, he hath a killing tongue and a quiet sword, by the
means whereof a breaks words and keeps whole weapons. For     30
Nym, he hath heard that men of few words are the best men,

---

Act 3, Scene 2   **19** preach] F (breach)   **23** wins] F; runs *Rann*   **23** SD *Exeunt . . . LLEWELLYN*] *Enter Fluellen and
beats them in* Q; *Exit* F   **30** whole weapons] F; weapons whole *Taylor conj.*

emphasised in his next scene, had already been launched on stage with Parson Evans in *Wiv*. It was imitated in plays of the rival companies such as *Patient Grissil, Sir John Oldcastle*, and *Satiromastix*. At this first appearance the idiom is not conspicuous. Both F and Q have 'breach' here where later they spell all his b's as p's. Q, however, adds an oath to his first words, 'Godes plud', that becomes a catchphrase throughout the Q text.

**19 dogs** After Henry has likened his soldiers to greyhounds, Llewellyn's term comes as an inversion.

**19 cullions** (1) rascals, (2) kitchen servants, (3) testicles.

**20 great duke** Probably an indirect allusion to Latin *dux*, a leader, but it is a characteristic Pistolian inflation. Llewellyn's first and last acts in the play are to beat Pistol.

**20 men of mould** men made of clay, earth. The phrase is from the Bishops' Bible.

**22 bawcock** A term of endearment, French *Beau coq.*

**22 lenity** mercy. See 3.7.96, where it relates to Bardolph.

**22 chuck** Another term of endearment.

**23 These** i.e. Pistol's pleading.

**23 Your honour** (1) Llewellyn's anger, (2) your dukeship.

**23 wins** Rann's conjectural emendation follows Nym's earlier usage at 2.1.97.

**23 SD** David Galloway has proposed that Llewellyn remains on-stage here, and that the boy's

speech is addressed to him. F does not mark any re-entry for Llewellyn with Gower at the beginning of the next scene. But for Llewellyn to stay behind after beating Bardolph and the others back to the breach would be odd, especially if he has to stay so long silent, and at Act 3, Scene 7 he has evidently not heard the boy's account of Pistol. Riverside adopts the idea that Llewellyn remains on-stage here and consequently numbers 3.3 as an extension of 3.2.

**24 swashers** swashbucklers, braggarts.

**25 boy to** (1) servant to, (2) younger than.

**25–6 though . . . serve** (1) if they would be my servant, (2) although they would like to bugger me.

**26 man** (1) servant, (2) sexual lover.

**26 antics** clowns.

**27–8 white-livered and red-faced** cowardly and a heavy drinker.

**28 a** i.e. he.

**28 faces it out** (1) has the face for it, (2) puts a bold front on it.

**30 breaks words** (1) talks a lot, (2) speaks broken English, (3) breaks promises, (4) (does not) break swords. The 'w' in 'sword' was pronounced, according to Cercignani (pp. 38, 112, 139). The fourth meaning justifies the subsequent phrase about whole weapons. There is also an allusion to farting, if *Err.* 3.1.75 is any precedent: 'A man may break a word with you, sir, and words are but wind.'

**31 men of . . . men** Proverbial (Dent W718, W26.1).

and therefore he scorns to say his prayers lest a should be
thought a coward, but his few bad words are matched with as
few good deeds, for a never broke any man's head but his own,
and that was against a post when he was drunk. They will steal      35
anything and call it purchase. Bardolph stole a lute-case, bore it
twelve leagues and sold it for three halfpence. Nym and
Bardolph are sworn brothers in filching, and in Calais they
stole a fire-shovel. I knew by that piece of service the men
would carry coals. They would have me as familiar with men's      40
pockets as their gloves or their handkerchiefs, which makes
much against my manhood if I should take from another's
pocket to put into mine, for it is plain pocketing up of wrongs. I
must leave them and seek some better service. Their villainy
goes against my weak stomach, and therefore I must cast it up.      45

                                                        *Exit*


3.3  *Enter* GOWER [*and* LLEWELLYN]

GOWER  Captain Llewellyn, you must come presently to the mines.
    The Duke of Gloucester would speak with you.
LLEWELLYN  To the mines? Tell you the Duke it is not so good to
    come to the mines, for, look you, the mines is not according to
    the disciplines of the war, the concavities of it is not sufficient.      5
    For, look you, th'athversary, you may discuss unto the Duke,

---

Act 3, Scene 3   6 athversary] F

**36 purchase** fair exchange.
**37 leagues** French miles, equal to about three English miles.
**38 filching** stealing.
**39 service** Domestic rather than military or sexual.
**40 carry coals** do menial work (Dent C464).
**43 pocketing up** tolerating offences, putting away stolen goods. Behind the phrase is the proverbial pocketing up of injury (Dent 170).
**45 cast it up** (1) give it up, (2) vomit it out.

**Act 3, Scene 3**
**0 SD GOWER** The name is probably from *2H4*, where a 'Master Gower' appears in Act 2, Scene 1 as a messenger going to the Lord Chief Justice and ignoring Falstaff's presence. As a captain here he seems to have a similar personality. He bears no resemblance to the Ancient Gower of *Pericles*.

**0 SD LLEWELLYN** See note to 3.2.18 SD. The two captains must enter by different doors, Gower looking for Llewellyn to bring him to the mines. Most editions have both entering by the same door.
**1 presently** immediately.
**1 mines** tunnels dug under the walls to plant explosives.
**5 concavities** concave sides, or cavities – i.e. depth. The depth must be insufficient if the enemy has dug beneath them.
**6 athversary** This spelling recurs at 3.7.80 and 84. Welsh pronunciation would normally offer the unvoiced t for d, never th. But in other plays Shakespeare always spells it as 'adversary', so the F spelling must be Shakespeare's.
**6 discuss unto** The intransitive use occurs in *Wiv.* at 1.3.73 (Nym) and 4.5.2 (the Hostess), in this play by Pistol at 4.1.37 and 4.4.4, 22–3.

look you, is digged himself, four yard under, the countermines!
By Cheshu, I think a will plow up all, if there is not better
directions.

GOWER The Duke of Gloucester, to whom the order of the siege is    10
given, is altogether directed by an Irishman, a very valiant
gentleman, i'faith.

LLEWELLYN It is Captain Macmorris, is it not?

GOWER I think it be.

LLEWELLYN By Cheshu, he is an ass, as in the world. I will verify    15
as much in his beard. He has no more directions in the true
disciplines of the wars, look you, of the Roman disciplines, than
is a puppy dog.

*Enter* MACMORRIS *and Captain* JAMY

GOWER Here a comes, and the Scots captain, Captain Jamy, with
him.                                                              20

LLEWELLYN Captain Jamy is a marvellous falorous gentleman, that
is certain, and of great expedition and knowledge in th'anchient

---

7 himself,] *Taylor;* ‿ F   7 under,] *Taylor;* ‿ F   8 Cheshu] F   13 SH LLEWELLYN] *Welch* F   16 has] F (h'as)
22 anchient] F; ancient *Taylor*

7 **digged . . . countermines** i.e. has counter-
mined to a depth of four yards below the English
mines.

**8 Cheshu** The Welsh use of unvoiced consonants, p, f, and ch for b, v, and j, is conspicuous
in the F spellings. Slurring the s is a characteristic shared by Llewellyn and Macmorris. The same
spelling recurs at line 15 below.

**8 plow** i.e. blow, as at 4.8.13. The next use of
Welsh p for b is not marked in F until 'pridge' at
3.7.9.

**12 gentleman** The captains are all noted in the
play as gentlemen, a social rank between the nobles
and the yeomen of 3.1.25.

**13 SH LLEWELLYN** From here on in F the
speech heading for Llewellyn become 'Welch', and
the later headings for Macmorris and Jamy are
'Irish' and 'Scot'.

**15 ass, as** Llewellyn's sibilants seem to be
unvoiced like his dentals, making 'ass' and 'hiss'.

**16 in his beard** Proverbial (Dent B143.1).

**17 the Roman disciplines** Humphreys finds
echoes in Llewellyn's emphasis on Roman warfare
of Thomas Digges's *Stratioticos*, which was reissued in 1590 by Richard Field, the Stratfordian
who published Shakespeare's poems.

**18 SD MACMORRIS** Holinshed (pp. 565–6)

mentions that at the siege of Rouen after
Agincourt the English forces were joined by 'the
lord of Kilmaine in Ireland, with a band of six-
teene hundred Irishmen, in maile, with darts and
skains after the maner of their countrie, all of them
being tall, quicke and nimble persons, which came
and presented themselves before the king lieng still
at the siege, of whom they were . . . gentlie received
& welcomed'.

**18 SD JAMY** According to Holinshed Henry did
have a Scottish James with him after Agincourt,
but he was a king, not a captain. See Appendix 2.
Neither Macmorris nor Jamy survive into Q, which
keeps little of this scene.

**19–20 and . . . him** Keith Brown has pointed
out how all the references to and speeches by Jamy
can be neatly cut from this scene, as if his presence
was a late addition. See Introduction, p. 66.

**22 expedition** Wright suggests that this is
Llewellyn's misuse of English, a compositor misreading, or a portmanteau word blending 'experience' and 'erudition'. Its normal meaning, quick
action, seems not unacceptable.

**22 anchient** Taylor notes F's 'aunchiant' at
3.7.10, 15, and elsewhere, and suggests it indicates
another distinctive Welsh pronunciation. But the
word is spelled 'aunchient' in F Act 3, Scene 7, so

wars, upon my particular knowledge of his directions. By
Cheshu, he will maintain his argument as well as any military
man in the world, in the disciplines of the pristine wars of the          25
Romans.

JAMY  I say guidday, Captain Llewellyn.

LLEWELLYN  Goodden to your worship, good Captain James.

GOWER  How now, Captain Macmorris, have you quit the mines?
Have the pioneers given o'er?                                              30

MACMORRIS  By Chrish law, 'tish ill done. The work ish give over,
the trumpet sound the retreat. By my hand I swear, and my
father's soul, the work ish ill done. It ish give over. I would
have blowed up the town, so Chrish save me law, in an hour.
O, 'tish ill done, 'tish ill done. By my hand, 'tish ill done.            35

LLEWELLYN  Captain Macmorris, I beseech you now, will you
vouchsafe me, look you, a few disputations with you, as partly
touching or concerning the disciplines of the war, the Roman
wars, in the way of argument, look you, and friendly
communication? Partly to satisfy my opinion, and partly for the           40
satisfaction, look you, of my mind, as touching the direction of
the military discipline, that is the point.

JAMY  It sall be vary guid, guid faith, guid captains baith, and I sall
'quite you with guid leave, as I may pick occasion, that sall I,
marry.                                                                    45

MACMORRIS  It is no time to discourse, so Chrish save me. The
day is hot, and the weather, and the wars, and the king, and the
dukes. It is no time to discourse, the town is besieched! An the

---

27 guidday] F (gudday)  28 Goodden] F (Godden)  43 baith] F (bath)  44 'quite] F (quit)  48 besieched] F
(beseech'd)  48 An] F (and)

this instance may be a compositor's misreading of
a for e in a non-standard word. Llewellyn's special pronunciation of this word has been registered
throughout in this edition with a non-standard
spelling.

27–8 guidday . . . Goodden Two regional pronunciations of the familiar greeting. The guttural
Scots u in 'good' is easy to standardise, but the
Welsh behind F's 'Godden' is more difficult. It may
be a version of 'Good e'en' (evening).

30 pioneers sappers, miners.

31 law Not quite the reference to Christ
in 'lord', but certainly an intensifying oath.
Macmorris repeats it at line 53. Llewellyn also
uses it at 4.7.128. For the theory, based on that
use, that Llewellyn's role in 4.7 and 4.8 was originally Macmorris's, see Thomas L. Berger, 'The

disappearance of Macmorris in Shakespeare's
*Henry V*', *Renaissance Papers 1985*, Durham NC,
1986, pp. 13–26.

43 captains Making the four regional voices
into army captains strongly implies that each of
them commands a similarly regional body of soldiers. The English Michael Williams is said at
4.7.132 to be in Gower's company. See Introduction, p. 32.

44 'quite requite, repay. See 2.2.161 n.

46 Chrish The F spelling indicates that
Macmorris slurs his sibilants. For this and other
pronunciations, see Introduction, pp. 69–70.

48 besieched i.e. besieged. Like Llewellyn,
Macmorris is given unvoiced consonants which in
standard English are voiced.

48 An If.

trumpet call us to the breach, and we talk and be Chrish do
nothing, 'tis shame for us all! So God sa' me, 'tis shame to          50
stand still, it is shame, by my hand. And there is throats to be
cut, and works to be done, and there ish nothing done, so
Christ sa' me law.

JAMY   By the mess, e'er these eyes of mine take themselves to
slumber I'll dee guid service, or I'll lig i'the grund for it. I owe   55
Got a death, and I'll pay't as valorously as I may, that sal I
surely do, that is the breff and the long. Marry, I wad full fain
hear some question 'tween you twae.

LLEWELLYN   Captain Macmorris, I think, look you, under your
correction, there is not many of your nation –                        60

MACMORRIS   Of my nation? What ish my nation? Ish a villain, and
a bastard, and a knave, and a rascal. What ish my nation? Who
talks of my nation?

LLEWELLYN   Look you, if you take the matter otherwise than is
meant, Captain Macmorris, peradventure I shall think you do           65
not use me with that affability as in discretion you ought to use
me, look you, being as good a man as yourself, both in the
disciplines of war, and in the derivation of my birth, and in
other particularities.

MACMORRIS   I do not know you so good a man as myself. So            70
Chrish save me, I will cut off your head!

GOWER   Gentlemen both, you will mistake each other.

JAMY   Ah, that's a foul fault.

*A parley*

---

55 I owe Got a death] *Craik;* ay, or goe to death F   58 hear] *Wilson;* heard F   60 nation – ] *Pope;* – . F   62 rascal.]
F; –? *Rowe*   73 SD *A parley*] F; alarum (*at end of* 3.4.0.1) Q

**49 be Chrish** Macmorris's pronunciation is
registered much less consistently in F than
Llewellyn's. He says 'By Chrish' at line 31. Here
the preposition seems a distinctive spelling.

**54 mess** mass – a Catholic oath. See
Introduction, p. 29.

**55–6 I . . . death** F misreads the Scottish
spellings in the manuscript. T. W. Craik first proposed his emendation in the *Times Literary Supple-
ment*, 26 February 1980. It prompted a correspon-
dence that ran on until 13 June.

**57 the breff . . . long** The proverbial idiom is
'the long and the short of it' (Dent L.419).

**58 hear** The F compositor misread e (heare) for
d. See Textual Analysis, p. 222.

**60 nation** It is intriguing to speculate what
Llewellyn was going on to say when Macmorris

interrupts him: that there were not many Irish in
Henry's army, perhaps, or something more directly
insulting about the 'wild Irish'. See Introduction,
p. 38.

**61–3 What . . . nation** For different readings of
this speech, see 'Why Captain Jamy in *Henry V?*',
*Archiv* 226 (1989), 365–73.

  **66 that** the sort of.

  **72 mistake** misunderstand.

  **73 SD *A parley*** A trumpet-call, either off-stage
or from the stage balcony, since Gower says it
comes from the town. See note to line 77 SD. A
'parley' was a standard signal to the enemy calling
for a truce so that the two sides could talk. Q marks
it as an '*alarum*' at the end of the entry that begins
Act 3, Scene 4.

GOWER  The town sounds a parley.

LLEWELLYN Captain Macmorris, when there is more better    75
    opportunity to be required, look you, I will be so bold as to tell
    you I know the disciplines of war, and there is an end.

                                                    *Exeunt*


3.4 *Enter the* KING [, EXETER] *and all his train before the gates*

KING  How yet resolves the governor of the town?
        This is the latest parle we will admit,
        Therefore to our best mercy give yourselves,
        Or like to men proud of destruction
        Defy us to our worst. For as I am a soldier,               5
        A name that in my thoughts becomes me best,
        If I begin the battery once again
        I will not leave the half-achieved Harfleur
        Till in her ashes she lie burièd.
        The gates of mercy shall be all shut up                    10

---

77 SD *Exeunt*] *Rowe; Exit* F

77 **there . . . end** Proverbial (Dent E113.1), also
used at 2.1.8 and in *Shr.*, *TGV*, *R2*, *1H4*, *2H4*,
*Ado*, and *TN*.
77 **SD** *Exeunt* F has a singular *Exit*. Taylor
argues that only Llewellyn leaves here and that
the others join Henry and the soldiers, making a continuous scene. Continuous staging on
Shakespearean stages made light of scene endings,
but it was usual to mark the general exit when
everyone leaves and a new scene starts. F regularly
uses a singular exit for a multiple departure. The
argument over the mines was in a 'scene' not
located in front of the gates, which is where Act 3,
Scene 4 takes place.

**Act 3, Scene 4**
0 SD EXETER Henry addresses Exeter at line 51.
F's '*all his Traine*' was probably meant to include
the lords as well as the soldiers, but Exeter's entry
needs to be specified.
1 **How . . . town?** Henry addresses the French
soldiers on the wall, the 'above' or balcony over
the central discovery-space, here representing the
town gates.
1 **How yet resolves** (1) Has he decided, (2) Is
he still resolute.

2 **latest parle** final parley, Harfleur's last chance
before the English renew their attack. What
happened to the renewed assault on the breach is
not mentioned.
4 **proud of** excited by (for a bitch to be proud
meant she was on heat). Henry claims that the
defenders are excited by destruction, and also by
the destruction their resistance will bring.
5 **Defy . . . worst** i.e. to do our worst, a proverbial saying (Dent W914).
5–6 **as . . . best** A more considered claim than
Bardolph's at 2.1.52–3. He gives himself the same
role in his wooing of Katherine at 5.2.142. This
speech is not in Holinshed or any of the sources.
As a threat to Harfleur it anticipates what actually
happened once the town surrendered, according to
Holinshed, but which in the play Henry at line 54
orders should not happen.
10–43 Henry's ultimatum is discussed in relation to the laws of war by E. A. Rauchut, '"Guilty
in defence"; a note on *Henry V*, 3.3.123', *SQ* 42
(1991), 55–7.
10 **gates of mercy** This threat echoes
Tamburlaine in front of Damascus (*1 Tamburlaine*
4.4 and 5.1). In the latter scene the Governor
invokes the fate of the Damascus virgins in terms
Henry now echoes.

And the fleshed soldier, rough and hard of heart,
In liberty of bloody hand shall range
With conscience wide as hell, mowing like grass
Your fresh fair virgins and your flowering infants.
What is it then to me if impious war,                                        15
Arrayed in flames like to the prince of fiends,
Do with his smirched complexion all fell feats
Enlinked to waste and desolation?
What is't to me, when you yourselves are cause,
If your pure maidens fall into the hand                                      20
Of hot and forcing violation?
What rein can hold licentious wickedness
When down the hill he holds his fierce career?
We may as bootless spend our vain command
Upon th'enragèd soldiers in their spoil                                      25
As send precepts to the Leviathan
To come ashore. Therefore, you men of Harfleur,
Take pity of your town and of your people
Whiles yet my soldiers are in my command,
Whiles yet the cool and temperate wind of grace                             30
O'erblows the filthy and contagious clouds

Act 3, Scene 4   23 career] F (Carriere)   27 ashore. Therefore] *Rowe;* –. / Therefore F

**11 fleshed** See 2.4.50 n. This image, with 'range' like an unleashed hunting-dog, and 'mowing' like Death the grim reaper, conflates the two least merciful spectres of Elizabethan life.

**12 In . . . hand** freely licensed to spill blood. 'Liberty' also meant sexual freedom, which anticipates the virgins of line 14.

**13 wide** open wide, loose.

**14 fresh fair . . . flowering** Extensions of the scythe image in 'mowing', but also an allusion to the French 'fleur' of Harfleur.

**15 impious war** Latin *bellum impium*, civil war. Harfleur was supposed to be English which would make the war a civil one instead of a foreign invasion.

**16 Arrayed** (1) Lined up, (2) Dressed. The war is personified as looking like a devil, while the allusion also fits the lines of soldiers standing in front of Harfleur's gates.

**17 smirched** blackened. Soldiers were blackened with gunpowder. Traditionally the devil was said to look like a collier.

**18 Enlinked** A 'link' was a torch for lighting travellers in dark streets.

**21 forcing** (1) physically violent, (2) stuffing, as of geese or capons in cooking.

**22 rein** (1) bridle, (2) kingship.

**24 as bootless** (1) with equal futility, (2) without loot.

**24 spend** expend, waste.

**25 spoil** pillaging and sacking the town. It was usual for the general commanding the attackers to release his soldiers to loot and pillage with the order to 'havoc'. See *JC* 3.1.273: 'Cry "Havoc!" and let slip the dogs of war.'

**26 precepts** writs of summons.

**26 Leviathan** a whale. The allusion is to the Leviathan in Job 41.1–3: 'No man is so fierce that dare stirre him up: who is able to stand before me? Or who hath geven me any thyng aforehand, that I may reward him againe? All thynges under heaven are myne. I wyll not keepe secret his great strength, his power, nor his comely proportion.'

**31 filthy** (1) stormy, (2) dirtying.

**31 clouds** i.e. of the storm and the smoke of battle.

Of heady murder, spoil and villainy.
If not, why, in a moment look to see
The blind and bloody soldier with foul hand
Defile the locks of your shrill-shrieking daughters,            35
Your fathers taken by the silver beards,
And their most reverend heads dashed to the walls,
Your naked infants spitted upon pikes
Whiles the mad mothers with their howls confused
Do break the clouds, as did the wives of Jewry                  40
At Herod's bloody-hunting slaughtermen.
What say you? Will you yield, and this avoid?
Or guilty in defence be thus destroyed?

*Enter* GOVERNOR [*above*]

GOVERNOR Our expectation hath this day an end.
The Dauphin, whom of succours we entreated,                     45
Returns us that his powers are yet not ready
To raise so great a siege. Therefore, great king,
We yield our town and lives to thy soft mercy.
Enter our gates, dispose of us and ours,
For we no longer are defensible.                                50

---

32 heady] F3; headly F2; headdy F2   35 Defile] *Rowe²;* Desire F   45 succours] F; succour Q   46 yet not] F; not yet
Q   50 defensible] F; defensive now Q

32 **heady** intoxicating.
33 **look** expect.
34 **blind** i.e. blind to reason.
35 **Defile** Rowe's emendation makes good sense.
The F text could be a long s/f wrong fount and
an l/r misreading. The 'foul hand' is more apt to
dirty than merely desire. There may also be a play
on thieves filing the other kind of locks, extended
with 'silver' in the next line.
35 **locks** (1) hair, (2) metal securing devices.
Chastity in *Ado* 4.1.198 is 'locked up', as with a
chastity belt.
38 **spitted** transfixed like roast pigs.
40 **break the clouds** (1) raise their howls to the
sky, (2) cause tears like a cloudburst.
41 **Herod** instigator of the Massacre of the Inno-
cents, described in Matthew 2.16–18: 'then Herod,
when he sawe that he was mocked of the wyse
men, was excedyng wroth, and sent foorth, and
slew all the chyldren that were in Bethlehem, and
in all the coastes, as many as were two yere olde, or

under, according to the tyme, which he had diligently searched out, of the wyse men. Then was
fulfylled that which was spoken of by Jeremie the
prophete, saying, In Rama was there a voyce hearde,
lamentation and great mourning, Rachel weping
for her children, and would not be comforted, for
they were not.'
43 **guilty . . . destroyed** i.e. be punished for
the crime of defending yourselves. Gentili was
unhappy over such actions. See Introduction, p. 23.
43 SD *above* Walter claims that the governor
could enter at stage level, but that would nullify
the subsequent exit below when Henry says 'Open
your gates'. The notation '*above*' signified the
balcony level over the central discovery-space in
the tiring house, which would have served as the
gates of the town. Capell's '*on the wall*' was based
on *3H6* 4.7.16 SD, where the Yorkist army is confronted by the Mayor of York '*on the Walls*'.
46 **Returns us** Gives us the reply.
46 **yet not** still not.

KING   Open your gates. Come, uncle Exeter,     [*Exit Governor above*]
        Go you and enter Harfleur. There remain
        And fortify it strongly 'gainst the French.
        Use mercy to them all. For us, dear uncle,
        The winter coming on, and sickness growing                    55
        Upon our soldiers, we will retire to Calais.
        Tonight in Harfleur will we be your guest,
        Tomorrow for the march are we addressed.

                              *Flourish, and enter the town*


**3.5**   *Enter* KATHERINE *and* [ALICE,] *an old gentlewoman*


KATHERINE   Alice, tu as été en Angleterre, et tu bien parles le
        langage.
ALICE   Un peu, madame.
KATHERINE   Je te prie, m'enseignez. Il faut que j'apprenne à
        parler. Comment appelez-vous la main en anglais?              5
ALICE   La main. Elle est appelée *de hand*.

---

54 all. For us, dear uncle, *Pope;* all for vs, deare Vncle. F    Act 3, Scene 5    3 Un] *Rowe; En* F    4 apprenne] F2; *apprend*
F   5 parler] F2; *parlen* F    5 Anglais] F (*Anglois*)    6 est] F (*&*)

**54 Use mercy** The town was sacked, according
to Holinshed.
**54 all. For us** Pope's emendation makes much
better sense than F's omission of the stop.
**56 retire to Calais** See 3.0.4 n.
**57 guest** Exeter must be his host, since he has
just given him command of Harfleur.
**58 SD** The trumpet-call here is standard for
the king's exit. The army marches in through the
central doorway or discovery-space in the tiring
house, below where the governor stood.

**Act 3, Scene 5**
**0 SD** In *Ado* and *AYLI* a tall and a short boy
played the chief women's parts. The same two, the
taller playing the young princess and the smaller
the old serving lady, may have been employed
for this scene. They offer a strong contrast to the
threats in the previous scene about shrill-shrieking
daughters and mad mothers. Possibly the two were
visualised as a pair of Frenchwomen representing
a normalisation of those extremes.
    **0 SD KATHERINE** No explicit indication is given

to the audience who the 'Madame' addressed by
'Alice' in line 3 might be. F names '*Katherine*' in
the entry direction, and '*Kath*' in the speech headings. The '*old gentlewoman*' of the entry direction is
'*Alice*' in the speech headings. Evidently the author
had the names in mind, but did not see much need
to tell the audience.
    **1–55** F sets the whole scene in italics. In this edi-
tion the usual form of italicising foreign words or
phrases has been maintained, but in reverse. For
modernisation and correction of the French, see
Introduction, pp. 68–9. The French is translated
in the footnotes.
    **1–2** 'Alice, you have been in England, and you
speak the language well.'
    **3** 'A little, madam.'
    **4–5** 'I beg you, teach me. I must learn to speak
it. How do you say hand in English?'
    **6** 'The hand. It is called *de hand*.'
    **6 est** F's recording of the French *est* is consis-
tently to use an ampersand, the Latin *et*.
    **6 de** Both French speakers use 'd' for English
'th'.

KATHERINE *De hand.* Et les doigts?

ALICE Les doigts, ma foi, j'ai oublié les doigts, mais je me
souviendrai les doigts. Je pense qu'ils sont appelés *de fingres.*
Oui, *de fingres.*                                                    10

KATHERINE La main, *de hand.* Les doigts, les *fingres.* Je pense que
je suis le bon écolier. J'ai gagné deux mots d'anglais vitement.
Comment appelez-vous les ongles?

ALICE Les ongles, nous les appelons *de nails.*

KATHERINE *De nails.* Écoutez! Dites-moi si je parle bien: *de hand, de*     15
*fingres,* et *de nails.*

ALICE C'est bien dit, madame. Il est fort bon anglais.

KATHERINE Dites-moi l'anglais pour le bras.

ALICE *De arm,* madame.

KATHERINE Et le coude.                                               20

ALICE *D'elbow.*

KATHERINE *D'elbow.* Je m'en fais la répétition de tous les mots que
vous m'avez appris dès à présent.

ALICE Il est trop difficile, madame, comme je pense.

KATHERINE Excusez-moi, Alice. Écoutez, *d'hand, de fingres, de*      25
*nails, d'arma, de bilbow.*

ALICE *D'elbow,* madame.

KATHERINE O Seigneur Dieu, je m'en oublié *d'elbow*! Comment
appelez-vous le col?

8 SH ALICE] *Theobald; Kath* F  9 souviendrai] F *(souemeray)*  9 sont] *Capell;* ont F  10 Oui] F *(ou)*  11 SH
KATHERINE] *Theobald; Alice* F  12 écolier] F *(escolier)*  14 nous] *Wilson; not in* F  19 arm] F *(Arme);* arma Q  20
le coude] F2; *de coudee* F  22 répétition] F (repeticio)

7 'De hand. And the fingers?'

8–10 'The fingers, my word, I've forgotten the
fingers, but I remember the fingers. I think they
are called *de fingres.* Yes, *de fingres.*'

11–13 'The hand, *de hand.* The fingers, *de
fingres.* I think I am a good pupil. I've learned two
words of English at once. What do you call the
nails?'

11 les Capell anglicises the F '*le*'. But neither
speaker is consistent in using the French or the
English article before each noun.

14 'The nails, we call them *de näils.*'

15–16 '*De näils.* Listen! Tell me if I speak
correctly: *de hand, de fingres,* and *de näils.*'

17 'That's well spoken, madam. It is very good
English.'

18 'Tell me the English for the arm.'

19 '*De arm,* madam.' Katherine subsequently

pronounces this word as *arma* (lines 26, 42, 52).
Q uses the same form here, but the F spelling indicates that Alice says it more accurately than her
mistress.

20 'And the elbow.'

21 '*D'elbow.*'

22–3 '*D'elbow.* I shall repeat all the words that
you have taught me so far.'

24 'It is too difficult, madam, I think.'

25–6 'Not so, Alice. Listen, *d'hand, de fingres,
de näils, d'arma, de bilbow.*' A bilbow was a short
sword, or alternatively a bar fastened to prisoners' legs. Drayton in *The Battaile of Agincourt*
(1627) writes of bilbows and foxes (see 4.4.8) being
sharpened in England ready for the invasion.

27 '*D'elbow,* madam.'

28–9 'Oh, good heavens, I forgot *d'elbow*! What
do you call the neck?'

ALICE *De nick*, madame.                                                          30

KATHERINE *De nick.* Et le menton?

ALICE *De chin.*

KATHERINE *De sin.* Le col, *de nick.* Le menton, *de sin.*

ALICE Oui. Sauf votre honneur, en vérité vous prononcez les mots
aussi droit que les natifs d'Angleterre.                                          35

KATHERINE Je ne doute point d'apprendre, par la grâce de Dieu,
et en peu de temps.

ALICE N'avez-vous pas déjà oublié ce que je vous ai enseigné?

KATHERINE Non, et je réciterai à vous promptement: *d'hand, de
fingre, de mailés* –                                                             40

ALICE *De nails*, madame.

KATHERINE *De nails, de arma, de ilbow* –

ALICE Sauf votre honneur, *de elbow.*

KATHERINE Ainsi dis-je. *D'elbow, de nick,* et *de sin.* Comment
appelez-vous les pieds et la robe?                                                45

ALICE *De foot*, madame, et *de count.*

KATHERINE *De foot* et *de count?* O Seigneur Dieu, ils sont les mots
de son mauvais, corruptible, gros et impudique, et non pour les
dames d'honneur d'user! Je ne voudrais prononcer ces mots

---

34 Sauf] *Rowe; Sans* F *; 37* en peu de temps] F *;* an pettie tanes, Ie parle milleur Q   40 *mailés –* ] F (*Maylees.*)   43
honneur] F (*honeus*)   44 dis-je] F (*de ie*)   45 robe] F (*roba*)   46 *De*] Q *; Le* F   47 ils sont] *Wilson; Il sont* F *; ce sont* F2

**30** '*De nick*, madam.' Both 'cul' and 'nick' were slang terms for the vulva, which leads up to Katherine's softer French sibilant for *chin* in her next word.

**31** '*De nick*. And the chin?'

**32** '*De chin.*'

**33** '*De sin.* The neck, *de nick*. The chin, *de sin.*'

**34–5** 'Yes. If it please your honour, you do indeed speak the words as accurately as the natives of England.'

**36–7** 'I have no doubt that I will learn, with God's grace, and very quickly.'

**38** 'Have you not already forgotten what I taught you?'

**39–40** 'No, and I'll recite it at once to you: *d'hand, de fingres, de mäilers*.' Possibly the mispronunciation of 'nails' is meant to sound like 'males'.

**41** '*De näils*, madam.'

**43** '*De näils, de arma, de ilbow* –' There is possibly a sexual pun here, similar to the 'bugle bow' of Q at 2.3.49.

**43** 'If it please your honour, *de elbow.*'

**44–5** 'That's what I said. *D'elbow, de nick, de sin.*
What do you call the feet and the dress?'

**46** '*De foot*, madam, and *de count*.' The French term Katherine hears is *foutre*, to fuck. Alice's attempt to say 'gown' comes out as French *con*, English 'cunt'. The F spelling, retained here, reflects Elizabethan pronunciation. John Harington has an epigram about a girl seduced by an earl which plays on the fact that he would not marry her and make her a countess: 'All Countesses in honour her surmount, / They have, she had, an honourable Count.' (Epigram 46, 'Of Lelia', *Letters and Epigrams*, ed. N. E. McClure, p. 269).

**46** *De* Alice's English is correct, and unlikely to slip back into French for the definite article, unlike Katherine. Q seems to have heard it correctly.

**47–53** '*De foot* and *de count?* Oh, good heavens, those are words that sound wicked, corrupting, and rude, and not for ladies of honour to use! I would not wish to pronounce such words in front of the lords of France for all the world! Tush! *De foot* and *de count*! None the less, I shall recite my whole lesson through once more: *de hand, de fingres, de näils, d'elbow, de nick, de sin, de foot,* the *count.*'

devant les seigneurs de France pour tout le monde! Foh! *De*          50
*foot* et *de count*! Néanmoins, je réciterai une autre fois ma leçon
ensemble: *de hand, de fingre, de nails, d'arma, d'elbow, de nick, de*
*sin, de foot*, le *count*.

ALICE Excellent, madame!

KATHERINE C'est assez pour une fois. Allons-nous à dîner.          55

                                              *Exeunt*


3.6 *Enter the King of* FRANCE, *the* DAUPHIN, *the* CONSTABLE
*of France, the Duke of* BOURBON, *and others*


FRENCH KING 'Tis certain he hath passed the River Somme.

CONSTABLE And if he be not fought withal, my lord,
    Let us not live in France. Let us quit all
    And give our vineyards to a barbarous people.

DAUPHIN *O Dieu vivant!* Shall a few sprays of us,          5
    The emptying of our father's luxury,
    Our scions, put in wild and savage stock,
    Spurt up so suddenly into the clouds
    And overlook their grafters?

---

51 Néanmoins] F (*neant moys*)  53 le *count*] F; de count Q, F3  55 SD *Exeunt*] *Exit* F  Act 3, Scene 6  0 SD BOURBON]
Q; *not in* F

**53 le** *count* The F version is a change from
the usual *de*. It may be an error, as F at line
46, but in this case it may serve to emphasise
Katherine's hesitation over pronouncing the words
'*de son mauvais*'.
    **54** 'Excellent, madam!'
    **55** 'That is enough for one turn. Let's go in to
dinner.'

**Act 3, Scene 6**
**0 SD BOURBON** For this scene Q introduces
Bourbon and gives him the speeches allocated in
F to Brittany. F lists Brittany from Holinshed but
omits him from the list of French nobles in 40–45,
where Bourbon is named. To give Bourbon a character before he takes over the Dauphin's lines at
Agincourt, he must speak in this scene.
    **1 Somme** A river on the plains halfway between
Harfleur and Calais, which are 170 miles or 270
kilometres apart.

**2 And if** This is probably an intensive, 'an if'.
    **2 withal** a relating term, carrying both the
preposition 'with' and 'as a consequence'.
    **5** *O Dieu vivant!* The Dauphin, the Consta-
ble, and Bourbon all start their speeches with
exclamatory phrases in French here and in Act 3,
Scene 8.
    **5–9** An extended image from family trees and
grafting plants.
    **5 sprays** sprigs, shoots. The English are all
taken to be descendants of the Norman French.
    **6 luxury** lust.
    **7 scions** grafted sprigs.
    **7 put in** grafted onto.
    **7 stock** parent plants.
    **8 Spurt** Sprout, shoot up.
    **9 overlook** (1) grow taller than, (2) dominate.
    **9 grafters** the trees from which the grafts were
taken.

BOURBON Normans, but bastard Normans, Norman bastards!                  10
  *Mort de ma vie*, if they march along
  Unfought withal, but I will sell my dukedom
  To buy a slobbery and a dirty farm
  In that nook-shotten isle of Albion.
CONSTABLE *Dieu de batailles*, where have they this mettle?              15
  Is not their climate foggy, raw and dull,
  On whom, as in despite, the sun looks pale,
  Killing their fruit with frowns? Can sodden water,
  A drench for sur-reined jades, their barley-broth,
  Decoct their cold blood to such valiant heat?                         20
  And shall our quick blood, spirited with wine,
  Seem frosty? Oh, for honour of our land
  Let us not hang like roping icicles
  Upon our houses' thatch whiles a more frosty people
  Sweat drops of gallant youth in our rich fields!                      25
  'Poor' may we call them, in their native lords!
DAUPHIN By faith and honour,
  Our madams mock at us and plainly say
  Our mettle is bred out, and they will give
  Their bodies to the lust of English youth                             30
  To new-store France with bastard warriors.

---

10 SH BOURBON] Q (*Bur.*), *Theobald; Brit.* F   11 *Mort de ma vie*] F (Mort du ma vie)*; Mordeu ma via* Q*; Mort Dieu! Ma vie! Wilson*   14 nook-shotten . . . Albion] F*; short nooke Ile of England* Q   26 'Poor' may we] *Keightley;* Poor we F*; Poor we may* F2*; Lest poor we Humphreys*

11 *Mort de ma vie* 'Death to my life.' The phrase is exclamatory, but does launch the sentence he goes on to speak.
13 **slobbery** wet and slimy (*OED* 1, citing this use). It is close to 'slubbered', meaning stained.
14 **nook-shotten** full of corners and 'angles'.
14 **Albion** An old name for England, Wales and Scotland. It is used twice in *2H6* and twice in *3H6*, once in a reference to Edward III as 'worthy Edward, king of Albion'. After James came to the English throne in 1603 Scotland's involvement made it a more problematic name. It does recur in a reference to ancient England in *Lear* 3.2.83.
16 **foggy . . . dull** Adjectives for unadventurous minds and weather. The underlying image is of 'humours'.
17 **as in despite** as if despising them.
18 **sodden water** boiled water, as in brewing beer.

19 **drench** dose or drink. See *1H4* 2.4.93.
19 **sur-reined jades** hard-ridden horses.
19 **barley-broth** beer. 'Broth', like 'drench', implies a health-giving function.
20 **Decoct** Warm up.
21 **quick** lively.
23 **roping** dangling like ropes. See 4.2.48, 'down-roping'.
25 **drops . . . youth** the blood of the young spilled in war. The whole speech contrasts the cold English weather and drink with the fiery French and finds it is the cold people who do the sweating.
26 **'Poor'** i.e. France's rich fields are owned by a people poor in their leadership.
26 **'Poor' may we** Keightley's reversal of the F2 insertion is more likely than Humphrey's invented 'Lest'. Eyeskip or an accidental omission by the F compositor would be more likely after the first word in the line.
29 **bred out** exhausted.

BOURBON They bid us to the English dancing-schools,
          And teach lavoltas high and swift corantos,
          Saying our grace is only in our heels,
          And that we are most lofty runaways.                    35
FRENCH KING Where is Montjoy the herald? Speed him hence,
          Let him greet England with our sharp defiance.
          Up, princes, and with spirit of honour edged
          More sharper than your swords hie to the field.
          Charles Delabret, High Constable of France,            40
          You Dukes of Orléans, Bourbon and of Berri,
          Alençon, Brabant, Bar and Burgundy,
          Jacques Châtillon, Rambures, Vaudemont,
          Beaumont, Grandpré, Roussi and Fauconbridge,
          Foix, Lestrelles, Boucicault and Charolais,            45
          High dukes, great princes, barons, lords and knights,
          For your great seats, now quit you of great shames.
          Bar Harry England that sweeps through our land
          With pennons painted in the blood of Harfleur.
          Rush on his host as doth the melted snow               50
          Upon the valleys, whose low vassal seat
          The Alps doth spit and void his rheum upon.
          Go down upon him. You have power enough,

32 SH BOURBON] Q (*Bur.*), *Theobald; Brit.* F    39 hie] F4; high F    40 Delabret] F (Delabreth)    42 Burgundy] F
(Burgonie)    43 Vaudemont] F (Vandemont)    44 Grandpré] F (Grand Pree)    45 Foix] *Capell;* Loys F    46 knights] *Pope*²
(*conj. Theobald*); kings F

33 **lavoltas . . . corantos** Two lively dance
steps, the first mainly high-leaping, the second
running.
34 **grace** (1) beauty, (2) rank.
35 **lofty** (1) high in rank, (2) high-leaping.
35 **runaways** (1) escaped horses, (2) fugitives
from battle.
36 **Montjoy** Actually a title for the royal herald
of the French, not a name. It was taken from
the French battle-cry, 'Montjoy St. Denis!' Quite
incidentally it was the name of Shakespeare's
Huguenot landlord in Cripplegate some time
before 1604, Christopher Mountjoy.
37 **sharp** (1) severe, keen, (2) damaging, as with
edged swords cited two lines below.
39 **hie** An archaic imperative. See *R2* 5.1.22,
*1H4* 4.4.1.
39 **field** i.e. battlefield.

40–5 These French names are taken largely from
Holinshed's list of those killed at Agincourt.
43 **Vaudemont** This is Holinshed's spelling. F
shows minim error.
47 **For** i.e. for the sake of.
47 **quit you** (1) get rid of, (2) acquit yourselves.
48 **Bar** (1) Stop, (2) Block his claim, a legal
term. See 1.2.12. The word recurs in 5.2.27.
49 **pennons** battle-flags, streamers used on
cavalry lances.
52 **void his rheum** empty his phlegm. This
image for avalanches has been compared to
Horace's burlesque (*Satires* 2.5.41), of a line
derided by Quintilian, 'Furius hibernas cana nive
conspuit Alpis'. This transfer of the burlesque,
which originally had Jupiter spitting snow onto the
Alps, is grandiloquent, but hardly a burlesque line
here.

And in a captive chariot into Rouen
Bring him our prisoner.
CONSTABLE                      This becomes the great.          55
Sorry am I his numbers are so few,
His soldiers sick, and famished in their march,
For I am sure when he shall see our army
He'll drop his heart into the sink of fear
And for achievement offer us his ransom.         60
FRENCH KING Therefore, Lord Constable, haste on Montjoy,
And let him say to England that we send
To know what willing ransom he will give.
Prince Dauphin, you shall stay with us in Rouen.
DAUPHIN Not so, I do beseech your majesty.            65
FRENCH KING Be patient, for you shall remain with us.
Now forth, Lord Constable and princes all,
And quickly bring us word of England's fall.

*Exeunt*


3.7 *Enter Captains, English and Welsh,* GOWER *and* LLEWELLYN

GOWER How now, Captain Llewellyn, come you from the bridge?
LLEWELLYN I assure you there is very excellent services committed
at the bridge.

---

60 for] F; fore *Taylor*

54 **a captive chariot** As in a Roman triumph
(the pronunciation of 'Rouen' was close to 'Rome').
Hall's and Holinshed's accounts of the French
preparations for Agincourt say that they prepared
a chariot to carry Henry captive in procession, a
prospect also mentioned in *Famous Victories*.

55 **becomes** is the appropriate action for.

59 **sink** Equivalent to the heart dropping into
the boots. 'Stomach' was both the source of
bravery, as in 4.3.35, and the 'sink' or cesspit of
the body, as in *Cor.* 1.1.105.

60 **for achievement** In heraldry 'achievement'
meant the full coat of arms with its outer adorn-
ments. By extension here it means battle honours.
The Constable says (1) that the only battle honour they will get will be Henry's ransom, (2) that
Henry will offer his ransom for (instead of) his own
honour. See Hulme, *Explorations*, pp. 289–91.

64–6 The French king's insistence is reported
by Holinshed, p. 552. In a scene reported fairly
roughly in Q, this exchange stands out clearly. See
Introduction, p. 65.

68 **fall** (1) of Henry in pride, (2) of the English
army in battle.

**Act 3, Scene 7**
0 SD Gower and Llewellyn must enter by
different doors, since they greet each other.

1 **the bridge** The cause of a skirmish on the
march to Calais. The bridge crossed the river
Ternoise, and Henry sent an advance guard to
secure it. In Holinshed the fight is described as
follows (p. 552): 'The king of England, hearing
that the Frenchmen approched, and that there was
an other river for him to passe with his armie by
a bridge, and doubting least if the same bridge
should be broken, it would be greatlie to his hinder-
ance, appointed certeine captains with their bands,
to go thither with all speed before him, and to
take possession thereof, and so to keepe it, till his
comming thither. Those that were sent, finding
the Frenchmen busie to break downe their bridge,
assailed them so vigorousile, that they discomfited
them, and tooke and slue them; and so the bridge

GOWER  Is the Duke of Exeter safe?

LLEWELLYN  The  Duke  of  Exeter  is  as  magnanimous  as     5
Agamemnon, and a man that I love and honour with my soul,
and my heart, and my duty, and my life, and my living, and my
uttermost power. He is not, God be praised and blessed, any
hurt in the woreld, but keeps the pridge most valiantly with
excellent discipline. There is an ancient lieutenant there at the     10
pridge. I think in my very conscience he is as valiant a man as
Mark Antony, and he is a man of no estimation in the world,
but I did see him do as gallant service.

GOWER  What do you call him?

LLEWELLYN  He is called Anchient Pistol.                              15

GOWER  I know him not.

*Enter* PISTOL

LLEWELLYN  Here is the man.

PISTOL  Captain, I thee beseech to do me favours. The Duke of
Exeter doth love thee well.

LLEWELLYN  Ay, I praise God, and I have merited some love at his     20
hands.

PISTOL  Bardolph, a soldier firm and sound of heart, and of buxom
valour, hath by cruel fate and giddy Fortune's furious fickle wheel,
that goddess blind that stands upon the rolling restless stone –

---

Act 3, Scene 7    7 life] Q; liue F    9 woreld] Q (worell); World F    10 ancient] F (aunchient); Ensigne Q    15 Anchient]
F (aunchient) ancient Q    22 and of] F; one of Q

was preserved till the king came, and passed the
river by the same with his whole armie.'

**4 Exeter** Holinshed notes that Exeter left Sir
John Fastolfe in charge at Harfleur, and joined the
king at Agincourt. Exeter was not involved at the
bridge over the Ternoise. He is presumably needed
here so that Pistol can ask Llewellyn to plead with
him for Bardolph's life.

**5–6 magnanimous as Agamemnon** as great-
minded as the leader of the Greeks at Troy. A pon-
derous mouthful for anyone with a Welsh accent.

**7 life** F's 'liue' may be another Welsh pronunciation, but the tendency towards unvoiced consonants makes it unlikely.

**9 woreld** Q's 'worell' seems a better indication
of the Welsh pronunciation than F, which spells
it 'orld' in Act 4, Scene 7. The F spelling, however, which may be another d/e misreading, calls
for something in between the two.

**10 ancient lieutenant** i.e. sub-lieutenant. See
Note on the Text, p. 70. For the spelling of 'ancient'

see note to 3.3.22. Llewellyn evidently pronounced
it in a non-standard way, judging by the F spelling
in Act 4, Scene 7. Gower in 5.1.63 uses 'ancient'
in its normal spelling, though we should note *Ado*
2.1.55–6, where Beatrice's 'state and aunchentry'
in F implies a non-Welsh pronunciation that uses a
long 'a' sound.

**13 as** Llewellyn compares Pistol to Mark
Antony, which indicates that he does not recall his
encounter with Pistol at 3.2.23.

**18 thee beseech** Pistol's inversions are all
poetic.

**22 buxom** vigorous, an unorthodox use of the
adjective.

**23–4 Fortune's . . . blind** It was proverbial
that Fortune is both fickle and blind (Dent F604,
606).

**24 that . . . stone** Pistol mixes two icons. Blind
Fortune turned the wheel of fortune, but it was the
victims who had to balance on the rolling stone.
Llewellyn's correction is pedantic but accurate.

LLEWELLYN By your patience, Anchient Pistol, Fortune is painted 25
plind, with a muffler afore her eyes to signify to you that
Fortune is plind. And she is painted also with a wheel to signify
to you, which is the moral of it, that she is turning and
inconstant and mutability and variation. And her foot, look you,
is fixed upon a spherical stone, which rolls and rolls and rolls. 30
In good truth, the poet makes a most excellent description of it.
Fortune is an excellent moral.

PISTOL Fortune is Bardolph's foe, and frowns on him. For he hath
stolen a pax, and hangèd must a be. A damnèd death! Let
gallows gape for dog, let man go free, and let not hemp his 35
windpipe suffocate! But Exeter hath given the doom of death,
for pax of little price. Therefore go speak. The duke will hear
thy voice, and let not Bardolph's vital thread be cut with edge
of penny cord and vile reproach! Speak, captain, for his life,
and I will thee requite. 40

LLEWELLYN Anchient Pistol, I do partly understand your
meaning.

PISTOL Why then, rejoice therefore.

LLEWELLYN Certainly, anchient, it is not a thing to rejoice at. For
if, look you, he were my brother I would desire the duke to use 45
his good pleasure and put him to execution. For discipline
ought to be used.

26 plind] Q (plinde); blinde F  26 her] Q; his F  27 plind] Q; blinde F  37 little] F; pettie Q

26 her F's reading may be a deliberate confusion, though the subsequent 'she' makes it unlikely.
32 moral emblem, symbol for a moral lesson.
33 Fortune . . . foe The mournful ballad 'Fortune my foe, why dost thou frown on me' was well known in Shakespeare's time. At the end of *The Knight of the Burning Pestle* (1607) it is sung as a punishment by the chief gull.
34 pax Holinshed (p. 552) mentions Henry executing one soldier for stealing a 'pix' from a church: 'Yet in this great necessitie, the poore people of the countrie were not spoiled, nor anie thing taken of them without paiment, nor anie outrage or offense doone by the Englishmen, except one, which was, that a souldier tooke a pix out of a church, for which he was apprehended, and the king not once remooved till the box was restored, and the offendor strangled.' A 'pix' was a box of communion wafers, a 'pax' a tablet depicting the crucifixion, kissed by the communicants. The change makes Bardolph steal a less valuable and less sacred object, but it is equally likely to have

been made to play on the Latin 'pax' (peace).
34 damnèd Pistol's verse-like emphasis, standard in the editions which versify his speeches, draws attention to the sacrilege that Bardolph has committed.
35 dog Dogs and cats were hanged for wrongdoing; hence 'hangdog' looks.
35 hemp i.e. rope.
37 little Q's adjective intensifies the plosive alliteration of Pistol's phrase.
38 vital thread At death, the Fates with their shears cut the thread of each person's life.
38-9 edge . . . cord Not the shears of Atropos but the hangman's cheap rope.
41-2 your meaning Principally Llewellyn indicates that he understands only in part Pistol's high style of language. But he may also be acknowledging the offer of a bribe.
43 therefore i.e. for that. The phrase is from Marlowe's *Massacre at Paris*, 1078, which Pistol first echoes in *2H4* 5.3.89. It was parodied by Jonson in *Poetaster* 3.4.256.

PISTOL  Die and be damned, and *fico* for thy friendship!
LLEWELLYN  It is well.
PISTOL  The fig of Spain!                              *Exit Pistol*    50
LLEWELLYN  Very good.
GOWER  Why, this is an arrant counterfeit rascal. I remember him now:
    a bawd, a cutpurse.
LLEWELLYN  I'll assure you, a uttered as prave words at the pridge
    as you shall see in a summer's day. But it is very well. What he    55
    has spoke to me, that is well, I warrant you, when time is serve.
GOWER  Why, 'tis a gull, a fool, a rogue, that now and then goes to
    the wars, to grace himself at his return into London under the
    form of a soldier. And such fellows are perfect in the great
    commanders' names, and they will learn you by rote where          60
    services were done – at such and such a sconce, at such a
    breach, at such a convoy; who came off bravely, who was shot,
    who disgraced, what terms the enemy stood on. And this they
    con perfectly in the phrase of war, which they trick up with
    new-tuned oaths. And what a beard of the general's cut and a       65
    horrid suit of the camp will do among foaming bottles and
    ale-washed wits is wonderful to be thought on. But you must
    learn to know such slanders of the age, or else you may be
    marvellously mistook.
LLEWELLYN  I tell you what, Captain Gower: I do perceive he is        70
    not the man that he would gladly make show to the woreld he is.
    If I find a hole in his coat I will tell him my mind.
                      [*A drum within*]

48 *fico*] F (*Figo*); figa Q    50 Spain!] *Spaine* within thy Iawe. / *Flew*. That is very well. / *Pist*. I say the fig within thy
bowels and thy durty maw. / *Exit Pistoll*. / *Flew*. Captain *Gour*, cannot you hear it lighten & thunder? Q    54 prave] F
(praue)    54 pridge] F (sute); shout Q    66 suit] F (sute); shout Q    71 woreld] F (World)

48 *fico* Dent cites 'a fig for him' as a proverbial
saying (F210). It also appears in *Wiv.* 1.3.20, *2H6*
2.3.64, and elsewhere. Usually it was accompanied
by an obscene gesture with the thumb.
50 The . . . Spain! Pistol's phrase is a variation
on the familiar 'turd in your teeth!' Q's extension
of this phrase, 'the figge of *Spaine* within thy jawe',
is more exactly equivalent and creates a rhyme
with 'thy durty maw'. It neatly elaborates Pistol's
exit line, but it is only one of many such extensions of the comic catchphrases, none of which are
authorial.
55 you . . . day Proverbial (Dent s967).
56 when . . . serve The leek which Llewellyn
forces Pistol to eat in Act 5, Scene 1 is a response
to Pistol's fig.
61 sconce   fortification   in   the   form   of
earthworks.

62 convoy military escort.
63 terms conditions for surrender.
64 con study, memorise.
64 trick up dress misleadingly.
65 beard . . . cut The Essex expedition to Cadiz
in 1596 created a fashion for 'Cadiz beards', square
instead of the usual pointed shape, in imitation of
Essex.
66 horrid . . . camp campaign gear. 'Horrid'
meant coarse, and possibly covered in blood; 'suit'
was homonymic for (1) clothes, (2) a shout, and (3)
shooting. The 'camp' was the military base in the
field.
72 a hole . . . coat Proverbial (Tilley H522).
72 SD *A drum within* Another stage direction
to be inferred from the context. Since the soldiers
are on foot, and the stage direction when the king
enters calls for a drum, it is a more likely warning

Hark you, the king is coming, and I must speak with him from the pridge.

*Drum and colours. Enter the* KING [,GLOUCESTER] *and his poor soldiers*

LLEWELLYN  God pless your majesty.                                    75
KING  How now, Llewellyn? Camest thou from the bridge?
LLEWELLYN  Ay, so please your majesty. The Duke of Exeter has very gallantly maintained the pridge. The French is gone off, look you, and there is gallant and most prave passages. Marry, th'athversary was have possession of the pridge, but he is   80 enforced to retire, and the Duke of Exeter is master of the pridge. I can tell your majesty, the duke is a prave man.
KING  What men have you lost, Llewellyn?
LLEWELLYN  The perdition of th'athversary hath been very great, reasonable great. Marry, for my part I think the duke hath lost   85 never a man, but one that is like to be executed for robbing a church, one Bardolph, if your majesty know the man. His face is all bubuckles and whelks, and knobs, and flames o'fire, and his lips blows at his nose, and it is like a coal of fire, sometimes plue and sometimes red. But his nose is executed and his fire's   90 out.
KING  We would have all such offenders so cut off, and we give express charge that in our marches through the country there be nothing compelled from the villages, nothing taken but paid

---

76 Camest] F (cam'st)*; come* Q*; com'st *Taylor   84 athversary] F (athuersarie)   88 flames o'fire] F (flames a fire)   92 we give] F*; we here give* Q

instrument here than a trumpet. See 3.0.33 SD, note.
   73 **from** about the fight at.
   74 SD *colours* banners, heading the march by the army.
   74 SD GLOUCESTER Gloucester speaks in the scene, but no other lord. The F stage direction emphasises the bedraggled state of the soldiers, so they cannot include the whole '*train*' of 3.4.0. It is now an army on the move, not an armoured besieging force.
   79 **passages** i.e. of arms, fighting.
   84 **perdition** sending to hell, losses.
   85–91 **Marry . . . out** Pistol had asked Llewellyn to intercede with the duke, not the king. In any case, Llewellyn makes no plea for him here.
   87 **if . . . man** Henry speaks to Bardolph at *1H4*

2.4.246 and in *2H4* Act 2, Scene 2. Llewellyn asks his question innocently. Most actors of the part make the most of the opportunity for showing the constraints on Henry's capacity to be merciful. In Holinshed the incident of the soldier being strangled for stealing a pix, set in a paragraph about Henry's 'lenity' (line 95), precedes the account of the battle for the Ternoise bridge which Llewellyn reports on at the beginning of the scene.
   88 **bubuckles** A portmanteau word, combining 'bubo' and 'carbuncle', boil-like swellings.
   88 **whelks** pimples.
   90 **his . . . executed** The victim's nose was slit. Bardolph has not yet been executed, so Llewellyn may only mean that his shining nose has gone out metaphorically.
   92–6 **We . . . language** See line 34, note.

for, none of the French upbraided or abused in disdainful          95
language. For when lenity and cruelty play for a kingdom, the
gentler gamester is the soonest winner.

*Tucket. Enter* MONTJOY

MONTJOY You know me by my habit.
KING Well then, I know thee. What shall I know of thee?
MONTJOY My master's mind.                                         100
KING Unfold it.
MONTJOY Thus says my king: 'Say thou to Harry of England,
though we seemed dead, we did but sleep. Advantage is a
better soldier than rashness. Tell him, we could have rebuked
him at Harfleur, but that we thought not good to bruise an      105
injury till it were full ripe. Now we speak upon our cue, and our
voice is imperial. England shall repent his folly, see his
weakness and admire our sufferance. Bid him therefore
consider of his ransom, which must proportion the losses we
have borne, the subjects we have lost, the disgrace we have     110
digested, which in weight to re-answer, his pettiness would
bow under. For our losses, his exchequer is too poor. For
th'effusion of our blood, the muster of his kingdom too faint a
number. And for our disgrace, his own person kneeling at our
feet but a weak and worthless satisfaction. To this add defiance,   115
and tell him for conclusion, he hath betrayed his followers,
whose condemnation is pronounced.' So far my king and
master, so much my office.

96 lenity] Q; leiuty F   106 cue] F (Q); kue Q

96 **lenity** F's spelling is a minim error, or a wrong fount or reversed letter. In this context of firm treatment of wrongdoers, it transfers the mercy that Pistol asks for Bardolph to the French peasants and creates an odd echo to Pistol's earlier plea to Llewellyn not to beat him, at 3.2.22.
96 **play** gamble, dice.
97 SD **Tucket** A trumpet-call announcing an arrival, not the same sound as the royal '*flourish*'. Derived from the Italian *toccata*, this is one of seven such calls altogether in Shakespeare's plays, counting the 'tucket sonance' at 4.2.35.
98 **habit** dress. Heralds wore a tabard or surcoat emblazoned with the arms of the authority they spoke for. This curt address is far less courteous than the speech of the French ambassador in Act 1, Scene 2. Henry's own equally curt reply responds to this undiplomatic tone. The short lines signal the overt hostility and arrogance in Montjoy

here which will intensify his subsequent humiliation at 4.7.57.
103 **Advantage** A superior position for making an attack.
105–6 **bruise an injury** squeeze an abscess.
106 **speak . . . cue** i.e. like an actor. It was a proverbial saying (C898.12), repeated in *Every Man Out of his Humour* 2.4.22.
107 **England** i.e. Henry.
108 **sufferance** restraint, forbearance.
112 **bow under** i.e., he is too petty to carry the weight, and would have to humble himself.
113 **muster** roll-call of soldiers (or all men).
115 **satisfaction** payment, compensation.
116–17 **betrayed . . . pronounced** The personal responsibility of the king for the fate of his subjects in his battles is debated in Act 4, Scene 1. Here there is an echo of the followers who betrayed Henry in Act 2, Scene 2.
118 **office** duty as herald.

KING  What is thy name? I know thy quality.
MONTJOY  Montjoy.                                                              120
KING    Thou dost thy office fairly. Turn thee back
        And tell thy king I do not seek him now,
        But could be willing to march on to Calais
        Without impeachment. For to say the sooth,
        Though 'tis no wisdom to confess so much                               125
        Unto an enemy of craft and vantage,
        My people are with sickness much enfeebled,
        My numbers lessened, and those few I have
        Almost no better than so many French,
        Who when they were in health, I tell thee, herald,                     130
        I thought upon one pair of English legs
        Did march three Frenchmen. Yet forgive me, God,
        That I do brag thus. This your air of France
        Hath blown that vice in me. I must repent.
        Go therefore, tell thy master here I am.                               135
        My ransom is this frail and worthless trunk,
        My army but a weak and sickly guard.
        Yet, God before, tell him we will come on
        Though France himself and such another neighbour
        Stand in our way. There's for thy labour, Montjoy.                     140
        Go, bid thy master well advise himself.
        If we may pass, we will. If we be hindered,
        We shall your tawny ground with your red blood
        Discolour. And so, Montjoy, fare you well.

**119 quality** (1) profession, (2) ability.

**124 impeachment** (1) hindrance, (2) being brought to trial.

**124 say the sooth** Proverbial (Dent *PLED* SS13.01).

**126 craft and vantage** resource and superior strength. 'Vantage' echoes Montjoy's 'advantage' at line 102.

**127–9** In Holinshed Henry makes no such admission. Here it softens the boast that follows.

**131–2 one . . . Frenchmen** Proverbial: 'One English can beat three French' (Dent E155).

**133 air** French boastfulness was also proverbial. This word, though, points specifically at F's Dauphin, about to be shown as a braggart in the next scene, as the 'heir' of France.

**136 trunk** (1) torso, corpse, (2) container for treasure.

**138 God before** See 1.2.307 n.

**139 France . . . neighbour** The king of France and another neighbour like him. There is a proverb behind this, brought out in Henry's joke at 4.1.6.

**140 There's . . . labour** According to Holinshed, Henry gave the French herald 'a princelie reward' (p. 552). Here it sounds more like a patronising wage hand-out, echoing the biblical proverb 'the labourer is worthy of his reward' (Luke 10.7, Bishops' Bible). The Geneva Bible translated the last word as 'wages', the Authorised Version of 1611 as 'hire'.

**141–4 Go . . . Discolour** Holinshed, p. 552: 'yet I wish not anie of you so unadvised, as to be the occasion that I die your tawnie ground with your red bloud'.

The sum of all our answer is but this:                       145
We would not seek a battle as we are,
Nor as we are we say we will not shun it.
So tell your master.
MONTJOY I shall deliver so. Thanks to your highness.        [*Exit*]
GLOUCESTER I hope they will not come upon us now.            150
KING  We are in God's hand, brother, not in theirs.
         March to the bridge. It now draws toward night.
         Beyond the river we'll encamp ourselves,
         And on tomorrow. Bid them march away.

                                                    *Exeunt*


3.8 *Enter the* CONSTABLE *of France, the Lord* RAMBURES,
ORLÉANS, BOURBON, *with others*


CONSTABLE Tut, I have the best armour of the world! Would it
    were day.
ORLÉANS You have an excellent armour, but let my horse have his
    due.
CONSTABLE It is the best horse of Europe.                    5
ORLÉANS Will it never be morning?
BOURBON My lord of Orléans, and my lord High Constable, you
    talk of horse and armour?
ORLÉANS You are as well provided of both as any prince in the
    world.                                                   10

---

154 on tomorrow. Bid] *Jackson;* on to morrow bid F, Q   Act 3, Scene 8   0 SD BOURBON] *Taylor;* Dolphin F   7 SH
BOURBON] Q (*Burb.*); Dolphin F

146–7 We . . . shun it Holinshed, p. 552, (immediately before the preceding quotation): 'I will not
seeke your maister at this time; but if he or his
seeke me, I will meet with them God willing.'
150 SH GLOUCESTER Gloucester may be
required to accompany Henry here because
Exeter's presence would have complicated the con-
versation with Llewellyn after Pistol's request to
Llewellyn to intercede with him for Bardolph's life.
But it may well be that a 'brother' is more useful
here than an 'uncle', in preparation for the 'band
of brothers' speech in Act 4, Scene 3.
154 on tomorrow. Bid Neither F nor Q makes
sense here. The context indicates that they are to
cross the captured bridge before nightfall, camp
there, and resume the march the next day. The

soldiers marched on with drum and colours at
the beginning of the scene. Now they march off.
Jackson's conjecture makes the best sense.

Act 3, Scene 8
0 SD The substitution of Bourbon for F's
'*Dolphin*' here is discussed in the Textual Analysis, pp. 231–3. Q specifies '*the foure French lords*',
including in the SH a '*Gebon*' who is not otherwise
identifiable.
1–2 Would . . . day The Constable by speaking
first sets himself out as the leader of the French
forces. He also indicates that it is a night scene,
before the battle.
3–4 my . . . due An allusion to the saying 'Give
everyone his due' (Dent D364).

BOURBON What a long night is this! I will not change my horse
with any that treads but on four pasterns. *Ch'ha!* He bounds
from the earth as if his entrails were hairs – *le cheval volant*, the
Pegasus, *qui a les narines de feu*! When I bestride him I soar, I
am a hawk! He trots the air. The earth sings when he touches          15
it. The basest horn of his hoof is more musical than the pipe of
Hermes.

ORLÉANS He's of the colour of the nutmeg.

BOURBON And of the heat of the ginger. It is a beast for Perseus.
He is pure air and fire, and the dull elements of earth and          20
water never appear in him but only in patient stillness while his
rider mounts him. He is indeed a horse, and all other jades you
may call beasts.

CONSTABLE Indeed, my lord, it is a most absolute and excellent
horse.                                                                25

BOURBON It is the prince of palfreys. His neigh is like the bidding
of a monarch, and his countenance enforces homage.

ORLÉANS No more, cousin.

BOURBON Nay, the man hath no wit that cannot from the rising of
the lark to the lodging of the lamb vary deserved praise on my       30
palfrey. It is a theme as fluent as the sea. Turn the sands into

---

12 pasterns] F2; postures F   12 Ch'ha!] F; Ça, ha! *Theobald;* ha, ha *Capell;* ah ha *Taylor*   14 qui a] *Capell;* ches F; chez
*Theobald*

---

**12 pasterns** The foot of a horse, between the
fetlock and the hoof.

**13 hairs** light-weight threads, as used to make
French tennis balls. There may also be a pun on
leaping hares.

**14 Pegasus** The flying horse (*cheval volant*)
of Greek mythology, thought to be ridden by
Perseus. When Perseus cut off the Medusa's head,
Pegasus was born from her blood. His hoof made
Hippocrene, the fountain of the Muses, emerge
on Mount Helicon. See T. W. Baldwin, 'Perseus
purloins Pegasus', *PQ* 20 (1941), 361–70. In *1H4*
4.1.108–10 Prince Hal mounted for battle is said to
ride a fiery Pegasus.

**14 qui a . . . feu** 'which has nostrils of fire'.

**16 musical** Developing a pun on 'horn' as a
hoof and as a hunting-horn.

**17 Hermes** The Greek god who invented the
lyre and the reed pipe.

**18 nutmeg** Since the colour of horses was
commonly related to their temperaments, and
since nutmeg is a mid-brown colour, Orléans
is possibly being sarcastic. But it is Orléans

who defends the speaker after he leaves, at lines
82–111. Possibly this speech should have been the
Constable's.

**19 Perseus** See note to line 14. The Bourbon
arms included a winged stag, emblazoned with the
word ESPERANCE.

**20 air and fire** The two elements that mounted.
The other two, earth and water, descended.

**25 horse** A response to Bourbon calling all
others beasts.

**26 palfreys** A word used for a saddle-horse
rather than a war-horse, and usually of the horses
ridden by ladies. At line 40 it is a 'courser', the
correct name for a war-horse.

**26 neigh** Also 'nay', a negation, as in Orléans'
next speech.

**29–30 rising . . . lamb** A familiar saying (Dent
B186).

**30 lodging** bedding-down.

**30 vary** speak variations on a theme – a basic
exercise in oratory.

**31 fluent** (1) flowing, (2) eloquent, infinitely
varied.

eloquent tongues and my horse is argument for them all. 'Tis a subject for a sovereign to reason on, and for a sovereign's sovereign to ride on, and for the world, familiar to us and unknown, to lay apart their particular functions and wonder at him. I once writ a sonnet in his praise, and began thus: 'Wonder of nature! . . .'			35

ORLÉANS I have heard a sonnet begin so to one's mistress.

BOURBON Then did they imitate that which I composed to my courser, for my horse is my mistress.			40

ORLÉANS Your mistress bears well.

BOURBON Me well, which is the prescript praise and perfection of a good and particular mistress.

CONSTABLE Nay, for methought yesterday your mistress shrewdly shook your back.			45

BOURBON So perhaps did yours.

CONSTABLE Mine was not bridled.

BOURBON Oh, then belike she was old and gentle, and you rode like a kern of Ireland, your French hose off, and in your strait strossers.			50

CONSTABLE You have good judgement in horsemanship.

BOURBON Be warned by me, then. They that ride so and ride not warily fall into foul bogs. I had rather have my horse to my mistress.

CONSTABLE I had as lief have my mistress a jade.			55

BOURBON I tell thee, Constable, my mistress wears his own hair.

CONSTABLE I could make as true a boast as that, if I had a sow to my mistress.

42 prescript praise] F; prescribed praise *Taylor*   55 lief] F (liue)

**32 argument** subject-matter.

**33 subject** (1) theme, (2) underling. The two meanings are picked up in sequence in the next two clauses beginning 'for'.

**35 particular** personal, individual.

**35 wonder at** marvel at, be overwhelmed by.

**41 bears** (1) breeds children, (2) carries her rider.

**42 prescript** prescribed. *OED* cites 'prescript formes' from 1586. Taylor modernises.

**44 shrewdly** sharply, shrewishly.

**47 mistress** i.e. my mistress was a woman, not a horse or a shrew. Shrewish women were sometimes made to wear bridles.

**48 old and gentle** i.e. (1) as a mistress, (2) as a horse.

**49–50 like a . . . strossers** like Irish foot-soldiers, who went bare-legged, like Bourbon with his mistress, or in tight trousers (strossers) instead of French leggings. *R2* refers to 'those rough rug-headed kerns' at 2.1.156. In *Oldcastle* 2672 an Irish murderer asks to be executed in his own clothes, including 'my strouces there'. See Illustration 7, p. 38 above.

**51 horsemanship** (1) managing horses, (2) managing whores.

**53 foul bogs** As in Ireland, and in foul women.

**55 jade** (1) inferior horse, (2) inferior woman.

**56 his own hair** Implying that the Constable's mistress wears a wig because she has lost her own hair through venereal disease.

**57 sow** Dent cites the proverbial comparison 'as meet as a sow to bear a saddle' (s672).

BOURBON 'Le chien est retourné à son propre vomissement, et la truie lavée au bourbier.' Thou makest use of anything.　　60

CONSTABLE Yet do I not use my horse for my mistress, or any such proverb so little kin to the purpose.

RAMBURES My lord Constable, the armour that I saw in your tent tonight, are those stars or suns upon it?

CONSTABLE Stars, my lord.　　65

BOURBON Some of them will fall tomorrow, I hope.

CONSTABLE And yet my sky shall not want.

BOURBON That may be, for you bear a many superfluously, and 'twere more honour some were away.

CONSTABLE Even as your horse bears your praises, who would　70 trot as well were some of your brags dismounted.

BOURBON Would I were able to load him with his desert. Will it never be day? I will trot tomorrow a mile, and my way shall be paved with English faces.

CONSTABLE I will not say so, for fear I should be faced out of my　75 way. But I would it were morning, for I would fain be about the ears of the English.

RAMBURES Who will go to hazard with me for twenty prisoners?

CONSTABLE You must first go yourself to hazard, ere you have them.　　80

BOURBON 'Tis midnight. I'll go arm myself.　　　　*Exit*

ORLÉANS The Duke of Bourbon longs for morning.

RAMBURES He longs to eat the English.

CONSTABLE I think he will eat all he kills.

ORLÉANS By the white hand of my lady, he's a gallant prince.　85

CONSTABLE Swear by her foot, that she may tread out the oath.

59 *vomissement*] F (vemissement)　59 *et la truie*] *Rowe*; est la leuye F　82 Duke of Bourbon] Q; Dolphin F

59–60 'Le chien . . . bourbier' A proverb (D458), here quoted from the Huguenot Bible, 2 Pet. 2.22. It is in Huguenot Bibles printed in 1540, 1551, and 1556, though it was altered in subsequent editions by the addition of a second *est retourné* for the sow. The version in the Bishops' Bible is 'The dogge is tourned to his owne vomite againe, and the sowe that was washed is turned againe to her wallowynge in the myre.' It was proverbial enough to be cited in the 1587 Holinshed *Chronicle of Ireland* (p. 133).
61 use i.e. sexually.
63–4 armour . . . stars A miniature by Nicholas Hilliard, in the National Maritime Museum, shows the Earl of Cumberland, the Queen's Champion, wearing armour covered with stars or suns. See Illustration 16, p. 219.
67 want be deficient.
72 his desert what he deserves.
75–6 faced . . . way (1) ashamed, (2) turned away.
78 go to hazard make a bet.
79 to hazard into danger.
84 eat . . . kills proverbial (Dent A192.2). Beatrice makes a similar jibe about Benedict in *Ado* 1.1.31–3.
86 tread . . . oath i.e. squash it. The sexual innuendo in treading (copulation) is also present, starting with the 'foot' that shocks Katherine at 3.5.46.

ORLÉANS He is simply the most active gentleman of France.

CONSTABLE Doing is activity, and he will still be doing.

ORLÉANS He never did harm that I heard of.

CONSTABLE Nor will do none tomorrow. He will keep that good name      90
still.

ORLÉANS I know him to be valiant.

CONSTABLE I was told that, by one that knows him better than
you.

ORLÉANS What's he?                                                    95

CONSTABLE Marry, he told me so himself, and he said he cared
not who knew it.

ORLÉANS He needs not, it is no hidden virtue in him.

CONSTABLE By my faith, sir, but it is. Never anybody saw it but
his lackey. 'Tis a hooded valour, and when it appears it will      100
bate.

ORLÉANS Ill will never said well.

CONSTABLE I will cap that proverb with 'There is flattery in
friendship.'

ORLÉANS And I will take up that with 'Give the devil his due.'       105

CONSTABLE Well placed. There stands your friend for the devil.
Have at the very eye of that proverb with 'A pox of the devil'.

ORLÉANS You are the better at proverbs, by how much 'a fool's
bolt is soon shot.'

CONSTABLE You have shot over.                                        110

ORLÉANS 'Tis not the first time you were overshot.

*Enter a* MESSENGER

MESSENGER My lord High Constable, the English lie within
fifteen hundred paces of your tents.

CONSTABLE Who hath measured the ground?

MESSENGER The lord Grandpré.

---

**88 Doing** Copulating.

**100–1 hooded . . . bate** An image from
falconry. Hawks were hooded until released to start
hunting, when the hawk would 'bate' or flap its
wings. Here it also means diminish.

**102 Ill . . . well** A straight proverb (Dent 141).
It launches the game of swapping proverbs, 103–
11. Such games appear in several plays.

**103 flattery** The usual proverb (Dent F349.1)
runs, 'there is falshood in friendship'. Shakespeare
invariably uses 'flattery' to mean deception.

**105 Give . . . due** Tilley D273.

**106 Well placed** i.e. like an arrow shot at a

target. Bourbon is like the devil.

**107 A pox . . . devil** More a curse than a
proverb, but accepted by Dent *PLED* P536.11.

**108–9 a fool's . . . shot** Dent F515, picking up
the archery reference from line 106.

**110 shot over** missed the target.

**111 overshot** (1) mistaken, (2) drunk. The same
joke appears in *LLL* 1.1.142 and 4.3.158.

**112 fifteen hundred** Holinshed says 250 paces.

**112 Grandpré** The name is from Holinshed,
though not from this context. Meaning 'large field',
it appears in the list of French nobles given by the
king at 3.6.44.

CONSTABLE A valiant and most expert gentleman. Would it were day! Alas, poor Harry of England! He longs not for the dawning as we do.

ORLÉANS What a wretched and peevish fellow is this king of England, to mope with his fat-brained followers so far out of his knowledge.

CONSTABLE If the English had any apprehension they would run away.

ORLÉANS That they lack, for if their heads had any intellectual armour they could never wear such heavy headpieces.

RAMBURES That island of England breeds very valiant creatures. Their mastiffs are of unmatchable courage.

ORLÉANS Foolish curs, that run winking into the mouth of a Russian bear and have their heads crushed like rotten apples. You may as well say that's a valiant flea that dare eat his breakfast on the lip of a lion.

CONSTABLE Just, just. And the men do sympathise with the mastiffs in robustious and rough coming on, leaving their wits with their wives. And then, give them great meals of beef and iron and steel, they will eat like wolves and fight like devils.

ORLÉANS Ay, but these English are shrewdly out of beef.

CONSTABLE Then shall we find tomorrow they have only stomachs to eat and none to fight. Now is it time to arm. Come, shall we about it?

ORLÉANS It is now two o'clock. But let me see, by ten
    We shall have each a hundred Englishmen!

*Exeunt*

112 shrewdly] F (shrowdly)

112 **mope** blunder aimlessly.

112 **apprehension** (1) good sense, understanding, (2) fear.

112 **mastiffs** The dog image is taken from Harrison's 'Description' in Holinshed's *Chronicles*, Volume I, p. 230: 'The mastiffe, tie dog, or banddog, so called bicause manie of them are tied up in chaines and strong bonds, in the daie time, for dooing hurt abroad, which is an huge dog, stubborne, ouglie, eager, burthensome of bodie (& therefore but of little swiftnesse) terrible and fearful to behold, and oftentimes more fierce and fell than anie Archadian or Corsican cur. Our Englishmen to the intent that these dogs may be more cruell and fierce, assist nature with some art, use and custome. For although this kind of dog be capable of courage, violent, valiant, stout and bold: yet will they increase these their stomachs by teaching them to bait the beare, the bull, the lion, and other such like cruell and bloudie beasts (either brought over or kept up at home, for the same purpose) without anie collar to defend their throats.' For the consistent application of dog images to soldiers through the play, see Introduction, p. 13.

112 **winking** with their eyes closed.

112 **sympathise with** match, resemble in spirit.

112 **give** i.e. if you give.

112 **shrewdly** F's spelling suggests a pun on death.

112 **stomachs** (1) appetites, (2) courage.

112 **Now . . . arm** The Constable makes the point that Bourbon went off to arm fifty lines or two hours too soon.

**4.0** [*Enter* CHORUS]

CHORUS   Now entertain conjecture of a time
                  When creeping murmur and the poring dark
                  Fills the wide vessel of the universe.
                  From camp to camp, through the foul womb of night,
                  The hum of either army stilly sounds,                                    5
                  That the fixed sentinels almost receive
                  The secret whispers of each other's watch.
                  Fire answers fire, and through their paly flames
                  Each battle sees the other's umbered face.
                  Steed threatens steed, in high and boastful neighs,              10
                  Piercing the night's dull ear. And from the tents
                  The armourers accomplishing the knights
                  With busy hammers closing rivets up
                  Give dreadful note of preparation.
                  The country cocks do crow, the clocks do toll,                    15
                  And the third hour of drowsy morning name.
                  Proud of their numbers and secure in soul
                  The confident and over-lusty French
                  Do the low-rated English play at dice,
                  And chide the cripple tardy-gaited night                             20
                  Who like a foul and ugly witch doth limp
                  So tediously away. The poor condemnèd English,
                  Like sacrifices, by their watchful fires

Act 4, Scene 0   4.0] *Pope; Actus Tertius* F   16 name] *Steevens²* (*conj. Tyrwhitt*); nam'd F   20 cripple] F (creeple)

**Act 4, Scene 0**

**4.0** Pope corrects F's editorial slip once again.

**1 entertain** give hospitality to.

**2 creeping** Usually with a pejorative association. It is present in *Sejanus* (1603) 1.1.175–7: 'Now observe the stoupes, / The bendings, and the falls / Most creeping base.'

**2 poring dark** the dark which makes eyes squint or pore over what they see.

**3 vessel** bowl, container.

**4 foul womb** The night, which gives birth to nightmares. The witch Hecate rode on the night mare. The image of a limping witch is picked up again at 21–2.

**5 stilly** (1) quietly, (2) always. A poetic usage repeating the Chorus's habit of strengthening adjectives by adding a terminal y, as in 'vasty'.

**8 paly** The same usage, this time with a heraldic connotation, as in 'umbered'.

**9 battle** the army drawn up ready to fight.

**9 umbered** (1) orange-brown, lit by the fires, (2) in shadow. A heraldic colour.

**12 accomplishing** fitting the knights into their armour.

**16 drowsy** i.e. for country people normally woken by cocks, not the armies.

**16 name** F's 'nam'd' indicates a d/e misreading. See Textual Analysis, p. 222.

**19 play at dice** In *Famous Victories* E3ʳ⁻ᵛ the French soldiers dice for their English prisoners, though none of them can win Henry.

**20 cripple** An extension of the 'creeping murmur' of line 2.

**21 witch** See line 4, note.

**23 watchful** A transferred epithet, though also 'watch-fires' (see *OED*, watch, *sb* 27). To 'watch' was to stay awake.

Sit patiently and inly ruminate
The morning's danger; and their gesture sad,         25
Investing lank-lean cheeks and war-worn coats,
Presented them unto the gazing moon
So many horrid ghosts. O now, who will behold
The royal captain of this ruined band
Walking from watch to watch, from tent to tent?      30
Let him cry 'Praise and glory on his head!'
For forth he goes and visits all his host,
Bids them good morrow with a modest smile,
And calls them brothers, friends and countrymen.
Upon his royal face there is no note         35
How dread an army hath enrounded him,
Nor doth he dedicate one jot of colour
Unto the weary and all-watchèd night,
But freshly looks and overbears attaint
With cheerful semblance and sweet majesty,      40
That every wretch, pining and pale before,
Beholding him, plucks comfort from his looks.
A largess universal like the sun
His liberal eye doth give to everyone,

---

27 Presented] F; Presenteth *Hanmer*

**24 inly** inwardly, silently.

**26 Investing** (1) laying siege to, (2) occupying.

**28 horrid ghosts** Horrifying ghosts only walked at night. 'Horrid' also implies that they are the dead covered in blood, as at 3.7.66. The 'horrid sights' of *JC* 2.2.16 are of graves giving up their dead.

**28 who will** who wishes to, who can imagine seeing (entertaining conjecture). The first Chorus at 1.0.4 also uses 'behold', renewed in this speech at lines 42 and 46, and in 52's 'sit and see'. See also Introduction, p. 9.

**29 royal . . . ruined** The alliteration contrasts leader and followers in ways that anticipate the campfire scene, 4.1.82–202.

**29 captain** A leader in the field, not the 'general' commander of 5.0.30.

**30 watch** Each 'watchful fire' had a company of soldiers 'watching', i.e. staying awake. The watchful sentries were elsewhere.

**32 host** army.

**34 brothers** See Introduction, pp. 30–3.

**36 enrounded** The English army was not literally surrounded. Its way to Calais was blocked by the French army.

**39 freshly looks** looks rosy-cheeked and wide awake.

**39 overbears attaint** (1) puts down the pressures on his mind, (2) overcomes false colouring, (3) ignores criminal charges.

**43–4 largess . . . everyone** See Chelidonius, *Of the Institution and firste beginning of Christian Princes*, trans. James Chillester, 1571: 'the Sunne . . . hath it not a representation of the chief & king, seeing that the Moone her self borroweth her light of him, and that by his course all things that bee under the globe & circle of the same bee made cleare and bright, have life and bee quickened, and being as it were dead and buried, be brought againe to their first being, state and strength?' This is from DI<sup>V</sup>-D2<sup>V</sup>, a passage about the kingdom of the bees which is not unlike the Archbishop of Canterbury's speech in 1.2.187–204.

**44 liberal** generous.

Thawing cold fear, that mean and gentle all                    45
Behold, as may unworthiness define,
'A little touch of Harry in the night'.
And so our scene must to the battle fly,
Where (O for pity!) we shall much disgrace,
With four or five most vile and ragged foils                    50
Right ill disposed in brawl ridiculous,
The name of Agincourt. Yet sit and see,
Minding true things by what their mockeries be.        *Exit*


**4.1** *Enter the* KING *and* GLOUCESTER [*and* BEDFORD *by another door*]

KING   Gloucester, 'tis true that we are in great danger.
The greater therefore should our courage be.
Good morrow, brother Bedford. God almighty,
There is some soul of goodness in things evil
Would men observingly distil it out.                            5
For our bad neighbour makes us early stirrers,
Which is both healthful and good husbandry.
Besides, they are our outward consciences
And preachers to us all, admonishing
That we should dress us fairly for our end.                     10

---

45 fear, that] F; –. Then *Theobald*   46 define,] F2; –. F   47 night.] *Rowe;* –, F   Act 4, Scene 1   3 Bedford] F; Clarence *Taylor*

**45 fear, that** Theobald's conjecture makes the Chorus address the audience as 'mean and gentle all', which contrasts with his more complimentary 'gentles all' of 1.0.8. Applied to the army it renews the distinction Henry makes between the 'noble English' and the 'yeomen' at 3.1.17 and 25.

**46 may unworthiness define** The Chorus gives a title to his own meanness in comparison with Henry's worth.

**47 A little touch** The Chorus's definition takes an echo from the touch of the linstock on the devilish cannon at 3.0.33, and also the healing touch of a king.

**50 four . . . foils** The small number of blunted swords normally used in fencing are a self-deprecating echo of Sidney's *Apology for Poetry*. Sidney mocks scenes where 'Two armies flye in

represented with four swords and bucklers, and then what harde heart will not receive it for a pitched field?' Jonson later echoed Sidney in mocking *Henry V*. See Introduction, p. 6. In fact the only battlefield confrontation with swords in the play is Pistol's with Le Fer in 4.4, which can fairly be described as a 'brawl ridiculous'.

**53 Minding** Putting in your mind, entertaining conjecture.

**Act 4, Scene 1**

**4 some . . . evil** Proverbial (Tilley N 328).

**6 neighbour . . . stirrers** Proverbial (Tilley N 107): 'He that has an ill neighbour has oftentimes an ill morning.' See 3.7.139 n.

**7 husbandry** farming, housekeeping.

**10 dress us** (1) clothe ourselves, (2) prepare ourselves.

Thus may we gather honey from the weed
And make a moral of the devil himself.

*Enter* ERPINGHAM

Good morrow, old Sir Thomas Erpingham.
A good soft pillow for that good white head
Were better than a churlish turf of France.                    15
ERPINGHAM  Not so, my liege. This lodging likes me better
Since I may say 'now lie I like a king'.
KING  'Tis good for men to love their present pains.
Upon example so the spirit is eased,
And when the mind is quickened, out of doubt           20
The organs, though defunct and dead before,
Break up their drowsy grave and newly move
With casted slough and fresh legerity.
Lend me thy cloak, Sir Thomas. Brothers both,
Commend me to the princes in our camp.                  25
Do my good morrow to them, and anon
Desire them all to my pavilion.
GLOUCESTER  We shall, my liege.
ERPINGHAM  Shall I attend your grace?
KING                                              No, my good knight.
Go with my brothers to my lords of England.          30
I and my bosom must debate awhile,
And then I would no other company.
ERPINGHAM  The Lord in heaven bless thee, noble Harry.
                                    *Exeunt* [*all but king*]
KING  God a mercy, old heart, thou speak'st cheerfully.

---

11 **honey . . . weed** Proverbial (Dent B205).

17 **now lie I** i.e. sleeping in the same condition as Henry. Given Henry's perversion of the proverb about ill neighbours, the other meaning of 'lie' is appropriate too.

18–23 G. C. Moore Smith conjectures that this speech should be an aside.

19 **Upon example** Sir Thomas is a model of cheerfulness. See line 34.

22 **drowsy grave** Sleep was commonly compared to death. Here it is not Lazarus rising from the dead, but snakes waking in the sun.

23 **casted slough** (1) skins shed, like snakes, (2) despondency rejected.

26 **anon** eventually, after a while.

34–282 This is the longest single episode in the play. First Henry is disguised and then in soliloquy and prayer, a wholly anonymous display of the 'little touch of Harry in the night' that the Chorus celebrates at 4.0.47.

34 This line is marked after Erpingham's departure in F, so it is a soliloquising comment indicating that Henry himself is not cheerful.

*Enter* PISTOL

PISTOL  *Qui vous là?*                                                    35
KING  A friend.
PISTOL  Discuss unto me, art thou officer, or art thou base,
  common and popular?
KING  I am a gentleman of a company.
PISTOL  Trail'st thou the puissant pike?                                  40
KING  Even so. What are you?
PISTOL  As good a gentleman as the emperor.
KING  Then you are a better than the king.
PISTOL  The king's a bawcock and a heart of gold, a lad of life, an
  imp of fame, of parents good, of fist most valiant. I kiss his dirty   45
  shoe, and from heartstring I love the lovely bully. What is thy
  name?
KING  Harry *le roi.*
PISTOL  Leroy? A Cornish name. Art thou of Cornish crew?
KING  No, I am a Welshman.                                                50
PISTOL  Knowest thou Llewellyn?
KING  Yes.
PISTOL  Tell him I'll knock his leek about his pate upon St Davy's
  day.

---

34 SD *Enter* PISTOL] F; *Enter the King disguised, to him Pistoll* Q   35 *Qui vous*] F (*Che vous*); *Qui va Rowe*   48 Harry *le roi*] F (*Harry le roy*)

35 *Qui vous là?* i.e. *Qui va là?*, a French sentry's challenge. Pistol's ignorance of French is affirmed in 4.4, so Rowe's correction is unnecessary. Since it is hardly the place to issue such a challenge, Pistol's bad French might be self-justifying.
38 popular At 1.1.59 the Archbishop speaks of Henry's youth spent in 'open haunts and popularity'.
39 a gentleman . . . company a man of 'gentle' rank serving as a common soldier, a volunteer. John Eliot's dedication to *Discourses of Warres*, 1591, cites the social range of soldiery. Writing about quarrels, he says 'if anie two have anie quarrell or difference betweene them, they must trie and end it by the combat, all justice troden underfoot. If he be a gentleman of a companie, a man at armes, yea but a single souldier, he must not pocket up the least looking in the face awrie, the lye given, or the least injurie that is, but he must crave revenge.' There are faint reminiscences of this elsewhere in the play.
40 Trail'st . . . pike? i.e. Are you an

infantryman? Pikes were wooden staves twelve feet and more in length, with a multi-bladed spearhead at one end. See Illustration 5, p. 31 above.
42 As . . . emperor Proverbial (G63.1). Llewellyn uses a similar saying at 4.7.123.
44 bawcock Another of Pistol's French terms. He uses it to Llewellyn at 3.2.22.
44–5 lad . . . imp youth, stripling. At *2H4* 5.5.38 Pistol addresses the newly crowned Henry as 'most royal imp of fame'. Henry recalls Falstaff's age and original name with 'my old lad o'the castle' at *1H4* 1.2.34.
46 bully roisterer, good fellow.
48 *le roi* i.e. the king. Medieval French *roi* was both spelt and pronounced 'roy'. See Introduction, p. 69.
49 crew A contemptuous term for a gang or rabble.
53–4 St Davy's day 1 March, when Welshmen wore leeks in their caps to celebrate their patron saint. Agincourt took place on 25 October.

KING  Do not you wear your dagger in your cap that day, lest he        55
  knock that about yours.
PISTOL  Art thou his friend?
KING  And his kinsman too.
PISTOL  The *fico* for thee, then.
KING  I thank you. God be with you.                                    60
PISTOL  My name is Pistol called.                             *Exit*
KING  It sorts well with your fierceness.

*Enter* LLEWELLYN *and* GOWER [*by separate doors*]

GOWER  Captain Llewellyn!
LLEWELLYN  So! In the name of Jesu Christ, speak fewer. It is the
  greatest admiration in the universal woreld when the true and       65
  ancient prerogatives and laws of the wars is not kept. If you
  would take the pains but to examine the wars of Pompey the
  Great you shall find, I warrant you, that there is no tiddle
  taddle nor pibble pabble in Pompey's camp. I warrant you, you
  shall find the ceremonies of the wars, and the cares of it, and     70
  the forms of it, and the sobriety of it, and the modesty of it, to
  be otherwise.
GOWER  Why, the enemy is loud. You hear him all night.
LLEWELLYN  If the enemy is an ass and a fool and a prating
  coxcomb, is it meet, think you, that we should also, look you, be    75
  an ass and a fool and a prating coxcomb, in your own
  conscience, now?
GOWER  I will speak lower.
LLEWELLYN  I pray you, and beseech you, that you will.
                            *Exeunt* [*Gower and Llewellyn*]

---

62 SD *Enter*] *This edn; Manet King. Enter* F  64 fewer] F; lewer Q; lower Q3, *Malone*  65 woreld] Q (worell); World
F  68–9 tiddle . . . pabble] F (tiddle tadle nor pibble bable)  79 *Exeunt*] *Exit* F

58 **kinsman** See 4.0.34 note. Kittredge saw this
as a reference to the old joke that all Welshmen are
related to each other.
  59 *fico* See 3.7.48 n.
  62 **sorts** consorts, fits.
  62 SD As before, the greeting indicates that
Gower and Llewellyn enter separately.
  64 **fewer** F's word is aptly ironic, given the
speaker, although Gower's defence at line 73

may justify Q's normalisation. Against that, if Q3
influenced F, F's reading must be a correction. See
Textual Analysis, pp. 222–4.
  65 **admiration** amazing thing.
  65 **universal woreld** Proverbial (Dent w 876.1).
  68–9 **tiddle taddle** tittle-tattle, chatter.
  74–5 **prating coxcomb** chattering fool. Country jesters and morris-men wore cock's combs.

KING  Though it appear a little out of fashion,                                80
    There is much care and valour in this Welshman.

      *Enter three soldiers, John* BATES, *Alexander* COURT *and*
                   *Michael* WILLIAMS

COURT  Brother John Bates, is not that the morning which breaks
    yonder?
BATES  I think it be. But we have no great cause to desire the
    approach of day.                                          85
WILLIAMS  We see yonder the beginning of the day, but I think we
    shall never see the end of it. Who goes there?
KING  A friend.
WILLIAMS  Under what captain serve you?
KING  Under Sir Thomas Erpingham.                              90
WILLIAMS  A good old commander, and a most kind gentleman. I
    pray you, what thinks he of our estate?
KING  Even as men wrecked upon a sand, that look to be washed off
    the next tide.
BATES  He hath not told his thought to the king?                95
KING  No. Nor it is not meet he should. For though I speak it to
    you, I think the king is but a man as I am. The violet smells to
    him as it doth to me. The element shows to him as it doth to
    me. All his senses have but human conditions. His ceremonies
    laid by, in his nakedness he appears but a man; and though his   100

---

90  Thomas] *Theobald;* John F

80–1 F prints these lines as verse. As in his soliloquy after the soldiers leave at line 202, Henry
speaks to himself in verse.
81 SD *John . . .* WILLIAMS This stage direction is unique in Shakespeare for its use of the
full names of ordinary people, and their anonymity.
There is no indication where the names might have
been taken from, nor why. They are unlikely to be
the names of actors, since the F manuscript was
nowhere marked for staging, and one of the names
is cited in the text. They are the third of three
distinctive trios, along with Bardolph, Pistol, and
Nym and Cambridge, Scroop, and Gray.
82 Brother A claim of amity, not kinship. See
Introduction, pp. 30–2.
87 Who . . . there? Unlike Pistol at line 35,
Williams issues his challenge in his native language.

90 Thomas Theobald's emendation corrected
the slip from line 24, where the name that appears
in Holinshed is given accurately. It was either an
authorial or compositorial error by contamination
from 'John Bates' four lines above.
92 estate condition, resources.
93 a sand a sandbank. The Goodwin Sands off
the Thames Estuary were notorious for shipwrecks.
96–7 though . . . you i.e. in confidence as common gossip. The proverbial phrase 'I say it who
shouldn't' (Tilley S114) is fitting, since it is the
phrase which usually precedes a boast. Here the
boast is offered as a secret and possibly subversive
thought about the king.
97 a man . . . am Proverbial (Dent M395.1).
98 element sky, weather.
99 ceremonies symbols of royalty.

affections are higher mounted than ours, yet when they stoop
they stoop with the like wing. Therefore when he sees reason of
fears as we do, his fears, out of doubt, be of the same relish as
ours are. Yet in reason no man should possess him with any
appearance of fear, lest he by showing it should dishearten his          105
army.

BATES  He may show what outward courage he will, but I believe,
as cold a night as 'tis, he could wish himself in Thames up to
the neck. And so I would he were, and I by him, at all
adventures, so we were quit here.                                        110

KING  By my troth, I will speak my conscience of the king. I think
he would not wish himself anywhere but where he is.

BATES  Then I would he were here alone. So should he be sure to
be ransomed and a-many poor men's lives saved.

KING  I dare say you love him not so ill to wish him here alone,          115
howsoever you speak this to feel other men's minds. Methinks I
could not die anywhere so contented as in the king's company,
his cause being just and his quarrel honorable.

WILLIAMS  That's more than we know.

BATES  Ay, or more than we should seek after, for we know enough          120
if we know we are the king's subjects. If his cause be wrong our
obedience to the king wipes the crime of it out of us.

WILLIAMS  But if the cause be not good the king himself hath a
heavy reckoning to make, when all those legs and arms and

---

116  minds. Methinks] *Rowe;* minds, me thinks F

---

**101 affections** emotions. In *JC*, while Brutus is
ruled by 'reason', Mark Antony is ruled by 'affections', the strength of emotion which makes him a
much better mob orator than Brutus.

**102 stoop** (1) (of hawks) dive, (2) (of humans)
climb down, be humbled.

**103 relish** taste, enjoyment.

**104 possess him** (1) obsess the king, (2) possess
himself.

**108 in Thames** i.e. in the river of London.

**110 so** so long as.

**111 my conscience** (1) what I believe, (2) what
I know.

**116 minds. Methinks** Rowe's emendation
strengthens what is left unclear in F.

**118 his . . . just** his legal suit being sound. See
Introduction, pp. 22–3.

**119 more . . . know** A conventional saying
(Dent M1155.1).

**121–2 If . . . of us** The doctrine of obedience
that required a subject or servant to do wrong

when so ordered by his master was a subject of
much debate. Pisanio in *Cym.* 3.2.14–15, on being
ordered to murder Imogen, says 'If it be so to do
good service, never / Let me be counted service-
able', and at 5.1.6–7 'Every good servant does not
all commands; / No bond, but to do just ones.'
John Norden, in *The Mirror of Honour*, 1597, writes
'When the cause is just no man may question
whether the warre bee lawfull. It is then just when
it seeketh to defend, and preserve the publique
quiet and Christian religion, and it is then lawful, when it is done by the authority of the Prince'
(A3). See Introduction, p. 22.

**123–4 if . . . make** Here Williams, in a speech
which deeply upsets the king, brings together the
law of nature and a proverbial dictum offering one
answer to Pisanio's problem quoted in the previous note: 'That which a man causeth to be done
he does himself' (Dent M387). The term 'reckoning' invokes the imagery of accounting, which runs
through the play from 1.0.17 onwards.

heads chopped off in a battle shall join together at the latter day     125
and cry all 'We died at such a place', some swearing, some
crying for a surgeon, some upon their wives left poor behind
them, some upon the debts they owe, some upon their children
rawly left. I am afeard there are few die well that die in a battle,
for how can they charitably dispose of anything when blood is     130
their argument? Now if these men do not die well it will be a
black matter for the king that led them to it, who to disobey
were against all proportion of subjection.

KING  So if a son that is by his father sent about merchandise do
sinfully miscarry upon the sea, the imputation of his     135
wickedness, by your rule, should be imposed upon his father
that sent him. Or if a servant, under his master's command
transporting a sum of money, be assailed by robbers and die in
many irreconciled iniquities, you may call the business of the
master the author of the servant's damnation. But this is not so.     140
The king is not bound to answer the particular endings of his
soldiers, the father of his son, nor the master of his servant, for
they purpose not their death when they purpose their services.
Besides, there is no king, be his cause never so spotless, if it
come to the arbitrament of swords can try it out with all     145
unspotted soldiers. Some, peradventure, have on them the guilt
of premeditated and contrived murder, some of beguiling
virgins with the broken seals of perjury, some, making the wars
their bulwark, that have before gored the gentle bosom of peace
with pillage and robbery. Now, if these men have defeated the     150
law and outrun native punishment, though they can outstrip

---

143 death] F; deaths Q     143 purpose] F; craue Q; propose *Taylor*

**125 latter day** The Day of Judgement. The
term is from the Bishops' Bible, Job 19.25.

**129 rawly** (1) young and dependent, (2) unprovided for.

**130 charitably** in Christian love.

**133 against all proportion** contrary to every
requirement.

**134–66** Henry's speech is redolent of the
'Homily against Disobedience and Wilful
Rebellion', read in churches every month. The
relevant sections are reprinted in the New
Cambridge *R2*, Appendix 3. For an analysis of
the rhetorical structure of the speech, see Brian
Vickers, *The Artistry of Shakespeare's Prose*, 1968,
pp. 164–5.

**139 irreconciled** Here and at lines 146 ('guilt'),
157 ('unprovided'), and 161, Henry alludes to the
expectation that a 'good' death requires making
one's peace with God by repenting one's sins.
Falstaff's death as reported in Act 2, Scene 3 lies
behind these references.

**140 author of** responsible for, the cause of.

**143 purpose their** Taylor's conjecture assumes
a compositorial slip misremembering the previous
word. But there is no reason to question an authorial repetition.

**151 native** local, by the laws of the country.
Gentili makes the point that all individuals are
subject to law, and only sovereigns can make war
against foreign countries.

men they have no wings to fly from God. War is His beadle,
war is His vengeance, so that here men are punished for
before-breach of the king's laws in now the king's quarrel.
Where they feared the death they have borne life away, and     155
where they would be safe they perish. Then, if they die
unprovided, no more is the king guilty of their damnation than
he was before guilty of those impieties for the which they are
now visited. Every subject's duty is the king's, but every
subject's soul is his own. Therefore should every soldier in the     160
wars do as every sick man in his bed, wash every mote out of
his conscience. And dying so, death is to him advantage; or, not
dying, the time was blessedly lost wherein such preparation was
gained. And in him that escapes it were not sin to think that,
making God so free an offer, He let him outlive that day to see     165
His greatness, and to teach others how they should prepare.

WILLIAMS  'Tis certain, every man that dies ill, the ill upon his own
head; the king is not to answer it.

BATES  I do not desire he should answer for me, and yet I
determine to fight lustily for him.     170

KING  I myself heard the king say he would not be ransomed.

WILLIAMS  Ay, he said so to make us fight cheerfully, but when our
throats are cut he may be ransomed and we ne'er the wiser.

KING  If I live to see it, I will never trust his word after.

WILLIAMS  You pay him then! That's a perilous shot out of an     175
elder gun, that a poor and a private displeasure can do against a
monarch. You may as well go about to turn the sun to ice with
fanning in his face with a peacock's feather. You'll never trust
his word after! Come, 'tis a foolish saying.

152 **beadle** policeman, agent of the law.

157 **unprovided** not prepared in spirit for death.

159 **the king's** i.e. due to the king.

161 **mote** dark spot, stain. In the Geneva Bible this word occurs in Matt. 7.3, 'the mote that is in thy brother's eye'. F's 'moth' gives the pronunciation, to judge from *LLL* 4.3.159.

162 **death . . . advantage** From the Bishops' Bible, Phil. 1.21: 'death is to me advantage'.

167–70 Williams is left uncertain, after the king's strong response. Bates interjects a less direct reaction, shrugging off the central question that

Williams is grappling with. Williams's doubt makes him react grudgingly to the suggestion of ransom at line 171. Q merges the two speeches of Williams and Bates, giving the amalgamation to the '3' speaker, who elsewhere takes Bates's lines.

167 **dies ill** i.e. in sin, 'unprovided'.

175 **You . . . then!** You punish him for it. If the king is above the law, as Elizabeth and later James declared, then no subject can inflict justice on a king. See *R2* 4.1.128.

176 **elder gun** pop-gun made from a hollowed-out elder stick.

178 **peacock** Representing vanity.

KING  Your reproof is something too round. I should be angry with     180
  you if the time were convenient.
WILLIAMS  Let it be a quarrel between us, if you live.
KING  I embrace it.
WILLIAMS  How shall I know thee again?
KING  Give me any gage of thine and I will wear it in my bonnet.       185
  Then, if ever thou darest acknowledge it, I will make it my
  quarrel.
WILLIAMS  Here's my glove. Give me another of thine.
KING  There.

                        [*They exchange gloves*]

WILLIAMS  This will I also wear in my cap. If ever thou come to me     190
  and say, after tomorrow, 'This is my glove', by this hand I will
  take thee a box on the ear.
KING  If ever I live to see it, I will challenge it.
WILLIAMS  Thou darest as well be hanged.
KING  Well, I will do it, though I take thee in the king's company.    195
WILLIAMS  Keep thy word. Fare thee well.
BATES  Be friends, you English fools, be friends! We have French
  quarrels enough if you could tell how to reckon.
KING  Indeed, the French may lay twenty French crowns to one
  they will beat us, for they bear them on their shoulders. But it     200
  is no English treason to cut French crowns, and tomorrow the
  king himself will be a clipper.

                                             *Exeunt soldiers*

---

198  reckon.] –. *Exit souldiers* F    202  SD *Exeunt soldiers*] Q; *not in* F

180 **round** blunt, rough.

185 **gage** A pledge to signify that the quarrel is acknowledged formally and the subsequent challenge will be met. There are two scenes in *R2* (1.1 and 4.1) where gloves are flung down on stage as gages in formal acknowledgement of a quarrel.

185 **bonnet** small hat, a term often used contemptuously, as at *R2* 1.4.31.

192 **a box . . . ear** A more humane action than cutting throats.

198 **quarrels** (1) disagreements, (2) crossbow arrows. The French archers used crossbows, not the English longbow.

198 **reckon** count – i.e. the numbers in the French army, all of whom have a quarrel, and crossbows to use, against the English.

198 In F, the soldiers depart here instead of after

Henry's last attempt at a joke to them.

199 **crowns** (1) the French *écu*, worth six shillings, (2) the tops of their heads.

200 **they . . . shoulders** The most explicit admission in this dialogue of the disparity in numbers, twenty to one, much higher odds than are claimed in 4.3 or in Holinshed.

201 **cut . . . crowns** (1) to trim gold off coins, (2) to chop heads.

202 **a clipper** (1) a hairdresser, (2) a counterfeiter of money.

202 SD Q correctly positions the soldiers' exit here. F's positioning at line 198 may indicate that Henry's last speech was an afterthought or a late insertion. Q omits the entire 'ceremony' speech of Henry that follows, taking him straight to his 'O God of battles' prayer at line 263.

Upon the king! 'Let us our lives, our souls, our debts, our
careful wives, our children and our sins, lay on the king.'
We must bear all.                                               205
O hard condition, twin-born with greatness,
Subject to the breath of every fool, whose sense
No more can feel but his own wringing.
What infinite heart's ease must kings neglect
That private men enjoy?                                         210
And what have kings that privates have not too,
Save ceremony, save general ceremony?
And what art thou, thou idol ceremony?
What kind of god art thou, that suffer'st more
Of mortal griefs than do thy worshippers?                      215
What are thy rents? What are thy comings-in?
O ceremony, show me but thy worth!
What? Is thy soul of adoration?
Art thou ought else but place, degree and form,
Creating awe and fear in other men,                            220
Wherein thou art less happy being feared
Than they in fearing?

218 What? Is] F (What? is); what is *Knight*   222   fearing?] *This edn*; –. F

203–10 The F compositor had some difficulty with lineation after the long prose passages. He versified the lines at 'souls / . . .
wives / . . . king / . . . condition /
. . . breath / . . . feel / . . . ease'. Subsequent editors
have tried different ways of versifying, but a half-
line has to intrude somewhere. This edition starts
with prose on the grounds that Henry is quoting
the soldiers, and then moves into verse for his own
thoughts. See Textual Analysis, p. 222.

203 **Upon . . . king** Henry is not echoing anything Williams or Bates actually says, though the
phrase does sum up Williams's argument at 123–33
about what the king's responsibility amounts to.

204 **careful** full of care, anxious.

206 **twin-born with** a twin of – i.e. a necessary
accompaniment.

208 **his own wringing** (1) what hurts just him,
(2) his belly-ache.

210 In verse a half-line is sometimes used to signify a brief pause or a significant silence. It seems
apt here, even though it may equally be a mark of
mislineation stemming from the F confusion after
line 203.

211 **privates** An abbreviation of the previous
line's 'private men', men who do not hold public
office. The military sense of a private soldier, whose
rank would put him in contrast with 'General
Ceremony' in the following line, is not recorded
before the eighteenth century.

216 **comings-in** income, benefits.

218 **What . . . adoration?** Whether this question is rhetorical and exclamatory or a real query
about the soul of ceremony is not entirely clear.
It makes better sense to read it as an enquiry
about whether its essence (soul) is merely adoration
rather than adopting Knight's attempt to make it
an enquiry about its adoring soul.

219 **place** public office. See Donne, 'The
Canonisation', stanza 1.

219 **degree** social rank.

219 **form** ritual in a set system, outward ritual.

222 **fearing?** The question mark is called for
by the syntax. F puts its question mark at line
220, after 'men', but the sentence continues.
The short line may again signify a pause, as at
line 210.

What drink'st thou oft, instead of homage sweet,
But poisoned flattery? Oh, be sick, great greatness,
And bid thy ceremony give thee cure.                                    225
Thinkst thou the fiery fever will go out
With titles blown from adulation?
Will it give place to flexure and low bending?
Canst thou, when thou command'st the beggar's knee,
Command the health of it? No, thou proud dream,                        230
That playst so subtly with a king's repose.
I am a king that find thee, and I know
'Tis not the balm, the sceptre and the ball,
The sword, the mace, the crown imperial,
The intertissued robe of gold and pearl,                               235
The farcèd title running 'fore the king,
The throne he sits on, nor the tide of pomp
That beats upon the high shore of this world;
No, not all these, thrice-gorgeous ceremony,
Not all these, laid in bed majestical,                                 240
Can sleep so soundly as the wretched slave
Who, with a body filled and vacant mind,
Gets him to rest, crammed with distressful bread;
Never sees horrid night, the child of hell,
But like a lackey from the rise to set                                 245

226 Thinkst] *Rowe;* Thinks F

223–4 **What . . . flattery?** Having addressed
ceremony, he now speaks to himself sarcastically
as the 'great greatness' to whom ceremony is the
physician. In *R2* 2.1.99 Henry's grandfather Gaunt
describes the king's flatterers as the physicians who
first made him sick. There may be some preparation here for the reference to Richard at 269–76.
227 **blown from adulation** corrupted, fly-
blown, by flattery.
228 **flexure** kneeling (by the flattering physicians).
230 **thou . . . dream** The addressee again
becomes ceremony.
232 **find** experience, test the quality of, judge.
233 **balm** (1) medicine, (2) anointing oil at the
coronation. G. C. Rothery, *The Heraldry of Shakespeare*, 1930, p. 114, suggests that this word should
be 'helm', since the royal helm or crown was the
first item in the regalia listed here. But the 'crown
imperial' is named later, immediately before the
coronation robe, the 'intertissued robe' of line 235.

236 **farcèd title** pompous name. A 'farced' or
'forced' piece of meat might be either force-fed or
stuffed. Compare the 'mighty whiffler' at 5.0.12.
237 **tide** flood-tide, which also ebbs.
241 **wretched slave** The antithesis of a king.
In a play which grades its countrymen so precisely (king, nobles, gentlemen-captains, yeomen
and 'mean' or base and common), this extreme
term is a mark of the intensity of Henry's feeling.
He repeats the word at line 254, specifically including it as the lowest type in his commonwealth. In
Rome slaves could not be citizens.
243 **crammed** A similar term to 'farced' at line
236.
244 **horrid night** Echoing the Chorus at 4.0.4
and 28.
245–6 **lackey . . . Phoebus** The comparison is
with a footman running (line 249) alongside his
master's carriage which, appropriately for a rising
sun-king, is the chariot of the sun.

Sweats in the eye of Phoebus, and all night
Sleeps in Elysium; next day after dawn
Doth rise and help Hyperion to his horse
And follows so the ever-running year
With profitable labour to his grave.                                     250
And but for ceremony such a wretch,
Winding up days with toil and nights with sleep,
Had the forehand and vantage of a king.
The slave, a member of the country's peace,
Enjoys it, but in gross brain little wots                                255
What watch the king keeps to maintain the peace,
Whose hours the peasant best advantages.

*Enter* ERPINGHAM

ERPINGHAM   My lord, your nobles, jealous of your absence,
    Seek through the camp to find you.
KING   Good old knight,                                                  260
    Collect them all together at my tent.
    I'll be before thee.
ERPINGHAM                    I shall do't, my lord.              *Exit*
KING   O God of battles, steel my soldiers' hearts.
    Possess them not with fear. Take from them now

---

248 Hyperion] F2; *Hyperio* F

**246 in . . . Phoebus** (1) under the gaze of the sun-god, (2) in the heat of the sun.

**247 Elysium** The Greek heaven, home of Phoebus the sun-god.

**248 Hyperion** Father of young Phoebus, charioteer of the sun. F's 'Hyperio' seems to be a misreading by the compositor of a tilde over the last letter.

**250 profitable** Not with just a narrowly financial benefit. In the 'world of profite and delight . . . / promised to the Studious Artisan' of Faustus's opening soliloquy in Marlowe's play (1.1.80–2) the concepts of both profit and artisan have been transformed by the Industrial Revolution.

**252 Winding up** Climbing up, closing.

**253 forehand** superior hand-hold in wrestling.

**254 member** a limb of the body politic.

**255 wots** knows. This poetic term starts a deliberate cacophony, since it has the same vowel sound as the two succeeding words, according to Cercignani (p. 24).

**256 watch** staying awake – as Henry and his army are said to do at 4.0.38.

**257 best advantages** makes best use of – an echo of 'vantage' at line 253, and more remotely of Henry's own reference to it at line 162.

**258 jealous of** anxious about. See 2.2.123 n.

**261** Henry had asked his brothers at line 27 to assemble them there.

**263 O God** F, which generally censors oaths in accordance with the Act of 1606, leaves this one alone. Q, which cuts all of the preceding speech, makes it a public prayer spoken in the company of Erpingham, Gloucester, and attendants.

**263 steel** harden – with a concealed pun on 'mettle'.

The sense of reckoning ere th'opposèd numbers          265
Pluck their hearts from them. Not today, O Lord,
Oh, not today, think not upon the fault
My father made in compassing the crown.
I Richard's body have interrèd new,
And on it have bestowed more contrite tears          270
Than from it issued forcèd drops of blood.
Five hundred poor I have in yearly pay
Who twice a day their withered hands hold up
Toward heaven to pardon blood. And I have built
Two chantries where the sad and solemn priests          275
Sing still for Richard's soul. More will I do,
Though all that I can do is nothing worth
Since that my penitence comes after all,
Imploring pardon.

                        *Enter* GLOUCESTER

GLOUCESTER  My liege.
KING                        My brother Gloucester's voice? Ay,          280
I know thy errand. I will go with thee.
The day, my friends, and all things stay for me.

                                                *Exeunt*

---

265 ere] *Moore Smith;* of F; That Q; if *Steevens (conj. Tyrwhitt);* or *Wilson*   265 numbers] *Pope;* – : F; multitudes which stand before them, Q   266 Pluck . . . them] F; May not appall their courage Q   272 I have] F; have I Q   278 all] F; not in Q; ill *Taylor conj.*   282 friends] Q; friend F

265 **reckoning ere** F does not make grammatical sense here, and may be a compositor's attempt to make sense of the line in the absence of a recognisable punctuation mark. Bates has already ticked off Williams and the disguised Henry for bickering when they should be 'reckoning' their French quarrels. Moore Smith's conjecture makes better sense than Tyrwhitt's, and its general sense is endorsed by Q.

266 **Not today** Shaheen, *Biblical References in Shakespeare's History Plays*, suggests that this phrase echoes the Psalm 115, *Non nobis*, which Henry orders sung after Agincourt. See 4.8.115.

269 **I . . . new** According to Holinshed, at the outset of his reign Henry 'caused the bodie of king Richard to be remooved with all funerall dignitie convenient for his estate, from Langlie to Westminster, where he was honorablie interred with queene

Anne his first wife, in a solemne toome erected and set up at the charges of the king' (pp. 543–4). The subsequent account of the five hundred poor and the chantries is not in Holinshed or Hall, though it is in Fabyan.

271 **forcèd** i.e. in the act of murder.

274–6 F mislines these three lines, possibly from trying to stretch them to the end of the page.

275 **chantries** Chapels where daily prayers are said for the dead.

278–9 **penitence . . . pardon** A neatly Protestant position. Good works, central to Catholic dogma, are less valuable than spiritual repentance, which is part of the Protestant doctrine of salvation by faith alone.

282 **friends** F makes this word into a response to Gloucester, who is a brother before he is a friend. Q has it correctly.

**4.2**   *Enter* BOURBON, ORLÉANS, RAMBURES *and* BEAUMONT

ORLÉANS   The sun doth gild our armour. Up, my lords!
BOURBON   *Montez à cheval!* My horse, varlet lackey! Ha!
ORLÉANS   Oh, brave spirit!
BOURBON   *Via les eaux et terres!*
ORLÉANS   *Rien puis l'air et feu?*                                    5
BOURBON   *Cieux*, cousin Orléans!

*Enter* CONSTABLE

            Now, my lord Constable?
CONSTABLE   Hark how our steeds for present service neigh.
BOURBON   Mount them, and make incision in their hides
            That their hot blood may spin in English eyes          10
            And dout them with superfluous courage! Ha!
RAMBURES   What, will you have them weep our horses' blood?
            How shall we then behold their natural tears?

*Enter* MESSENGER

MESSENGER   The English are embattled, you French peers.
CONSTABLE   To horse, you gallant princes, straight to horse!     15
            Do but behold you poor and starvèd band
            And your fair show shall suck away their souls,
            Leaving them but the shells and husks of men.

---

Act 4, Scene 2   0 SD BOURBON] *Taylor; Dolphin* F armour. Up,] *Capell;* armour up, F; armour, up F2   2 SH BOURBON]
*Taylor; Dolph.* F   2 *Montez à cheval*] *Monte Cheual* F   2 varlet] F (*Verlot*).   4 terres] terre F   5 *Rien puis*] F; Rien plus
*Sisson*   6 *Cieux*] F (*Cien*); Ciel *Theobald*   11 dout] F (doubt)   16 yon] F (yond)   18 shells] F (shales)

**Act 4, Scene 2**

**1 armour. Up** Another F confusion over punctuation.

**2** *Montez à cheval!* 'Mount up!' or 'To horse!'

**2 varlet lackey** A lackey was a personal servant, as in line 26. 'Varlet' was a name of contempt.

**4** *Via . . . terres!* At 3.8.20 he had declared his horse to be made of air and fire. Now the rising elements are to confront the baser ones of earth and water, of which the English are made. *Via* is an imperative meaning through or over: 'Go through water and earth.'

**5** *Rien . . . feu?* 'No air and fire then?'

**6** *Cieux* 'the heavens'.

**8 Hark** It is not unimaginable that noises off were provided, to signify excited horses.

**9 incision** A medical term. Blood-letting with spurs would let out some of the hot spirits.

**10 spin** gush, or spurt (*OED v* 8). Drayton's 'Nymphidia', published with his poem 'The Battaile of Agincourt' in 1627, has a line 'The blood out of their Helmets span' (*The Works of Michael Drayton*, ed. J. William Hebel, 5 vols., 1961, III, 144). *OED* misattributes this reference to the Agincourt poem.

**11 dout them** put them out, douse them.

**12 weep** Rambures picks up the 'English eyes' of line 10.

**14 embattled** drawn up in line of battle.

**16 yon** The F 'yond' is a compositor spelling, changing the usual Shakespearean form, restored here.

**18 shells** F's 'shales' was a distinct form which later merged with the modern spelling.

There is not work enough for all our hands,
Scarce blood enough in all their sickly veins                    20
To give each naked curtal-axe a stain,
That our French gallants shall today draw out
And sheathe for lack of sport. Let us but blow on them,
The vapour of our valour will o'erturn them.
'Tis positive 'gainst all exceptions, lords,                      25
That our superfluous lackeys and our peasants
Who in unnecessary action swarm
About our squares of battle were enough
To purge this field of such a hilding foe,
Though we upon this mountain's basis by                          30
Took stand for idle speculation,
But that our honours must not. What's to say?
A very little little let us do
And all is done. Then let the trumpets sound
The tucket sonance and the note to mount,                        35
For our approach shall so much dare the field
That England shall crouch down in fear, and yield.

*Enter* GRANDPRÉ

GRANDPRÉ  Why do you stay so long, my lords of France?
Yon island carrions, desperate of their bones,
Ill-favouredly become the morning field.                         40
Their ragged curtains poorly are let loose
And our air shakes them passing scornfully.

25 'gainst] F2; against F    35 sonance] F (sonuance)    39 Yon] F (Yond)

21 **curtal-axe** A weapon not quite the same as the modern cutlass, which takes its name from it. It was a short, broad-bladed sword for chopping.
28 **squares of battle** military formations, usually, as here, made of cavalry.
29 **hilding** contemptible.
30–1 **Though . . . speculation** A reference to the French king's account of Edward III at Crécy, 'on mountain standing' (2.4.55–63).
31 **Took . . . speculation** stood idly by as spectators.
35 **tucket . . . mount** the trumpet-call to march, and the mounting call. Paul A. Jorgensen, *Shakespeare's Military World*, p. 22, notes that the sequence is the wrong way round. Francis Markham, an authority on military music, wrote that it should be '*Butte sella*, Clap on your saddles; *Mounte Cavallo*, mount on horseback, *Tucquet*,

march; *Carga, carga*, An Alarme to charge'. The Constable reverses the second and third of these trumpet-calls. Two other tuckets are marked in F, for the French herald at 3.7.97 SD and at 4.3.78 SD.
36 **dare** terrify. Larks were 'dared' on the ground, and netted by fowlers.
38 SD GRANDPRÉ Remarked as the noble who measured the distance between the two armies at 3.8.115.
39 **island** *OED* does not cite this adjectival use until 1621.
39 **carrions** i.e. already corpses, not birds of prey.
39 **desperate of** careless about.
40 **Ill-favouredly become** Look ugly on.
41 **curtains** (1) window-curtains, opened at dawn, (2) battle ensigns.
42 **passing** exceedingly.

Big Mars seems bankrupt in their beggared host,
And faintly through a rusty beaver peeps.
The horsemen sit like fixèd candlesticks                              45
With torch staves in their hand, and their poor jades
Lob down their heads, dropping the hides and hips,
The gum down-roping from their pale dead eyes,
And in their pale dull mouths the gemelled bit
Lies foul with chewed-grass, still and motionless.                    50
And their executors the knavish crows
Fly o'er them all, impatient for their hour.
Description cannot suit itself in words
To demonstrate the life of such a battle,
In life so lifeless, as it shows itself.                              55
CONSTABLE  They have said their prayers, and they stay for death.
BOURBON  Shall we go send them dinners and fresh suits,
And give their fasting horses provender,
And after fight with them?
CONSTABLE  I stay but for my guidon. To the field!                    60

---

46 hand] F; hands *Taylor*  47 dropping] F; drooping F2  49 pale] F; palled *Hudson*  49 gemelled] *This edn*; Iymold F; gimmal *Theobald*; gimmalled *Delius*  50 chewed-grass] F (chaw'd-grasse)  50 still] F; stiff *Vaughan conj.*  52 them all, impatient] F; them, all impatient *Rowe*; --------- *Taylor*  60 guidon. To] *Rann*; Guard: on / To F

**43 Mars** The Roman god of war, compared to Henry in the sixth line of the play.

**44 rusty beaver** The face-guard of a helmet, which is rusty from lack of use and because the host or army Mars leads is short of money, bankrupt, and beggared.

**45 fixèd candlesticks** In *The White Devil* 3.1.68–70 Flamineo says 'he showed like a pewter candlestick fashioned like a man in armour, holding a tilting staff in his hand, little bigger than a candle of twelve i'th'pound'.

**47 Lob down** Droop.

**47 dropping** The case for F2's normalisation is strong, but in *Ham.* 1.2.11 Claudius speaks of 'one auspicious and one dropping eye'.

**49 pale** Taylor suggests a d/e misreading, punning on 'made pale' and 'covered with a funeral pall'. The frequency with which the F compositor mistook a terminal d for e or vice versa makes this attractive, but the collocation of the two 'd' sounds would be very awkward.

**49 gemelled** F's 'Iymold' can be modernised in different ways, according to whether the bit had a 'gimmal', or hinge, or a 'gemel', a double ring. The two terms were not always differentiated. *OED sb* 2 gemel was the term for coupled bars, also used in heraldry; *sb* 4 gemel is a double ring; *sb* 5 a hinge. Since this term covers both possibilities, it seems the preferable spelling.

**50 chewed-grass** F's spelling indicates that it is a compound word stressed on the first syllable.

**51 executors** (1) managers of their estates after death, (2) killers. The term is picked up from 'carrions' at line 39.

**52 all, impatient** Taylor's omission of any punctuation underlines the point that either of the two ways of punctuating these words is possible. Rowe's reading puts more emphasis on their deaths, F's on the English army's long wait. Where the possible readings are equal, F should be preferred.

**54 a battle** an army drawn up ready to fight.

**57–9** Bourbon's impatience makes this a scornful mock-proposal. The Constable's reply is defensive over the delay.

**60 guidon** a standard or pennant. Rann's emendation makes sense of the Constable's next two lines, which come from a note in Holinshed, p. 554: 'They thought themselves so sure of victorie, that diverse of the noble men made such hast towards the battell, that they left manie of their servants and men of warre behind them, and some of them would not once staie for their standards: as amongst other the duke of Brabant, when his standard was not come, caused a baner to be taken from a trumpet and fastened to a speare, the which he commanded to be borne before him in steed of his standard.'

I will the banner from a trumpet take
And use it for my haste. Come, come, away!
The sun is high and we outwear the day.

*Exeunt*

**4.3** *Enter* GLOUCESTER, BEDFORD, EXETER, ERPINGHAM
*with all his host,* SALISBURY *and* WESTMORLAND

GLOUCESTER   Where is the king?
BEDFORD   The king himself is rode to view their battle.
WESTMORLAND   Of fighting men they have full threescore thousand.
EXETER   There's five to one. Besides, they all are fresh.
SALISBURY   God's arm strike with us! 'Tis a fearful odds.                    5
    God be wi'you, princes all. I'll to my charge.
    If we no more meet till we meet in heaven
    Then joyfully, my noble lord of Bedford,
    My dear lord Gloucester and my good lord Exeter,
    And my kind kinsman, warriors all, adieu.                                10
BEDFORD   Farewell, good Salisbury, and good luck go with thee.
EXETER   Farewell, kind lord. Fight valiantly today.

*[Exit Salisbury]*

    And yet I do thee wrong to mind thee of it,
    For thou art framed of the firm truth of valour.

---

Act 4, Scene 3   0 SD BEDFORD] F; *Clarence* Q   0 SD WESTMORLAND] F; WARWICK *Taylor.*   2 SH BEDFORD] F;
CLARENCE *Taylor.*   10 my kind kinsman] F; *my Lord of Warwick* Q   12] *Theobald; after 14* F   12 SH EXETER] F; *Clar*
Q   12 SD *Exit Salisbury*] *Rowe; not in* F, Q

**Act 4, Scene 3**

**0 SD** SALISBURY *and* WESTMORLAND These
two names look like an afterthought, since the
stage army is complete with Erpingham's '*host*'.
Salisbury was the famous fighter whose death was
dramatised in *1H6*, Act 1, Scene 4. Henry hails
him as one of the great names of Agincourt at
line 54. Westmorland is a more unusual inclusion,
since his presence is unhistorical. The reason may
be that he was Henry's kinsman, a point Henry
emphasises when he speaks to him at line 19. See
Introduction, p. 35. Taylor, adopting the Q change
of characters, argues that Warwick's name but not
Westmorland's appears in Henry's list at 53–4, and
that he should be substituted for Westmorland. But
Westmorland's name fits the metre better at line 19,
and the list at 53–4 is of names already famous, like
the anachronistic Talbot from *1H6*. The Warwick
in this list is most likely the equally anachronistic
'kingmaker' Warwick of the Henry VI plays.

**3 threescore thousand** Holinshed is not clear

about the French numbers. At p. 553, after listing the French battle order, he writes 'Thus the
Frenchman being ordered under their standards
and banners, made a great shew: for suerlie they
were esteemed in number six times as manie or
more, than was the whole companie of the Englishmen, with wagoners, pages and all.' Westmorland's
figure of 60,000 would make the English force ten
thousand, where Holinshed's figures make about
15,000. Exeter's odds would make the English
12,000.

**10 kinsman** Westmorland's son was married to
Salisbury's daughter, which gives historical justification to the insistence on kinship.

**12–14** Styan Thirlby conjectured that the F
sequence of lines indicates a late insertion of two
lines in the F copy. Q, for which the reporter playing Exeter was present, gets the sequence right,
although it puts in the mistaken SH for Clarence
probably by a memory of the name two lines
before.

BEDFORD He is as full of vâlour as of kindness, 15
        Princely in both.

*Enter the* KING

WESTMORLAND         O that we now had here
        But one ten thousand of those men in England
        That do no work today.
KING                       What's he that wishes so?
        My cousin Westmorland. No, my fair cousin.
        If we are marked to die, we are enough 20
        To do our country loss. And if to live,
        The fewer men, the greater share of honour.
        God's will, I pray thee wish not one man more.
        By Jove, I am not covetous for gold,
        Nor care I who doth feed upon my cost. 25
        It yearns me not if men my garments wear.
        Such outward things dwell not in my desires.
        But if it be a sin to covet honour,
        I am the most offending soul alive.
        No, faith, my coz, wish not a man from England. 30
        God's peace, I would not lose so great an honour
        As one man more, methinks, would share from me,
        For the best hope I have. Oh, do not wish one more!
        Rather proclaim it, Westmorland, through my host
        That he which hath no stomach to this fight 35
        Let him depart. His passport shall be made,

---

26 yearns] F (yernes)    34 Westmorland] F; presently Q

**16 SD** The king's entry unobserved here repeats his previous anonymity. Possibly he returns Erpingham his cloak while Westmorland is speaking. It is a crowded scene in any case, making it easy for him to enter quietly behind a group of soldiers.

**17 one ten thousand** A fraction: one in ten thousand.

**19–67** Henry starts by addressing Westmorland specifically, but the speech is of course to the whole 'host', as his reference to 'we few' at line 60 makes clear. Holinshed on p. 553 has a marginal note, 'K Henries oration to his men', in a paragraph which begins, 'calling his capteins and soldiers about him, he made to them a right grave oration, mooving them to plaie the man'. See Appendix 2.

**22 The . . . honour** Proverbial (Tilley D35).

**23–4 God's will . . . By Jove** Johnson said of this that 'The king prays like a Christian, and swears like a heathen.'

**26 yearns** grieves. See 2.3.3 n.

**28 a sin . . . honour** Again proverbial, paraphrasing the proverb 'he that seeks honour is least worthy of it' (Dent H566).

**30 coz** An abbreviation for 'cousin', used in full at line 19.

**33 best hope** i.e. of salvation.

**35 stomach** (1) appetite, (2) courage.

**36 passport** Not the modern document but a paper to give foreigners, and especially soldiers, in a strange country right of passage. *OED* records 'letters of passport' in *c.* 1500, and 'passport' in this sense from 1546.

And crowns for convoy put into his purse.
We would not die in that man's company
That fears his fellowship to die with us.
This day is called the Feast of Crispian.                    40
He that outlives this day and comes safe home
Will stand a-tiptoe when this day is named,
And rouse him at the name of Crispian.
He that shall see this day and live old age
Will yearly on the vigil feast his neighbours,               45
And say 'Tomorrow is Saint Crispian.'
Then will he strip his sleeve and show his scars,
And say 'These wounds I had on Crispin's day.'
Old men forget, yet all shall be forgot
But he'll remember, with advantages,                         50
What feats he did that day. Then shall our names,
Familiar in his mouth as household words,
Harry the king, Bedford and Exeter,
Warwick and Talbot, Salisbury and Gloucester,
Be in their flowing cups freshly remembered.                 55
This story shall the good man teach his son,
And Crispin Crispian shall ne'er go by
From this day to the ending of the world
But we in it shall be remembered.
We few, we happy few, we band of brothers —                  60

---

44 see . . . live old] F; live . . . see old *Pope;* see . . . live t'old *Keightley conj.*   48 And . . . day.'] Q, *Malone; not in* F   53–4 Bedford . . . Gloucester] F; *Bedford* and *Exeter, Clarence* and *Gloster, / Warwick* and *Yorke* Q   59 remembered] F, Q (remembred); rememberèd *Rowe*

---

**37 crowns for convoy** money (French) to pay for passage.

**38 We** The royal pronoun, meaning Henry personally, but by implication also those present who share his opinion.

**38 die** Coleridge conjectured that this should be 'live', but the mood is too mordant.

**39 fellowship** This comes close to the brotherhood of line 60, though the word has more ambiguous associations, as in the dismissiveness of Henry calling Williams 'fellow' at 4.8.51.

**40 Feast of Crispian** There were actually two saints, Crispinus and Crispianus, martyred together in A.D. 287. The date was 25 October.

**44 see . . . live** Pope reverses the verbs, partly because of a shift in the use of prepositions between 1599 and 1725. In 1599 prepositions could be omitted before some verbs with an indirect object, mostly verbs inviting elision, such as 'say' or 'ask'.

See Abbott, 198–201 (pp. 131–5).

**45 vigil** the preceding night. Knights used to maintain a vigil of prayer on the eve of their saint's day.

**50 with advantages** i.e. with some touches added to the picture.

**53–4** A roll-call of the figures made famous in *1H6*. Warwick and Talbot are not otherwise mentioned in this play, while York, who died at Agincourt, is ignored.

**57 Crispin Crispian** See 40 n. Holinshed reported, p. 552, 'the five and twentieth of October in the yeare 1415, being then fridaie, and the feast of Crispine and Crispinian'. This note, in blackletter at the end of the page, breaks the second name at the end of a line: 'Crispine and Crispini- / an'. Possibly this caused the fusion of the two saints.

**60–3** See Introduction, pp. 33–4.

For he today that sheds his blood with me
Shall be my brother; be he ne'er so vile
This day shall gentle his condition –
And gentlemen in England, now abed,
Shall think themselves accursed they were not here,                65
And hold their manhoods cheap whiles any speaks
That fought with us upon Saint Crispin's Day.

*Enter* SALISBURY

SALISBURY  My sovereign lord, bestow yourself with speed.
        The French are bravely in their battles set,
        And will with all expedience charge on us.                  70
KING  All things are ready, if our minds be so.
WESTMORLAND  Perish the man whose mind is backward now!
KING  Thou dost not wish more help from England, coz?
WESTMORLAND  God's will, my liege, would you and I alone,
        Without more help, could fight this royal battle!           75
KING  Why, now thou hast unwished five thousand men,
        Which likes me better than to wish us one.
        You know your places. God be with you all.

*Tucket. Enter* MONTJOY

MONTJOY  Once more I come to know of thee, King Harry,
        If for thy ransom thou wilt now compound                    80
        Before thy most assurèd overthrow.
        For certainly thou art so near the gulf
        Thou needs must be englutted. Besides, in mercy,
        The Constable desires thee thou wilt mind
        Thy followers of repentance, that their souls               85

63 **gentle his condition** raise his social status to that of a gentleman by making him a king's brother.
64 **now abed** The scene is set after dawn, when all peasants would have risen. Gentlemen rose much later.
65–6 See Textual Analysis, p. 224.
69 **bravely** (1) boldly, (2) handsomely, flauntingly.
70 **with all expedience** with speed, as soon as they can.
76 **five . . . men** It would be wrong to calculate from this that the entire English army numbered only 5,002. See 3 n.

78 SD See 4.2.35 n. The trumpet-call for the charge might have been expected, but this is the same sound as at 3.7.97 SD, and introduces the same character.
80 **compound** make a bargain. The offer is in Holinshed. Q omits all but the first two lines with the enquiry about a ransom.
82–3 **gulf . . . englutted** swallowed up in a pit. Hell's mouth was sometimes called a 'gaping gulf'. The French king uses the same image, with a different function, at 2.4.10.
84 **mind** bring to mind, remind.
85 **repentance** See 4.1.139 n.

May make a peaceful and a sweet retire
From off these fields where, wretches, their poor bodies
Must lie and fester.
KING                                  Who hath sent thee now?
MONTJOY  The Constable of France.
KING  I pray thee bear my former answer back.                          90
Bid them achieve me, and then sell my bones.
Good God, why should they mock poor fellows thus?
The man that once did sell the lion's skin
While the beast lived, was killed with hunting him.
A many of our bodies shall no doubt                                    95
Find native graves, upon the which, I trust,
Shall witness live in brass of this day's work.
And those that leave their valiant bones in France,
Dying like men, though buried in your dunghills,
They shall be famed, for there the sun shall greet them              100
And draw their honours reeking up to heaven,
Leaving their earthly parts to choke your clime,
The smell whereof shall breed a plague in France.
Mark then abounding valour in our English,
That being dead, like to the bullet's crazing                        105
Break out into a second course of mischief
Killing in relapse of mortality.
Let me speak proudly. Tell the Constable
We are but warriors for the working day.

104 abounding] F; abundant Q    105 crazing] F, Q; grazing F2

86 **retire** a happy withdrawal, not a sour retreat
in battle.

89 Not the king, as it was last time, nor the
Dauphin, but the general commanding the French
army. This question-and-answer may be part of the
Dauphin's demotion from this act.

93–4 **The man . . . him** Proverbial (Dent B132),
from Aesop's fable about a man hunting a bear. The
change to a lion denotes the royal quarry and the
heraldic use of lions on the royal coat of arms. For
longish memories, the first reference to Henry in
relation to lions appeared in Falstaff's excuse over
his cowardice at Gadshill (*1H4* 2.4.224), but there
the lion Falstaff was refusing to attack the true
prince.

96 **native** i.e. in England. The word is oddly
recurrent in the play. See 1.2.17; 2.4.64, 96; 3.6.26;
4.1.151.

97 **in brass** in funeral monuments. The phrase

became a proverb (B607.1).

98 Picking up Montjoy's final point from 87–8.

100–1 **the sun . . . honours** They have been
promised honours, or at least gentrification, by the
sun-king at 61–3.

102 **clime** (1) region, (2) climate.

104 **abounding** (1) plentiful, (2) leaping. The
word also carries a faint smell of tennis balls. In
royal tennis the rebound generated the 'chase'.

105 **crazing** (1) further breakage, (2) ricochet.
The familiar term 'grazing' carries only the second
sense. 'Crazing' suggests the damage a fragmented
bullet causes after its first impact.

107 **relapse of mortality** while decaying in
death, causing death on the rebound.

109–11 **warriors . . . field** A deliberately pedestrian image. They look workmanlike, because their
colourful clothes are dirty from marching in the
wet to the battlefield.

Our gayness and our gilt are all besmirched                          110
With rainy marching in the painful field.
There's not a piece of feather in our host
(Good argument, I hope, we will not fly)
And time hath worn us into slovenry.
But by the mass, our hearts are in the trim,                         115
And my poor soldiers tell me yet ere night
They'll be in fresher robes, or they will pluck
The gay new coats o'er the French soldiers' heads
And turn them out of service. If they do this –
As, if God please, they shall – my ransom then                       120
Will soon be levied. Herald, save thou thy labour.
Come thou no more for ransom, gentle herald.
They shall have none, I swear, but these my joints,
Which if they have, as I will leave 'em them,
Shall yield them little. Tell the Constable.                         125

MONTJOY  I shall, King Harry. And so fare thee well.
Thou never shalt hear herald any more.                        *Exit*

KING  [*Aside*] I fear thou wilt once more come again for a ransom.

*Enter* YORK

YORK  My lord, most humbly on my knee I beg
The leading of the vanguard.                                         130

---

117 or] F; for *Hanmer;* as *Taylor*   118 the] F; your Q   124 'em] *Rowe;* vm F, Q3; am Q   128 again] F; *not in Taylor*   130 vanguard] F (vaward)

**111 field** It is still more a farmer's field than a battlefield. The word recalls the vasty fields of 1.0.12, 1.2.129, and 3.6.25, which become the world's best garden in Burgundy's speech at 5.2.36.

**113 fly** (1) speed like birds, (2) run away from the battle.

**114 time** the working day of line 109.

**115 in the trim** (1) fashionable, (2) fit.

**117 or** Q and F agree on 'or', which is a less obvious construction than Hanmer's or Taylor's conjectures. But the F reading is emphatic – the English will either be in their fresh clothes or they will take the gay coats from the French. Henry's poor soldiers have not said any such thing to him on stage.

**119 service** (1) work as soldiers, (2) serving a lord (being a 'lackey') and wearing his livery.

**121 soon** i.e. easily, because the soldiers will be enriched by loot from the French.

**128 I fear . . . ransom** F's prose is surprising, and may indicate a misreading of the manuscript. Wilson seeks to adjust the F reading, arguing that 'once more' and 'again' are tautologous and one should go. But Henry's statement itself is surprising. He must be expressing his own doubt about the outcome of the battle, which would justify a prose aside. The prospect of a ransom looms large in the next scene, but on an entirely different level. This edition records the line as an aside, revealing doubts that Henry will not admit to his soldiers.

**128 SD York** does not appear elsewhere in the play. He is named in Holinshed as asking to lead the 'vaward', being 'of an haughty corage' (p. 553). This brief appearance prepares for the news of his death in the battle, reported in 4.6.11–32 and 4.8.95.

**130 vanguard**   F   reproduces   Holinshed's spelling, a distinct abbreviated form.

KING  Take it, brave York. Now soldiers, march away,
        And how Thou pleasest, God, dispose the day.

                                                        *Exeunt*


4.4  *Alarm. Excursions. Enter* PISTOL, FRENCH *soldier*, BOY

PISTOL  Yield, cur!
FRENCH  *Je pense que vous êtes le gentilhomme de bon qualité.*
PISTOL  Quality? 'Colin o custure me'. Art thou a gentleman? What
        is thy name? Discuss.
FRENCH  *O Seigneur Dieu!*                                    5
PISTOL  O Seigneur Due should be a gentleman. Perpend my
        words, O Seigneur Due, and mark: O Seigneur Due, thou
        diest on point of fox, except, O Seigneur, thou do give to me
        egregious ransom.
FRENCH  *Oh, prenez miséricorde! Ayez pitié de moi!*          10
PISTOL  Moy shall not serve. I will have forty moys, or I will fetch
        thy rim out at thy throat, in drops of crimson blood.


Act 4, Scene 4  1 Yield] F (Yeeld); Eyld Q  3 Quality] F (Qualtitie)  3 Colin o custure me] *Malone;* calmie o custure me F  11 or] *Theobald;* for F

**Act 4, Scene 4**
**0 SD** *Alarm* Most likely a drum roll, since the two soldiers enter on foot.
**0 SD** *Excursions* This word is the only indication in F that any battle action was depicted on stage. Q's stage direction, '*Enter Pistoll, the French man, and the Boy*' where the scene is transposed until after Act 4, Scene 5 and the French acknowledgement of defeat, is less pointed, though less tantalising. Q's stage directions make no note of battle noises, except for a single '*alarum*' at the end of Act 4, Scene 6 that prompts Henry's order to kill the prisoners.
**1–9** It has been proposed that the first lines are an early draft for the lines that follow, since Pistol repeats the demand for his prisoner's name, first made at 3–4, at 18.
**1 Yield** Q's 'Eyld' probably gives the pronunciation. Cercignani notes the occasional loss of initial y, as with 'yearn', at 2.3.3 and 5, also spoken by Pistol.
**2 *Je . . . qualité*** 'I think you are a gentleman of high rank.'
**3 'Colin o custure me'** Malone identified this as the refrain of a popular Irish song, 'callin og o' stor', Maiden, my treasure, printed in Clement

Robinson's *Handful of Pleasant Delights* (1584). F. W. Sternfeld, *Elizabethan and Jacobean Studies*, ed. H. Davis and H. Gardner, 1959, p. 163, lists four melodies and thirteen references to it from the time. Pistol's quotation of the Irish vaguely follows the French he has just heard. If he knows its meaning it could also be an exclamation at the prospect of a ransom.
**5 *O . . . Dieu!*** See 3.5.28–9 n.
**6–7 Due** i.e. as in the acknowledgement of a due debt.
**6 Perpend** Hear, understand. Used as an inflated or mock-pompous term at *Wiv.* 2.1.94, *AYLI* 3.3.47, *TN* 5.1.280, and *Ham.* 2.2.105.
**8 fox** An old-fashioned broadsword.
**8 except** unless.
**9 egregious** exceptional.
**10 *Oh . . . moi!*** 'Oh, have mercy! Take pity on me!'
**11 Moy** Pistol hears the French '*moi*' (pronounced as 'moy' in Middle French) as a half, or moiety.
**11 or** Theobald's emendation creates the choice lost in the F reading.
**12 rim** i.e. a clipping cut with a knife from his coin. See 4.1.201 n.

FRENCH   *Est-il impossible d'échapper la force de ton bras?*

PISTOL   Brass, cur? Thou damnèd and luxurious mountain goat,
     offer'st me brass?                                                                              15

FRENCH   *Oh, pardonnez-moi!*

PISTOL   Sayest thou me so? Is that a tun of moys? Come hither,
     boy. Ask me this slave in French what is his name.

BOY   *Écoutez. Comment êtes-vous appelé?*

FRENCH   *Monsieur le Fer.*                                                                          20

BOY   He says his name is Mr Fer.

PISTOL   Mr Fer. I'll fer him, and firk him, and ferret him. Discuss
     the same in French unto him.

BOY   I do not know the French for fer and ferret and firk.

PISTOL   Bid him prepare, for I will cut his throat.                                                 25

FRENCH   *Que dit-il, monsieur?*

BOY   *Il me commande à vous dire que vous faites-vous prêt, car ce soldat
     ici est disposé tout à cette heure de couper votre gorge.*

PISTOL   *Oui, coupe la gorge, par ma foi,* peasant, unless thou give me
     crowns, brave crowns, or mangled shalt thou be by this my          30
     sword.

FRENCH   [*Kneels*] *Oh! Je vous supplie, pour l'amour de Dieu, me
     pardonner! Je suis le gentilhomme de bonne maison. Gardez ma vie,
     et je vous donnerai deux cents écus.*

PISTOL   What are his words?                                                                         35

BOY   He prays you to save his life. He is a gentleman of a good
     house, and for his ransom he will give you two hundred crowns.

---

13 *la*] F (*le*)   21 Mr Fer] F (M. *Fer*)   28 *tout à cette heure*] F (*tout asture*)   29 *Oui, coupe la gorge*] F (Owy, cuppele gorge)

13 *Est-il . . . bras?* 'Is it impossible to escape the strength of your arm?'

14 **luxurious** lecherous – thought to be an attribute of goats (Dent G167). Llewellyn receives similarly charged invective, at 5.1.25.

16 *Oh . . . moi!* 'Oh, I beg your pardon.'

17 **tun of moys** box of half-coins. The container is a reminder of the tennis balls in Act 1, Scene 2.

19 *Écoutez . . . appelé?* 'Listen. What's your name?'

20 **le Fer** In French the name means 'iron'.

22 **firk . . . ferret** whip or beat, hunt, rifle his pockets.

25 **prepare** i.e. for death.

26 *Que . . . monsieur?* 'What does he say, sir?'

27–8 *Il . . . gorge* 'He orders me to tell you that you should prepare yourself, because this soldier here is inclined to cut your throat at once.'

28 *à cette heure* Sixteenth-century French pronunciation used an elliptical form sometimes transcribed as 'asteure', or 'ast'heure'. The ellipsis has been removed, since modern French is used in this edition. See J. W. Lever, 'Shakespeare's French fruits', *S. Sur.* 6 (1953), 79–90, and Cercignani, p. 46.

32 SD *Kneels* Le Fer is certainly kneeling at line 43. Such an action implies a parody of the conspirators in Act 2, Scene 2.

32–4 *Oh . . . écus* 'Oh! I beg you, for the love of God, to pardon me! I am a gentleman of good family. Save my life, and I will give you two hundred crowns.'

PISTOL Tell him my fury shall abate, and I the crowns will take.

FRENCH *Petit monsieur, que dit-il?*

BOY *Encore qu'il est contre son jurement de pardonner aucun prisonnier.* 40
*Néanmoins, pour les écus que vous l'ayez promis, il est content à vous*
*donner la liberté, le franchisement.*

FRENCH *Sur mes genoux je vous donne mille remerciements, et je*
*m'estime heureux que je suis tombé entre les mains d'un chevalier – je*
*pense le plus brave, vaillant, et très distingué seigneur d'Angleterre.*    45

PISTOL Expound unto me, boy.

BOY He gives you upon his knees a thousand thanks, and he
esteems himself happy that he hath fallen into the hands of one
(as he thinks) the most brave, valorous and thrice-worthy
seigneur of England.                                                          50

PISTOL As I suck blood, I will some mercy show. Follow me.

BOY *Suivez-vous le grand capitaine.*

                      *[Exeunt Pistol and French soldier]*

I did never know so full a voice issue from so empty a heart.
But the saying is true, the empty vessel makes the greatest
sound. Bardolph and Nym had ten times more valour than this         55
roaring devil i'th'old play, that everyone may pare his nails with
a wooden dagger, and they are both hanged, and so would this
be if he durst steal anything adventurously. I must stay with the
lackeys with the luggage of our camp. The French might have a
good prey of us if he knew of it, for there is none to guard it       60
but boys.                                                      *Exit*

---

41 *l'ayez promis*] F (*layt a promets*)   42 *la liberté*] F (*le liberte*)   43 *je*] F (*se*)   43 *remerciements*] F (*remercions*); *remerciement*
F2   44 *je suis tombé*] Theobald; *Ie intombe* F   44 *mains*] F (*main.*)   44–5 *je pense*] F (*Ie peuse*); *comme je pense* Taylor   45
*distingué*] Capell; *distinie* F   52 *Suivez-vous*] Rowe; *Saaue vous* F   52 SD *Exeunt . . . soldier*] Not in F

39 *Petit . . . dit-il?* 'Little sir, what does he say?'
40–2 *Encore . . . franchisement* 'Again that it
is contrary to his oath to pardon any prisoner.
Nonetheless, for the crowns you have promised him
he is content to give you liberty, your freedom.'
43–5 *Sur . . . d'Angleterre* 'Oh my knees I give
you a thousand thanks, and I think myself happy to
have fallen into the hands of a gentleman – I think
the most gallant, valiant, and distinguished lord of
England.'
51 **suck blood** i.e. as a leech. See 2.3.43–4.
51 **I . . . show** Two scenes later Pistol's profits
are lost by Henry's order to kill the prisoners.
52 *Suivez-vous . . . capitaine* 'Follow the great

captain.' Pistol is promoted again.
54–5 **empty . . . sound** Proverbial (Dent v36).
It has been heard before at *2H4* 1.3.74–5.
56–7 **roaring . . . dagger** In the morality plays
the devil had a property dagger of lath. It is also
referred to in *2H6* 4.2.1 and in *TN* 4.2.108. Paring
the devil's nails was proverbial (Dent N12).
57 **both hanged** We have been told before of
Bardolph's fate, but not Nym's.
59 **luggage** heavy baggage. It is used in *1H4*
5.4.147. Llewellyn uses it again at 4.7.1.
59–61 **The French . . . boys** A forewarning that
the boy will be killed as Bardolph and Nym have
been.

**4.5** *Enter* CONSTABLE, ORLÉANS, BOURBON, *and* RAMBURES

CONSTABLE   *O diable!*
ORLÉANS   *O Seigneur! Le jour est perdu, tout est perdu!*
BOURBON   *Mort de ma vie*, all is confounded, all!
   Reproach and everlasting shame
   Sits mocking in our plumes.                              5
              *A short alarm*
   *O méchante fortune!* Do not run away.
CONSTABLE   Why, all our ranks are broke.
BOURBON   O perdurable shame, let's stab ourselves.
   Be these the wretches that we played at dice for?
ORLÉANS   Is this the king we sent to for his ransom?            10
BOURBON   Shame, and eternal shame, nothing but shame!
   Let us die! In once more, back again,
   And he that will not follow Bourbon now
   Let him go hence, and with his cap in hand
   Like a base pander hold the chamber door,               15

---

Act 4, Scene 5   0 SD BOURBON] Q (*Enter the foure French Lords*); *Burbon, Dolphin* F   2 *Seigneur*] F2; *sigueur* F   2 *est perdu . . . est perdu*] *Rowe; et perdia . . . perdie* F   3 SH BOURBON] *This edn; Or.* Q; *Dol.* F   3 *Mort de ma vie*] F (*Mor Dieu ma vie*); *Mort Dieu! Ma vie! Wilson (conj. Greg)*   4 Reproach] F; Reproach, reproach *Capell*   8 SH BOURBON] *This edn; Dol.* F; *not in* Q   12 die! In once more,] *This edn*; dye in once more ‸ F; Lets die with honour Q; die in honour! Once more, *Knight*; die in harness: once more, *Wilson*; die in arms: once more, *Walter*   15 pander] F; leno Q

### Act 4, Scene 5

**0 SD** Q's entry direction reads '*Enter the foure French Lords.*' The quality of its transcription here is good enough to indicate that a reporter was present, probably Bourbon, although the text is cut to 18 lines and speeches are attributed to different speakers.

**0 SD BOURBON** F records both Bourbon and the Dauphin.

**1 *O diable!*** 'Oh hell!'

**2 *O . . . perdu!*** 'Oh God! The day is lost, everything's lost!'

**3 *Mort . . . vie*** 'Death of my life'. This exclamation is used by Brittany in F at 3.6.11. Q gives it to the Constable here.

**5 mocking . . . plumes** See *R2* 3.2.162–3, and Introduction, pp. 14–15.

**6 *O . . . fortune!*** 'O evil fortune!'

**7 SH CONSTABLE** Taylor follows Q in this scene, putting the speech by Orléans (20–22) ahead of the Constable's and Bourbon's disdaining order (18–19 and 23–4), and cutting 7–11. This underrates the point about the French

disorder, which indirectly prompts the attack on the 'luggage' just anticipated by the boy. On the other hand it reduces the focus on Bourbon (the Dauphin in F), who is given no further lines in the scene, and whose urgent exhortation not to run away would have been made more ridiculous if he were than promptly to depart. As it stands in F, Bourbon's urgent demand not to flee (line 6) drains away in the recriminations. Possibly that is the point.

**8 perdurable** everlasting.

**12 die! In** As before (see 3.4.54, 4.1.116, 4.2.52), F's punctuation seems deficient. The key word is the preposition, which means both going 'in' to battle again, and exiting into the tiring house.

**13 Bourbon** The identification of Bourbon in this speech as the aggressive speaker suggests that he had not yet been identified in the F text as the figure to replace the Dauphin.

**15 pander** Q's 'leno' is a sophisticated alternative word for F's more familiar term, meaning a bawd or pimp. Its rarity has led to the assumption that its existence in Q shows an authorial revision.

Whilst by a slave, no gentler than my dog,
His fairest daughter is contaminate.
CONSTABLE  Disorder, that hath spoiled us, friend us now.
　　　Let us on heaps go offer up our lives.
ORLÉANS  We are enough yet living in the field                    20
　　　To smother up the English in our throngs,
　　　If any order might be thought upon.
BOURBON  The devil take order now, I'll to the throng.
　　　Let life be short, else shame will be too long.

　　　　　　　　　　　　　　　　　　　　　　*Exeunt*

**4.6** *Alarm. Enter the* KING *and his train, with prisoners*

KING  Well have we done, thrice-valiant countrymen.
　　　But all's not done, yet keep the French the field.

　　　　　　　　*[Enter* EXETER *by another door]*

EXETER  The Duke of York commends him to your majesty.
KING  Lives he, good uncle? Thrice within this hour
　　　I saw him down, thrice up again and fighting.                  5
　　　From helmet to the spur all blood he was.
EXETER  In which array, brave soldier, doth he lie
　　　Larding the plain; and by his bloody side,
　　　Yoke-fellow to his honour-owing wounds,
　　　The noble Earl of Suffolk also lies.                           10

---

16 Whilst by a slave] *Pope;* Whilst a base slaue F; Who least by a slaue Q    17 contaminate] *Capell;* contaminated F;
contamuracke Q    20 SH ORLÉANS] F; *Con.* Q    24 SD *Exeunt.*] *Exit.* F

**16 a slave** F repeats the adjective from the
previous line.
**16 slave . . . gentler** The language indicates
social outrage at the contamination of gentry by
lower classes. The comparison of the slave with a
dog reintroduces the imagery of soldiers as dogs
and the ravishing of virgins from Henry's Harfleur
threats at 3.4.11–14 and 20–3. See Introduction,
p. 13.
**17 contaminate** made impure, by the slave
raping the gentlewoman. F's misreading is a d/e
error. See Textual Analysis, p. 222.
　　**18 spoiled** robbed, despoiled.
　　**19 on heaps** i.e. in disorder.
　　**24 Let . . . long** The proverb which says that it

is better to die with honour than live with shame
(Dent H576) is called in question by Bourbon's
later appearance on stage as Henry's prisoner in
Act 4, Scene 7. Since F allocates this speech to
Bourbon, that evidently was the original point.

**Act 4, Scene 6**
　　**2 SD** Exeter does not enter with the king's train
at the beginning of the scene, but comes from elsewhere on the battlefield with his news. York had
the leading of the vanguard (4.3.131).
　　**8 Larding** Enriching. The word is also used of
Falstaff's sweat when he runs away at Gadshill
(*1H4* 2.2.191).

Suffolk first died, and York, all haggled over,
Comes to him where in gore he lay insteeped,
And takes him by the beard, kisses the gashes
That bloodily did yawn upon his face.
He cries aloud 'Tarry, my cousin Suffolk.                            15
My soul shall thine keep company to heaven.
Tarry, sweet soul, for mine, then fly abreast,
As in this glorious and well-foughten field
We kept together in our chivalry.'
Upon these words I came, and cheered him up.                         20
He smiled me in the face, raught me his hand,
And with a feeble grip says 'Dear my lord,
Commend my service to my sovereign.'
So did he turn, and over Suffolk's neck
He threw his wounded arm, and kissed his lips,                       25
And so, espoused to death, with blood he sealed
A testament of noble-ending love.
The pretty and sweet manner of it forced
Those waters from me which I would have stopped,
But I had not so much of man in me,                                  30
And all my mother came into mine eyes
And gave me up to tears.

KING                                       I blame you not,
For hearing this I must perforce compound
With wilful eyes, or they will issue too.

---

Act 4, Scene 6   14 face.] F; face, And Q, *Pope*   15 my] F; dear Q   34 wilful] *This edn;* mixt-full F; mistful *Warburton*

11–27 An account notably similar to the account of the deaths of the Talbots, father and son, in *1H6* Act 4, Scene 7.
  11 **haggled** hacked and mangled.
  12 **insteeped** soaked.
  14 **yawn** Wounds are represented as mouths in a development of this image in *JC* 3.1.260.
  15 **He** Q's reading makes it a repetitive 'and . . . and' sentence, less breathless than F.
  19 **chivalry** (1) mounted nobles in battle array, (2) honour in battle. The honour is the 'service' of line 23.
  20 **cheered him up** Not quite the modern idiom, though close. In *2H4* 4.2.113 the exhortation 'cheer up yourself, look up' is not dissimilar.
  21 **raught** reached.
  26–7 The complex word play here merges marriage and death. The blood that seals a testament of

marriage is the breach of virginity. The testament of death is the last will made by a dying man. The wax used to seal legal documents such as wills is always red.
  31 **my mother** womanly moisture. A complex theory of human physiology lies behind the identification of the 'mother' (hysteria) in men being also the softness inherited from the mother which brings tears. (*OED sb* 1d, 12b, 13).
  33 **compound** make a bargain (such as ransom, 4.3.80). The image picks up Exeter's 'gave me up', or surrendered.
  34 **wilful** F's reading makes no sense, and Warburton's is an eighteenth-century sentimentalisation not used anywhere else by Shakespeare. Warburton evidently had his own doubts about his emendation, because his own copy of his edition in the Folger Shakespeare Library has both the

*Alarm*

But hark, what new alarm is this same?                          35
The French have reinforced their scattered men.
Then every soldier kill his prisoners.
Give the word through.

*Exeunt*

**4.7** *Enter* LLEWELLYN *and* GOWER

LLEWELLYN  Kill the poys and the luggage! 'Tis expressly against
the law of arms. 'Tis as arrant a piece of knavery, mark you
now, as can be offert, in your conscience now, is it not?
GOWER  'Tis certain. There's not a boy left alive, and the cowardly
rascals that ran from the battle ha' done this slaughter. Besides,    5
they have burned and carried away all that was in the king's
tent, wherefore the king most worthily hath caused every
soldier to cut his prisoner's throat. Oh, 'tis a gallant king!

---

38 *Exeunt*] F; *Pist.* Couple gorge. *Exit omnes.* Q   **Act 4, Scene 7**   **4.7** *Actus Quartus* F   **3** offert, in] F; –. In *Wilson*

emendation and the accompanying note crossed out
by his hand. The problem is to identify what the
F 'mixt-full' might have been a misreading of. In
Shakespeare 'mixt' is usually accompanied by a
preposition such as 'with' or 'together'. The four
minims which start the word cannot readily be
made to read anything but mi- unless the number of
strokes is altered, and x in Elizabethan hands could
not be misread as anything but another consonant, perhaps p or b, though they do not fit either.
There is a 'mindfull' in *Lucrece*, but that does
not develop the image launched in 'compound'.
'Wilful', if written in the manuscript used for F
as 'will-full', most nearly suits the range of possible readings in the handwriting. It also sets the reason, which has to bargain or compound, against the
will, which ignores reason. The other word which
may possibly be related to the image, 'issue' (come
forth), cannot be made to match any of the more
plausible readings.

**37** The rapid change from tears to slaughter is
in part a demonstration of how English 'order'
contrasts with the French disorder of the previous scene. Taylor proposes that Henry's entry
'*with prisoners*' at the beginning of the scene must
mean that the throats are cut on stage. See note in
Taylor, p. 65, and Introduction, p. 25. The Q

version, however, has no prisoners on stage, in
a scene which has a large speaking part for one
of the reporters. Thus if Q does recall the staged
version, it was evidently not a particularly memorable slaughter. Moreover, Pistol's added 'Couple
gorge' in Q is a comic catchphrase insertion which
would lose all its comedy if immediately enacted
with blood on stage. Q is not a good guide to the
original staging here.

**Act 4, Scene 7**

**1 Kill . . . luggage** Llewellyn's first word echoes
Henry's of only two lines earlier. Its transfer to
the killing of inanimate objects, slipping in the
Eastcheap boy indirectly, makes a joke that jolts
the word out of its initial shock value. The boy
had used the term 'luggage' at the end of Act 4,
Scene 4. Gower confirms that the boy must be dead
in line 4.

**3 offert, in** Wilson proposes an alternative
punctuation, which, given the uncertainty in F
of setting punctuation from this section of the
manuscript, has some plausibility. But without any
more obviously superior reading, F should stand.

**7 wherefore** i.e. as a result. Gower mistakes
Henry's reason for giving the order, which has just
been witnessed on stage. See Introduction, p. 25.

LLEWELLYN   Ay, he was porn at Monmouth. Captain Gower, what
   call you the town's name where Alexander the Pig was born?          10
GOWER   Alexander the Great.
LLEWELLYN   Why, I pray you, is not 'pig' great? The pig, or the
   great, or the mighty, or the huge, or the magnanimous, are all
   one reckonings, save the phrase is a little variations.
GOWER   I think Alexander the Great was born in Macedon. His          15
   father was called Phillip of Macedon, as I take it.
LLEWELLYN   I think it is e'en Macedon where Alexander is porn. I
   tell you, captain, if you look in the maps of the woreld I warrant
   you sall find, in the comparisons between Macedon and
   Monmouth, that the situations, look you, is both alike. There is     20
   a river in Macedon, and there is also moreover a river at
   Monmouth. It is called Wye at Monmouth, but it is out of my
   prains what is the name of the other river. But 'tis all one, 'tis
   alike as my fingers is to my fingers, and there is salmons in
   both. If you mark Alexander's life well, Harry of Monmouth's        25
   life is come after it indifferent well, for there is figures in all
   things. Alexander, God knows, and you know, in his rages and
   his furies and his wraths and his cholers and his moods and his
   displeasures and his indignations, and also being a little
   intoxicates in his prains, did in his ales and his angers, look      30
   you, kill his best friend Cleitus.
GOWER   Our king is not like him in that. He never killed any of his
   friends.
LLEWELLYN   It is not well done, mark you now, to take the tales out of
   my mouth ere it is made and finished. I speak out in the figures     35

---

9 Monmouth. Captain Gower,] Q; *Monmouth* Captaine *Gower:* F   12 great] F2; grear F   14 variations] F; variation Q   17
e'en Macedon] *Oxford;* in *Macedon* F; Macedon indeed Q   18 woreld] F (Orld); worell Q   35 made] F; made an end Q

**9 Monmouth** A town on the border of Wales
and England, on the River Wye.

**9 Monmouth . . . what** Q's punctuation seems
preferable to F's here, because it makes Llewellyn
more meditative, though either form of punctuation makes sense.

**11 Alexander the Great** King of Macedon,
356–23 B.C., conqueror of the known world, and
cutter of the gordian knot. See 1.1.46 n.

**14 variations** The plural for 'reckonings' and
'variations' may have been designed as another
Welsh pronunciation. The plurals recur in the list
at 27–9 and 'tales' at 34. Possibly F's word is a
minim misreading of 'variatious', though Q's reading indicates that it is not.

**15 Macedon** A country rather than a town.

**17 e'en Macedon** The Oxford conjecture is
plausible, since it gives the F text the extra emphasis
that is in the Q reading.

**26 figures** emblematic significance, symbols.

**31 Cleitus** Alexander's foster-brother and
fellow-soldier. He was killed by Alexander in a
drunken quarrel. The story was told in the *Homily
Against Gluttony and Drunkennesse.*

**32–3 killed . . . friends** A resonant statement.
Besides the report of Falstaff's death in Act 2,
Scene 3, the deaths of both Bardolph and Nym
have been registered by 4.4.57. They no longer
qualify, and to Gower never have qualified, as the
king's friends.

and comparisons of it. As Alexander killed his friend Cleitus,
being in his ales and his cups, so also Harry Monmouth,
being in his right wits and his good judgements, turned away
the fat knight with the great belly doublet. He was full of jests
and gypes and knaveries and mocks – I have forgot his name.                 40
GOWER   Sir John Falstaff.
LLEWELLYN   That is he. I'll tell you, there is good men porn at
     Monmouth.
GOWER   Here comes his majesty.

*Alarm. Enter* KING *Harry*, [EXETER, GLOUCESTER, WARWICK,
     *and English* HERALD,] *and* BOURBON *with prisoners. Flourish*

KING   I was not angry since I came to France                              45
          Until this instant. Take a trumpet, herald.
          Ride thou unto the horsemen on yon hill.
          If they will fight with us, bid them come down,
          Or void the field. They do offend our sight.
          If they'll do neither, we will come to them,                     50
          And make them skirr away as swift as stones
          Enforcèd from the old Assyrian slings.
          Besides, we'll cut the throats of those we have,
          And not a man of them that we shall take
          Shall taste our mercy. Go and tell them so.                      55
                                                    [*Exit English Herald*]

---

47 yon] F (yond)

**37 ales and his cups** A proverbial phrase (Dent
C911).
   **39 great belly doublet** A doublet so stuffed as
to protrude like a fat stomach. Given the familiar
image of Falstaff as immensely fat, the last word
may be a joke addition, though not Llewellyn's
joke.
   **40 gypes** gibes, sharp jokes.
   **40–1 forgot . . . Falstaff** Taylor ('The fortunes
of Oldcastle', p. 96) suggests that this is a theatre
in-joke about the change of Falstaff's name from
Oldcastle in *1H4* to Falstaff in *2H4*.
   **44 SD WARWICK** His first appearance. He has
been named amongst Agincourt's likely heroes in
Act 4, Scene 3 along with Talbot (see 4.3.54 n.).
His one line in the play comes at 4.8.18.
   **44 SD BOURBON** Bourbon has nothing to say in
this scene, but his presence may reflect his replacing the Dauphin at Agincourt. His mute presence after his boasting in Act 3, Scene 8, and Act
4, Scene 2 and his conspicuousness as the most

lordly of the prisoners makes him the on-stage
target for Henry's threat to cut more throats at
line 53.
   **44 SD Flourish** The entry starts with a drum roll
signalling an '*alarm*', and ends with a trumpet-call
signalling a royal entrance.
   **46 Until this instant** Henry has evidently only
just learned of the attack on the 'luggage'. The
statement implicitly contradicts Gower's version at
the beginning of the scene.
   **46 trumpet** i.e. a trumpeter. Heralds never blew
their own trumpets.
   **47 yon** See 4.2.16 n.
   **51 skirr** skip, like a stone.
   **52 Assyrian slings** The Geneva Bible refers
(Judith 9.9) to the Assyrian 'shield, spear, and
bow, and sling'. This the Bishops' Bible translates
as 'their charets, arrowes, and speares'. They are
mentioned three times in Marlowe's *Tamburlaine*
and are parodied by Falstaff in *2H4* 5.3.82. See
Introduction, p. 27 n. 1.

*Enter* MONTJOY

EXETER  Here comes the herald of the French, my liege.

GLOUCESTER  His eyes are humbler than they used to be.

KING  How now, what means this, herald? Know'st thou not
    That I have fined these bones of mine for ransom?
    Com'st thou again for ransom?

MONTJOY                  No, great king.    60
    I come to thee for charitable licence,
    That we may wander o'er this bloody field
    To book our dead, and then to bury them,
    To sort our nobles from our common men,
    For many of our princes – woe the while –    65
    Lie drowned and soaked in mercenary blood,
    So do our vulgar drench their peasant limbs
    In blood of princes, while the wounded steeds
    Fret fetlock deep in gore, and with wild rage
    Yerk out their armèd heels at their dead masters,    70
    Killing them twice. Oh, give us leave, great king,
    To view the field in safety, and dispose
    Of their dead bodies.

KING               I tell thee truly, herald,
    I know not if the day be ours or no,
    For yet a-many of your horsemen peer    75
    And gallop o'er the field.

MONTJOY           The day is yours.

KING  Praisèd be God, and not our strength, for it.
    What is this castle called that stands hard by?

MONTJOY  They call it Agincourt.

---

58 How now] F; Gods will Q   60 SH MONTJOY] F (*Her.*)   68 while the] *This edn;* and with F; and their *Malone;* and our *Taylor*

**55 SD** In Holinshed the French herald returns to Henry on the morning after the battle.

**57** Gloucester's comment prepares the ground for the sarcasm in Henry's question to the herald.

**58 How now** Q's reading may indicate the censoring of an oath in the F copy.

**59 fined** settled the price of.

**60 Com'st ... ransom** The two previous visits were at 3.7.97 and 4.3.78.

**60 SH MONTJOY** F's speech heading is '*Her*'.

**61 charitable licence** i.e. a concession made from Christian kindness.

**63 book** put on record.

**66 mercenary** See 'Why Jamy in *Henry V*?', pp. 372–3.

**68 while the** F needs correcting, since it seems to have anticipated 'and with' from the next line immediately below it. Malone's 'their' picks up a word from the preceding line and makes the vulgar own the steeds.

**70 Yerk** This word is not quite the modern 'jerk'; it is a larger gesture, closer to 'lash'.

**75 peer** (1) look across, and probably (2) appear.

KING   Then call we this the field of Agincourt,                                    80
       Fought on the day of Crispin Crispianus.
LLEWELLYN   Your grandfather of famous memory, an't please your
       majesty, and your great-uncle Edward the Plack Prince of
       Wales, as I have read in the chronicles, fought a most prave
       pattle here in France.                                                       85
KING   They did, Llewellyn.
LLEWELLYN   Your majesty says very true. If your majesties is
       remembered of it, the Welshmen did good service in a garden
       where leeks did grow, wearing leeks in their Monmouth caps,
       which your majesty know to this hour is an honourable badge of   90
       the service. And I do believe your majesty takes no scorn to
       wear the leek upon St Tavy's day.
KING   I wear it for a memorable honour,
       For I am Welsh, you know, good countryman.
LLEWELLYN   All the water in Wye cannot wash your majesty's           95
       Welsh plood out of your pody, I can tell you that. God pless it
       and preserve it, as long as it pleases His Grace – and his
       majesty too.
KING   Thanks, good my countryman.
LLEWELLYN   By Cheshu, I am your majesty's countryman! I care       100
       not who know it. I will confess it to all the woreld. I need not to
       be ashamed of your majesty, praised be God, so long as your
       majesty is an honest man.
KING   God keep me so.

81 Crispin Crispianus.] F; (*Crispin Crispianus.*); *Cryspin Cryspin* Q; Cryspin, Crispianus. Q3   99 countryman] Q, F2;
countrymen F   101 woreld] F (Orld)   104 God] Q, F3; Good F

81 **Crispin Crispianus** A case where the same
influence that altered Q3 may have affected F. See
Textual Analysis, p. 224.
  82 **grandfather** i.e. great-grandfather, Edward
III. See 1.2.103–10.
  84–5 **prave pattle** i.e., Crécy.
  88–9 **a garden . . . grow** This legend has no
definite origin, unless it refers to the Welsh battle
against the Saxons in A.D.540. See 91–2 n.
  89 **Monmouth caps** round, brimless headgear
with a high crown, worn by ordinary soldiers
(M. C. Linthicum, *Costume in the Drama of Shakespeare and his Contemporaries*, 1936, p. 226). They
were proverbial (Dent M1105). At line 138 and
4.8.27 Llewellyn wears a 'cap'.
  90 **badge** distinctive emblem.
  91–2 **to wear . . . day** The Welsh tradition of
wearing leeks to commemorate the victory of 540
against the Saxons on St David's day, 1 March,

does not emerge until several decades after this
reference. Elizabeth, however, did adopt Welsh traditions, and celebrated St David's day. Some of
the traditions may have developed long before they
were first recorded in print. The play is unlikely to
have begun this one.
  94 **I am Welsh** Henry was born at Monmouth,
but only one of his great-grandfathers, not Edward
III, was Welsh. Historically his chief acquain-
tance with Wales was his long training in siege
warfare during the succession of rebellions against
his father.
  97–8 **His Grace . . . too** Llewellyn adds
'majesty' to clarify his reference to God's grace.
Henry has been called 'his grace' by Canterbury
1.1.78, Westmorland at 1.2.125, and Bedford at
2.2.1.
  99 **countryman** A slightly more removed
relation than the brotherhood of 4.3.60.

*Enter* WILLIAMS

Our heralds go with him.
Bring me just notice of the numbers dead                         105
On both our parts.

[*Exeunt Montjoy, Gower and English heralds*]
Call yonder fellow hither.

EXETER   Soldier, you must come to the king.

KING   Soldier, why wear'st thou that glove in thy cap?

WILLIAMS   An't please your majesty, 'tis the gage of one that I
should fight withal, if he be alive.                              110

KING   An Englishman?

WILLIAMS   An't please your majesty, a rascal that swaggered with
me last night, who if a live and ever dare to challenge this
glove, I have sworn to take him a box o'th'ear; or if I can see
my glove in his cap, which he swore as he was a soldier he        115
would wear, if a live, I will strike it out soundly.

KING   What think you, Captain Llewellyn, is it fit this soldier keep
his oath?

LLEWELLYN   He is a craven and a villain else, an't please your
majesty, in my conscience.                                        120

KING   It may be his enemy is a gentleman of great sort, quite from
the answer of his degree.

LLEWELLYN   Though he be as good a gentleman as the devil is, as
Lucifer and Beelzebub himself, it is necessary, look your grace,
that he keep his vow and his oath. If he be perjured, see you      125
now, his reputation is as arrant a villain and a Jack Sauce as

---

113 a live] *Capell;* aliue F   116 a live] aliue F; a lived *Taylor*   123 gentleman] F (Ientleman)   126 Jack Sauce] F (Iack sawce)

106 SD GOWER See 135 n.

112 **swaggered** The term used of Pistol at *2H4*
2.4.56, 'a swaggering rascal'; the Hostess plays
involuntarily on the word, lines 67–70.

113 **a live** Capell's emendation makes good
sense, because it supplies a pronoun for the
following verb.

117–20 **What . . . conscience** In performance,
Llewellyn's attention is often distracted during
Williams's reply, so that he only hears Henry's
question about the oath without knowing what
the reason for the oath is. His failure to connect
Williams's story with what follows at 4.8.7–39 thus
becomes less obtuse. Henry's follow-up, however,

makes this rather awkward.

121 **great sort** high social rank.

121–2 **from . . . degree** so superior that it would
not be fitting for him to answer a common soldier's
challenge.

123 **as good . . . devil** Proverbial (Dent D 240.1).
*Lear* 3.4.127 has 'the Prince of Darkness is a
gentleman'.

124 **look your grace** Llewellyn's most regular
catchphrase is 'look you'. Here it is modified by
the stumble at line 97. It is repeated at 4.8.24.

126 **Jack Sauce** The proverbial name for a male
rascal (Dent J 23.1).

ever his black shoe trod upon God's ground and His earth, in
my conscience, law.

KING  Then keep thy vow, sirrah, when thou meet'st the fellow.

WILLIAMS  So I will, my liege, as I live.                                130

KING  Who serv'st thou under?

WILLIAMS  Under Captain Gower, my liege.

LLEWELLYN  Gower is a good captain, and is good knowledge and
literatured in the wars.

KING  Call him hither to me, soldier.                                     135

WILLIAMS  I will, my liege.                                    *Exit*

KING  Here, Llewellyn, wear thou this favour for me, and stick it in
thy cap. [*Gives him Williams's glove*] When Alençon and myself
were down together I plucked this glove from his helm. If any
man challenge this, he is a friend to Alençon and an enemy to        140
our person. If thou encounter any such, apprehend him, an
thou dost me love.

LLEWELLYN  Your grace does me as great honours as can be
desired in the hearts of his subjects. I would fain see the man
that has but two legs that shall find himself aggrieffed at this      145
glove, that is all. But I would fain see it once, an't please God
of His grace, that I might see.

---

143 does] F (doo's)   145 aggrieffed] F (agreefd)   147 might see] F; would but see him Q; would see *Taylor*

**127 black shoe** Black was the devil's colour.
It was also the colour of the most fashionable
footwear, appropriately enough given that the devil
is a gentleman.

**127 upon God's ground** Proverbial (Dent
G460.1).

**127 His earth** Llewellyn's habit of doubling his
terms probably means that he is referring here to
God's territory with both of them, although if the
devil is a gentleman he should also be spacious in
the possession of dirt, like Osric in *Ham.*

**128 law** It has been conjectured that this exclamation, characteristic of Macmorris, is a relic from
an early draft in which the Irishman returned for
this scene, his dialogue being later transferred to
Llewellyn.

**129 sirrah** A downward form of address, to an
underling.

**134 literatured** A vivid polysyllable to pronounce in Llewellyn's voiceless consonants.

**135 Call him hither** Gower was on stage at
line 43, and neither F nor Q marks his departure.

He could most easily have left the stage with the
heralds at line 106.

**137 this favour** a badge, in this case the distinctive glove.

**139 down together** 'Down' suggests that they
were off their feet, but it may mean no more than
dismounted, for hand-to-hand combat. It makes a
neatly oblique way of introducing a direct reference
to one of Henry's own contributions in the battle. Holinshed, p. 544, reports 'The king that daie
shewed himself a valiant knight, albeit almost felled
by the duke of Alanson; yet with plaine strength
he slue two of the dukes companie, and felled the
duke himself; whome when he would have yelded,
the kings gard (contrarie to his mind) slue out of
hand.'

**139 helm** Armoured battle headgear. 'Helmet'
is actually a diminutive form. See 1.0.13 n.

**141 an** if.

**143 does** It is possible that the F spelling marks
a particular pronunciation of the vowel.

KING  Know'st thou Gower?

LLEWELLYN  He is my dear friend, an't please you.

KING  Pray thee go seek him and bring him to my tent.                    150

LLEWELLYN  I will fetch him.                                *Exit*

KING  My lord of Warwick, and my brother Gloucester,
     Follow Llewellyn closely at the heels.
     The glove which I have given him for a favour
     May haply purchase him a box o'th'ear.                        155
     It is the soldier's. I by bargain should
     Wear it myself. Follow, good cousin Warwick.
     If that the soldier strike him, as I judge
     By his blunt bearing he will keep his word,
     Some sudden mischief may arise of it,                         160
     For I do know Llewellyn valiant,
     And, touched with choler, hot as gunpowder,
     And quickly will return an injury.
     Follow, and see there be no harm between them.
     Go you with me, uncle of Exeter.                              165

                                             *Exeunt*


**4.8** *Enter* GOWER *and* WILLIAMS

WILLIAMS  I warrant it is to knight you, captain.

                *Enter* LLEWELLYN

LLEWELLYN  God's will and His pleasure, captain. I beseech
you now, come apace to the king. There is more good toward
you, peradventure, than is in your knowledge to dream of.

---

**149 an't]** F (and)

**150 go seek him** Henry has already sent Williams for Gower, in Llewellyn's hearing. This order appears to correct the first by directing Gower not 'hither' (line 135) but to the king's tent. The object is to ensure that Llewellyn, now with the glove on show, meets Williams who has been authorised to challenge him over it.

**154 for a favour** (1) as a badge, (2) as a privilege.

**155 haply** by chance, or good fortune.

**160 Some sudden mischief** Not for striking a superior, but from Llewellyn's violent reaction.

**162 touched . . . gunpowder** Being hot, his anger will act like a linstock applied to the gunpowder in a cannon. See 3.0.33 n.

**163 return** As in returning gunfire.

**163 injury** (1) insult, (2) hurt.

**Act 4, Scene 8**

**1 to knight you** See Introduction, p. 33. Knighting a captain on the battlefield was the standard way to honour a company, as well as its captain. Llewellyn's summons then seems to confirm Williams's expectation.

WILLIAMS  [*To Llewellyn*] Sir, know you this glove?                    5
LLEWELLYN  Know the glove? I know the glove is a glove.
WILLIAMS  I know this, and thus I challenge it.
                                *Strikes him.*
LLEWELLYN  God's blood, an arrant traitor as any's in the
    universal world, or in France, or in England!
GOWER  [*To Williams*] How now, sir? You villain!              10
WILLIAMS  Do you think I'll be forsworn?
LLEWELLYN  Stand away, Captain Gower. I will give treason his
    payment into plows, I warrant you.
WILLIAMS  I am no traitor.
LLEWELLYN  That's a lie in thy throat. I charge you in his     15
    majesty's name apprehend him, he's a friend of the Duke
    Alençon's.

                *Enter* WARWICK *and* GLOUCESTER

WARWICK  How now, how now, what's the matter?
LLEWELLYN  My lord of Warwick, here is, praised be God for it, a
    most contagious treason come to light, look you, as you shall   20
    desire in a summer's day. Here is his majesty.

                *Enter* KING *and* EXETER

KING  How now, what's the matter?
LLEWELLYN  My liege, here is a villain and a traitor, that, look

---

**Act 4, Scene 8**  8 God's blood] F ('Sblood); Gode plut, and his Q   8 any's] F (anyes); any is F2   13 into plows] F; in due blows *Steevens*

**6 I know . . . glove** Llewellyn is markedly slower than Williams in identifying the mate of the glove he has just been given.

**7 SD** *Strikes him* Editors add a stage direction to make Williams take the glove from Llewellyn's cap before striking him. But the blow is evidently a box on the ear (4.1.192), delivered on the glove where it hangs from Llewellyn's cap (line 24), as Henry predicted.

**8 God's blood** The F exclamation is markedly quiet compared with Q's. It was routine for Q to elaborate on the catchphrases and regional idioms, which probably explains the 'and his' addition. But the F abbreviation looks like censorship of an oath, so the full oath as in Q seems right.

**8–9 the universal world** See 4.1.65 n.

**10 You villain** Williams is in Gower's company, subject to his direct command.

**11 be forsworn** break an oath. He has the king's authority to keep it.

**13 into plows** Steevens sought to correct Llewellyn's grammar. Nobody has yet proposed 'in two blows'.

**15 a lie . . . throat** By Touchstone's criteria this is the lie direct (*AYLI* 5.4.83), worse than a lie in the teeth. It was a proverbial phrase (Dent T268).

**15 I charge you** Directed to Gower, as Williams's captain, even though Llewellyn has just ordered Gower to stand back.

**20 contagious** infectious, pernicious.

**21 in . . . day** The bright day throws light on the treason. A proverbial phrase (Dent S967), used by Llewellyn before at 3.7.54.

your grace, has struck the glove which your majesty is take out
of the helmet of Alençon.                                               25
WILLIAMS  My liege, this was my glove – here is the fellow of it –
and he that I gave it to in change promised to wear it in his cap.
I promised to strike him if he did. I met this man with my glove
in his cap, and I have been as good as my word.
LLEWELLYN  Your  majesty,  hear  now,  saving  your  majesty's   30
manhood, what an arrant, rascally, beggarly, lousy knave it is!
I hope your majesty is pear me testimony and witness and will
avouchment that this is the glove of Alençon that your majesty
is give me, in your conscience now.
*[Gives glove to king]*
KING  Give me thy glove, soldier. Look, here is the fellow of it.   35
'Twas I indeed thou promisèd to strike,
And thou hast given me most bitter terms.
LLEWELLYN  An't please your majesty, let his neck answer for it, if
there is any martial law in the world.
KING  How canst thou make me satisfaction?                             40
WILLIAMS  All offences, my lord, come from the heart. Never
came any from mine that might offend your majesty.
KING  It was our self thou didst abuse.
WILLIAMS  Your majesty came not like yourself. You appeared to
me but as a common man – witness the night, your garments,   45
your lowliness. And what your highness suffered under that
shape, I beseech you take it for your own fault and not mine,
for had you been as I took you for, I made no offence.
Therefore I beseech your highness pardon me. *[Kneels]*
KING  Here, uncle Exeter, fill this glove with crowns              50
And give it to this fellow. Keep it, fellow,

36 promisèd] F (promised'st)   38 An't] F (And)

24 **struck the glove** See 7 SD n.
26 **this** i.e. the one still in Llewellyn's cap.
27 **in change** in exchange.
32–3 **will avouchment** will vouch, testify.
36 **promisèd** F's 'promised'st', conflating second person past and present, is a recurrent feature of Compositor A's work.
40 **satisfaction** compensation. In chivalry such a question would lead to a duel. A duel between a king and a common soldier would be unthinkable, as Henry has already acknowledged at 4.7.121–2.
43 **our self** The term renews Henry's concern with his former self of 1.2.267–80 and *2H4* 5.5.52–4.

49 SD *Kneels* A gesture acknowledging unequal status and asking pardon is necessary here. Henry keeps his distance, deputing Exeter to hand the glove back.
50 **this glove** Henry has both gloves, having matched them at line 35. One glove filled with crowns is presumably enough payment for Williams's victimisation in Henry's game.
51 **fellow** In the Crispin's day speech at 4.3.39 Henry spoke of the 'fellowship' of his army. At line 35 of this scene he refers to the 'fellow' of Williams's glove. This use is a third sense, distancing the commoner from the king.

And wear it for an honour in thy cap
Till I do challenge it. Give him the crowns.
And captain, you must needs be friends with him.

LLEWELLYN  By this day and this light, the fellow has mettle          55
enough in his belly. Hold, there is twelve pence for you, and I
pray you to serve God and keep you out of prawls and prabbles
and quarrels and dissentions, and I warrant you it is better
for you.

WILLIAMS  I will none of your money.                                 60

LLEWELLYN  It is with a good will. I can tell you it will serve you to
mend your shoes. Come, wherefore should you be so pashful?
Your shoes is not so good. 'Tis a good silling, I warrant you, or
I will change it.

*Enter* HERALD

KING  Now, herald, are the dead numbered?                            65
HERALD  Here is the number of the slaughtered French.
                    [*Gives him paper*]
KING  What prisoners of good sort are taken, uncle?
EXETER  Charles, Duke of Orléans, nephew to the king;
John, Duke of Bourbon, and Lord Boucicault.
Of other lords and barons, knights and squires,                     70
Full fifteen hundred, besides common men.

---

58 dissentions] F    63 silling] F; shilling Q

**52 for an honour** i.e. the honour of having
challenged the king with it.

**53 challenge it** question its honour.

**55 mettle** A mettle/metal pun. Williams has
mettle in his belly so needs no more metal in his
purse.

**56 twelve pence,** i.e. a shilling. Llewellyn,
although just placed as a distant 'captain' by
Henry, tries to copy his 'brother' with more limited
resources.

**57–8 prawls . . . dissentions** A possibly
subconscious memory of *Rich's Farewell*, quoted
already at 2.1.61. At sig. x3ᵛ, Rich writes of
'troubles, tumultes, broyles, Brabbles, Murthers,
Treasons'.

**61 a good will** i.e. I give it freely and with good
intentions.

**63 shoes . . . good** Henry replied to the French
herald at 4.3.116–9 that his 'poor soldiers' would
clothe themselves from the French.

**64 change it** Neither F nor Q indicates whether
Williams accepts Llewellyn's offer, and in performance it has been handled in various ways.
But Williams cannot refuse the king's gift, and
there is little reason for him to do anything but
accept Llewellyn's. It would be a sign of anger
cooling.

**64 SD HERALD** An English herald, not Montjoy.

**66 SD *paper*** Henry specifies 'this note' at
line 72.

**67 of good sort** See 4.7.121 n.

**68–96** This list paraphrases Holinshed, p. 555.
Each listing of names, of the French prisoners at
68–9 and of the French dead at 84–92, begins with
two of the characters who appear on stage in Act
3, Scene 8, 4.2 and 4.5.

**68 Orléans** Named in Act 2, Scene 4 and 3.6,
on stage in 3.8, 4.2 and 4.5.

**69 Bourbon** On stage in Act 2, Scene 4 (Q
version), 3.6, 3.8, 4.2, 4.5 and 4.7.

KING  This note doth tell me of ten thousand French
　　　　That in the field lie slain. Of princes in this number
　　　　And nobles bearing banners, there lie dead
　　　　One hundred twenty-six. Added to these,                         75
　　　　Of knights, esquires and gallant gentlemen,
　　　　Eight thousand and four hundred, of the which
　　　　Five hundred were but yesterday dubbed knights.
　　　　So that in these ten thousand they have lost
　　　　There are but sixteen hundred mercenaries.                      80
　　　　The rest are princes, barons, lords, knights, squires,
　　　　And gentlemen of blood and quality.
　　　　The names of those their nobles that lie dead:
　　　　Charles Delabret, High Constable of France;
　　　　Jacques of Châtillon, Admiral of France;                       85
　　　　The Master of the Crossbows, Lord Rambures;
　　　　Great Master of France, the brave Sir Guiscard Dauphin,
　　　　John, Duke of Alençon; Antony, Duke of Brabant,
　　　　The brother to the Duke of Burgundy;
　　　　And Edward, Duke of Bar. Of lusty earls:                       90
　　　　Grandpré and Roussi, Fauconbridge and Foix,
　　　　Beaumont and Marle, Vaudemont and Lestrelles.
　　　　Here was a royal fellowship of death.
　　　　Where is the number of our English dead?
　　　　　　　　[*Takes another paper*]
　　　　Edward, the Duke of York, the Earl of Suffolk,                 95
　　　　Sir Richard Keighley, Davy Gam, esquire.
　　　　None else of name, and of all other men
　　　　But five and twenty. O God, Thy arm was here!

---

90 earls:] *This edn;* Earles, F  92 Vaudemont] F (*Vandemont*)  92 Lestrelles] F (*Lestrale*)  96 Keighley] *Taylor;* Ketly F;
Kikely *Wilson*

80 **mercenaries** The two references to French
mercenaries, here and at 4.7.66, are both additions
to the lists in Holinshed. See 4.7.66 n.
　84 **Constable** On stage in Act 2, Scene 4, 3.6,
3.8, 4.2 and 4.5.
　86 **Rambures** On stage in Act 3, Scene 8, 4.2
and 4.5.
　88 **Alençon** See 4.7.139 n.
　90 **earls:** The colon is required by analogy with
the first listing at line 83.
　94 SD *another paper* Each set of names is read
from the herald's list. Here Henry asks for the
separately listed English tally. As with the French

lists, it starts with two names already given prominence (4.6.3–32).
　96 **Keighley** Holinshed spells this otherwise
unknown name 'Kikely'. Editors have tried different renderings. F's 'Ketly' is distinct from Holinshed and seems to link the name with the town
of Keighley in Yorkshire, which is nowadays pronounced 'Keithley', a sound not far from the F version.
　98 **five and twenty** Holinshed gives this total,
adding that more plausible estimates of the English
dead from French as well as English sources range
between one hundred and six hundred.

And not to us, but to Thy arm alone
Ascribe we all. When, without stratagem,                    100
But in plain shock and even play of battle,
Was ever known so great and little loss
On one part and on th'other? Take it, God,
For it is none but Thine.
EXETER                        'Tis wonderful.
KING  Come, go we in procession to the village,            105
    And be it death proclaimèd through our host
    To boast of this, or take that praise from God,
    Which is His only.
LLEWELLYN  Is it not lawful, an't please your majesty, to tell how
    many is killed?                                       110
KING  Yes, captain, but with this acknowledgement,
    That God fought for us.
LLEWELLYN  Yes, in my conscience, He did us great good.
KING  Do we all holy rites.
    Let there be sung *Non nobis* and *Te Deum*,          115
    The dead with charity enclosed in clay,
    And then to Calais, and to England then,
    Where ne'er from France arrived more happy men.

                                            *Exeunt*

102 loss] *Pope; –?* F   103 th'other?] *Pope; –,* F   105 we] F2; me F   109 an't] F (and)   113 in] Q; *not in* F   114 rites] F (Rights)

100 **without stratagem** This ignores the tactics with the hidden archers and the protective stakes, which all the sources make much of. Holinshed, marking the paragraph in the margin 'A politike invention', writes (p. 553): 'he sent privilie two hundred archers into a lowe medow, which was neere to the vauntgard of his enimies, but separated with a great ditch, commanding them there to keep themselves close till they had a token to them given, to let drive at their adversaries . . . he caused stakes bound with iron sharpe at both ends, of the length of five or six foot to be pitched before the archers, and of ech side the footmen like an hedge, to the intent that if the barded horses ran rashlie upon them, they might shortlie be gored and destroied . . . This device of fortifieng an armie was at this time first invented.'
105 **village** Not Agincourt, which was a castle,

but Maisoncelles, unnamed in Holinshed.
107 **boast . . . God** The saying 'Give God thanks and make no boast' (Dent B487.1) is also used in *Ado* 3.3.17, and *AYLI* 2.5.28–9.
113 **in my conscience** In F Llewellyn uses the full phrase on six other occasions (in Act 3, Scene 7, 4.1, 4.7, and line 34 above), so F's omission of the first word here is probably due to compositor eyeskip.
115 *Non nobis . . . Deum* Psalm 115, and the hymn of thanksgiving, *Te Deum laudamus*, We praise thee, O Lord. They were one Psalm in the Vulgate but two in the Elizabethan Book of Common Prayer, where their Latin titles survived. Holinshed reports that Henry ordered *In exitu Israel*, the Vulgate Psalm 114 of which *Non nobis* formed the second part, to be sung, and told the soldiers to kneel at *Non nobis*.

**5.0** *Enter* CHORUS

[CHORUS]  Vouchsafe to those that have not read the story
        That I may prompt them, and of such as have,
        I humbly pray them to admit th'excuse
        Of time, of numbers, and due course of things
        Which cannot in their huge and proper life        5
        Be here presented. Now we bear the king
        Toward Calais. Grant him there. There seen,
        Heave him away upon your wingèd thoughts
        Athwart the sea. Behold the English beach
        Pales-in the flood with men, with wives, and boys,        10
        Whose shouts and claps out-voice the deep-mouthed sea,
        Which, like a mighty whiffler 'fore the king,
        Seems to prepare his way. So let him land,
        And solemnly see him set on to London.
        So swift a pace hath thought that even now        15
        You may imagine him upon Blackheath,
        Where that his lords desire him to have borne
        His bruisèd helmet and his bended sword
        Before him through the city. He forbids it,

Act 5, Scene 0  5.0] *Actus Quintus* F  10 flood] *Pope;* flood; F  10 with men, with wives, and boys] F2; with Men, Wiues, and Boyes F; with men, maids, wives, and boys *Taylor*

**Act 5, Scene 0**

**5.0** F correctly heads this Act *Actus Quintus.*

**1 read** Presumably in Holinshed, but possibly also in broadside ballads.

**2 prompt** i.e. like actors on a stage.

**3 admit** accept.

**4 time** The brief stage time now spoken of covers the five years which elapsed between Act 4's Agincourt in 1415 and the Treaty of Troyes agreed in Act 5, which was signed in 1420.

**5 proper** i.e. in their own reality, a renewal following from the reference to 'numbers' of the Chorus's 'ciphers' apology in 1.0.17.

**10 Pales-in** Puts a fence round, as in the Irish Pale.

**12 whiffler** attendant who clears the way for a procession. John Stow, author of the *Annals of England*, 1592, which Shakespeare may have consulted, and of the *Survey of London*, 1603, was twice a whiffler for the Merchant Taylors' procession when a mayor from that guild was elected, in 1561 and 1568. The account of Henry's reception in England, which is not in Holinshed, may have come from Stow's *Annals*, p. 351.

**15 So swift . . . thought** See 3.0.1–3 n.

**16 Blackheath** A stretch of open ground south of Greenwich near London on the road from Dover.

**17–19** This account is resonant with the report of Henry's father Bullingbrook and his welcome by London in *R2* 5.2.3–21. Both the *R2* account and this one were regularly made into stage pageants in Victorian productions.

**17 to have borne** to arrange to have carried in front of him in the kind of procession which used whifflers.

**18 bended sword** The adjective hints at the humility of a bended knee as well as the damage of battle.

**19 He forbids it** Holinshed, p. 556, reports that 'The king like a grave and sober personage, and as one remembring from whome all victories are sent, seemed little to regard such vaine pompe and shewes as were in triumphant sort devised for his welcomming home from so prosperous a journie, in so much that he woold not suffer his helmet to be caried with him, whereby might have appeared to the people the blowes and dints that were to be seene in the same.'

Being free from vainness and self-glorious pride,                20
Giving full trophy, signal and ostent
Quite from himself to God. But now behold
In the quick forge and working-house of thought,
How London doth pour out her citizens,
The mayor and all his brethren in best sort,                     25
Like to the senators of th'antique Rome,
With the plebeians swarming at their heels,
Go forth and fetch their conquering Caesar in –
As, by a lower but by loving likelihood
Were now the general of our gracious empress,                    30
(As in good time he may) from Ireland coming,
Bringing rebellion broachèd on his sword,
How many would the peaceful city quit
To welcome him? Much more, and much more cause,
Did they this Harry. Now in London place him –                  35

---

29 but by loving] F; but loving *Rowe;* but high-loving *Taylor*    35 him –] *This edn (Theobald parenthesis); –.* F

**21 trophy . . . ostent** Synonyms for the marks of triumph in war, emblems and displays. At 5.1.64 Gower calls the St David's day leek a 'memorable trophy of predeceased valour'.

**23 forge and working-house** a workshop for shaping iron. The term is presented as a doublet. Behind the concept of the mind as a smithy is the proverbial phrase 'the mind is a mint'. See Thompson and Thompson, *Meaning and Metaphor,* p. 205.

**23 thought** Thought is 'quick' because it is not only alive but speedy, as the Chorus several times insists. It starts with 'imaginary forces' at 1.0.18, adding speed to the 'imagined wing' at 3.0.1–3.

**25 brethren** the aldermen of the city of London.

**25 in best sort** in their best civic dress.

**26 antique** ancient.

**27 swarming** Annabel Patterson points out that bees swarm when they are following a new leader. For an account of this metaphor and the reference to Essex that follows, see *Shakespeare and the Popular Voice,* pp. 81–8.

**29 but by loving** This phrase is lodged in a six-foot line which launches a four-line parenthesis, of which the first three lines all have more than the standard ten syllables. Even if 'general', 'gracious', and 'empress' are made dissyllables, and 'rebellion' is elided into three syllables, the rhythm spills out of its metrical pattern. It may be a late insertion that loses the rhythm by being tacked on to a

half-line at 34 or 35, but it is difficult to see exactly what may have comprised the insertion. Rowe's excision of F's 'by' is an attempt to regularise the metre, but it is invalidated by the following overspills. Taylor's emendation, assuming that the F compositor read the hyphenated 'hy' as 'by', links it to 'lower', but otherwise has little to commend it.

**29–35** A parenthesis almost certainly tied to the period between April and September 1599, when Essex was commanding the English troops in Ireland. See Introduction, p. 6. Its survival in F so far past the time when it would have been appropriate is the strongest indication that the copy for F was not a playhouse transcript but an authorial draft made at that time and not subsequently altered.

**30 our gracious empress** Implicitly compared with 'Caesar' at line 28.

**32 broachèd** (1) impaled, (2) broken open.

**33–4 How many . . . him?** When Essex returned from the Cadiz expedition in 1596 there was a comparably enthusiastic reception for him.

**35–9** The F punctuation at lines 35, 37 and after 'them' in 39 is awkward. Both the lamentation of the French and the Holy Roman Emperor's visit to England place Henry in London, so a parenthesis explaining it (36–9) seems necessary. Editors have rearranged the F punctuation of these lines in a variety of ways. Taylor (pp. 301–2) posits the omission of a line at 39, where the parenthesis ends.

As yet the lamentation of the French
Invites the king of England's stay at home,
The emperor's coming in behalf of France
To order peace between them – and omit
All the occurrences, whatever chanced,                              40
Till Harry's back return again to France.
There must we bring him, and myself have played
The interim, by remembering you 'tis past.
Then brook abridgement, and your eyes advance
After your thoughts, straight back again to France.      *Exit*   45


5.1 *Enter* LLEWELLYN *and* GOWER


GOWER  Nay, that's right. But why wear you your leek today?
   St Davy's day is past.
LLEWELLYN  There is occasions and causes why and wherefore in
   all things. I will tell you ass my friend, Captain Gower. The
   rascally, scald, beggarly, lousy, pragging knave Pistol, which you    5

---

37 home,] – : F; – . *Taylor*   39 them – ] – : F   Act 5, Scene 1   4 ass] F (asse)

**36 As . . . lamentation** Since the lamentation
continues, and so to.
**38 emperor** The Holy Roman Emperor
Sigismund visited England in 1416.
**39 order** (1) demand, (2) compose, arrange.
**39–40 and . . . chanced** This phrase encom-
passes a series of further negotiations: incur-
sions into France, successful sieges of French
strongholds, and the struggles between successive
Dauphins and the Dukes of Burgundy. An omission
from the F text has been conjectured in the middle of line 39. Capell proposed 'but these now/We
pass in silence over.' Oxford suggested that a reference to the death of the Dauphin has been lost.
No insertion is really necessary.
**42–3 played . . . interim** performed through
the intervening period.
**43 remembering** reminding.
**44 brook abridgement** tolerate the shortening.
It has been suggested that the phrase is a pun on
Henry Brooke, Lord Cobham, the Lord Chamberlain who in 1596–7 ordered the change of name
from Oldcastle to Falstaff in *1H4*. Pollard suggested
equally plausibly that it is a reference to a legal
textbook, Robert Brook's *La graunde abridgement*,
published in 1573 and reissued in 1576 and 1583.

**Act 5, Scene 1**
**0 SD** The scene is evidently set in France in
the immediate wake of the battle. At the end of
the scene Pistol sets off for the return journey to
England with his scars to claim that he got them
in 'the Gallia wars', of which the only occurrences
in the play are Harfleur and Agincourt. As before
(see 2.0.41 n.) the Chorus breaks up the flow of
events when they involve the low-life characters.
Johnson thought that Act 5, Scene 1 should be the
last scene of Act 4.
**1 Nay . . . right** A mid-speech entrance. Gower
is responding to another of Llewellyn's pronounce-
ments.
**2 St Davy's day** See 4.1.53–4 n. From what
Llewellyn says about Pistol's insult, this is the day
after St David's day, i.e. 2 March. Agincourt was
25 October.
**3 why and wherefore** Proverbial (Dent W332)
as well as a chronic doubling of terms.
**5 rascally** Etymologically a 'rascal' was the runt
in a deer herd, a laggard not usually thought worth
hunting.
**5 scald** covered with scabs.
**5 lousy** Meant more literally than today.

and yourself and all the world know to be no petter than a
fellow, look you now, of no merits, he is come to me, and
prings me pread and salt yesterday, look you, and bid me eat
my leek. It was in a place where I could not breed no conten-
tion with him, but I will be so bold as to wear it in my cap till I    10
see him once again, and then I will tell him a little piece of my
desires.

*Enter* PISTOL

GOWER   Why, here he comes, swelling like a turkey-cock.

LLEWELLYN   'Tis no matter for his swellings, nor his turkey-cocks.
God pless you, Anchient Pistol, you scurvy, lousy knave, God    15
pless you.

PISTOL   Ha, art thou bedlam? Dost thou thirst, base Trojan, to
have me fold up Parca's fatal web? Hence! I am qualmish at the
smell of leek.

LLEWELLYN   I peseech you heartily, scurvy, lousy knave, at my    20
desires and my requests and my petitions, to eat, look you, this
leek. Because, look you, you do not love it, nor your affections
and your appetites and your digestions does not agree with it, I
would desire you to eat it.

PISTOL   Not for Cadwallader and all his goats.    25

LLEWELLYN   There is one goat for you.

*Strikes him [with cudgel]*

Will you be so good, scald knave, as eat it?

PISTOL   Base Trojan, thou shalt die!

LLEWELLYN   You say very true, scald knave, when God's will is. I
will desire you to live in the meantime, and eat your victuals.    30
Come, there is sauce for it. [*Strikes him*] You called me yester-

---

15 Anchient] F (aunchient)    23 digestions] F (disgestions)    23 does] F (doo's)

**13 swelling . . . turkey-cock** Proverbial for
pride (Dent T612). In *TN* 2.5.26–7 it is used of
Malvolio.

**17 bedlam** An abbreviation meaning an inhabi-
tant of the Bethlehem madhouse in south London.

**18 fold up . . . web** Webs can be folded, but the
Fates (Parcae) wove threads which they cut when
they ended people's lives.

**18 qualmish** nauseated.

**25 Cadwallader** a legendary Welsh hero
(d. 664).

**25 goats** Wales being mountainous, it was noted
for its goats. Pistol's last appearance onstage was

with Le Fer, whom he called a 'luxurious mountain goat' at 4.4.14. The same insult was evidently
levelled at Llewellyn, to judge from line 32.

**27 eat it** The leek is Llewellyn's direct response
not only to the salt-and-pepper insult but to the fig
of Spain at 3.7.50.

**29 when . . . is** The full proverb (N311) is that
'nothing is more certain than death, and nothing
more uncertain than its time.' It also occurs in *2H4*
3.2.29–30.

**31 sauce for it** The 'sauce' must be the blood
he draws from Pistol's head, the 'ploody coxcomb'
of line 38.

day 'mountain-squire', but I will make you today a squire of
low degree. I pray you, fall to. If you can mock a leek, you can
eat a leek.

GOWER   Enough, captain. You have astonished him.                35

LLEWELLYN   By Cheshu, I will make him eat some part of my
leek, or I will peat his pate four days. Bite, I pray you. It is good
for your green wound, and your ploody coxcomb.

PISTOL   Must I bite?

LLEWELLYN   Yes, certainly, and out of doubt and out of question   40
too, and ambiguities.

PISTOL   By this leek, I will most horribly revenge – [*Llewellyn
threatens him*] I eat and eat, I swear!

LLEWELLYN   Eat, I pray you. Will you have some more sauce to
your leek? There is not enough leek to swear by.                45

PISTOL   Quiet thy cudgel, thou dost see I eat.

LLEWELLYN   Much good do you, scald knave, heartily. Nay, pray
you throw none away. The skin is good for your broken coxcomb. When you take occasions to see leeks hereafter, I pray
you mock at 'em, that is all.                                   50

PISTOL   Good.

LLEWELLYN   Ay, leeks is good. Hold you, there is a groat to heal
your pate.

PISTOL   Me a groat?

LLEWELLYN   Yes, verily, and in truth you shall take it, or I have    55
another leek in my pocket which you shall eat.

PISTOL   I take thy groat in earnest of revenge.

LLEWELLYN   If I owe you anything, I will pay you in cudgels. You
shall be a woodmonger, and buy nothing of me but cudgels.
God b'wi' you, and keep you, and heal your pate.        *Exit*   60

---

36 By Cheshu] Q (by Iesu); I say F   37 days] F; days and foure nights Q   42–3 revenge – I] reuenge . I F; –; *Rowe;* – .
*Capell*

32–3 **squire . . . degree** A parodic use of
the titles of medieval romances, in contrast with
Llewellyn's high mountain degree.
35 **astonished** dazed, stunned.
36 **By Cheshu** F's opening is uncharacteristi-
cally mild in comparison with Q's and may reflect
editorial softening of oaths in the F text.
37 **pate** scalp.
38 **green** fresh.
38 **coxcomb** (1) jester's cap, (2) head of a fool.
42 **revenge –** Some vivid gesture by Llewellyn
is required to make Pistol change his attitude so

quickly. The offer of 'more sauce to your leek'
means more blood on Pistol's scalp, an offer he
presumably declines by eating the rest of the leek.
44 **Eat** i.e. rather than swear.
48 **your** Pistol's, but also the abstract 'one's'.
The wearing of leeks by Welsh soldiers was thought
to be for their curative properties.
52 **groat** A fourpenny coin.
54 **Me a groat?** Llewellyn gave Williams a
shilling, three times the value of the groat.
57 **in earnest of** as a deposit for a debt owed
by Llewellyn.

PISTOL  All hell shall stir for this!

GOWER  Go, go, you are a counterfeit cowardly knave. Will you
mock at an ancient tradition began upon an honourable respect,
and worn as a memorable trophy of predeceased valour, and
dare not avouch in your deeds any of your words? I have seen    65
you gleeking and galling at this gentleman twice or thrice. You
thought because he could not speak English in the native garb
he could not therefore handle an English cudgel. You find it
otherwise, and henceforth let a Welsh correction teach you a
good English condition. Fare you well.                    *Exit*  70

PISTOL  Doth fortune play the hussy with me now? News have I
that my Doll is dead i'th'Spital of a malady of France, and
there my rendezvous is quite cut off. Old I do wax, and from
my weary limbs honour is cudgelled. Well, bawd I'll turn, and
something lean to cutpurse of quick hand. To England will I    75
steal, and there I'll steal.
      And patches will I get unto these cudgelled scars,
      And swear I got them in the Gallia wars.          *Exit*

63 began] F; begun *Capell*  71 hussy] F (huswife)  72 Doll] F, Q; Nell *Capell*  72 of a] F; of *Pope*  78 swear] Q;
swore F

**62–70** Q omits all of this speech, although Gower
is thought to have been one of the reporters.

**66 gleeking and galling** jibing and scoffing,
making galls.

**69–70 a . . . condition** i.e. honourable respect
for the Welsh.

**71 fortune . . . hussy** A paraphrase of the saying 'fortune is a strumpet' (Dent F603.1). 'Hussy'
is a difficult word to render in modern English. F's
'hussif' marks the gradual shift from respectable
housewife to eighteenth-century strumpet, which
had hardly begun in 1599. Pistol has already
urged his wife the Hostess towards 'housewifery'
at 2.3.49.

**72 Doll** Doll Tearsheet is Falstaff's Doll in *2H4*.
She is mentioned by name at 2.1.61 but does not
make an appearance in this play. Editors have been
bothered by Pistol calling her 'my' Doll when he
is married to the Hostess, and have conjectured
that originally this was written as an exit speech
for Falstaff. The Act 2, Scene 1 reference sets her
in the lazar hospital in Spitalfields, which fits this
account of her death. It is quite possible to read
the reference as indicating that Pistol, as the sole
survivor of the Eastcheap company, thought he had
acquired Falstaff's Doll as well as the Hostess, and
now knows she is gone too. He evidently has no
intention of returning to become 'mine host Pistol', which is what Nym had mocked him with in
Act 2, Scene 1.

**72 malady of France** i.e. venereal disease.

**73 rendezvous** refuge. See 2.1.14 n.

**73 Old** i.e. an ancient. He finally accepts an
honest name as he leaves the army.

**73 wax** grow.

**74 honour** This word carries a faint echo of
Falstaff's 'honour' catechism and has been linked
with 'Doll' to persuade some editors that the
speech was originally Falstaff's.

**74 bawd** It seems odd to declare a voca-
tion as pimp in response to news of Doll's
death, but 'bawd' was often linked with 'cutpurse'
as a characterisation of underworld occupations.
Pistol's choice exactly echoes Gower's account of
him at 3.7.53 as 'a bawd, a cutpurse'.

**75 something lean to** incline to become.

**76 steal . . . steal** An *antanaclasis*. See 1.0.13 n.
Pistol is again penniless, having lost his ransom at
Agincourt thanks to Henry's order to cut the prisoners' throats. Here the *antanaclasis* echoes his own
declaration at 2.1.87: 'I'll live by Nym and Nym
shall live by me', which plays on the meaning of
'nim', to steal. It emphasises his status as sole survivor.

**77–8 And . . . wars** It seems worth retaining
these two lines as verse, since they rhyme and are
designed as a closure.

**78 Gallia wars** The term has a faint echo of
Caesar's *Gallic Wars*, well known to all students of
school Latin. Canterbury uses it at 1.2.216.

**5.2** *Enter at one door* KING *Henry*, EXETER, BEDFORD,
WESTMORLAND *and other lords. At another,* QUEEN *Isabel, the*
[FRENCH] KING, [*the Princess* KATHERINE *and* ALICE,] *the Duke
of* BURGUNDY, *and other French*

KING    Peace to this meeting, wherefor we are met.
        Unto our brother France and to our sister,
        Health and fair time of day. Joy and good wishes
        To our most fair and princely cousin Katherine.
        And as a branch and member of this royalty,                  5
        By whom this great assembly is contrived,
        We do salute you, Duke of Burgundy.
        And princes French, and peers, health to you all.
FRENCH KING    Right joyous are we to behold your face,
        Most worthy brother England, fairly met.                     10
        So are you, princes English, every one.
QUEEN    So happy be the issue, brother England,
        Of this good day, and of this gracious meeting,
        As we are now glad to behold your eyes,
        Your eyes which hitherto have borne in them                  15
        Against the French that met them in their bent

---

Act 5, Scene 2    9 face,] F; –. *Taylor*    11 princes English] F (princes (English))    12 England] F2; Ireland F

**Act 5, Scene 2**

**0 SD** ALICE F records her only as '*Lady*' in the
speech headings, but she must be the same lady as
the 'Alice' of Act 3, Scene 5.

**0 SD** BURGUNDY Strictly speaking, Burgundy
(Philip the Good) was a French lord. But the
dukedom of Burgundy had for centuries been an
appanage largely independent of French rule, and
quite apart from his opposition to the Dauphin's
party he made an effective mediator between the
two kings. See line 5 n. The Burgundy named as
a French duke at 3.6.42 and 4.8.89 was actually
Philip's father, who was killed by a stratagem of
the Dauphin's forces in 1419. Holinshed reports
these events on pp. 560, 571. This scene delivers
his account of the Treaty of Troyes, which was
drawn up and agreed in 1420.

**1 wherefor** i.e. the reason why we are meeting
is to make peace.

**2 our brother** Henry speaks consistently of
kinship with the French royal family. Here
'brother' has a different association from its use for
the soldiers at Agincourt. It is a courteous form of
address, as with the French king's and queen's use
below.

**5 this royalty** the royal family. Burgundy has
been identified at 4.8.89 as brother to the Duke of
Brabant, but not himself a member of the French
royal line. Henry may be emphasising that the
mediator and peacemaker belongs on the French
side.

**9 face,** Taylor's punctuation turns this response
first to Burgundy and only then to the English
king. If Burgundy enters with the French train,
as F makes him, this is pointless as well as discourteous to Henry. Q starts this speech with 'Brother
of England . . . '

**12 issue** outcome, an allusion to the 'peace' of
Henry's first words, though possibly also a hint over
the presence of the princess Katherine.

**12 England** In Hand D of *Sir Thomas More*,
the word is spelt 'Ingland'. A similar manuscript
spelling might have misled F's Compositor A into
reading it as 'Ireland'. See Textual Analysis, p. 222.

**13 gracious** (1) handsome, (2) blessed by God's
grace, (3) generous.

**15** F's lineation goes wrong here, putting the last
two syllables into the next line.

**16 bent** (1) aim, as in archery, (2) customary
use.

The fatal balls of murdering basilisks.
The venom of such looks we fairly hope
Have lost their quality, and that this day
Shall change all griefs and quarrels into love.                    20
KING    To cry amen to that, thus we appear.
QUEEN    You English princes all, I do salute you.
BURGUNDY    My duty to you both, on equal love,
            Great kings of France and England. That I have laboured
            With all my wits, my pains and strong endeavours,        25
            To bring your most imperial majesties
            Unto this bar and royal interview,
            Your mightiness on both parts best can witness.
            Since then my office hath so far prevailed
            That face to face and royal eye to eye                    30
            You have congreeted. Let it not disgrace me
            If I demand before this royal view
            What rub or what impediment there is
            Why that the naked, poor and mangled peace,
            Dear nurse of arts, plenties and joyful births,           35
            Should not in this best garden of the world,
            Our fertile France, put up her lovely visage?
            Alas, she hath from France too long been chased,
            And all her husbandry doth lie on heaps,
            Corrupting in it own fertility.                           40

17 **balls** (1) eyeballs, (2) cannon balls.

17 **basilisks** (1) mythical beasts that killed by the sight of their eyes (proverbial: B99.1), (2) large cannon.

19 **that** i.e. the loss of venom. Behind the word lies the image of a snake and Satan's invasion in that shape which changed the love in Eden into 'griefs and quarrels'. The queen is broaching the central image of Burgundy's great speech which follows.

22 This line completes the queen's greeting to the opposing contingent, matching that of her husband at line 11.

23–67 Burgundy adopts in part the role of the Holy Roman Emperor (5.0.38–9), seeking to make peace. Q cuts the speech from 45 lines to 4.

27 **bar** court of justice, place of trial.

28 **on both parts** Burgundy makes his speech from centre stage. Possibly a gesture to each side is called for here, since the French and the English 'princes' are assembled on opposite sides of the stage, as the two salutations by the French king

and queen indicate. The word 'interview' suggests an exchange of looks between the kings, a reading confirmed by the 'royal view' of the two monarchs at line 32.

31 **congreeted** greeted each other. See 1.2.182 n. Both 'congreeing' and 'congreeted' are first used in this play.

33 **rub** obstacle.

35 **nurse** feeder and wet-nurse.

36 **best . . . world** See line 19 n. In *R2* 2.1.42 Gaunt describes England as 'this other Eden'. A proverb said 'Lombardy is the garden of the world' (1414).

37 **put up** raise, show – like a flower to the sun. The whole image of 34–7 combines peace as a ravished maiden with peace as a lovely flower.

39 **husbandry** harvest.

39 **on heaps** in disorder. See 4.5.19 n.

40 **it** An old genitive. 'Its' was not common before the 1620s. The normal usage in Shakespeare's time was 'his'.

Her vine, the merry cheerer of the heart,
Unprunèd, dies. Her hedges, even-pleached,
Like prisoners wildly overgrown with hair
Put forth disordered twigs. Her fallow leas
The darnel, hemlock and rank fumitory                                    45
Doth root upon, while that the coulter rusts
That should deracinate such savagery.
The even mead, that erst brought sweetly forth
The freckled cowslip, burnet, and green clover,
Wanting the scythe, all uncorrected, rank,                               50
Conceives by idleness, and nothing teems
But hateful docks, rough thistles, kecksies, burs,
Losing both beauty and utility.
And as our vineyards, fallows, meads and hedges,
Defective in their natures, grow to wildness,                            55
Even so our houses, and ourselves, and children
Have lost, or do not learn for want of time
The sciences that should become our country,
But grow like savages, as soldiers will
That nothing do but meditate on blood,                                   60
To swearing and stern looks, diffused attire,
And everything that seems unnatural.

45 fumitory] F (femetary)  50 scythe, all] *Rowe²;* Sythe, withall F; scythe withal *Riverside*  54 And as] *Capell;* And all
F; An all *Taylor*  55 natures] F; nurtures *Warburton*  55 wildness.] F; –, *Capell*  61 diffused] F (defus'd)

41 vine . . . heart Proverbial: 'Good wine makes a merry heart' (Dent w460).
42 even-pleached interlaced uniformly.
44 fallow leas arable land left untilled.
45 darnel . . . fumitory wild plants, the weeds most likely to spring up on tilled land. See the list of weeds that grow amongst corn in *Lear* 4.3.3–6.
46 coulter plough blade.
47 deracinate uproot – a Latinism.
47 savagery wildness – with a hint about the warfare which has produced this condition.
48 mead meadow, grassland (unlike the 'leas' of line 44).
48 erst formerly.
49 cowslip . . . clover meadow plants good for cattle feed.
50 all F's 'withall' is not easy to accommodate, either in syntax or metre. It may indicate a deletion in the manuscript which was not recorded clearly.
50 rank Already used for 'rank fumitory' at line 45, it is an adjective commonly associated

with weeds and noxious stagnation. In *Ham.* 3.3.36 Claudius calls his hidden act of murder 'rank'.
51 Conceives by idleness Idleness generates weeds.
51 teems flourishes.
52 docks . . . burs wild weeds.
52 kecksies dry stalks.
54 And as Taylor stops the sentence at line 53 and makes 54–6 an if . . . so sentence. This ignores the reference to the Fall in 55. Capell's emendation makes good sense, since it leads to 'Even so' at 56.
54 vineyards . . . hedges This line summarises the contents of lines 41–8, picking 'vineyards' from 41, 'fallow' from 44, 'meads' from 48, and 'hedges' from 42.
55 Defective . . . natures Creatures of the fallen world, outside Eden.
58 sciences knowledge, learning.
59 savages . . . soldiers See line 47 n.
61 diffused disorderly.

Which to reduce into our former favour
You are assembled; and my speech entreats
That I may know the let why gentle peace                                65
Should not expel these inconveniences
And bless us with her former qualities.

KING    If, Duke of Burgundy, you would the peace
Whose want gives growth to th'imperfections
Which you have cited, you must buy that peace                           70
With full accord to all our just demands,
Whose tenors and particular effects
You have, inscheduled briefly, in your hands.

BURGUNDY    The king hath heard them, to the which as yet
There is no answer made.

KING                                    Well then, the peace,                    75
Which you before so urged, lies in his answer.

FRENCH KING    I have but with a cursitory eye
O'er-glanced the articles. Pleaseth your grace
To appoint some of your council presently
To sit with us once more, with better heed                              80
To re-survey them. We will suddenly
Pass our accept and peremptory answer.

KING    Brother, we shall. Go, uncle Exeter,
And brother Bedford, and you brother Gloucester,
Westmorland, Huntington, go with the king,                              85
And take with you free power to ratify,
Augment or alter as your wisdoms best
Shall see advantageable for our dignity,
Anything in or out of our demands,
And we'll consign thereto. Will you, fair sister,                       90
Go with the princes or stay here with us?

---

72 tenors] F (Tenures)    77 cursitory] *Wilson;* curselarie F; cursenary Q; cursorary Q3    84 Bedford] This ed.; Clarence
F    85 Westmorland] *This edn; Warwick,* and F

63 **reduce into** return to.
63 **favour** (1) preference, approval, (2) appearance, face.
65 **let** prevention, hindrance.
66 **inconveniences** intrusions, injuries.
68 **would** wish for.
69 **want** lack, absence.
69 **imperfections** i.e. manifestations of the
fallen world.
70 **you . . . peace** Henry identifies Burgundy
with 'this royalty' (line 5) of France.

72 **tenors** tendency, general aims.
74–5 **The . . . made** Burgundy speaks directly
for the French side in the negotiations.
77 **cursitory** A seventeenth-century variant of
'cursory'. See Hulme, *Explorations*, p. 216.
81 **suddenly** with speed, at once.
82 **accept and peremptory** agreed and
final.
83–5 Henry flourishes his brothers and kinsmen.
Huntington has not appeared before.
90 **consign** agree, sign to.

QUEEN  Our gracious brother, I will go with them.
          Happily a woman's voice may do some good
          When articles too nicely urged be stood on.
KING  Yet leave our cousin Katherine here with us.                  95
          She is our capital demand, comprised
          Within the forerank of our articles.
QUEEN  She hath good leave.

                  *Exeunt all but King and Katherine* [*and Alice*]
KING                      Fair Katherine, and most fair,
          Will you vouchsafe to teach a soldier terms
          Such as will enter at a lady's ear                        100
          And plead his love-suit to her gentle heart?
KATHERINE  Your majesty shall mock at me. I cannot speak your
          England.
KING  O fair Katherine, if you will love me soundly with your
          French heart I will be glad to hear you confess it brokenly with   105
          your English tongue. Do you like me, Kate?
KATHERINE  *Pardonnez-moi*, I cannot tell vat is 'like me'.
KING  An angel is like you, Kate, and you are like an angel.
KATHERINE  [*To Alice*] *Que dit-il – que je suis semblable à les anges?*
ALICE  *Oui, vraiment, sauf votre grâce, ainsi dit-il.*              110
KING  I said so, dear Katherine, and I must not blush to affirm it.
KATHERINE  *O bon Dieu, les langues des hommes sont pleines de
          tromperies!*
KING  What says she, fair one? That the tongues of men are full of
          deceits?                                                   115

---

93 Happily] F; Haply F4   98 SD *Exeunt . . . but*] *Exeunt omnes manet* F   107 vat] *Rowe*; wat F

93 **Happily** F's 'Haply', which is used at 4.7.155, means more emphatically 'by good luck' than it does here.
94 **articles** clauses, conditions, details.
94 **too nicely urged** too insistently upheld, and so becoming barriers to acceptance of the whole treaty.
96 **our capital demand** the chief article in the treaty. She is so because Henry's demand for the French crown has been moderated to a claim for his heirs to inherit the title. No mention is made of the Dauphin's alternative title.
98–253 The resemblance of this scene to the one in *Famous Victories* is fairly close. See Appendix 1.
102 **mock** Pistol has been punished in the

previous scene for his 'mocks' at Welsh differences from the 'native garb'.
107 *Pardonnez-moi* 'Excuse me'.
107 **vat** The French Dr Caius in *Wiv.* uses 'vat' for 'what' nine times. The same F spelling occurs in this scene at lines 164 and 237. It has been used consistently throughout here.
109 *Que . . . anges?* 'What does he say – that I am like the angels?'
109 *à les* Modern French *aux*. This may be either Shakespeare's ignorance or Middle French. See Introduction, pp. 68–9. F is too exact here to be modernised.
110 *Oui . . . dit-il* 'Yes, truly, begging your grace's pardon, he said that.'
112–13 *O . . . tromperies!* Henry translates this correctly.

ALICE  *Oui,* dat de tongeus of de mans is be full of deceits, dat is
de princess.

KING  The princess is the better Englishwoman. I'faith, Kate, my
wooing is fit for thy understanding. I am glad thou canst speak
no better English, for if thou couldst thou wouldst find me such    120
a plain king that thou wouldst think I had sold my farm to buy
my crown. I know no ways to mince it in love, but directly to
say 'I love you'. Then if you urge me farther than to say 'Do
you in faith?', I wear out my suit. Give me your answer, i'faith
do, and so clap hands and a bargain. How say you, lady?    125

KATHERINE  *Sauf votre honneur,* me understand well.

KING  Marry, if you would put me to verses, or to dance for your
sake, Kate, why, you undid me. For the one I have neither
words nor measure, and for the other I have no strength in
measure, yet a reasonable measure in strength. If I could win a    130
lady at leapfrog, or by vaulting into my saddle with my armour
on my back, under the correction of bragging be it spoken I
should quickly leap into a wife. Or if I might buffet for my love
or bound my horse for her favours I could lay on like a butcher
and sit like a jackanapes, never off. But before God, Kate, I    135
cannot look greenly, nor gasp out my eloquence, nor I have no
cunning in protestation, only downright oaths, which I never
use till urged, nor never break for urging. If thou canst love a
fellow of this temper, Kate, whose face is not worth sun-
burning, that never looks in his glass for love of anything he    140

---

116 tongeus] F   117 princess] F; princess say *Keightley*   126 well] F; vell *Capell*

**116 tongeus** The F spelling indicates a non-
native pronunciation, as with 'mans' for 'men' and
'de' for 'the'.
**118 the . . . Englishwoman** i.e. better for
preferring honesty.
**121 a plain king** See Introduction, pp. 13–14.
**122 mince it** play the mincing, affected,
courtier.
**124 I wear . . . suit** (1) my plea for love is
exhausted, (2) my plain clothes are worn out.
**125 clap . . . bargain** shake or clasp hands in
acknowledgement of a deal (like yeomen making a
bargain). Proverbial (Dent H109.1).
**126 me . . . well** On the evidence of Henry's
renewal of his 'suit' in his next speech, there should
be a 'no' before or after 'understand'. On the other
hand there is very likely a concealed pun on the
French 'entendre', (1) to understand, (2) to agree,

make a bargain.
**129 measure** (1) verse metre, (2) rhythm in
dancing, (3) restraint.
**130 reasonable measure** good capacity.
**131 leapfrog** *OED* records this as the first mention of the game in print. To 'leap' also meant to
mount sexually, as did 'vaulting'. The innuendo
becomes more explicit at line 133.
**133 buffet for** fight with fists – as an apprentice
butcher might do.
**134 bound my horse** make my horse leap.
**134 lay on** The same phrase was applied to
fighting and to sex. See *Mac.* 5.8.33 and *Oth.* 4.1.35.
**135 jackanapes** monkey.
**136 look greenly** behave like a lovesick girl.
**137 protestation** repeated claims.
**139–40 face . . . sun-burning** i.e. Henry is
already brown. See *Tro.* 1.3.283.

sees there, let thine eye be thy cook. I speak to thee plain
soldier. If thou canst love me for this, take me. If not, to say to
thee that I shall die is true, but for thy love, by the Lord, no.
Yet I love thee too. And while thou livest, dear Kate, take a
fellow of plain and uncoined constancy, for he perforce must      145
do thee right, because he hath not the gift to woo in other
places. For these fellows of infinite tongue that can rhyme
themselves into ladies' favours, they do always reason
themselves out again. What? A speaker is but a prater, a rhyme
is but a ballad, a good leg will fall, a straight back will stoop, a   150
black beard will turn white, a curled pate will grow bald, a fair
face will wither, a full eye will wax hollow – but a good heart,
Kate, is the sun and the moon, or rather the sun and not the
moon, for it shines bright and never changes, but keeps his
course truly. If thou would have such a one, take me. And take     155
me, take a soldier. Take a soldier, take a king. And what sayest
thou then to my love? Speak, my fair, and fairly, I pray thee.

KATHERINE  Is it possible dat I sould love de *ennemi* of France?
KING  No, it is not possible you should love the enemy of France,
Kate. But in loving me you should love the friend of France,        160
for I love France so well that I will not part with a village of it. I
will have it all mine; and, Kate, when France is mine and I am
yours, then yours is France, and you are mine.
KATHERINE  I cannot tell vat is dat.
KING  No, Kate? I will tell thee in French, which I am sure will     165
hang upon my tongue like a new-married wife about her
husband's neck, hardly to be shook off. *Je quand sur le possession*

---

158 *ennemi*] F (*ennemie*)   164 vat] *Rowe*; wat F   167 *sur le possession*] *suis le possesseur Taylor (conj. Fuzier)*

---

**141 thy cook** to dress and garnish the
(sunburnt) dish. Proverbial: 'Let his eye be the best
cook' (Dent E242.1).
**142–3 to say . . . no** A conventional anti-
Petrarchan sentiment. Compare Llewellyn to Pistol
at 5.1.29.
**145 uncoined** not stamped like a coin, i.e. not
current. There is again a bawdy innuendo, since
'coin' puns on 'quaint', like Kate's 'gown' in Act 3,
Scene 5.
**146–7 he hath . . . places** Developing the
'uncoined' image, that not being current he
cannot be spent anywhere else.
**147–8 rhyme . . . reason** 'Rhyme and reason'
was proverbial (Dent R98.1).
**149 prater** i.e. always talking, with the implication that boasting prevents sexual doing.
**150 ballad** i.e. popular, cheap. Broadsheet

ballads were the scandal sheets of their day, telling
lurid tales in doggerel.
**154 his** its.
**158 *ennemi*** F uses a spelling which cannot be
intended as an English pronunciation.
**162–3 when . . . mine** Henry echoes the old
cliché about marriage.
**165–72** Q offers a much shorter version of this
speech, with Katherine repeating each of Henry's
phrases with the pronouns reversed to show that
she understands.
**167–8 *Je quand . . . moi*** 'I when on the possession of France, and when you have possession of
me . . .' Henry's French, an attempt to render his
English of 162–3, is even worse than Katherine's
English, despite her modest disclaimer at 173–4.
**167 *sur le possession*** Jean Fuzier has proposed

de France, *et quand vous avez le possession de moi* – let me see,
what then? Saint Denis be my speed! – *Donc vôtre est France, et
vous êtes mienne.* It is as easy for me, Kate, to conquer the    170
kingdom as to speak so much more French. I shall never move
thee in French, unless it be to laugh at me.

KATHERINE  *Sauf votre honneur, le français que vous parlez, il est
meilleur que l'anglais lequel je parle.*

KING  No, faith is't not, Kate. But thy speaking of my tongue and I    175
thine most truly falsely must needs be granted to be much at
one. But Kate, dost thou understand thus much English? Canst
thou love me?

KATHERINE  I cannot tell.

KING  Can any of your neighbours tell, Kate? I'll ask them. Come, I    180
know thou lovest me, and at night when you come into your
closet you'll question this gentlewoman about me, and I know,
Kate, you will to her dispraise those parts in me that you love
with your heart. But good Kate, mock me mercifully, the
rather, gentle princess, because I love thee cruelly. If ever thou    185
beest mine, Kate, as I have a saving faith within me tells me
thou shalt, I get thee with scambling, and thou must therefore
needs prove a good soldier-breeder. Shall not thou and I,
between Saint Denis and Saint George, compound a boy, half
French half English, that shall go to Constantinople and take    190

---

173 *français*] F (*Francois*)    174 *meilleur*] F (*meilleus*)    174 *l'anglais*] F (*l'Anglois*)

a mistranscription of this passage by a compositor lacking French who misread *suis* as *sur*, and set
*le possession* twice, instead of *la possession*, for the
initial *le possesseur*. It would be grammatically correct to have *le possesseur*, and an initial misreading
might have generated the wrong gender for *possession* seven words later, making a better French
paraphrase of Henry's own English at 162–3. But
much of the joke is Henry's poor French, and the
F text may have it rightly wrong.
  169 **Saint Denis** The patron saint of France.
  169–70 *Donc . . . mienne* 'Then France is yours
and you are mine.'
  173–4 *Sauf . . . parle* 'With respect, the French
that you speak, it is better than the English that I
speak.'
  176 **truly falsely** true in meaning, false in
grammar.

176–7 **at one** alike, and of one mind.
  181 **thou** The second-person singular was commonly used when speaking of 'love'. When he
moves on to other matters Henry changes to the
routine plural. He does the same in his next long
speech at 201–23.
  182 **closet** bedroom.
  185 **cruelly** i.e. painfully, an obvious antonym
to 'mercifully'.
  187 **with scambling** through the struggles of
war. See 1.1.4 n.
  190 **Constantinople** The Turks captured
Constantinople, the city used as the base for most
of the Crusades, in 1453. This reference to Henry's
son becoming a crusader is the final reference
to the Jerusalem motif which began in *R2*. See
Introduction, pp. 12–13.

the Turk by the beard? Shall we not? What sayest thou, my fair flower de luce?

KATHERINE　I do not know dat.

KING　No, 'tis hereafter to know, but now to promise. Do but now promise, Kate, you will endeavour for your French part of such　195 a boy, and for my English moiety take the word of a king and a bachelor. How answer you, *la plus belle Katherine du monde, mon très cher et divin déesse?*

KATHERINE　Your majesty 'ave *fausse* French enough to deceive de most *sage demoiselle* dat is *en France*.　200

KING　Now fie upon my false French. By mine honour, in true English, I love thee, Kate. By which honour I dare not swear thou lovest me, yet my blood begins to flatter me that thou dost, notwithstanding the poor and untempering effect of my visage. Now beshrew my father's ambition! He was thinking of civil　205 wars when he got me. Therefore was I created with a stubborn outside, with an aspect of iron, that when I come to woo ladies I fright them. But in faith, Kate, the elder I wax the better I shall appear. My comfort is that old age, that ill layer-up of beauty, can do no more spoil upon my face. Thou hast me, if　210 thou hast me, at the worst; and thou shalt wear me, if thou wear me, better and better. And therefore tell me, most fair Katherine, will you have me? Put off your maiden blushes. Avouch the thoughts of your heart with the looks of an empress. Take me by the hand and say 'Harry of England, I am　215 thine.' – which word thou shalt no sooner bless mine ear withal

---

199 'ave] F (aue)

192 **flower de luce** The French heraldic lily, fleur-de-lis. Edward III quartered it on his arms to signify his claim to the French crown. In the early Henry VI plays the loss of the French emblem from the English coat is mentioned several times (*1H6* 1.1.80, *2H6* 5.1.11).

194 **to know** i.e. sexually, in begetting a son.

196 **moiety** half-share.

197–8 **la . . . déesse?** 'The most lovely Katherine of the world, my very dear and divine goddess?' The lack of agreement between French adjective and noun in *cher* and *divin* is confirmed by *mon*. The others might have their feminine endings concealed in F, but *mon* is unmistakable as Henry's error, using English agreement rather than French and creating the '*fausse* French'

which Katherine promptly comments on.

199 *fausse* (1) 'inaccurate', (2) 'deceitful'.

200 *sage demoiselle* 'wise young lady'.

204 **untempering** discouraging, making less sharp than a sword.

205–6 **thinking . . . me** The father's state of mind at conception was thought to influence the child's mind, a theory burlesqued in the opening chapter of *Tristram Shandy*.

207 **aspect** appearance – as when clad in armour.

209 **layer-up** preserver – as on a sick-bed.

210 **spoil** looting and destruction, as in war.

211 **wear** (a) be clothed in, (b) tolerate.

213 **maiden blushes** Proverbial (Dent B479.1).

but I will tell thee aloud 'England is thine, Ireland is thine,
France is thine, and Henry Plantagenet is thine', who, though I
speak it before his face, if he be not fellow with the best king
thou shalt find the best king of good fellows. Come, your          220
answer in broken music, for thy voice is music, and thy English
broken. Therefore, queen of all, Katherine, break thy mind to
me in broken English. Wilt thou have me?

KATHERINE  Dat is as it sall please de *roi mon père*.

KING  Nay, it will please him well, Kate; it shall please him, Kate.    225

KATHERINE  Den it sall also content me.

KING  Upon that I kiss your hand, and I call you my queen.

KATHERINE  *Laissez, mon seigneur, laissez, laissez! Ma foi, je ne veux*
*point que vous abaissiez votre grandeur, en baisant la main d'une de*
*votre seigneurie indigne serviteur. Excusez-moi, je vous supplie, mon*   230
*très puissant seigneur.*

KING  Then I will kiss your lips, Kate.

KATHERINE  *Les dames et demoiselles, pour être baisées devant leurs*
*noces, il n'est pas la coutume de France.*

KING  Madam, my interpreter, what says she?                        235

ALICE  Dat it is not be de *façon pour les* ladies of France – I cannot
tell vat is *baiser en* Anglish.

KING  To kiss.

ALICE  Your majesty *entends* bettre *que moi*.

224 sall] *Wilson*; shall F   229 abaissiez] *Wilson*; abbaisse F   229 grandeur] F (*grandeus*)   229–30 d'une de votre seigneurie
indigne] *Wilson*; d'une nostre Seigneur indignie F   231 très puissant] F (*tres-puissant*); treis puissant *Taylor*   234 noces] F
(*nopcesse*)   237 vat] *Rowe*; wat F   237 baiser] *Hanmer*; buisse F   239 entends] *This edn*; entendre F

218 **Plantagenet** The royal family's name from
1154 to the death of Richard III in 1485.
220 **king . . . fellows** Proverbial: 'The king of
good fellows is appointed for the queen of beggars'
(Dent K66).
221 **broken music** an instrumental part-song,
or music in parts.
222 **break** break open.
224 **de . . . père** 'the king my father'.
225 **it . . . well** Henry knows that his marriage
to Katherine is the first article in the Treaty of
Troyes. The Chorus to Act 3 has already mentioned that the French king has offered Henry his
daughter (3.0.30). Katherine presumably does not
know. Its position as Henry's 'capital demand' is
affirmed at line 297.
228–31 **Laissez . . . seigneur** 'Let go, my lord,
let go, let go! On my word, I would never wish
you to lower your dignity by kissing the hand of an
unworthy servant of your lordliness. Excuse me, I

beg you, my most mighty lord.' Katherine's shock
indicates that Henry's talk of being a king of good
fellows has not altered her respect for his rank. She
should kiss his hand.
231 **très puissant** Taylor's '*treis*' is a French form
of 'thrice'.
232 **kiss your lips** A more egalitarian gesture
than kissing hands.
233–4 **Les . . . France** 'For ladies and girls to be
kissed before marriage is not the custom in France.'
236 **façon pour les** 'fashion for the'.
237 **Anglish** F's spelling must be designed to
indicate Alice's pronunciation.
239 **entends** The Oxford editors note the idea
that the French infinitive in F may have been assimilated from the next word.
239 **bettre** An odd intrusion of Franglais. In F
the English word is given a French spelling and
italicised as a French word.

KING  It is not a fashion for the maids in France to kiss before they    240
are married, would she say?

ALICE  *Oui, vraiment.*

KING  O Kate, nice customs curtsy to great kings. Dear Kate, you
and I cannot be confined within the weak list of a country's
fashion. We are the makers of manners, Kate, and the liberty    245
that follows our places stops the mouth of all find-faults, as I
will do yours, for upholding the nice fashion of your country in
denying me a kiss. Therefore patiently, and yielding. [*Kisses
her*] You have witchcraft in your lips, Kate. There is more
eloquence in a sugar touch of them than in the tongues of the    250
French Council, and they should sooner persuade Harry of
England than a general petition of monarchs. Here comes your
father.

*Enter the French power* [FRENCH KING, QUEEN *Isabel*,
BURGUNDY], *and the English lords* [EXETER, WESTMORLAND]

BURGUNDY  God save your majesty. My royal cousin, teach you our
princess English?    255

KING  I would have her learn, my fair cousin, how perfectly I love
her, and that is good English.

BURGUNDY  Is she not apt?

KING  Our tongue is rough, coz, and my condition is not smooth, so
that having neither the voice nor the heart of flattery about me I    260
cannot so conjure up the spirit of love in her that he will appear
in his true likeness.

BURGUNDY  Pardon the frankness of my mirth if I answer you for
that. If you would conjure in her you must make a circle, if
conjure up love in her in his true likeness he must appear    265
naked and blind. Can you blame her then, being a maid yet

---

**243 nice** (1) delicate, (2) unimportant.

**244 weak list** feeble barriers – as in jousting.

**245–6 the liberty . . . places** the freedom conferred by our status.

**246 stops the mouth** Proverbial usually of a kiss (Dent M1264).

**246–7 as . . . yours** i.e. stop her mouth by kissing her.

**254 cousin** For Burgundy to address Henry as 'cousin' means either that he claims the brotherhood of royalty, or that Henry's claim of a right by blood to the French crown makes him kin, or possibly that as one of the vice-regal French dukes he himself will soon be related by marriage to Henry.

In his reply Henry emphasises Burgundy's choice of a familial claim. At lines 273 and 280 he calls Katherine Burgundy's cousin.

**258 apt** (1) to learn English, (2) sexually promising.

**259 Our tongue** (1) the English language, (2) the soldierly speech of Henry.

**261 he will** Cupid, the god of love, will.

**264 conjure . . . circle** The magician's magic circle was commonly used for a sexual pun. see *Rom.* 2.1.24.

**266 naked and blind** The infant Cupid ('his') as the god of love was usually depicted blindfolded when he shot his arrows.

rosed over with the virgin crimson of modesty, if she deny the
apperance of a naked blind boy in her naked seeing self? It
were, my lord, a hard condition for a maid to consign to.

KING  Yet they do wink and yield, as love is blind and enforces.          270

BURGUNDY  They are then excused, my lord, when they see not
what they do.

KING  Then, good my lord, teach your cousin to consent winking.

BURGUNDY  I will wink on her to consent, my lord, if you will
teach her to know my meaning; for maids well summered and     275
warm kept are like flies at   Bartholomew-tide, blind, though
they have their eyes, and then they will endure handling which
before would not abide looking on.

KING  This moral ties me over to time, and a hot summer; and so I
shall catch the fly, your cousin, in the latter end, and she must   280
be blind too.

BURGUNDY  As love is, my lord, before it loves.

KING  It is so. And you may, some of you, thank love for my
blindness, who cannot see many a fair French city for one fair
French maid that stands in my way.                                   285

FRENCH KING  Yes, my lord, you see them perspectively, the cities
turned into a maid, for they are all girdled with maiden walls
that war hath never entered.

281 too] F2; To F   282 before it] F; before that it *Taylor*   288 never entered] *Rowe;* entered F

267–8 deny the appearance refuses to admit
(1) the sight, and (2) the entry.

268 naked . . . self her self being naked, and
seeing the naked boy.

269 a hard condition Another sexual innuendo.

269 consign to sign her consent to – as in the
wedding contract.

274 wink on her This has more of the modern
meaning of 'wink'.

275 know my meaning i.e. teach her about sex.

275 summered cared for.

276 warm kept Warmth in the blood was
thought to intensify lust.

276 Bartholomew-tide St Bartholomew's day
was 24 August, the height of summer, when flies
are most sluggish.

277–8 they will . . . on i.e. women will
lose their reserve about being sexually handled.
Burgundy's grossly sexual language makes Henry's
images of sex as warfare seem by comparison positively genial.

279 moral comparison, inference.

280 in . . .end (1) at the end of summer,
(2) in Katherine's sexual organ. Henry objects
to Burgundy's double-talking implication that he
must wait till the end of the summer when Katherine will be as blind as Cupid.

282 As . . . loves A cryptic play on the proverbial
blindness of love until the loved object is seen.
Taylor's emendation reverses the point, making
Burgundy claim that Henry is blind to what
Katherine is.

283 some of you A sharp reminder of the other
articles in the treaty, which the lords now returned
have been negotiating.

284–5 one . . . way Remotely, this anticipates
*1H6* where Joan of Arc successfully led the fight
against the English.

286 perspectively in a 'prospective glass', or a
distanced and distorted view.

287 girdled . . . walls The opening Chorus
(1.0.19) describes the playhouse circumference as
'the girdle of these walls'.

288 never Rowe's insertion makes sense of F's
nonsense.

KING  Shall Kate be my wife?

FRENCH KING  So please you.                                           290

KING  I am content, so the maiden cities you talk of may wait on
her, so the maid that stood in the way for my wish shall show
me the way to my will.

FRENCH KING  We have consented to all terms of reason.

KING  Is't so, my lords of England?                                  295

WESTMORLAND  The king hath granted every article,
His daughter first, and then in sequel all
According to their firm proposèd natures.

EXETER  Only he hath not yet subscribèd this:
where your majesty demands that the King of France, having     300
any occasion to write for matter of grant, shall name your
highness in this form and with this addition, in French: *Notre
très cher fils Henri, roi d'Angleterre, héritier de France*; and thus in
Latin: *Praeclarissimus filius noster Henricus, rex Angliae et heres
Franciae.*                                                          305

FRENCH KING  Nor this I have not, brother, so denied
But your request shall make me let it pass.

KING  I pray you then, in love and dear alliance,
Let that one article rank with the rest,
And thereupon give me your daughter.                                310

FRENCH KING  Take her, fair son, and from her blood raise up
Issue to me, that the contending kingdoms
Of France and England, whose very shores look pale
With envy of each other's happiness,
May cease their hatred. And this dear conjunction                   315

297 then in] F2; in F; so in *Taylor*

291 **content, so** content, so long as.

292 **her, so** her, thus.

293 **my will** (1) my sexual desire, (2) what my
son may inherit.

297–8 **in . . . natures** Largely what the
Archbishop of Bourges brought to offer England
before the invasion, noted and scorned by the
Chorus at 3.0.28–31. The terms are substantially less than Henry set out to secure when he
declared 'No king of England if not king of France'
(2.2.188). Essentially he has accepted the rever-
sion of the title from the French king, a promise
clinched by the hand of his daughter. The alternative claimant, the Dauphin, whose claim was to be
reinvigorated by Joan of Arc, gets no mention. Nor

does the fact that this marriage renews the situation
for Henry's son that Edward III inherited.

301 **for matter of grant** when composing title
deeds, granting land.

302–3 *Notre . . . France* 'our very dear son
Henry, king of England, heir to France'.

304 *Praeclarissimus* A slip in Hall, which carried through Holinshed into Shakespeare's text. It
should be '*praecarissimus*', most beloved. The word
used means 'most famous'.

308 **dear** (1) beloved, (2) costly. The same pun
is used above at 2.2.57 and below at line 315.

313 **look pale** i.e. the white cliffs of Dover and
Calais. See 1.0.21.

315 **conjunction** (1) marriage, (2) alliance.

      Plant neighbourhood and Christian-like accord
      In their sweet bosoms, that never war advance
      His bleeding sword 'twixt England and fair France.
LORDS  Amen.
KING  Now welcome, Kate, and bear me witness all        320
      That here I kiss her as my sovereign queen.
                    *Flourish*
QUEEN  God, the best maker of all marriages,
      Combine your hearts in one, your realms in one.
      As man and wife, being two, are one in love,
      So be there 'twixt your kingdoms such a spousal     325
      That never may ill office or fell jealousy,
      Which troubles oft the bed of blessèd marriage,
      Thrust in between the paction of these kingdoms
      To make divorce of their incorporate league,
      That English may as French, French Englishmen,   330
      Receive each other. God speak this 'amen'.
ALL  Amen.
KING  Prepare we for our marriage; on which day,
      My lord of Burgundy, we'll take your oath
      And all the peers, for surety of our leagues.     335
      Then shall I swear to Kate, and you to me,
      And may our oaths well kept and prosperous be.
                    *Sennet. Exeunt*

**5.3** *Enter* CHORUS

CHORUS  Thus far with rough and all-unable pen
      Our bending author hath pursued the story,

319 SH LORDS] F; *All Capell*   328 paction] *Theobald;* pation F   332 SH ALL] F

**316 neighbourhood** Before Agincourt, Henry claimed that their bad neighbours, the French army, did the English the good service of making them early risers.

**319 SH LORDS** Capell introduces here the more comprehensive support of everyone that is signalled at line 332. Although it is not indicated whether this applause comes from the English lords or both sides, it seems worth retaining the F speech headings.

**322 God . . . marriages** Proverbial: 'Marriages are made in heaven' (Dent M688).

**329 incorporate league** The alliance will make them one body, like husband and wife in the marriage service. The word 'divorce' sharpens the marriage metaphor.

**332 SH ALL** See 319 n.

**334 Burgundy** In *The Famous Victories* Burgundy and the Dauphin are made to kiss Henry's sword. Nashe reported that he had seen the French king and Dauphin doing it on stage.

**337 SD** *Sennet* A trumpet fanfare, often used by a body of players to signal their entrance or exit.

**Act 5, Scene 3**
**1–14** A sonnet. The Prologue and Act 2 Chorus to *Rom.* are also in sonnet form.
**2 bending** (1) bowing, (2) leaning over his pen. The prologue to the Mousetrap play in *Ham.* 3.2.150 says 'Here stooping to your clemency'. Henry also uses 'bending' at 4.1.228.

In little room confining mighty men,
Mangling by starts the full course of their glory.
Small time, but in that small, most greatly lived                               5
This star of England. Fortune made his sword
By which the world's best garden he achieved,
And of it left his son imperial lord.
Henry the Sixth, in infant bands crowned king
Of France and England, did this king succeed,                                   10
Whose state so many had the managing
That they lost France and made his England bleed,
Which oft our stage hath shown – and for their sake,
In your fair minds let this acceptance take.                          [*Exit*]

**3 little room** a small space, not an enclosed room, though the prison image is behind 'confining'.

**4 Mangling by starts** Distorting by lack of smoothness.

**4 course** (1) story, (2) gallop, (3) hunt.

**5 Small time** Henry died in 1422 at the age of 35. Strictly, the 'small time' is the business described by the Chorus as 'Turning th'accomplishment of many years / Into an hourglass' (1.0.30–1)

**6 Fortune** Machiavelli's three qualities needed for political success are *gloria*, *fortuna*, and *virtu*, all of which Henry demonstrates. Since he is insistent that the victory at Agincourt should be given to God, the Chorus's change here is peculiarly pointed.

**7 the . . . garden** Not Eden but France, according to Burgundy at 5.2.36.

**8 his son** Henry VI was less than a year old when his father died.

**9 infant bands** swaddling clothes. 'Bands' and 'bonds' were not always differentiated.

**11 state** estate, with the narrower sense of 'throne' or 'chair' of state as well as the broader one of 'condition'.

**13 oft . . . shown** i.e. Shakespeare's Henry VI plays.

**14 this** this play.

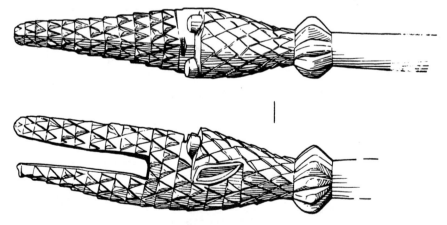

15 The head of a linstock (3.0.33), discovered in the wreck of the Mary Rose (The Mary Rose Trust)

16 The third Earl of Cumberland dressed as the Queen's Champion, from a miniature painted by Nicholas Hilliard in about 1591. The *impresa* on his shield shows the earth, sun and moon, and his armour has suns (or stars) picked out on it in gold. In front of his hat we wears the queen's glove as a gage (National Maritime Museum). See 3.8.64–5

# TEXTUAL ANALYSIS

The Folio text (F) is the better of the two versions with close links to the original performance script that we have. Printed, in all likelihood, from the manuscript that the author submitted to the company, like the majority of the First Folio plays not previously printed in quarto form, it lacks the staging adjustments, the regularised speech headings and the text corrections of a regular prompt-book, but it is still the best available record of the author's original idea of how he expected it to be staged. This original idea apparently changed as the play was rehearsed and prepared for the stage. The other text with primary authority, the Quarto printed in 1600 (Q), has many differences from the F text. Mostly they indicate that this copy underwent a far rougher kind of transmission from Shakespeare's text to the printed page. Some of the Quarto's variants, however, may indicate features of the play as finally performed in 1599–1600.

The first kind of alteration from the author's manuscript that is visible in the principal text, F, was editing to prepare it for the press. The F manuscript certainly underwent some changes before it was handed to the printers of the Folio. Most obviously the editors censored oaths containing references to God, a routine exercise after the Act of 1606 to restrain the use of oaths in plays. In 4.7.58, for instance, Henry's greeting to the French herald, which in Q is 'Gods will', in F is the innocuous 'How now'. At 104 Q's 'God' appears as the softer 'Good'. Llewellyn's oaths are similarly quieter in F, though that might equally well be the author's original restraint and an intensification of his verbal violence in Q, or an author-created violence that the F censor softened. The most solemn invocations of God's name, Henry's prayer beginning 'O God of battles' at 4.1.263, and his praise for the victory at 4.8.98 and 112, are the same in both texts, but in most cases the F text follows the general F practice of replacing references to God with appeals to the heavens, or something even milder. It seems likely that most of these oaths would have been altered by the F editors. A more positive indication that this editing does show its presence in the F text, and that it was not authorial, is the insertion of wrongly positioned act breaks. The mark for Act 2 was misplaced before the Chorus for Act 3, Act 4 was marked as Act 3, and 4.7 was then marked as Act 4, before the correctly placed insertion of Act 5.

The second form of alteration to the F text was the process of printing itself. The play was set, on quires h–k2, by the two principal compositors out of the five or more who set the whole of the First Folio, A and B.[1] Copyright problems with

1 Charlton Hinman, *The Printing and Proofreading of the First Folio of Shakespeare*, 2 vols., 1963, II, 98.

the copy for *Richard II* and *1* and *2 Henry IV* advanced its setting ahead of its historical predecessors, and mistakes in calculating the length of the delayed text led to some misnumbering in F, with the result that quire h, the first twelve pages of *Henry V*, became the second of two sets of pages numbered 69–80. There were few other problems. The two compositors worked together on the first two formes that the play took, with Compositor A setting the rest by himself. Compositor B set h3, h3v and h4a, i4v, i5, and i6va (2.0.18–2.2.174; 4.4.34–4.7.131; 5.1.33–5.2.11) while Compositor A set all the other text. Compositor A spelled Nym's name as 'Nim' in 2.3 (h4r and v), and Compositor B spelled it as 'Nym' in 2.1. (h3r and v) and 4.4 (i4v). No press corrections have been found in any part of the Folio text for the play.[1] Subsequent folio editions (F2 in 1632, F3 in 1664 and F4 in 1685) all copied their text from F, making a few commonsense corrections.

A number of errors in F appear to derive from the compositors' misreadings of the manuscript, which seems to have been written in a hand not unlike that of the allegedly Shakespearean Hand D in *Sir Thomas More*.[2] Two obvious misreadings where terminal e has been read for terminal d are at 1.2.74 and 82, where Holinshed's 'Lingard' and Ermengard' become in F 'Lingare' and 'Ermengare'. To these might be added six other instances. In two, d was mistaken for e: 2.3.14 'table' for 'babld', and 2.4.108 'priuie' for 'privèd'. There are four where e was misread as d: 1.2.72 'find' for 'fine', 3.3.58 'heard' for 'heare', 4.0.16 'nam'd' for 'name', and 4.5.17 'contaminated' for 'contaminate'. Both compositors were involved in these misreadings, Compositor A doing seven of them, B doing 4.5.17.

It is also likely that a hand similar to Hand D could have caused the misreading 'Ireland' for 'Ingland' at 5.2.12 and 'in-land' for 'Ingland' (QI: 'England') at 1.2.142, both by Compositor A. Two other evident misreadings of manuscript copy are 3.1.24 'me' for 'men', and 4.1.248 '*Hyperio*' for 'Hyperion', where a tilde over the vowel in the manuscript to signify a following 'n' was missed by Compositor A. Walter[3] has also proposed some misreadings of e for minims: 2.1.32 'hewne' for 'here', 2.3.21 'vp-peer'd' for 'upward', 3.8.12 'postures' for 'pasterns', 4.0.20 'creeple' for 'cripple', 5.2.45 'Femetary' for 'fumitory', and 5.2.77 'curselarie' for 'cursitory'. Of these, 2.1.31 was by Compositor B, while Compositor A set the others. Compositor A's habit, known from some of his other texts, of rendering 'yon' as 'yond' appears at 4.2.16 and 39, and 4.7.47. There is a little apparent mislineation by Compositor A at 4.1.203–10, after a long passage of prose, at 4.8.36–7, where a line of prose is divided into two lines of verse, and at 4.8.111, where it may mark a pause in speech. All of these possible mislineations occur in passages where prose and verse are mixed, and the transition is difficult to identify precisely, especially in the first example.

The Oxford editors have seen some influence of the Pavier Q3, printed in 1619 by one of the consortium which published the Folio, in the F version. They suggest that

1 Hinman, *Printing and Proofreading of the First Folio*, 11. 14, 24, 31, 35.
2 See Scott McMillin, *The Elizabethan Theatre and 'The Book of Sir Thomas More'*, 1987; Giles E. Dawson, 'Shakespeare's Handwriting', *S.Sur. 43* (1990), 119–28, esp. 123–5.
3 J. H. Walter (ed.), *Henry V*, 2.1.36 n.

*Bates.* Be friends you Englifh fooles, be friends, wee
haue French Quarrels enow, if you could tell how to rec-
kon.                                                *Exit Souldiers.*
    *King.* Indeede the French may lay twentie French
Crownes to one, they will beat vs, for they beare them
on their fhoulders : but it is no Englifh Treafon to cut
French Crownes, and to morrow the King himfelfe will
be a Clipper.
Vpon the King, let vs our Liues, our Soules,
Our Debts, our carefull Wiues,
Our Children, and our Sinnes, lay on the King :
We muft beare all.
O hard Condition, Twin-borne with Greatneffe,
Subiect to the breath of euery foole, whofe fence
No more can feele, but his owne wringing.
What infinite hearts-eafe muft Kings neglect,
That priuate men enioy ?
And what haue Kings, that Priuates haue not too,
Saue Ceremonie, faue generall Ceremonie ?

17a F, 4.1.197–212 (detail)

    *King.* Giue me thy Gloue Souldier ;
Looke, heere is the fellow of it :
'Twas I indeed thou promifed'ft to ftrike,
And thou haft giuen me moft bitter termes.
    *Flu.* And pleafe your Maieftie, let his Neck anfwere
for it, if there is any Marfhall Law in the World.
    *King.* How canft thou make me fatisfaction ?
    *Will.* All offences, my Lord, come from the heart : ne-
uer came any from mine, that might offend your Ma-
ieftie.
    *King.* It was our felfe thou didft abufe.

17b F, 4.8.35–43 (detail)

it was used as a printed text available to be consulted by the F compositors
where the manuscript copy was indecipherable.[1] This is potentially an important
question, since any unauthorised alterations in Q3 that were incorporated in F would
eliminate its authority in those instances. No alterations of much significance have
been found, however. In three cases the editors of the Oxford *Textual Companion*
suggest that an error in Q passed to Q3 and thence into F. At 1.2.74 they consider that

1 See Stanley Wells and Gary Taylor (eds.), *The Oxford Shakespeare. A Textual Companion*, 1987, p. 376.

F's '*Lingare*' may have been influenced by Q's '*Inger*'. Given the other occurrences of the same slip noted above, a d/e misreading of Holinshed's 'Lingard' is more likely in this case. At 3.3.8, F's 'Cheshu' is thought to have derived from Q's 'Iesus' through Q3's 'Ieshu', on the grounds that the 'sh' spelling is anomalous in F. This is another of the problems of transliterating Llewellyn's Welsh dealt with in the Note on the Text. The third case is 4.3.117, where Q and F agree in reading 'or they will pluck', which Hanmer emended to 'for they will pluck' and Taylor to 'as they will pluck'. The QF reading is not obviously wrong in this instance.

Despite these uncertain cases, there is, as in other plays for which a Pavier quarto already existed, a little evidence to support the view that a few of the Pavier Q3 readings may have been taken from an authoritative text, possibly the manuscript copy used to set F. Q3 was certainly printed from a copy of Q, as its loss of a speech heading at 4.3.76 indicates. Q has the catchword '*King. Why*' on $E_2{}^r$, but the speech starts on $E_2{}^v$ without the two words. Q3's $E_2{}^v$ reprints the Q version without inserting the missing speech heading. But at 4.3.65–6 and 4.7.81, Q3 corrects Q with readings that are peculiarly close to F and may well have been taken, like several other Pavier quarto readings, from the same manuscript that was used to set F.[1] This of course devalues Q3 as an authority independent of F and destroys the Oxford case for Q contaminating F through Q3.

Other apparent inadequacies in the F text may have been the consequence of its manuscript copy being a draft not completely prepared for the stage. The variable lords and their speech headings, and especially the Dauphin's presence at Agincourt, together with irregular speech headings such as the Hostess as '*Woman*' in Act 2, Scene 3, with '*Welch*', '*Irish*', '*Scot*' in Act 3, Scene 3, seem to indicate unsystematised authorial copy. This is a crucial question, since any firm indication that the copy for F was not fully revised for the stage might justify using Q in its place where Q seems to offer a more sensible version. But that depends on what we think the origin of Q's copy is.

The Quarto text (Q) had a quite different origin from F, and has a quite different kind of authority. It was printed in 1600 by Thomas Creede, who issued a number of plays in quarto, including some of Shakespeare's. He had registered *The Famous Victories of Henry V* with the Stationers' Company in 1594 and issued a quarto of that text in 1598. It looks as if his registration of *The Famous Victories* was expected to count for Shakespeare's play too.[2] His imprint on the title-page of Q declares that he was printing it for Thomas Millington and John Busby, 'And are to be sold at his house in Carter Lane, next the Powle head.' Whose house the 'his' indicates is not clear. Creede sold from several shops, but the inclusion of Millington and Busby suggests that they were the booksellers who marketed it and the address was very likely Millington's.[3]

---

1 See Paul Werstine, review of Wells and Taylor, *Modernising Shakespeare's Spelling, with Three Studies of 'Henry V'*, in *S.St.* 16 (1983), 382–91.
2 Rights over the play texts were not entirely clear-cut. Even after the transfer of the Shakespeare text to Pavier, Creede evidently retained the rights for *The Famous Victories*, since his successor Bernard Alsop reprinted it in 1617.
3 I am grateful to Peter Blayney for supplying me with this point, together with much other information about the circumstances of printing in the period 1598–1608.

The Chamberlain's Men released a number of their more popular plays to the press between 1597 and 1600. They lost their playhouse, the Theatre, by April 1597. Their financial backer had sunk his resources into building the new Blackfriars indoor theatre as its replacement, which they were then forbidden to use. Until they dismantled the Theatre and used its scaffolding to begin building the Globe in 1599 their finances were in trouble. Through those years good texts of eleven of their plays were sold to the press for issuing in quarto form. Two of them, *Romeo and Juliet* in 1599 and probably *Love's Labour's Lost* in 1598, appear to have been given to the printers to replace unauthorised earlier versions. The others were chiefly their major successes, *Richard III*, *Richard II*, 1 *Henry IV*, *The Merchant of Venice* and *A Midsummer Night's Dream*, some of which were reprinted several times in these years. In 1599 and 1600 the Admiral's Men also went through a phase of publishing their plays, possibly as a reaction to the competition from the new Globe and the new boy companies, possibly to help finance the building of their own new playhouse, the Fortune.[1] This flurry of publication came to an end in 1601. The few later quartos of Shakespeare plays, notably *Merry Wives*, printed in 1602, *Hamlet* in 1603, and *Pericles* in 1608, seem not to have been texts issued by the company.

In the Stationers' Register an entry authorised by the wardens and dated 14 August 1600 transferred the rights for several plays already in print, including 'The historye of Henrye the v$^{th}$ w$^{th}$ the battell of Agencourt' to Thomas Pavier. Pavier subsequently used Creede to reprint it in 1602 (Q2), and Jaggard made another reprint, one of the so-called 'Pavier quartos', with a title-page dated 1608, in 1619 (Q3). The transfer entry on 14 August 1600 has occasioned much debate, because it is preceded in the Register by a note on a preliminary leaf naming four of the Chamberlain's Men's plays, in what has been called a 'staying entry'. Under a note 'to be staied', it brackets together these titles:

> *as yow like yt:* / a booke
> HENRY THE FFIFT: / a booke
> *Every man in his humour.* / a booke
> *The commedie of muche A doo about nothinge.*
>     a booke /

This was evidently not itself an official entry, since it was made on a preliminary leaf and not authorised by a warden. It seems to be a memorandum to himself by the clerk about some future business. Two of the four plays apparently named in the list were recorded regularly, with authorisation by a warden, ten days later on 14 August, including the transfer of *Henry V*, and a third on 23 August. The fourth play, *As You Like It*, was not entered and never appeared in print until the Folio in 1623.

---

1 The composers of the title-pages for plays published in 1598–1602 used only slightly varying terminology to advertise their wares. In thirteen instances, including the quarto of *Henry V*, Chamberlain's Men's plays and the Paul's Boys' plays are described as performed 'sundry times' by their companies, and twice it is 'diverse times'. The Admiral's plays twice have 'sundry times', but three times they are 'lately acted'. This may be a slight mark of different agencies producing the plays for the press. If so, it affirms the legitimacy of the printers whatever the origin of their copy.

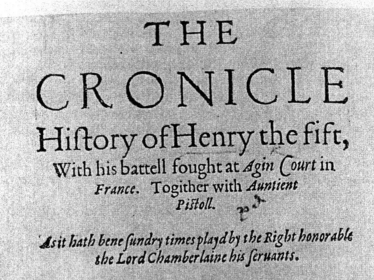

# THE
# CRONICLE

Hiſtory of Henry the fift,

With his battell fought at *Agin Court* in
*France*. Togither with *Auntient*
*Piſtoll.*

*As it hath bene ſundry times playd by the Right honorable
the Lord Chamberlaine his ſeruants.*

LONDON.

Printed by *Thomas Creede*, for Tho. Millington, and Iohn Busby. And are to be
ſold at his houſe in Carter Lane, next
the Powle head. 1600.

18 The Q title-page

The entry on 23 August is noteworthy, because it is part of the entry for another Chamberlain's company play that was printed in a quarto in 1600, *2 Henry IV*. This entry reads

Entred for their copies under the hands of the wardens Two bookes, the one called *Much a Doo about nothing. Tother the second parte of the history of kinge Henry the iiii^{th} with the humours of Sir JOHN FFALLSTAFF:* Wrytten by master Shakespere.

These seem to be regular entries of new copy, the wording taken from the books' title-pages.

The debate over the 'staying entry' and its four plays was generated by the question of 'piracy' and the so-called 'bad' or memorial quartos, the 'divers stolen and surreptitious copies' which Heminges and Condell deplored in their preface to the Folio in 1623.[1] The 'staying entry' has been thought to be part of an attempt to prevent piratical printers from printing unauthorised copies of the plays. This view is complicated by the evidently authorised nature of the copy for the quartos of *Much Ado* and *2 Henry IV* which appeared in the same year. Judging from the texts as printed, the copy for both of them was of a similar character, the authorial drafts given to the company from which the prompt-book and parts were customarily made, similar to most of the copy for the Folio plays, including F *Henry V*. Evidently the 1600 quartos of *Much Ado* and *2 Henry IV* were not printed from stolen copy. *Every Man In*, entered on 14 August, was also printed from an 'authorised' text in 1601. Of the four marked in the 'staying entry', only the 1600 Quarto of *Henry V* stands out as a 'stolen' text.

It seems, however, quite likely that the transfer of the *Henry V* rights ten days after the 'staying entry' was a coincidence. It reads like a regular transfer by a printer who had rights to the play from the previous entry for *The Famous Victories* in 1594, and who evidently had already obtained and printed Shakespeare's play before the transfer on 14 August to Pavier. Quite possibly the '*Henry V*' noted in the 'staying' memorandum was not the Agincourt play but *2 Henry IV*, which was waiting along with the other plays from the Chamberlain's for an official entry and subsequent publication. The succinct name '*HENRY the FFIFT*' could have been a summary note of the title taken by the clerk from the manuscript's title-page.[2] The published Quarto's full title reads: '*THE /* Second part of Henrie the fourth, continuing to his death, */ and coronation of Henrie /* the fift. With the humours of sir John Fal */ staffe, and swaggering Pistol*.' The clowns' parts would not have supplied a main title, but the new King Henry coming at the end of the main title might.

This reading of the entries has some significance for the question of the Stationers' concern about stolen copy. If the clerk's note on 4 August about staying the four 'bookes' was merely in anticipation of their being subsequently registered for printing for the first time, it is reasonable to assume that the three plays entered in the fortnight that followed, and which were printed in 1600 and 1601, were part of a routine transaction noting plays

---

1 The debate is summarised by Richard Knowles (ed.), *The New Variorum As You Like It*, 1977, pp. 353–64.
2 This reading of the evidence about the 'staying entry' was originally proposed in an unpublished paper by Peter Blayney, 'Shakespeare's fight with *what* pirates?', presented at the Folger Shakespeare Library in May 1987.

that had just been released by the Chamberlain's Men for the press, and which were to be officially entered later. They were not part of any dramatic intervention by the players either to stop publication of the *Henry V* Quarto or to ensure that the players, rather than Creede, profited by the publications. The text named in the 14 August transfer, 'The historye of Henrye the v$^{th}$ w$^{th}$ the battell of Agencourt', copies the Quarto's title-page closely, and was almost certainly taken directly from it, because the book was already in print and the transaction was merely a routine transfer of the rights.

Nonetheless, the copy for the Quarto of *Henry V* is not likely to have been an 'authorised' text. It seems to have been made up from memory by two or three of the players, possibly the same players who gave the printers the equally unauthorised Quarto of *Merry Wives* printed two years later. The concept of 'memorial' or 'reported' texts has been a subject for much debate throughout the twentieth century.[1] The debate itself gave rise to the concept of 'pirated' quartos, and the recent questioning of that concept has thrown some doubt on the theory of 'memorial' transmission. Despite those doubts, it does seem almost certain that the copy for Q *Henry V* was made up by some of the players. What is unclear is why they did it, since the money they would have been paid by the printer would not have been substantial, and the labour of making up the transcript was not a small one. Doubts over the motive have fed the supposition that it was made first as an acting text, and only handed to the printer subsequently. My analysis of Q deepens that uncertainty, because it indicates that the Q copy was prepared for reading, not for acting. Its value as an authoritative source for the original staging of the play must therefore be called in question.

The original player of Ancient Pistol, who seems to have been one of the transcribers along with Exeter and Gower, may also have played the linguistically extravagant Host of the Garter in *Merry Wives*. Such clownish parts, we might speculate, would be appropriate for the player who had taken the clown's roles in the company since 1594, Will Kemp. We know that he left the company in late 1599, selling his 10% investment in the Globe to four of his fellows, one of them Shakespeare. This may be coincidence, but it does seem possible that after leaving he settled down with two of the minor players to produce a version that would bring some profit from a printer. Such a trick might explain the enigmatic statement in his book about his famous morris dance from London to Norwich, *Kemps nine daies wonder*, printed in 1600, that 'Some sweare in a Trenchmore I have trode a good way to winne the world: others that guesse righter, affirme, I have without good help daunst my selfe out of the worlde.'[2] Whether or not it was the dance to Norwich that took him out of the Globe, he certainly did leave the company in 1599, going across the Channel (Dover to Calais) at the end of the year to try more dancing exploits. On his return he joined Worcester's Men at the Rose, neighbour and rival to the Globe.

---

1 For affirmative views about memorial quartos, see Gary Taylor, 'We happy few: the 1600 abridgment', in *Three Studies*, 1979. For a more sceptical view, see Paul Werstine, 'Narratives about printed Shakespearean texts: 'foul papers' and 'bad' quartos', *SQ* 41 (1990), 65–86.
2 Epistle Dedicatory, A3. The book was entered in the Stationers' Register on 22 April 1600.

Most of the attempts to identify the origin of Q have identified it as a player's text, transcribing a version made for a reduced cast, probably made up for performance by the company while on tour away from their London base. It certainly was heavily cut; it lacks the six choruses, some characters are merged or missing, notably Macmorris and Jamy, and several inessential speeches have gone, including the whole of Act 1, Scene 1, 3.1, Henry's 'ceremony' soliloquy from 4.1, and 4.2. These sections, with other cuts amounting to almost half of the F version, are thought to have been left out either as economies for a shorter provincial performance or because none of the reporting players was on stage for these scenes and so had difficulty remembering the lines. All such ideas are speculative, and there is no firm evidence to uphold any of them. Players who had left Shakespeare's company might well have made use of their memories to write out a playbook, either for the press or another company. If they joined a travelling company they might have made it as a new prompt-book for future performances. They could not have expected to use the new text in London, where it would be recognised as another company's, but a shortened version for fewer players would have a use on tour. So some contrivance of that kind might have produced the copy for the Q text. But the version that reached the printer contains features which strongly suggest it was not primarily designed for acting.

There is evidence to suggest that it was prepared for the reader, not the stage. In three places the cuts make nonsense of the Elizabethan tradition of continuous staging, where characters leaving at the end of one scene do not immediately re-enter for the next scene. Shakespeare's plays never require characters to re-enter as soon as they have left the stage,[1] but in Q that happens three times. At the end of Act 4, Scene 1 in Q Gloucester goes off with Henry, and immediately returns to start 4.3. At the end of 4.4, which in Q comes after 4.5, the direction is *Exeunt omnes*, including Pistol. He is then marked to return in the mass entry that begins 4.6. Llewellyn and Gower depart at the end of 4.8, and in the absence of an intervening Chorus they re-enter directly for 5.1's scene with Pistol and the leek. On this evidence, it seems Q cannot have been prepared as an acting text. It was written for the printers, not the stage.[2]

Much debate has been caused by the radical cutting and merging of characters in Q.[3] *Henry V* uses an exceptionally large number of characters on stage. The consequent need for doubling and cutting to fit so many parts to a limited number of players would be the first kind of change that might be expected in adapting the F manuscript for stage use. Consequently the cuts in the Q text and its characters have provoked considerable speculation about whether they might indicate the most likely patterns of doubling in the original performances. This is a question complicated by the fact that more players would have been available for London performances than for plays taken on tour. The

1  See Irwin Smith, 'Their exits and reentrances', *SQ* 18 (1967), 7–16; Andrew Gurr, '*The Tempest*'s tempest at Blackfriars', *S.Sur. 41* (1988), 91–102.
2  If this is the case, the much-debated issue of casting the Q version for fewer players than the F version becomes a minor matter, as I believe it is.
3  See Gary Taylor, 'We happy few: the 1600 abridgment', and Thomas L. Berger, 'Casting *Henry V*', *S.St.* 20 (1988), 89–104. On the question whether the 'memorial' quartos were cut for smaller companies to perform, see Scott McMillin, 'Casting the *Hamlet* quartos: *The limit of eleven*', in *The 'Hamlet' First Published. Q1, 1603: Origins, Forms, Intertextualities*, ed. Thomas Clayton, 1992, pp. 179–94.

radical cutting of scenes with extra players such as Jamy and Macmorris might be explained by a text made for provincial touring. But the Chorus, a major omission from Q, would not have been a problem of doubling, and another explanation has to be found for that cut. The Chamberlain's Men in London had a company large enough to perform the full F text, and the Q cuts are open to other explanations than the limits in theatrical resources for touring. The cutting and merging of characters, and the possibilities in either text for doubling, cannot be more than a matter for entertaining speculation.

Q was set by formes, by cast-off copy which seems to have been in a very rough and irregular shape.[1] The composition process was fairly leisurely, on sheets A–G. Its printing was not exactly a meticulous job, since some of the standard formatting such as the italicising of stage directions is distinctly irregular. Speech headings and most of the stage directions were set in italics, but several stage directions are in roman, and there is little rigour or consistency in the setting generally. Twice speech headings recorded as catchwords fail to appear at the head of the following page.[2]

The central question about the Q text is the precise nature of its copy. Certainly its scribes knew the play well, and probably the version of the play performed on the London stage. There are several relics of lines cut from the F text relocated in other scenes of Q. The couplet which is placed at the end of Act 4, Scene 2 in the F text, for instance, is transferred rather awkwardly to 3.8 in the Quarto, which otherwise omits the whole of 4.2. Inserting it at the end of 3.8 puts the sun high in the sky before dawn. Many lines are attributed to different speakers, and not all the speech headings make sense. Pistol in 4.1 and other speakers are given headings for successive speeches. At F's 4.8.72 in Q Exeter incongruously extends his speech so that he reads the whole list of the dead at Agincourt, including Henry's 'This note doth tell me . . .'. The progressive loss of closeness in the correlation between F and Q seems to indicate growing weariness in the Q scribes, and therefore a motive more modest than transcribing a performable version of the play, still less a prompt-book. This evidence, like the three exits with immediate re-entries, suggests that, although the Q authors knew the whole play, they recomposed it with more regard for readability than performance.[3] What this says about the reliability of Q as evidence for the script as originally performed in London is not encouraging. Besides the evident casualness, some influence more positive than memory alone affected the transcript from which Q was made. Possibly the transcribers made it up with a travelling group of players in mind, but if so it was only as a hypothetical performance text that had never been tried on stage. More likely they simply prepared it as a readable version for the money it brought them from the printers.

---

1 Thomas L. Berger, 'The printing of *Henry V*, Q1', *The Library*, sixth series, i (1979), 114–25.
2 At 1.2.33 (Canterbury) and 4.3.76 (Henry). Catchwords were of doubtful importance even when setting by formes, but printers were usually meticulous in following the practice.
3 Kathleen Irace, who has done a careful computer analysis of the memorial quarto texts, concludes that Q was made from a fully F-related text. She finds that at least three actors, Exeter, Gower, and Pistol, must have prepared the text, each of them doubling in smaller roles. She suggests that the reduced Q text was possibly prepared from F by the players for a touring group.

That being so, it is necessary to exercise caution in taking Q readings over into F. At one level, a transcription of the heard phrase might correct an F phrase that was misread in his copy by the F compositor. The Welsh, Irish, and Scottish dialect forms similarly can gain from a phonetic transcription. But Q's intensified use of catchphrases and oaths by the comic characters is more dubious, as is the transfer of speeches from one character to another. The reattribution of speeches, and particularly the substitution of Warwick for Westmorland and Clarence for Bedford, may be the result of compression made necessary so that parts could be doubled when the play was cast for the London stage. But it may also be simply the result of a hazy memory of the names of the lesser nobles and who spoke what. The only strong evidence for Q to contain the changes made between F's copy and the performed text is the replacement of the Dauphin by Bourbon.

Thomas Nashe's comment in *Pierce Penilesse* (1592) about the early version of the play makes it clear that the Dauphin was presented as the anti-hero to Henry. Nashe specifies that the Dauphin and the French king were shown making their submission on stage to Henry, as happens in the printed text of *The Famous Victories*. Nashe objects to 'any Collian, or clubfisted Usurer' who will not see

what a glorious thing it is to have *Henrie* the fifth represented on the Stage, leading the French King prisoner, and forcing both him and the Dolphin to sweare Fealty.[1]

Evidently the Dauphin was the omnipresent villain in the early stage versions of the story. In *3 Henry VI* Shakespeare himself describes how Henry had 'made the Dauphin stoop'. *The Famous Victories* recurs three times to the tennis-balls insult and makes the Dauphin kneel to Henry in the final scene, although, as in Shakespeare's play, the French king's ban on his presence at Agincourt is recorded. Up to Act 3 in Shakespeare's version the Dauphin occupies the same role of antagonist that he does in *The Famous Victories*. Until his father orders him not to go to Agincourt (3.6.64–6), Shakespeare's play emphasises his role as Henry's opposite. Besides the tennis balls, and Exeter's direct reply to the Dauphin in Act 2, Scene 4, he is ordered in 2.4.6 to join the French dukes strengthening the towns against the English, and at 3.4.45–7 the Governor of Harfleur specifically blames the Dauphin for not bringing the town relief. Henry puns on his antagonist with 'this your heir of France' at 3.7.133. In 3.8 in the F text the Dauphin is at the battle, but in 4.5 he is accompanied by Bourbon, and Bourbon is the only French prisoner named in the entry stage direction at the beginning of 4.7. Bourbon and Orléans are specified as prisoners in 4.8.68–9. The Dauphin gets no further mention there or in Act 5.

Historically, the Dauphin had little validity as Henry's principal antagonist apart from the tennis-balls insult. He was ordered to stay with the king at Rouen, and he did not fight at Agincourt. In fact the sender of the tennis balls, if historically that act ever did take place, died not long after the battle. Between it and the Treaty of Troyes celebrated in the final act of the play three different men held the title of Dauphin. It seems that Shakespeare hesitated between the alternative versions offered by his two

1 *Works*, ed. R. B. McKerrow, 5 vols., 1904–10, I, 213.

main sources.[1] The earlier play or plays made the Dauphin into Henry's chief antagonist and showed him humiliated and stripped of his inheritance at the end. Holinshed, who for the earlier plays Shakespeare had been careful to follow in considerable detail and with considerable accuracy, disintegrates this stage figure. It is quite conceivable that in the course of composition, or of writing out the draft that he gave to the company and that was eventually turned into the F text, Shakespeare shifted the basis of his thinking about the Dauphin's role from his presentation in the early stage-play to the figures in Holinshed.

There may also have been, perhaps, a question of giving offence to the French ambassador in 1599. On the one hand, the Dauphin was a useful culprit in place of the French king. A detail in Holinshed that is notably avoided in the play is the French king's recurrent bouts of madness, or 'frenzie' as Holinshed called it, and he is not given any name as he is in *The Famous Victories*. Whether because he was Katherine's father, or for diplomacy, he is given sane and largely impersonal authority in Shakespeare's text. Making the Dauphin the chief culprit took a heavy load off the French king. But his later presence, quite apart from the anomaly of his unhistorical appearance at Agincourt, set up new problems which may not have occurred to the author until Act 5 was looming in his mind.

The largest reason for his thinking about eliminating the Dauphin from the second half of the play I suspect had its source in the dynastic issue. With his French marriage Henry renewed the position that drew Edward III into the Hundred Years War. The Dauphin's disappearance from the treaty scene (Act 5, Scene 2) softens the political edge of the play's closure. It also conceals the fact that the treaty required the Dauphin to be deposed in favour of Henry as 'héritier de France', the king's new heir, a point that *The Famous Victories* gives some emphasis to. Even more to the point, it minimises the parallelism of Henry's position with that of Edward III, which had a similar pattern of early victory (Crécy and Agincourt) followed by a long period of attrition that ended in almost total loss of the English possessions in France. The F text shows signs of unresolved hesitancy about what to do with the Dauphin's role in the play. It seems likely that the Q text shows how that question was resolved.

The Q version not only reattributes the Dauphin's speeches in Act 3, Scene 8 and 4.5 to Bourbon, but builds up his part by giving him lines in earlier scenes, 2.4 and 3.6. This change has some awkward consequences for the presentation of the French nobles in 3.8. It was easy to stress the latent discords in the French camp when the Dauphin praises his own valour and writes sonnets to his 'palfrey'. The subsequent antagonism, shown in the proverb-swapping game between the Constable and Orléans, grows out of Orléans' defence against the Constable's contempt for the Dauphin. That, with Rambures' tactful attempts to distract them both, makes a neat contrast to the 'brothers' of the English camp. Substituting Bourbon for the Dauphin reduces the

---

1 This point was first made very cogently by Gary Taylor, in the one-volume Oxford edition of *Henry V* published in 1982. His discussion in that edition of the textual problems, pp. 12–26, was the first to take Q seriously as a version of the original staged text.

force of this scene as a contrast to the English scene, and he is given no other significant role except as mute prisoner in 4.7 (Gary Taylor, whose analysis of the substitution is generally admirable, has no evidence for claiming that Bourbon leads the counter-attack and is responsible for killing the boys).[1] The substitution by Q of Bourbon for the Dauphin at Agincourt, and the subsequent disappearance of the Dauphin in both versions, seems to indicate what the final resolution of this hesitancy was for the staged text. Its side effects remain as one of the many awkwardnesses in the play.

1 Taylor, p. 25.

# Appendix 1: Theatre sources – *The Famous Victories*

*The Famous Victories of Henry V* is the only surviving example, besides Shakespeare's, of several plays about Henry and Agincourt staged in the 1580s and 1590s. The Queen's Men had a play in the 1580s, in which their leading tragedian Knell played Henry and Tarlton took the clown's role. This may have been the version Nashe wrote about in *Pierce Penilesse* in 1592, and which Shakespeare alludes to in *3 Henry VI*. Both Nashe and Shakespeare report that their version made the Dauphin submit to Henry in the final scenes. Another play about 'harey the v' appears in *Henslowe's Diary* as a 'ne' play, performed thirteen times between 28 November 1595 and 15 July 1596. Neither of these versions was necessarily the same as the one that appears in the printed text under the name *The Famous Victories of Henry the fifth: Containing the Honourable Battell of Agin-court.*

A play of that name was entered in the Stationers' Register in 1594, by the man who issued the published text of 1598, Thomas Creede. Creede in 1594 printed ten plays in quarto, four of them from the Queen's Men, which finally gave up playing in London in the summer of that year. When he put out the quarto of *The Famous Victories* four years later it was also identified as a Queen's Men's play, specifying on the title-page 'As it was plaide by the Queenes Majesties Players'. This implies that his text was the old play referred to in the anecdote about Richard Tarlton. The joke, reproduced in *Tarlton's Jests*, has an air of truth about it.

At the Bull at Bishops-gate was a Play of Henry the fift, wherein the Judge was to take a box on the eare, and because he was absent that should take the blow, *Tarlton* himselfe (ever forward to please) tooke upon him to play the same Judge, besides his owne part of the Clowne: and *Knel* then playing *Henry* the fift, hit *Tarlton* a sound boxe indeed, which made the people laugh the more because it was he: but anon the Judge goes in, and imediately *Tarlton* (in his Clownes cloathes) comes out, and askes the Actors what newes; O (saith one) hadst thou been here, thou shouldest have seene Prince *Henry* hit the Judge a terrible box on the eare. What man, said *Tarlton*, strike a Judge? It is true yfaith, said the other, No other like, said *Tarlton*, and it could not be but terrible to the Judge, when the report so terrifies me, that me thinkes the blow remaines still on my cheeke, that it burnes againe.[1]

The Bull was an inn located in Gracechurch Street near London Bridge, where there were several inns used for staging plays up to 1594. *The Famous Victories* has a scene where the Lord Chief Justice is struck by the prince, and it is immediately followed by one between Dericke the clown and his feed John Cobler. Unfortunately, in the previous scene Dericke appears on stage along with the Lord Chief Justice, so it would have been difficult for the anecdote to fit easily into the *Famous Victories* text as we have

---

1 *Tarlton's Jests*, 1600, p. 13.

it. But the absence of any player from a performance would have called for some hasty adjustments, and Dericke's first comic scene with the Justice might have been cut in favour of the ear-boxing scene.

On the face of it, therefore, the quarto play entitled *The Famous Victories* might have been the play performed by Knell and Tarlton in the mid-1580s, the one which Nashe and Shakespeare knew. It certainly has a final scene where the Duke of Burgundy and the Dauphin have to kiss Henry's sword in an act of submission. But it is a very short and defective text. Half the length of a Shakespeare play at 1,550 lines, it covers the whole story of the prodigal prince, from his Gadshill robbery to the peace with France and his wedding with Princess Katherine. Between 1594 when Creede registered the text he got from the Queen's Men and 1598 when he printed it, two of Shakespeare's most popular plays telling the same story of Prince Hal had intervened, so there is an obvious question whether Shakespeare's plays influenced the text that Creede finally printed. If not, the question is how much the earlier play influenced Shakespeare. And since one-third of *The Famous Victories* deals with Henry as king, and has a similar set of equivalences, we have to ask the same questions about *Henry V*, and whether Shakespeare's play was not already on stage in 1598 when *The Famous Victories* was printed.

It is always a tricky question deciding which of two similar stories came first. Usually the more gifted author is credited with the greater inventiveness and is therefore given precedence. In this case, the reverse must be true. Shakespeare knew either *The Famous Victories* or a stage version from which it derived when he wrote his *Henry V*. He may well also have known the stage version when he wrote his own two plays about the prodigal prince. The evidence is not entirely positive, and comes perilously close to a circular argument in places. But taking the pieces of evidence cumulatively, it does seem most likely that Shakespeare took his outline for the story of Henry as king and a few of his details from his memory of the old Queen's Men's play. The chief uncertainty is how much the 1598 text of *The Famous Victories* preserves from its original.

*The Famous Victories* is shaped as a prodigal son play, a kind that had been widely popular for more than twenty years, especially with citizen audiences. It uses Hall and Stow for its account of the young prince's wild youth, and keeps to Hall for its basic information about Henry's career in France. All of the points from Hall that appear in Shakespeare's version where they differ from Holinshed could have been mediated to him through the earlier play. The earlier play certainly uses Hall and not Holinshed. It specifies, for instance, that Henry's first landing in France for the siege of Harfleur was at 'Kidcocks', which follows Hall's 'Caux, comonly called Kyd Caux'. Holinshed calls it 'Kidcaur'. In *The Famous Victories* the tennis balls come in a 'tun', as in Hall, not Holinshed's 'barrell'. *Henry V* has 'tun', probably from Hall via the earlier play, although Holinshed's word-play on courts is tied in with it. In the few other cases where Shakespeare uses Hall he could have similarly taken the details from the old play. He seems to have done so when he took Cuthbert Cutter's nickname 'Gadshill' for the thief in *1 Henry IV*. In general, Shakespeare picked what he wanted from his memory of a performed version of *The Famous Victories* to mix with his current reading of Holinshed. The sword covered in crowns (*Henry V*, 2.0.9) can certainly be related more readily to the comic scene between Dericke and the French soldier than it can to an illustration of Edward III's emblem reproduced in the 1577 Holinshed,[1] which Wilson thought must have been Shakespeare's source for the image, but which it is doubtful Shakespeare ever consulted. More notably, if the 1598 Quarto of *The Famous Victories* does represent the old play truly, then the comic presentation of 'Jockey', Sir John Oldcastle, as chief among the robber companions to the young Henry, must have come to Shakespeare from the Queen's Men's play.[2]

There are very few close verbal parallels between *The Famous Victories* and Shakespeare's plays. If there were more, they would strengthen the case for Shakespeare's version getting on stage first, since his words are by far the more memorable. At points like Scene 8 of *The Famous Victories*, where the dying Henry IV says to his son about the crown 'For God knowes my sonne, how hardly I came by it', the Shakespearean version offers a mighty enhancement: 'God knows, my son, / By what by-paths and indirect crook'd ways / I met this crown' (*2H4* 4.2.311–13). The same is true of the faint verbal resemblances in *Henry V*, such as the Crispin's Day speech (*Famous Victories*, Scene 14, 66–73), the numbers of the Agincourt dead (Scene 15, 5–12), and the identification of the name Agincourt (Scene 15, 40–6). The closest verbal parallel between the two versions is Kate's response to Henry in the final scene, 'How should I love thee, which is my father's enemy?', which is not far from Shakespeare's 5.2.158: 'Is it possible dat I sould love de *ennemi* of France?' But the parallelisms are so largely of story and incident and the verbal parallels so remote that it is necessary to assume either that the composer of *The Famous Victories* Quarto had an appallingly imprecise memory for verse or that Shakespeare used his own words for a story, the outline and some details of which were familiar from the earlier play. The latter seems altogether more likely.

It is difficult to identify specific points of dependency, but a short list of the main features that are in *The Famous Victories* and missing from Shakespeare's play does at least show some things that were the common currency of Henry's story as it was staged before Shakespeare. Of these the prominence given to the Dauphin is certainly the greatest. In *The Famous Victories* his insult with the tennis balls features in Henry's decision to make war, and is mentioned twice more at points when his role as Henry's antagonist is being foregrounded. The Dauphin is present in the run up to Agincourt, though not shown at the battle itself, and he is present and made to kiss Henry's sword as a gesture of submission at the end. His disinheritance is firmly emphasised there. At Agincourt the famous tactic with the archers and their protective stakes is mentioned twice, and command of the archers, which in Hall was given to Erpingham, in *The Famous Victories* is given to the Earl of Oxford, whose prominence throughout the play is one of its minor peculiarities. Oxford joins Exeter as Henry's firmest adviser, taking much of the part that Shakespeare gives to Westmorland in the opening debate about the war. It is he who offers the famous tag about winning France

---

1 J. Dover Wilson (ed.), *Henry V*, The New Shakespeare, p. 132, and see 2.0.9–11 n.
2 A suggestive account of the Oldcastle/Falstaff story is given by Gary Taylor, 'The fortunes of Oldcastle', *S.Sur. 38* (1985), 85–100.

by starting on Scotland, though he puts it the wrong way round. In fact the reversal makes Oxford the good adviser, because where in Shakespeare Westmorland quotes it as an argument for starting with Scotland, and Exeter counters with the opposite view, in *The Famous Victories* Oxford's reversal gives him Exeter's winning argument. At Agincourt he asks for the vanguard, and, told it has already been promised to York, is given the archers as a consolation. He joins an honour-roll of English nobles at Agincourt who had Elizabethan descendants: Derby, Kent, Nottingham, Huntington, Willoughby and Northumberland.[1] Other distinct features of *The Famous Victories* are that before Agincourt the French soldiers are shown dicing for the English, and the chair prepared for Henry to be carried in after Agincourt is also noted more prominently than in Shakespeare. Names taken from Hall, such as the Archbishop of Bourges, who becomes the French ambassador, and King Charles himself, do not appear in Shakespeare's version. Mercenary troops are specified out of Hall that get no direct mention in Shakespeare.

Some of these features in *The Famous Victories* are glanced at so obliquely in Shakespeare's play that one wonders if they are not being taken for granted. And yet the whole story of Henry as king told by the 1598 Quarto takes less than one-fifth the number of lines of Shakespeare's play. Their omission in Shakespeare cannot all be just streamlining or overfamiliarity. Much of Shakespeare's additional detail comes from a close reading of Holinshed, though even there the selection of detail suggests an originality in the approach amounting to much more than a variant telling of a familiar story. The three major events featured in Shakespeare's play that do not appear in *The Famous Victories* are first the conspiracy at Southampton, which is omitted entirely from the 1598 Quarto. The reasons for that, and the further omission it entails, are considered in the Introduction, pp. 19–21. Secondly, the siege of Harfleur is mentioned only in passing by the Archbishop of Bourges and then by Henry as 'this good lucke of winning this Towne'. One battle was enough. The third substantial omission is the killing of the prisoners. The firing of the king's tents is mentioned twice, by Dericke after the battle and by Henry to King Charles in the treaty scene, where the French king swears it was not the Dauphin's doing, but nothing is said about the more substantial offence, killing the French prisoners.

1  The Earl of Oxford as patron of companies of players and as playwright has been given an extraordinary amount of attention in recent years, considering that the available evidence about his activities and his writing is far smaller than for Shakespeare. Possibly the credit given to Oxford in *The Famous Victories* may reflect a desire to gain access to him as a patron, or possibly the play had fallen into the hands of a company he was patron to. Laurence Dutton was a leader of an Oxford's company in 1583 when he was taken from it to help make the Queen's Men. Oxford then ran a boy company through John Lyly, though by 1585 he seems to have had another adult company, which is noted as playing at Norwich in 1585–6, Ipswich in 1586–7, and Maidstone in 1589–90. An Oxford's company merged with Worcester's to perform at the Boar's Head in 1602. This company may have been in existence in the vicinity of 1598, when *The Famous Victories* was published, because they are named on the title-page of *The Weakest Goeth to the Wall*, published in 1600. But the 1598 Quarto is unequivocal in ascribing the play to the old Queen's Men, who had disappeared in 1594, close to the time when the play was first entered for publication. Conceivably Dutton, of whom there is no record after 1590 when he was still a Queen's Man, reverted to his old Oxford allegiance after 1594. Rather less conceivably he might have had a hand in preparing the text of *The Famous Victories* for the printer in 1598. But that still does not explain why the Queen's and not Oxford's should be named on the title-page.

The most fundamental difference between Shakespeare's play and *The Famous Victories* is Shakespeare's elimination of the prodigal son aspect of the story. In the old play the young prince is truly wild, truly a thief, and truly boxes the Lord Chief Justice on the ear. His conversion, in a talk with his father, is sudden and complete. It makes a model before-and-after tale, with a strong colouring from a local twist to the biblical parable that the late sixteenth-century prodigal tales normally gave it. Their emphasis was not the virtues of love and parental forgiveness but the lesson that the penitent son receives in learning the virtue of good and thrifty behaviour. Shakespeare's story transforms that trite moralism from the moment Hal delivers his 'I know you all' soliloquy at the end of the second scene of *1 Henry IV*. For some implications of that change, see Introduction, p. 29.

A reasonably good version of the text of the whole of *The Famous Victories* with notes is given in Geoffrey Bullough, *Narrative and Dramatic Sources*, IV, 299–343.

# Appendix 2: Historical sources – Holinshed's *Chronicles*


Shakespeare must have owned his own copy of the second and enlarged edition of Raphael Holinshed's multi-volume *Chronicles of England, Scotland, and Ireland*, published in 1587. It was his primary source for *Richard II* and the plays that followed. In places for *Henry V*, particularly in Act 1, Scene 2, and for the names of the dead at Agincourt in 4.7, he appears to have had his copy at his elbow, versifying directly from it. He made use not only of Holinshed's account of Henry's wars in France but the 'Description of England' supplied by William Harrison for Volume I, and very likely referred to the Chronicles of Scotland and Ireland as well. He consulted the 'Description' for its account of English dogs, and may well have quarried the Chronicle of Scotland for information about the Scottish James that Henry took with him to France. Given his interest in Ireland and the Essex campaign going on there in 1599, he may also have taken note of the highly prejudicial account by John Hooker of the Irish in that volume.

One distinctive consequence of Shakespeare's reading of Holinshed is apparent in his choice of the Scots 'Jamy'. In the Chronicle of England's history, Holinshed reports that at some time after Agincourt Henry brought to France the young King James I of Scotland to accompany him in the wars. A captive of the English from the age of 11, James fought for Henry in several conflicts in France, including the siege of Melun, where he tried to persuade the Scots who were fighting for the French to change sides, without success. When the siege was won Henry had twenty of them executed for disobedience to their king. James was the chief mourner at Henry's funeral in 1422. His whole story is given in much more detail in Holinshed's Chronicle of Scotland. In the play, Captain Jamy is a long way from being a Scottish prince. But the name itself keeps jumping out from Holinshed's story of Henry's reign.

Holinshed relied on a variety of sources for his work. Edward Hall's earlier history of 1548, *The Union of the two noble and illustrious families of Lancastre and Yorke*, is regularly cited in Holinshed's marginal notes, along with Robert Fabyan's *New Chronicles of England and France* (1516), Richard Grafton's *Chronicle at Large* (1569), and the Latin of Polydore Virgil likewise. John Stow's *Chronicles of England* (1580), reissued as the *Annals* in 1592, was not an influence on Holinshed, who had died before his 1587 edition appeared, though Shakespeare seems to have known it. Stow's *Summarie of the Chronicles of England. Diligently collected and abridged . . .*, a duodecimo book printed in 1598, has a few pages on 'Henry of Monmouth'. It is chiefly notable for twice using Pistol's version (2.1.39) of the word 'marvellous'. At L3 Henry is described as 'of marvailous great strength', and at L4 'he fought the battail at Agincourt, where he had a marvailous victorie'.

The commentary notes to this edition quote a number of the passages in Holinshed that are used in the play. A complete transcript of Holinshed, which is needful to see what Shakespeare omitted as well as what he used, is not possible here for reasons of space. Texts of the 1587 Holinshed are available in either the Everyman edition (no. 800), *Holinshed's Chronicle, As Used in Shakespeare's Plays*, ed. Allardyce and Josephine Nicoll, London, 1927, New York, 1951; or in the more selective *Shakespeare's Holinshed: an edition of Holinshed's Chronicles, 1587; source of Shakespeare's History Plays, King Lear, Cymbeline, and Macbeth*, ed. Richard Hosley, New York, 1968. What follows attempts to track Holinshed's own account and the direct uses that were made of it for the play, with a few notes about possibly significant omissions.

Holinshed opens his account at Henry IV's death in 1413. In the opening paragraph on Henry V's reign he records the most notable event of that year, the shipwreck of the young Scottish prince James at Flamborough, which led to his eighteen-year detention in England. The next paragraph describes Henry's accession. Henry's youthful attachment to 'misrulie mates of dissolute order and life' and his striking the Lord Chief Justice are noted before his transformation to doing good, both pious and practical, at his ascension to the throne. He set St George's day as a feast-day against the wishes of the Archbishop of Canterbury, who wanted St Dunstan, he formally reinterred Richard II at Westminster, and he gave a fairly gentle admonishment to Sir John Oldcastle, accused of heresy by the Archbishop, as a 'straied sheepe'.

The next six paragraphs give an account of Lollard risings, with details of Oldcastle's imprisonment and escape. Other events of these years in the reign at home and abroad are listed, none of which are used in the play. Its incidents recur with the seventh paragraph, recounting Parliament's renewal of the bill against the clergy, cited in the play at 1.1.1. Archbishop Chichele's oration about Henry's claim to the French crown, and the Salic Law, follows, introduced as a 'sharpe invention, that he should not regard the importunate petitions of the commons'. The play copies the terms of the oration and the subsequent debate quite closely. The diplomatic exchanges between the two countries that followed are tightly compressed in the play from Holinshed's ten paragraphs. On the other hand, Holinshed's two concise paragraphs about the Cambridge conspiracy at Southampton are expanded in the play, though a subsequent two paragraphs about Cambridge's claim to the throne, the basis for his plotting, are omitted. A paragraph speculating about Oldcastle's involvement in the Cambridge conspiracy is also cut.

Holinshed's next eleven paragraphs, on the preparations for invasion, the arrival at 'Caur, commonlie called Kidcaur, where the river of Saine runneth into the sea', and the siege and victory at Harfleur, are compressed in the play, which invents a good deal that is not in Holinshed. The material points about the surrender of the town follow the book, although Holinshed's reports of rapine by the English are ignored. The play then follows the book's account of the march towards Calais, apart from a page about Henry dubbing some new knights and some skirmishes and displays of valour over crossing the Somme. Much of Holinshed's detailing over the preparations for battle on both sides is compressed or omitted from the play's fourth act, including a long paragraph about the invention of the archers' stakes. Westmorland's wish for more English soldiers is reported as an anonymous voice, but Holinshed's version of the king's reply gives the gist of what he says in the play. Otherwise Act 4, apart from its insertions of Pistol's gambols and the long debate with the three soldiers, is fairly loyal to Holinshed's much more exhaustive account. The play's retailing of the deaths of York and Suffolk is largely Shakespeare's own, as are the French scenes. The play uses nothing from Holinshed's account of the main battle-lines, the long three-hour struggle, and the named nobles killed or wounded in the field. The only major use made of Holinshed's long lists of names is for the dead on both sides. Nothing is retailed of the French vanguard and the English assaults on their middle battle. Among the smaller incidents that the play cuts are Henry's heroism in saving his brother: 'The duke of Glocester the kings brother was sore wounded about the hips, and borne downe to the ground, so that he fell backwards, with his feet towards his enimies, whom the king bestrid, and like a brother valiantile rescued from his enimies, & so saving his life, caused him to be conveied out of the fight.'

The play trims other incidents such as Henry's attack on the French rear and their confused retreat, and the names of the French leaders who attacked the English 'tents & pavillions'. The play's different versions of that attack also pass by Holinshed's scrupulous note that for the 'treason and haskardie in thus leaving their camp at the very point of fight, for winning of spoile where none to defend it, verie manie were after committed to prison, and had lost their lives, if the Dolphin had longer lived'. Henry's subsequent and clinching order to kill the French prisoners is given a quite different treatment from Holinshed's account, which is quoted in the Introduction, p. 24.

Apart from the game with Williams and Llewellyn, the play follows Holinshed closely for the aftermath of the battle, with the French Herald's return, the lists of the dead on both sides, the naming of the field as Agincourt, and the king's own behaviour in victory and after, 'like a grave and sober personage'. The fifth Chorus, summarising Henry's arrival at Calais and shipping to Dover, the welcome at Blackheath, and the Holy Roman Emperor's visit, covers fifteen of Holinshed's paragraphs. It leaps over the five years of further campaigns in France, going straight from Agincourt in 1415 to the peace negotiations at Troyes in 1420.

Holinshed has an account of the long struggles, sieges, battles and peace talks that occupied Henry in France up to 1419. The high point of the campaign in Normandy was the successful siege of Rouen. The arrival of the Irish led by Lord Kilmain occurs here, as does Henry's threat about Bellona which is echoed in the Prologue. A succession of French sieges, the changes of Dauphin, and the quarrel between the Burgundians and the Dauphin's followers are all passed over in the play. Holinshed's intervening paragraphs contain not only the exploits of the Scottish King James and the arrival of the Irish soldiery but the last Oldcastle rebellion and the first meeting of Henry with the princess Katherine at Troyes, which took place some time before the assembly of royalty and nobles who met to settle the treaty. Burgundy's arrangement of the treaty meeting and its terms in 1420 takes another forty-five paragraphs, mostly to quote the terms of the treaty.

Holinshed's account tells of Henry's first meeting with the Duke of Burgundy, when he told him he would marry the king's daughter. Burgundy, then still trying to make an alliance with the Dauphin's party, scorned this claim at the time. He was, however, murdered at a meeting with the Dauphin later in 1419. Burgundy's heir then allied himself with the king against the Dauphin, and the meeting at which the Treaty of Troyes would be signed was set up. Burgundy's oath at Troyes is given in Latin and English. Henry's marriage to Katherine, 'solemnized and fullie consummate', on 3 June 1420, gets a concise note, after which Holinshed lists the thirty-three articles of the treaty. The five terms of a further secret treaty between Henry and Burgundy against the Dauphin are also quoted, the Dauphin then being the only active enemy to the English. In what follows, the ensuing 'civill discord' in France, mostly fighting between the Dauphin's supporters with Henry's English army, is described, including, after a paragraph about the regency in Scotland, the exploits of James and Henry at the siege of Melun.

The remainder of Holinshed's account of Henry's life lists his return to England for Katherine's coronation in 1421, giving in great detail the subsequent banquet at Westminster, the continuing battles in France, the birth of the future Henry VI, and Henry's death, which came when he was once again on campaign in France, in 1422. Nothing of Henry's speech about the treaty, including his attack on the misdoings of the new Dauphin Charles, murderer of the late Duke of Burgundy, appears in the play. The last sixty-two paragraphs, recounting the renewed sieges and battles against the Dauphin up to Henry's death, the birth of Henry's son, and the ceremonials of the death and funeral itself, are also omitted. Holinshed's concluding eulogy gets a fairly precise echo in Shakespeare's Epilogue:

Thus ended this puissant prince his most noble and fortunate reign, whose life (saith Hall) though cruell Atropos abbreviated; yet neither fire, malice nor fretting time shall appall his honour, or blot out the glorie of him that in so small time had doone so manie and roiall acts.

# Appendix 3: Background sources – Richard Crompton, *The Mansion of Magnanimitie*

Crompton's book was entered to R. Blower in the Stationers' Register on 15 May 1598, transferred to W. Ponsonby on 13 December, and printed by Shakespeare's printer and fellow-Stratfordian Richard Field for Ponsonby with the date 1599 on the title-page. Its full title is: 'The Mansion of Magnanimitie. Wherein is shewed the most high and honorable acts of sundrie English Kings, Princes, Dukes, Earles, Lords, Knights and Gentlemen, from time to time performed in defence of their Princes and Countrie: set forth as an encouragement to all faithfull subjects, by their examples resolutely to addresse them selves against all forreine enemies.' It was dedicated to the Earl of Essex, the dedication closing with the statement that

I have thought it convenient to dedicate this little Treatise to a man of such state, and unto your honour chiefly, to the ende you may therein see the notable actes of Chivalrie performed in that service, that thereby you may be incouraged to followe their steppes, and increase the fame, honour, and renowme, which you have attayned in your late valiant service at CALES IN SPAINE, and else where.

Its first section is 'An oration to be made by the General to the whole armie afore the battel', conceived as the kind of speech which Essex ought to have made at Cadiz, since the enemy is Spanish. The marginal gloss gives its main thrust: *'The cause of the war must be published, that it may appeare to arise upon just occasions, which much doth encourage the souldier to fight.'*

The book seems to have been mostly written in 1596, at the time of Essex's Cadiz expedition, or very shortly after. Crompton states in chapter 5, for instance, that England has not been invaded since William the Conqueror, 'which is about 529 yeares past' (D3), and in chapter 11 that the Spanish tried another invasion after the Armada 'in the beginning of winter about three yeares past', which was thwarted by a shipwreck near Ferrol. We know that was 1592, which like the calculation of 529 years after 1066 would make the year of composition for these chapters 1595. There is a section about the Cadiz expedition also in chapter 11 which notes the capture of prisoners for ransom and speculates about what will happen as if the date were 1596. Given the force of the arguments then being put to recusants by Parsons and Allen, an appeal to nationalism over religious allegiance would have been pertinent in any part of this decade.

Unlike writers such as John Eliot and John Norden, whose works made direct use of the Bible to endorse the rightness of fighting for one's country,

Crompton appeals rather to loyalty and patriotism. The General's oration declares war to be honourable: 'Everie man is borne once to die, and how, when, or where, is most uncertaine: and to give our lives for our countrie, hath alwayes amongst all nations (and among the heathen) bene reputed an honorable thing' (A4ᵛ). And God of course fights for the faithful: 'Wherby it doth appear, that it is not the great multitude of men of war, horses, & chariots, but the lord God that giveth victory in battell' (D3ᵛ).

In the first chapters the fear of a Spanish invasion lies behind the whole discourse. In chapter 3 William the Conqueror's imposition of Norman authority to 'despoil' the English nobles is presented as a shameful mark of the troubles of invasion. Chapter 5 invokes the spirit of Henry V and Agincourt, and the subsequent victories of Talbot (of *1 Henry VI*), climaxing in a poem in honour of Talbot (E4ᵛ-F1). Chapter 6, ostensibly on sedition, concludes with a section about Agincourt as an illustration of a quotation from Cicero, which is translated as follows:

*All things are miserable in civill warres, but nothing is more miserable then the victory it selfe, which although it happen to the best sort, yet it maketh them cruell, inso much that though they be not so by nature, yet of necessity they are compelled so to be, for many things by the overcommer at the pleasure of such, by whose ayd he doth overcome, even against his will are to be done.* When king *Henry* the fift not having above fifteene thousand men, gave a great overthrow to the French king at *Agincourt* in *Fraunce*, where he had assembled to the number of forty thousand of the flower of all his countrey, & had taken many prisoners of the french, both Nobles and others, the french as they are men of great courage and valour, so they assembled themselves againe in battell array, meaning to have given a new battell to king *Henry*, which king *Henry* perceiving, gave speciall commaundement by proclamation, that every man should kill his prisoners: whereupon many were presently slaine, whereof the French king having intelligence, dispersed his army, and so departed: whereby you may see the miseries of warre, that though they had yeelded and thought themselves sure of their lives, paying their ransome, according to the lawes of armes, yet uppon such necessary occasion, to kill them was a thing by all reason allowed, for otherwise the king having lost diverse valiant Captaines and souldiers in this battell, and being also but a small number in comparison of the French kings army, & in a strong countrey, where he could not supply his neede upon the sudden, it might have bene much daungerous to have againe joyned with the enemy, and kept his prisoners alive, as in our Chronicles largely appeareth. (G2ᵛ-G3)

Crompton does not make it clear whether he regarded Henry's invasion of France as technically a civil war, which might have justified his quotation from Cicero and his use of Agincourt with its slaughter of Henry's prisoners as his instance.

Chapter 7 moves straight on to Popish plots in the context of the Papal proclamation of 33 Elizabeth (1590), which incited Catholic subjects to undertake acts of sedition against their heretical rulers. The Pope's 'plots & practises' are designed 'to move, stirre up, and perswade as many of her highnesse subjects as they dare deale with all, to renounce their allegeance due to her Majestie and her Crowne, & upon hope by forreyn invasion to be enriched' (H1). The English Jesuits Parsons and Allen are named as producing for the Spanish king lists of subversives living near the coasts who would support him when he invaded England. By a lengthy leap, or leapfrog from the end of the previous chapter, Crompton then cites cases of English prisoners at Resendale and Gravelines being murdered by their Spanish captors – acts of 'horrible murther' out of 'bloudie inhumanitie' (H3). Erasmus and Augustine are both invoked against rebellion, and the marginal gloss states 'No subject can rebell for any cause. *Rom.* 13'. The chapter concludes by asking the Pope 'Can he find by the word of God, that it is lawfull for the subject to rebell against his Prince for any cause whatsoever?' (11ᵛ).

The next three chapters trace the same argument, rehearsing the statutes against treason and citing King John, Holinshed, the 'Booke of Martyrs', and even the Marprelate controversy. Chapter 11 lists English victories against foreigners, including those wars 'against the French and Scots', but chiefly devoting itself to victories against Spain, including Essex at 'Cales'. On the latter Crompton applauds the moderation in the leaders:

The said noble Earles of *Essex* and *Nottingham*, knowing the loosenesse of soldiers, very honorably caused the Ladies and gentlewomen (wherof there were diverse in that Citie) with the rest of the women and children, with 500 men to be safely conveyed out of the Citie, and a straite proclamation made, that none should offer to any of them any violence upon paine of deathe, and shortly after they fired the towne, and tooke the seas.                    (N4)

Chapter 12 returns to the central issue, treason, concluding that all should join against the common enemy although divided by religion.

John Norden's *The Mirror of Honor*, written at the same time as Crompton's treatise but published earlier, in 1597, offers a more biblical approach to the same subject. Also dedicated to Essex, its main argument is more or less 'onward Christian soldiers', using Norden's extensive knowledge of the Bible to uphold the concept of a just and Christian war. In the epistle *To the Reader*, he writes

[War] is a pernicious evil, as of it selfe, but by circumstances it is both lawfull and expedient, not that *it openeth the way to heaven by slaughter and bloud*, as *Scipio of Affricke* boasted, but that it is the way to redeeme most wished peace. When the cause is just no man may question whether the warre bee lawfull. It is then just when it seeketh to defend and preserve the publique quiet and Christian religion, and it is then lawful, when it is done by the authority of the Prince . . .
    As touching the justice and lawfulnes of the cause present, it sufficeth us to know it is to preserve our state, the superiour Magistrate commandeth it, and wee are to obey it in treble dutie, to God, our Soveraigne and commonweale, to the end . . . Our present warre is a defence against hostile offence, which (as every man seeth) threatneth unto us the dreadfull devouring sword.                    (A3)

They that covet to vanquish, and not to bee vanquished, must relie wholly on him that disposeth of victorie, and to use souldiers, munition and policie as his meanes: for if they be blessed by him, they are holie, otherwise they may bee aswell instruments of their owne, and of the confusion of such as trust in them as of their safetie.                                     (B1)

Such assertions about the rigours of war and the laws of human justice that ought to be applied to them have echoes, sometimes distinct, sometimes faint, in Henry's dispute with his soldiers in Act 4, Scene 1 of *Henry V* and at other points such as the French king's citation of the Bible at 2.4.59–64.

# READING LIST

All of the books mentioned in abbreviated form in the notes to the Introduction and in the commentary are listed here in full. The list includes useful reference works and a selection of books and articles which might be found useful in further studies of the play. It does not include articles which deal with specific details and which are given in full at the appropriate point in a commentary note.

Abbott, E. A. *A Shakespearian Grammar*, 1879

Barton, Anne. 'The king disguised: Shakespeare's *Henry V* and the comical history', in *The Triple Bond: Plays, Mainly Shakespearean, in Performance*, ed. Joseph G. Price, 1975, pp. 92–117

Beauman, Sally (ed.). *The Royal Shakespeare Company's Production of 'Henry V' for the Centenary Season at the Royal Shakespeare Theatre*, 1976

Berger, Harry Jr. 'Harrying the stage: *Henry V* in the tetralogical echo chamber', *The Shakespearean International Yearbook* 3, 2003, pp. 131–55

Berger, Thomas L. and Williams, George Walton. 'Notes on Shakespeare's *Henry V*', *Analytical and Enumerative Bibliography* 12 (2001), 264–87

Berry, Ralph. *The Shakespearean Metaphor*, 1978. (Chapter 4 is about *Henry V*.)

Bevington, David M. *Tudor Drama and Politics: A Critical Approach to Topical Meaning*, 1968

Blake, Norman. 'Shakespeare's text: introduction and commentary', *Studies in English Language and Linguistics* 4 (2002), 23–36, esp. 28–9, 32–4

Boris, Edna Zwick. *Shakespeare's English Kings, The People and the Law*, 1978

Bradshaw, Graham. *Misrepresentations: Shakespeare and the Materialists*, 1993, chapter 1.

Brennan, Antony. *Henry V*, Harvester New Critical Introductions to Shakespeare, 1992

Brissenden, Alan. *Shakespeare and the Dance*, 1981

Bullough, Geoffrey (ed.). *Narrative and Dramatic Sources of Shakespeare*, IV, 1960. (Selectively reprints source texts.)

Calderwood, J. L. *Metadrama in Shakespeare's Henriad: 'Richard II' to 'Henry V'*, 1979

Campbell, Lily B. *Shakespeare's 'Histories': Mirrors of Elizabethan Policy*, 1974. (Chapter 15 gives evidence for *Henry V* as a sustained dramatisation of Elizabethan ideas about war.)

Candido, Joseph, and Forker, Charles R. *'Henry V': An Annotated Bibliography*, 1983

Cercignani, Fausto. *Shakespeare's Works and Elizabethan Pronunciation*, 1981

Champion, Larry S. *Perspectives in Shakespeare's English Histories*, 1980

Cox, John D. *Shakespeare and the Dramaturgy of Power*, 1989. (The personality of Henry is examined especially on pp. 104–12.)

Dent, R. W. *Shakespeare's Proverbial Language: An Index*, 1981
    *Proverbial Language in English Drama, exclusive of Shakespeare, 1495–1616*, 1984
Dillon, Janette. *Language and Stage in Medieval and Renaissance England*, 1998, pp. 177–82
    'Tiring-house wall scenes at the Globe; a change in style and emphasis', *Theatre Notebook* 53 (1999), 163–73
Duffin, Ross W. *Shakespeare's Songbook*, 2004
Edwards, Philip, *Threshold of a Nation*, 1979. (On the involvement with Ireland.)
Erne, Lukas. *Shakespeare as Literary Dramatist*, 2003
Goddard, Harold C. *The Meaning of Shakespeare*, 1951. See pp. 215–68. (The Chorus gives the popular view of Henry, but the action tells the truth.)
Goldman, Michael. *Shakespeare and the Energies of Drama*, 1972. (Chapter 5 is on 'Henry V: the strain of rule'.)
Grady, Hugh. *Shakespeare, Machiavelli, and Montaigne: Power and Subjectivity from 'Richard II' to 'Hamlet'*, 2002, chapter 5.2
Greenblatt, Stephen. *Shakespearean Negotiations: The Circulation of Social Energy in Renaissance England*, 1988
Hillman, Richard. *Shakespeare, Marlowe and the Politics of France*, 2002
Hinman, Charlton. *The Printing and Proofreading of the First Folio of Shakespeare*, 2 vols., 1963
Holderness, Graham. *Shakespeare Recycled: The Making of Historical Drama*, 1992. (Chapter 7, 'Reproductions', considers Henry played as an actor in Olivier's 1944 film.)
Homan, Sidney. *Shakespeare's Theater of Presence. Language, Spectacle and the Audience*, 1986. (Chapter 7 is on *Henry V*.)
Howard, Jean and Rackin, Phyllis. *Engendering a Nation: A Feminist Account of Shakespeare's English Histories*, 1997. (A chapter on *Henry V* is on pp. 186–215.)
Hulme, Hilda M. *Explorations in Shakespeare's Language*, 1964
Jones, Emrys. *The Origins of Shakespeare*, 1977
Jorgensen, Paul A. *Shakespeare's Military World*, 1956
Knowles, Ronald. *Shakespeare's Arguments with History*, 2001
Loehlin, James. *Shakespeare in Performance: Henry V*, 1996
McAlindon, Tom. *Shakespeare Minus 'Theory'*, 2004. (A chapter on war and peace in *Henry V* concludes the study of the two *Henry IV* plays set out in *Shakespeare's Tudor History*, 2001.)
    'Natural Closure in *Henry V*', *The Shakespearean International Yearbook* 3, 2003, pp. 156–71
McMillin, Scott. 'Casking the *Hamlet* quartos: The limit of eleven', in *The 'Hamlet' First Published. Q1, 1603: Origins, Forms, Intertextualities*, ed. Thomas Clayton, 1992, pp. 179–94
Marcus, Leah. *Puzzling Shakespeare: Local Reading and its Discontents*, 1988
Meron, Theodor. *Bloody Constraint: War and Chivalry in Shakespeare*, 1998

Neill, Michael. 'Translating the Irish: the tongues of *Henry V*', in *Putting History to the Question: Power Politics, and Society in English Renaissance Drama*, 2002, pp. 357–72

Ornstein, Robert. *A Kingdom for a Stage: The Achievement of Shakespeare's History Plays*, 1972

Patterson, Annabel. 'Back by popular demand: the two versions of *Henry V*', *Renaissance Drama* n.s.19 (1988), 29–62, revised as chapter 4 of *Shakespeare and the Popular Voice*, 1989
   *Reading Holinshed's Chronicles*, 1994, pp. 131–53

Pierce, Robert B. *Shakespeare's History Plays: The Family and the State*, 1971

Prior, Moody E. *The Drama of Power: Studies in Shakespeare's History Plays*, 1973
   'Comic theory and the rejection of Falstaff', *S.St.* 9 (1976), 159–71

Quinn, Michael (ed.). '*Henry V*': *A Casebook*, 1969. (Includes extracts from Johnson (1769), Hazlitt (1817), Masefield (1911), and others, and essays by Van Doren (1939), Knights (1962) and Sprague (1964).)

Rabkin, Norman. 'Rabbits, ducks, and *Henry V*', *SQ* 28 (1977), 279–96. (Revised and reprinted as 'Either/or: responding to *Henry V*', in *Shakespeare and the Problem of Meaning*, 1981, chapter 2.)

Rackin, Phyllis. *Stages of History: Shakespeare's English Chronicles*, 1990

Scoufos, Alice-Lyle. *Shakespeare's Typological Satire: A Study of the Falstaff–Oldcastle Problem*, 1979

Siegel, Paul N. *Shakespeare's English and Roman History Plays. A Marxist Approach*, 1986

Sisson, C. J. *New Readings in Shakespeare*, 2 vols., 1956. (The section on textual cruxes in *Henry V* is at II, 56–67)

Smidt, Kristian. *Unconformities in Shakespeare's History Plays*, 1982. (See chapter 8, 'The Disunity of *King Henry V*'.)

Smith, Emma. *King Henry V*, Shakespeare in Production, 2002

Smith, Gordon Ross. 'Shakespeare's *Henry V*: another part of the critical forest', *Journal of the History of Ideas* 37 (1976), 3–26. (A thoroughly sceptical survey, expounding the anti-hero view.)

Sprague, Arthur C. *Shakespeare's Histories: Plays for the Stage*, 1964

Taunton, Nina. *1590s Drama and Militarism: Portrayals of War in Marlowe, Chapman and Shakespeare's 'Henry V'*, 2001

Taylor, Gary. 'The fortunes of Oldcastle', *S.Sur.* 38 (1985), 85–100

Thompson, Ann, and Thompson, John O. *Shakespeare: Meaning and Metaphor*, 1987

Tilley, M. P. *A Dictionary of the Proverbs in England in the Sixteenth and Seventeenth Centuries*, 1950

Tyler, Sharon. 'Minding true things: the Chorus, the audience, and *Henry V*', in *The Theatrical Space*, ed. James Redmond, Themes in Drama 9, 1987, 69–80

Van Laan, Thomas. *Role-Playing in Shakespeare*, 1978

Vickers, Brian. *The Artistry of Shakespeare's Prose*, 1968

Wells, Stanley, and Taylor, Gary. *Modernising Shakespeare's Spelling, with Three Studies in the Text of 'Henry V'*, 1979

Werner, Sarah. 'Firk and foot: the boy actor in *Henry V*', *Shakespeare Bulletin* 21 (2003), 19–27

Wilcox, Lance. 'Katherine of France as victim and bride', *S.St.* 17 (1985), 61–76

Wilder, John. *The Lost Garden: A View of Shakespeare's English and Roman History Plays*, 1978. (See especially pp. 58–63, 112–15.)

Williamson, Marilyn. 'The episode with Williams in *Henry V*', *Studies in English Literature 1500–1900* 9 (1969), 275–82